BUTLER'S
LIVES OF THE SAINTS

NEW

FULL EDITION

DECEMBER

BUTLER'S
LIVES OF THE SAINTS

NEW FULL EDITION

Patron
H. E. CARDINAL BASIL HUME, O.S.B.+
Archbishop of Westminster

BUTLER'S LIVES OF THE SAINTS

NEW
FULL EDITION

DECEMBER

Revised by
KATHLEEN JONES

BURNS & OATES

THE LITURGICAL PRESS
Collegeville, Minnesota

First published 2000 in Great Britain by
BURNS & OATES
Wellwood, North Farm Road,
Tunbridge Wells, Kent TN2 3DR

First published 2000 in North America by
THE LITURGICAL PRESS
St John's Abbey, Collegeville,
Minnesota 56321

ISBN 0 86012 261 1   Burns & Oates
ISBN 0-8146-2388-3   The Liturgical Press

Library of Congress Catalog Card Number: 95-81671

Typeset by Search Press Limited
Printed in the United States of America

CONTENTS

Contents

PREFACE

The liturgical calendar for December leads us to the coming of the Christ-Child. The four Sundays of Advent recall Israel's long period of waiting for the promised Messiah: Christmas celebrates the fulfillment of the promise, when the Word was made flesh. The infinite variety of the Godhead was made manifest in time and space: in a human being of a particular height and colouring, a particular race and gender, in a particular place and period of history. The life of the Church began when he chose his apostles; and at Pentecost, as the Sunday Missal records, Christ "filled the Church with the power of his Spirit and sent it out into the world." The risen Christ lives on in men and women, young and old, of many races and different cultures, in succeeding generations. Those in whom the flame burns brightly, and who are recognized by the Church, are called saints or blessed. They reflect a wide variety of human experience.

Because of the liturgical importance of Advent and Christmas, some saints formerly commemorated in December have had their feasts moved to other months in the year; but the "December saints" still provide an ample variety of Christian example.

Many died for their faith: Stephen, the proto-martyr, has his feast on the day after Christmas, and other martyrs range from early Christians of Rome and Alexandria and Antioch through to English martyrs of the Reformation, the martyrs of Thailand (12th, 16th, 18th, and 19th), and a young African nun, Anuarite Nengapeta, martyred in the Congo in 1964 (1st).

There are four great Doctors of the Church: Ambrose of Milan (7th), John Damascene (4th), John of the Cross (14th), and Peter Canisius (21st). Other scholars include John Ruysbroeck (2d) and Jacopone of Todi (25th), who wrote in their own local dialects and whose work remained relatively obscure for centuries. Both have been the subject of considerable study in recent years. There are also unlettered saints, such as Servulus, the beggar of Rome (23d), whose lives demonstrate the power of faith with great simplicity.

Among the missionaries is the great Francis Xavier (3d), who took the Faith to the virtually unknown cultures of India and Japan. Among the defenders of the Faith against kings and emperors is Thomas Becket (29th), killed in his cathedral at Canterbury. There are princes and peasants, bishops and hermits, rich and poor, all part of the same company.

In his editorial preface to *A Dictionary of Saints* (1958; since revised as *A New Dictionary of Saints*, 1993) Donald Attwater commented that the saints publicly recognized are not necessarily representative of all the people who have led lives of great sanctity: "If it be a question of *canonized* and *beatified* saints . . . there are far more clergy and religious than lay people, and also far more bishops than priests, and men than women." He goes on to point out that "purely natural factors come into play" in the selection of candidates for recognition. This is a question of social visibility: bishops are more prominent than other clergy, the major religious Orders can forward the "cause" of their own candidates to Rome, and men have through the centuries had greater opportunities for public recognition than women.

The comment helps to explain why, of nearly two hundred entries in this volume, only forty-two relate to women and nearly all of them are virgins, widows, or foundresses of religious Orders. St Gregory Nazanzien's eulogy on his married sister Gorgonia, praising her devotion to her husband and children, is one of the few recognitions of women's contribution to family life. A new generation of women scholars is now beginning to provide more information on women saints.

Recent canonizations and beatifications have included people who bring fresh perspectives on sainthood from the eighteenth and nineteenth centuries. Among them are Nicholas Stensen (5th), the eminent Danish scientist who became a bishop; Margaret d'Youville (23d), a Canadian woman who faced great hardship at the time of the English conquest of Quebec; two Polish patriots, Albert Chmielkowski (25th) and Honoratus Kosminski (16th), who kept the Catholic tradition alive in the days of Tsarist oppression; and two industrial workers from the Rhineland who founded organizations for young artisans: Peter Friedhofen (21st) and Adolf Kolping (4th).

The study of the lives of saints began as a mixture of tradition, folk-lore, and illustrative example. Serious historical study on the subject is a comparatively recent development and owes much to the Society of Bollandists, who have drawn attention to inadequate manuscripts, mistranslations, unreliable datings, and many other possible sources of error in what has been handed down to us. Attempts to get closer to historical truth are to be welcomed: we do the saints no service if we embroider holy lives with pious improbabilities. On the other hand, a desire for historical precision should not lead to the rejection of all incomplete or doubtful accounts, particularly from periods or societies where written records were poor or have not been preserved. For some of the early saints, particularly in the Byzantine Church and the Celtic Church, the evidence is often sketchy; but oral tradition and place names are relevant to historical study. Archetypes, cults, and even myths, as Jung reminds us, are also evidence, if interpreted with discretion. If the accounts that follow are laced with "probably," "possibly," and "according to tradition," this is to ensure that no more weight is placed on the evidence than it can reasonably stand.

Many people have helped with this revised account of the December saints. Thanks are especially due to the consultants, who have provided invaluable (mostly cautionary) advice; to the librarians and staff of the Catholic Central Library, the University of York Library, and the Minster Library at York, who have responded patiently to many difficult queries (and often sent me to other libraries for the answers); to the members of religious Orders who have found the time and taken the trouble to provide information from their own records; to Dr Lucy Cohen of The Catholic University of America in Washington D.C. for much interest and support and particularly for help with Mother Cabrini; to Fr Czekly Bela of the Archbishop's Library at Esztergom for information on Archbishop Sebastian; to Mr William Pike, Editor of *The Vision*, the Kampala daily newspaper, for assistance with the story of Sister Anuarite; to Fr Saemundur Vigfusson for setting me right on Bishop Thorlac of Skalholt; and above all to Paul Burns, managing editor of the series, for encouraging me to range over nearly two thousand years of history in search of some remarkable and inspiring people.

3 June 1999, Feast of the Martyrs of Uganda
Kathleen Jones

Abbreviations and Short Forms

A.A.S.   *Acta Apostolicae Sedis.* Rome, 1908-.

AA.SS.   *Acta Sanctorum,* 64 vols. Antwerp, 1643-.

AA.SS.OSB.   L. d'Achéry and J. Mabillon. *Acta Sanctorum Ordinis Sancti Benedicti,* 9 vols. Paris, 1668-1701.

Anal.Boll.   *Analecta Bollandiana* (1882-).

Anstruther   G. Anstruther, O.P. *The Seminary Priests: a Dictionary of the Secular Clergy,* 4 vols. Ware, Ushaw, and Great Wakering, 1968-77.

A.S.C.   G. N. Garmonsway. *The Anglo-Saxon Chronicle* (trans. and ed.). London, 1972.

Auréole Séraphique Léon de Clary, O.F.M. *L'auréole séraphique.* Eng. trans., *Lives of the Saints and Blessed of the Orders of St Francis,* 4 vols. Taunton, 1887.

Baluze-Mansi   J. D. Mansi. *Tutelensis Miscellanea Novo Ordine Digesta opera et studio,* ed. S. Baluze. Lucca, 1761.

Bardenhewer   O. Bardenhewer. *Geschichte der altkirchlichen Literatur,* 5 vols. Freiburg, 1902-32.

B.D.E.C.   J. Gillow (ed.). *Biographical Dictionary of English Catholics,* 5 vols. London and New York, 1887.

Bibl.SS.   *Bibliotheca Sanctorum,* 12 vols. Rome, 1960-70; Suppl. 1 (*Prima Appendice*). Rome, 1987.

BS(R)   Benedictines of Ramsgate. *The Book of Saints.* Ramsgate, 1989.

Christian Worship L. Duchesne. *Christian Worship and its Evolution* (trans. M. L. McClure). 5th ed. London, 1919.

C. E.   C. Heberman (ed.). *The Catholic Encyclopaedia,* 17 vols. and index. London and New York. 1907-14.

C.M.H.   H. Delehaye. *Commentarius Perpetuus in Martyrologium Hieronymianum*: *AA.SS.* vol. 64. 1940.

C.T.S.   Catholic Truth Society.

D.A.C.L.   F. Cabrol and H. Leclercq (eds.). *Dictionnaire d'archéologie chrétienne et de liturgie,* 15 vols. Paris, 1907-53.

D.C.B.   W. Smith and H. Wace. *Dictionary of Christian Biography,* 4 vols. London, 1877-87.

D.C.B. (1911)   H. Wace and W. C. Piercy (eds.). *Dictionary of Christian Biography* (one vol. updated). London, 1911.

D.Cath.Biog.	J. J. Delaney and J. E. Tobin (eds.*)*. *Dictionary of Catholic Biography*. London, 1961.
D.E.C.H.	S. L. Ollard and G. Crosse (eds.). *Dictionary of English Church History*. London and Oxford, 1912; 3d. ed. 1971.
de Villegas	Alonso de Villegas Selvado. *Flos Sanctorum*. 1623. Eng. trans., *The Lives of the Saints*, vol. 2. E.R.L. 356, 1977.
D.H.G.E.	A. Baudrillart *et al.* (eds.). *Dictionnaire d'histoire et de géographie ecclésiastiques*. Paris, 1912- .
Dict.Sp.	M. Viller, S.J. *et al.* (eds.). *Dictionnaire de spiritualité*. Paris, 1937-.
D.I.P.	*Dizionario degli Istitute di Perfezione*, 10 vols. Rome, 1974- .
D.N.B.	L. Stephen *et al.* (eds.). *Dictionary of National Biography*, 63 vols. London, 1885-.
D.T.C.	A. Vacant, A. Mangenot, and E. Amann (eds.). *Dictionnaire de théologie catholique*, 15 vols. Paris, 1903-50.
Duchesne, *Fastes*	L. Duchesne. *Fastes Épiscopaux de l'ancienne Gaule*, 3 vols. 4th edition, Paris, 1908.
D.N.H.	F. Holböck (ed.). *Die neuen Heiligen der katholische Kirche*, 3 vols. to date. Stein am Rhein, 1991-4.
E.H.R.	*English Historical Review* (1886-).
E.R.L.	D. M. Rodgers (ed.). *English Recusant Literature (1558-1640)*. Ilkley and London, 1970.
Eusebius, *H. E.*	Eusebius, *Historia Ecclesiasticae*. See N.P.N.F., 1.
F.B.S.	Marion A. Habig. *The Franciscan Book of Saints*. Chicago, rev. ed., 1979.
Florez	Enrique (Henrique) Florez. *España Sagrada: Indice*. Madrid, 1877; 2d ed. 1946.
Golden Legend	Jacob de Voragine. *The Golden Legend* (trans. W. G. Ryan), 2 vols. Princeton ed. 1993.
Haddan and Stubbs	A. W. Haddan and W. Stubbs. *Councils and Ecclesiastical Documents*, 3 vols. Oxford, 1869-78.
Hefele-Leclerc	C. J. Hefele. *Histoire des Conciles d'après les documents originaux* (ed. H. Leclercq *et al.*), vols 1-9. Paris, 1907-.
Hefele-Clark	*History of the Christian Councils*. Eng. trans. of the above, ed. W. R. Clark and H. N. Oxenham, 2 vols. London, 1871-6, with English commentaries.

Hieronymianum	See *C.M.H.*
Heist, *V.S.H.*	W. W. Heist. *Vita Sanctorum Hiberniae.* 2 vols. Brussels, 1963.
Irish Saints	D. D. C. Pochin Mould. *The Irish Saints.* Dublin and London, 1964.
Jaffé	P. Jaffé. *Regesta Pontificum Romanorum.* 1885; rp. Graz, 1956.
L.E.M. 1	Bede Camm (ed.). *Lives of the English Martyrs*, first series, 2 vols. London, 1904-5.
L.E.M. 2	E. H. Burton and J. H. Pollen (eds.). *Lives of the English Martyrs*, second series, on the martyrs declared Venerable 1583-8. London, 1915.
L.D.H.	J. Torsky (ed.). *Lexicon der Deutschen Heiligen.* Cologne, 1959.
Lib. Pont.	L. Duchesne (ed.). *Liber Pontificalis,* 2 vols. Paris, 1886-92.
Liber Pontif.	Raymond Davis (ed.). *The Book of Pontiffs: Liber Pontificalis.* Liverpool, 1889.
M.G.H.	G. Pertz *et al.* (eds.). *Monumenta Germaniae Historiae, Scriptores,* 64 vols. Hanover, 1839-1921. Sub-series include *Auctores Antiquissimi, Epistolae Selectae*, and *Scriptores Rerum Merovingicarum.*
Mann	H. K. Mann. *The Lives of the Popes in the Middle Ages.* London, 1925.
Mazzara	B. Mazzara (ed.). *Leggendario Francescano,* 12 vols. Rome, 1721.
Mortier	D. A. Mortier. *Histoire des maîtres généraux O.P.*, 4 vols. Paris, 1923.
M.M.P.	R. Challoner, *Memoirs of Missionary Priests.* 1741-2; new ed. by J. H. Pollen. London, 1924.
N.D.B.	*Neue Deutsche Biografie.* Berlin, 1952- .
N.C.E.	*New Catholic Encyclopedia,* 14 vols. New York, 1967.
N.L.A.	C. Horstmann, (ed.). *Nova Legendae Angliae* 2, vols. Oxford, 1901.
N.P.N.F.	P. Schaff and H. Wace (eds.). The Nicene and Post-Nicene Christian Fathers. 1887-1900; second series rp. Grand Rapids, Michigan, 1979. Vol. 1: Eusebius of Caesarea; vol. 2: Socrates, *Historia Ecclesiastica;* Sozomen, *Historia Ecclesiastica;* vol. 3: Rufinus, *Historia Ecclesiastica;* vol. 6: Jerome; vol.10: Ambrose.

N.S.B. 1	Thierry Lelièvre. *100 nouveaux saints et bienheureux de 1963 à 1984.* Paris, 1983.
N.S.B. 2	Thierry Lelièvre. *Nouveaux saints et bienheureux de 1984 à 1988.* Paris, 1989.
O.D.P.	J. W. Kelly (ed.). *The Oxford Dictionary of Popes.* Oxford, 1986.
O.D.S.	D. H. Farmer. *The Oxford Dictionary of Saints.* 3d. ed., Oxford and New York, 1993.
Pastor	L. Pastor. *History of the Popes from the Close of the Middle Ages,* 40 vols. (various eds. and trans.). 6th ed., London, 1938.
P.B.	F. Guérin (ed.). Vie des Saints des Petits Bollandistes: *Décembre*: vol. 14 of 17. Paris, 1880.
P.G.	J. P. Migne (ed.). *Patrologia Graeca,* 162 vols. Paris, 1857-66.
P.L.	J. P. Migne (ed.). *Patrologia Latina,* 221 vols. Paris, 1844-64.
Plummer, *V.S.H.*	C. Plummer (ed.). *Vitae Sanctorum Hiberniae,* 2 vols. Oxford, 1910; 2d ed. 1968.
Procter	J. Procter (ed.). *Short Lives of the Dominican Saints.* London, 1900.
Propylaeum	H. Delehaye *et al.* (eds.). *Propylaeum ad Acta Sanctorum Decembris: AA.SS.* 65. Brussels, 1940.
Quentin	H. Quentin, *Les martyrologes historiques du Moyen Age.* Paris, 1908.
R.H.E.	*Revue d'histoire ecclésiastique* (1900-).
R.S.	Rolls Series: *Rerum Britannicaum Medii Aevi Scriptores.* London, 1858-.
Rufinus, *H.E.*	Se N.P.N.F. 3.
Ruinart	T. Ruinart. *Acta Martyrum Sincera.* Paris, 1859.
Saints in Italy	L. Menzies. *The Saints in Italy.* London, 1924.
S.B.I.	A. Bond and N. Mabin. *Saints of the British Isles.* Bognor Regis, 1980.
Socrates, *H.E.*	See N.P.N.F. 2.
Sozomen, *H.E.*	See N.P.N.F. 2.
Stanton	R. Stanton. *A Menology of England and Wales.* London, 1892.

Synax.Const.	H. Delehaye (ed.). *The Synaxary of Constantinople*, in *AA. SS.*, 64. 1902.
Wadding	L. Wadding (ed.). *Annales seu Trium Ordinum a S. Francisco Institutorum*, 25 vols. Rome, 1931-47.
William Worcestre	J. H. Harvey (ed.). *Itineraries*. Cambridge, 1969.

1

ST EDMUND CAMPION, *Martyr* (*c.* 1540-81)

Edmund Campion was the son of a bookseller in the city of London and showed great promise as a boy. He was admitted at the age of ten to the Bluecoat School and in 1553, when he was about thirteen years of age, was chosen to make a speech of welcome to Queen Mary I. At fifteen he was given a scholarship to St John's College, Oxford, then newly founded. Two years later he was appointed a junior fellow, and he gained a great reputation as an orator. He was chosen to speak at the re-burial of Lady Dudley (Amy Robsart); at the funeral of the college's founder, Sir Thomas White; and before Queen Elizabeth I when she visited Oxford in 1566.

Campion's talents and personality earned him the goodwill and patronage of the queen, Sir Robert Cecil, and the Earl of Leicester: Cecil called him "one of the diamonds of England." His career seemed assured, but he became increasingly doubtful about the Elizabethan religious settlement. He took the Oath of Supremacy under the Act of 1559, but he had grown up in Queen Mary's reign, when Catholics had seen full relations with the Holy See restored. On Elizabeth's accession, those relations were again broken.

His allegiance to the Church as defined under the settlement was much shaken by his reading of the early Fathers. Though he was persuaded by the bishop of Gloucester to receive the diaconate, he was troubled at the prospect of becoming a priest under the new dispensation. He became the centre of a group of personal disciples who shared his concerns. The Grocers' Company, which had funded his studies, was seriously worried about his religious allegiance.

Campion resolved to leave England. In 1569, when he ended his term as junior proctor, he left Oxford "full of remorse of conscience and detestation of mind." He went to Dublin, where the new religious settlement was being widely ignored, but he was not at home there. In his *Short History of Ireland*, he appears very much as a young Oxford don observing a race of foreigners:

> The people are thus inclined: religious, franke, amorous, irefull, sufferable of paines infinite, very glorious, many sorcerers, excellent horsemen, delighted with warres, great almes-givers, passing in hospitalitie: the lewder sort both clarkes and laymen are sensuall and loose to lechery above measure. The same being vertuously bred up are such mirrours of holinesse and austeritie, that other nations retaine but a shewe or shadow of devotion in comparison of them.

1

In 1570 a papal Bull of Pope Pius V charged Elizabeth I with heresy, formally deposed her from the throne of England, and excommunicated her. All who continued to obey her laws were to be subject to the same anathema. The English Parliament responded in the following year with a statute declaring it to be high treason to affirm that Elizabeth was not, or ought not to be, queen, or that she was a heretic, schismatic, tyrant, infidel, or usurper of the crown. Catholics such as Campion were thus presented with a stark choice.

He returned to England in 1571. Knowing that he was in danger as a suspected person, he came in disguise. He was present in Westminster Hall at the trial of Bd John Storey (1 June), Oxford's first professor of civil law, who had taken a major part in the condemnation and execution of Protestants in Queen Mary's reign. Campion would have heard the arguments at the trial, his keen mind assessing them and working out the dictates of his own conscience. He would have seen Storey condemned and sentenced. After the trial he left England again for the Continent; he was stopped on the way for having no passport but was allowed to proceed on giving up his luggage and money.

Fr William Allen, later Cardinal Allen, had founded the English College at Douai two years earlier. It was already becoming a centre for study and mission for clergy and laity who were opposed to the Elizabethan settlement. Campion took his B.D. at Douai and was ordained sub-deacon. In 1573 he went to Rome and was admitted to the Society of Jesus. As there was as yet no English Jesuit province in communion with Rome, he was sent to the province of Bohemia, and after his novitiate at Brno he went to the college of Prague to teach.

In view of the great success of the Jesuits among the Protestants of Germany, Bohemia, and Poland, Pope Gregory III was persuaded to send a mission to England, and at the end of 1579 Edmund Campion and Robert Persons were chosen as the first to be sent. They were very well aware of the probable consequences: on the night before Campion left Prague one of the fathers wrote above the door of his cell: *P. Edmundus Campianus, Martyr.* The spirits of the missioners were high; in Geneva, where Ralph Sherwin (1 Dec., below) was one of the party, Campion amused his companions by pretending to be an Irish serving-man named Patrick who knew no Latin. When he was leaving Geneva he disputed recklessly with a Protestant minister at the city gate. Persons travelled to England disguised as a soldier returning from the Low Countries, while Campion was disguised as a jewel merchant, with his companion, a coadjutor Brother named Ralph Emerson, as his servant.

The Jesuits were not welcomed by all Catholics. Many felt the proselytizing zeal of the Society to be a threat to political and social stability, and the two were asked to declare on oath that "their coming was only apostolical, to treat of matters of religion in truth and simplicity, and to attend to the gaining of souls without any pretence or knowledge of matters of state." Their arrival was known to the government and not initially opposed, but attitudes were hardening on both sides. These events took place while the Spanish Armada was being prepared and the threat of invasion was increasing. Though Campion and his supporters saw their work as high intellectual and spiritual adventure, the risks that their intervention would be seen in political rather than religious terms became very serious.

During his time in London Campion ministered to Catholics in prison and wrote a challenge to the Privy Council known as *Campion's Brag*, in which he described his mission as "one of free cost to preach the Gospel, to minister the sacraments, to instruct the simple, to reform sinners, to confute errors; in brief, to cry alarm spiritual against foul vice and proud ignorance, wherewith many of my dear countrymen are abused."

Campion's Brag was written for publication in the event of his arrest, to try to secure him a fair hearing. It was composed hastily, but it plainly stated the reasons for his mission. The document soon spread from hand to hand and became a manifesto for the mission. Campion had to leave London and worked in Berkshire, Northamptonshire, and Oxfordshire, where he made some notable converts. He wrote to the Jesuit father general in Rome: "I ride about some piece of the country every day. The harvest is wonderful great. . . . I cannot long escape the hands of the heretics. . . . I am in apparel to myself very ridiculous; I often change it, and my name also. I read letters sometimes myself that, in the first front, tell news that Campion is taken, which roused in every place where I come so filleth my ears that fear itself hath taken away all fear."

He went to Lancashire, where he preached almost daily, pursued by spies and several times narrowly missing arrest. His sermons were still remembered fifty years later by those who had heard them. During this time he was writing a Latin treatise, *Decem Rationes*, in which he expounded ten reasons why he had challenged the most learned Anglicans openly to discuss religion with him. It was extremely difficult to get this work printed. Eventually the work was carried out on a secret press at the house of Dame Cecilia Stonor in Stonor Park, Berkshire. Lady Stonor was later to die in prison for her part in this enterprise. Owing to a shortage of type, the treatise had to be set one page at a time, and it took half a dozen typesetters (dressed as gentlemen to disarm suspicion) nine weeks to set it. On Oxford's Commemoration Sunday, 27 June 1581, four hundred copies were found distributed on the benches of the university church. The publication of *Decem Rationes* caused a tremendous sensation, and efforts to capture Campion were redoubled.

After the publication of *Decem Rationes* he decided to retire to Norfolk; on the way he stayed at a house in Lyford, near Wantage, where he celebrated Mass and preached to some forty people. Someone informed the authorities: the house was searched three times in twelve hours, and Campion and two other priests were eventually found in hiding, concealed above the gateway. They were taken to the Tower of London, in bonds for the latter part of the journey, and Edmund was labelled "Campion, the seditious Jesuit." After three days in prison he was interviewed by the earls of Bedford and Leicester and, it is said, by the queen herself, who tried to persuade him and then to bribe him into giving up his cause. All attempts at persuasion or bribery failed, and he was racked. People who were known to have sheltered him were arrested, and to demoralize his supporters still further it was falsely rumoured that he had betrayed them. While still suffering from the effects of torture he was four times confronted by Anglican churchmen whose questions, objections, and insults he answered with spirit. Among those present who were permanently affected by his words and bearing was Philip Howard, earl of Arundel, afterwards himself a martyr and now canonized (19 Oct.).

Campion was racked again, so fiercely that, when asked the next day how he felt, he could only reply, "Not ill, because not at all." No admission was obtained from him, so on 14 November he was indicted at Westminster Hall with Ralph Sherwin, Thomas Cobham, Luke Kirby, and others on the charge of having plotted at Rome and Reims to raise a rebellion in England and of having come to England for that purpose. When told to plead he was too weak to move his arms, and one of his companions, kissing his hand, held it up for him.

Campion conducted his own defence and that of the other defendants very ably, protesting their loyalty to the queen, contesting the evidence, discrediting the witnesses, and arguing that their only offence was their religion. The packed jury took an hour to bring in a verdict but eventually pronounced them guilty. Before sentence of death was passed, Campion addressed the court: "In condemning us, you condemn all your own ancestors. . . . God lives. Posterity will live. Their judgment is not so liable of corruption as that of those who now sentence us to death."

Campion's sister came with a message offering him a good benefice if he would return to the established Church, but this he refused. He freely forgave a man named Eliot, who had both betrayed him and given evidence against him, giving him a letter of recommendation to a nobleman in Germany. On 1 December 1581, a wet, muddy day, Campion, Sherwin, and Alexander Briant (see below) were drawn together to Tyburn. On the scaffold Campion again refused to give an opinion of the papal Bull against Elizabeth and publicly prayed for her: "Your queen and my queen, unto whom I wish a long reign with all prosperity." There the three were barbarously executed. Some of Campion's blood splashed on a young man named Henry Walpole, who also became a Jesuit and a beatified martyr (7 Apr.). Among Walpole's poems on the life and death of Campion is a lyric, "Why do I use my paper and ink," which was beautifully set to music by William Byrd, himself frequently "presented" for recusancy.

Edmund Campion was beatified in 1886 and canonized as one of the Forty Martyrs of England and Wales by Pope Paul VI on 25 October 1970. His feast is kept not only by the Society of Jesus and in the dioceses of Northampton and Plymouth but also in Brno and Prague.

4

The *Decem Rationes* is published in *E.R.L.*, 1, with a translation, and in several other versions, including E. Campion, *Ten reasons proposed to his adversaries . . .*, ed. J. H. Pollen (1914). See also R. Persons, *On the Life and Martyrdom of Father Edmund Campion*, facsimile edition, ed. T. Allfield (1970); Cardinal William Allen, *A Brief Historie of the Glorious Martyrdom of twelve reverend Priests*, ed. J. H. Pollen (1908); Henry More, *Historia Missionis Anglicanus Societatis Jesu* (1660), published as *The Elizabethan Jesuits*, trans. and intro. Francis Edwards (1981), books 2 and 3. For a modern biography see Evelyn Waugh, *Edmund Campion* (1935), especially the bibliography, pp. 224–5. For general background see J. Bossy, *The English Catholic Community 1570–1850* (1975). On Campion's relics see Bede Camm, *Forgotten Shrines* (1911), pp. 377–8.

St Tudwal, *Bishop* (Sixth Century)

Three place names on the Lleyn peninsula, the northern arm of Cardigan Bay, commemorate the name of Tudwal, Tugdual, or Tual. He does not appear in ancient Welsh calendars, but his cult is strong in Brittany, where he is reported to have settled at Lan Pabu in Léon with his mother, his sister, and some monks. He made several other monastic foundations. His cousin, Deroc, was the local ruler, but Tudwal is said to have travelled to Paris to obtain confirmation of his titles to land from the Frankish king Childebert I, who insisted that he should become a bishop. He became the first bishop of Treher, now Tréguier, and ended his days in the monastery there.

Tudwal's Island East (*Ynys Tudwal*), a small uninhabited island off Abersoch in the Lleyn peninsula, has an ancient ruined chapel dedicated to St Tudwal and thought to have been his hermitage. This is mentioned in the local taxation documents of 1291.

Tudwal's name appears in a Breton litany of the tenth century. In art he is depicted as a bishop, holding a dragon by his stole. Tréguier, Laval, and Chartres all claim part of his relics. He is known as *Pabu* (Father) in Brittany.

Anal. Boll. 8 (1889), pp. 158–65; Haddan and Stubbs, 2, p. 82; Stanton, p. 714; M. Miller, *The Saints of Gwynedd* (1979), p. 15.

Note: The new Roman Martyrology will commemorate him on 30 November, which will be followed in future editions of this work.

St Agericus, *Bishop* (*c.* 521-88)

St Agericus, or Airy, was born at or near Verdun, perhaps at Harville, about the year 521. His parents had long been childless and prayed for a son, and Thierry, king of Austrasia, consented to be his godfather when their prayers were answered. Agericus became one of the clergy of the church of SS Peter and Paul at Verdun; when he was thirty-three he was appointed the tenth bishop. He was visited there by St Gregory of Tours (17 Nov.) and St Venantius Fortunatus (14 Dec.), both of whom praised his work. Fortunatus wrote in a celebrated Latin couplet: "The poor receive relief, the despairing hope, the naked clothing; whatever you have, all have."

King Sigebert I and his son Childebert, who succeeded him, favoured Agericus and accepted his counsel. He obtained pardon for a condemned malefactor at Laon but failed to save a nobleman named Bertefroi and his companions, who came to him for sanctuary and protection after a failed revolt: Bertefroi was murdered in the bishop's own chapel by royal officers. Agericus died in 588, still mourning his failure to save Bertefroi. He was buried in the church of SS Andrew and Martin, which he had built at Verdun, and an abbey, established there in the eleventh century, was dedicated in his honour.

See Hugh of Flavigny's biography in *P.L.*, 154, 126–31; *D.H.G.E.*, 1223–4; P.B., pp. 17–18, from the *Histoire de Verdun*.

St Eligius, *Bishop* (*c*. 588–660)

Of all the Merovingian saints, St Eligius (Eloi, or Loy) brings us most closely into touch with Christian life and liturgical practice in the seventh century. His name, like those of his father, Eucherius, and his mother, Terrigia, shows him to be of Roman Gaulish extraction. He was born in the Haute-Vienne, near Limoges, about 588 and developed a remarkable talent for metalwork. Eucherius apprenticed him to a goldsmith who was master of the mint at Limoges. When his apprenticeship was completed he went across the Loire into Frankish territory and became known at the court of Clotaire II in Paris. The king gave him materials to make a chair of state, including gold and precious stones, and from these Eligius contrived to make two thrones instead of one. Clotaire admired his ability as a designer and his honesty and took him into the royal household, giving him the post of master of the mint at Marseilles. His name is still to be seen on several gold coins struck in Paris and Marseilles in the reigns of Clotaire II and Dagobert I.

Eligius came into some conflict with Clotaire II when the latter asked him to swear an oath of allegiance. He had scruples about the implications of such an oath, since he did not know what he might be called on to do or approve as a consequence of it, so he made excuses. Clotaire pressed him and was displeased at his refusal: Eligius was, after all, a foreigner, so his allegiance could not be taken for granted. Eventually the king realized that the issue was a matter of conscience and not lack of loyalty. Then he assured Eligius that his conscience was a better pledge of fidelity than other men's oaths.

King Clotaire's regard for and trust in Eligius was shared by his son Dagobert I, though, like many monarchs, Dagobert was more prepared to take advice about his public life than his private life. He admired Eligius and kept him at court. The court was based in Paris but moved frequently to different parts of Gaul. Eligius was so influential that strangers to the court usually visited him first, and he became a sort of gatekeeper to the royal presence.

He was given some magnificent commissions. The *Vita S. Eligii* states that among other works he made the reliquaries of St Martin at Tours and St Denys in Paris. The latter was splendidly ornamented with precious metals and surmounted by a jewelled cross. He is also credited with reliquaries for SS Quintinus, Crispin, and Crispinian at Soissons, St Lucian, St Germanus of Paris, and St Genevieve.

His skill as a workman, his official position, and his friendship with the king soon made him a wealthy man. He dressed magnificently, sometimes all in silk (a rare material in France in those days), and his clothes were embroidered with gold and adorned with precious stones. He also gave large sums in alms: when a stranger asked the way to his house, he was told, "Go to such a street, and it's where you see a crowd of poor people."

At court Eligius sought the company of such men as Sulpicius, Bertharius, Desiderius and his brother Rusticus, and above all, Audoenus, all of whom became bishops and are commemorated as saints. St Audoenus, known in France as St Ouen (24 Aug.), must have been a boy when Eligius first knew him. For many years he was credited with the sole authorship of the *Vita S. Eligii*. This is now regarded as largely the work of a later monk of Noyon, though he may have drawn on a manuscript written by St Audoneus. The *vita* describes *Eligius* at this time as "tall, with a fresh complexion, his hair and beard curling without artifice; his hands were shapely and long-fingered, his face full of angelic kindness and its expression grave and unaffected."

Both Eligius and Audoenus developed a strong vocation to the monastic life, but Dagobert was unwilling to part with them, though he helped them to found monasteries. He gave Eligius the estate of Solignac in his native Limousin for the foundation of a monastery; the monks, who followed the combined Rules of St Columban (23 Nov.) and St Benedict (11 July), were noted later for their good work in various arts. The original charter of Solignac, signed by Eligius, is preserved in the archives of Limoges. Dagobert also gave Eligius a house in Paris, which he converted into a monastery for women. He asked for an additional piece of land to complete the buildings, which Dagobert granted him, but he found that he had used rather more land than he was given and went to ask the king's pardon. Dagobert was surprised at his careful honesty and said to his courtiers, "Some of my officers do not scruple to rob me of whole estates, whereas Eligius is afraid of having one inch of ground which is not his."

Eligius was chosen to be bishop of Noyon and Tournai at the same time as his friend Audoenus was made archbishop of Rouen. They were consecrated together at Noyon—an unusual practice, since bishops were usually consecrated in their own cathedral churches. The date is sometimes given as 635, but Vacandard adduces good reasons for placing it on 13 May 641.

Eligius proved to be as good a bishop as he had been a layman, and his zeal and pastoral care were outstanding. His missionary activities took him into Flanders, where he preached in Antwerp, Ghent, and Courtrai. The inhabitants of Courtrai reviled him as a foreigner and a Roman, but Eligius took care of their sick, protected them from oppression, and showed them by example how Christians behaved. Every year at Easter he baptized those whom he had brought to a knowledge of God in the previous twelve months.

The author of the *vita* says that Eligius preached to the people every Sunday and feast-day and gives an abstract of several of his discourses united in one. This appears to borrow heavily from the sermons of St Caesarius of Arles (27 Aug.), who died in 543, but it may be the author rather than the saint who did the borrowing. One homily that does appear to be the work of Eligius is a very interesting discourse in which the preacher warns his hearers against superstititious and heathen practices:

> Do not trust those who put their faith in magical practices, in fortune-tellers, sorcerers, in wizards: do not seek from them help for any cause or infirmity: do not consult them for anything, for whoever commits such a sin loses straighta-way the grace of baptism. . . . When you begin on a task or a journey, make the sign of the Cross in the name of Jesus Christ, recite the Sunday prayers, and the enemy will not cause you any harm.

His listeners were warned against the observances of New Year's Day and Midsummer's Day. Charms, the use of omens, lustrations, secret groves and temples, midnight revels, calling on the names of the old Greek gods, and many other practices were strictly forbidden. Christians were urged to place their faith in the Creed, the Lord's Prayer, anointing in time of sickness, and the body and blood of Christ.

Eligius was a powerful preacher, not afraid to use the threat of hell-fire for those who knew the Faith and disobeyed its teaching. He taught the wealthy that they must help the poor and that to let people starve was an act of homi-cide.

Eligius established a house of nuns at Noyon and brought his protegée St Godeberta (11 Apr.) from Paris to administer it. He was very active in promot-ing the cult of local saints, and it was during his episcopate that several of the reliquaries mentioned above were made either by him or under his direction.

He took a leading part in the ecclesiastical life of his day, and for a short time immediately before his death he was a valued counsellor of the queen-regent, St Bathild (30 Jan.). They had in common not only political views but a deep solicitude for slaves: Bathild had been carried off from England and sold as a child. The Council of Chalon (*c.* 647) forbade the sale of slaves out of the kingdom and decreed that they must be free to rest on Sundays and holidays. Eligius had long made a practice of personally ransoming slaves—men and women, Romans, Britons, Gauls, Moors, and Saxons. They were given the choice of entering a monastery, remaining in the world, or returning to their own homes. Some of them remained in his service and were his faithful assist-ants throughout his life. One, a Saxon named Tillo, is numbered among the saints (7 Jan.). He was the first among the seven disciples of Eligius who followed him from the workshop when he became a bishop.

The only certainly authentic writing of Eligius is an affectionate letter to his friend St Desiderius (Didier) of Cahors (15 Nov.): "Remember your Eligius, O my Desiderius, who art dear to me as mine own self, when your soul pours itself out in prayer to the Lord," he writes, "I greet you with all my heart and the most sincere affection. Our faithful companion, Dado, greets you as well." Dado is his friend and colleague Audoenus.

When he had been bishop of Noyon for nineteen years, Eligius contracted a fever and died on 1 December 660. Bathild made preparations for moving his body to her monastery at Chelles; others wished it to be transported to Paris, but the people of Noyon so strenuously opposed a move that the body of their pastor was left with them, and his remains now rest in the cathedral.

Eligius was for long one of the most popular saints in France, and his feast was universal in north-western Europe during the later Middle Ages. Chaucer's Prioress swears "by Saint Loy." He is the patron saint of all kinds of smiths and metalworkers, and he is also invoked on behalf of farriers and horses, because of the legendary tales about horses that have become attached to his name. He practised his art as a metalworker all his life, and a number of existing artefacts are attributed to him.

The best text of the *Vita S Eligii* is that edited by B. Krusch in *M.G.H., Scriptores rer. Merov.*, 4, pp. 654-761; see also *P.L.*, 87, 481-94, with homilies attributed to him, pp. 593-654; *Anal.Boll.* 9 (1890), pp. 423-36; S. R. Maitland's account of "the goldsmith who became a bishop" in *The Dark Ages* (1845), pp. 81, 122, 141-57; E. Vacandard in *D.T.C.*, 4, pp. 340-9; P. Parsy, *Saint Eloi* (1904), in the series Les saints; P.B., pp. 4-16. On missionary sermons and the homiletic influence of St Caesarius see W. Levison, *England and the Continent . . .* (1946), app. 10, pp. 302-14, "Venus, A Man."

There are paintings showing him at work as a jeweller in the Lehman Collection in New York and the Dr Sternheim Collection in Amsterdam.

Bd John of Vercelli (*c*. 1205-83)

John was born near Vercelli in Piedmont about the year 1205. Our knowledge of him starts in the 1240s, when he was prior of the Dominicans at Vercelli. After filling various offices and undertaking missions, he was elected sixth master general of the Order of Preachers in 1264, an office which he held with great distinction for nineteen years.

John was rather short of stature—in his first letter to his brethren he describes himself as "a poor little man"—but made up for his lack of size by a remarkable energy, and he was tireless in his visitation and correction of the Dominican houses of Europe. On these journeys he kept all the fasts prescribed by the Church and by his Order.

On his election to the papacy in 1271 Bd Gregory X (10 Jan.) gave John and his friars the task of pacifying the quarrelling States of Italy, and three years later he was ordered to draw up a *schema* for the Second Council of Lyons. At the council he met Jerome of Ascoli (later Pope Nicholas IV), who had succeeded St Bonaventure (15 July) as minister general of the Franciscans, and the two addressed a joint letter to the whole body of friars. Later they were sent together by the Holy See to mediate between Philip III of France and Alfonso X of Castile. John was a skilful negotiator and peacemaker.

By this time, the Inquisition that followed Simon de Montfort's campaign against the Cathars (1209-31) had been over for some years. Gregory X selected John of Vercelli to spread devotion to the name of Jesus, which the Council of Lyons had prescribed in reparation for the Albigensian heresy, and John addressed all the provincial priors accordingly. It was decided that there should be an altar of the Holy Name in every Dominican church and that confraternities against blasphemy and profanity should be formed. In 1278 John sent a visitor to England, where some friars had been attacking the teaching of St Thomas Aquinas (28 Jan.), then recently dead. Two years later he came himself to Oxford, where a general chapter was held.

John refused episcopacy and a curial office at Rome. He wished to resign the generalate of his Order but was induced to keep it until his death. His cult was confirmed in 1903.

There is a full Life in French by P. Mothon, trans. into Italian as *Vita del B Giovanni de Vercelli* (1903). See also Mortier, 2, pp. 1-170; Procter, p. 158.

Note: The new Roman Martyrology will commemorate him on 30 November, which will be followed in future editions of this work.

BB Richard Whiting, Hugh Faringdon, and John Beche,
Abbots and Martyrs (1539)

In 1534 the clergy were summoned to take the Oath of Supremacy, recognizing King Henry VIII as head of the Church in England. With the exception of St Thomas More and St John Fisher (both 22 June), the Carthusian monks, and the Franciscan Observants, few stood out in immediate opposition. The abbots of Glastonbury, Reading, and Colchester all took the oath with their monks, like many others, in the hope of preserving their monasteries through a period of royal tyranny; but as the suppression of the monastic Orders gathered force, all three reached the point of no return.

Glastonbury holds a unique place among the religious centres of Europe and has long been a focus for special veneration. The deaths of Richard Whiting, the last abbot of Glastonbury, and that of the abbey's treasurer and sacrist for their faith during the persecutions of Henry VIII's reign form a well-attested part of its history.

Richard Whiting was born at Wrington in Somerset, probably soon after 1460, and educated at Cambridge (possibly Magdalene College). He became a monk early, took his M.A. in 1483, was ordained priest in 1501, and returned to Cambridge for his S.T.D. in 1505. For some years he held the post of chamberlain in the monastery at Wells, and in 1525 Cardinal Wolsey chose him as the new abbot on the death of Abbot Bere. He was described in the letter of commission as "an upright and religious monk, a provident and discreet man, and a priest commendable for his life, virtues and learning." St Thomas More was one of the signatories.

In 1535, following the passing of the Act of Supremacy, the king's commissioners visited Glastonbury, reported that the monks were kept in such good order that they could not offend, and assured the monks that no harm was intended against them.

A year later the lesser monasteries were suppressed, and by the time the greater ones were condemned Glastonbury was the only monastery left in Somerset. The commissioners arrived in September 1539. They impounded various documents—a book against the king's divorce, copies of papal Bulls, and a Life of St Thomas Becket—and questioned Abbot Richard. He refused to surrender his charge and was said to have showed "his cankerous and traitorous mind against the King's Majesty and his succession." He was taken to the Tower of London.

Thomas Cromwell received from the commissioners a "book of evidences" accusing Abbot Richard of "sundry and divers treasons." This is not extant, and its contents are unknown, but Cromwell subsequently noted in his *Remembrances*: "Item, the Abbot of Glaston to be tried at Glaston and executed there"—which indicates that the case was pre-judged. There is a good deal of uncertainty as to what actually took place—whether Abbot Whiting was tried in London or in Wells or both—but he was condemned to death. The indictment was not made public and has not survived. If it was for high treason he would have had a right to be tried by his peers in the House of Lords. The available evidence suggests that it was rather for the specific offence of denying the royal supremacy.

Abbot Richard arrived at Wells with his escort on Friday 14 November 1539. On the following day he was hurried to Glastonbury, where he asked permission to make a farewell visit to his abbey. This was refused; he did not know that by that time the abbey was deserted and the community scattered. He was dragged on a hurdle to the top of the Tor, a hill some five hundred feet high, and there, aged and sick as he was, hanged and dismembered. Before the evening his head was displayed above the gate of his monastery.

The treasurer of the abbey church, Bd John Thorne, and the sacristan, Bd Roger James, were executed in the same manner. They were charged with sacrilege in that they had hidden various treasures of their church to save them from the king's hands; and this may have been a charge against their abbot. They are both also commemorated on this day.

Abbot Hugh of Reading was commonly called Faringdon after his birthplace in Berkshire, but his surname was Cook, and he bore, or assumed, the arms of Cook of Kent. He became a monk at Reading and was elected abbot in 1520. It was an important office, carrying a seat in the House of Lords and in Convocation, and the holder was a county magistrate. Though hostile chroniclers have suggested that he was "utterly without learning," the master of Reading Gram-

11

mar School dedicated a book on rhetoric to him, and he maintained an excellent discipline in his monastery.

Dom Hugh was opposed to the preachers of the new Protestant doctrines, whom he called "heretics and knaves," but he was on very good terms with Henry VIII for some years—perhaps necessarily, as Reading is so close to Windsor. The king visited him and called him "my own abbot." The abbot sent presents to the king—hunting-knives, and trout netted in the river Kennet. He went further: when the king's divorce became an issue, he signed the petition to Pope Clement VII for the annulment of Henry's marriage to Catherine of Aragon and gave the king a list of books likely to help his case. In 1536 he signed Convocation's articles of faith, which virtually acknowledged the royal supremacy over the Church in England. At the end of 1537 he still enjoyed the royal favour, and he took a prominent part in the funeral of Queen Jane Seymour.

A few weeks later Abbot Hugh offended the king by repeating to Thomas Cromwell and the abbot of Abingdon a rumour that the king was dead. He was examined by a commission but released. Even so, though he had gone further than many of his peers in assenting to the king's wishes, he reached his sticking-point. When Henry VIII embarked on the suppression of the greater monasteries, it was known that Abbot Hugh would not surrender. In the summer of 1539 he was sent to the Tower of London, charged with treason.

With him were tried Bd John Eynon, a priest of St Giles' church at Reading, and Bd John Rugg, a prebendary of Chichester living in retirement at Reading Abbey. Eynon had been in trouble for writing and distributing a copy of Robert Aske's proclamation of the Pilgrimage of Grace in 1536; Rugg was charged with having possession of a relic of the hand of St Anastasius "knowing that His Majesty had sent visitors to the said abbey to put down such idolatry." These two priests may have been monks, but this is not certain. As with the abbot of Glastonbury, the terms of the indictment are not known, but it was not doubted at the time that all three were charged with denying the royal supremacy. Abbot Hugh spoke clearly on the scaffold: the supremacy of the Holy See in spiritual matters was, he said, "the common faith of those who had the best right to declare the true teaching of the English church." The execution of all three took place outside Reading Abbey gateway. John Eynon and John Rugg are both also commemorated on this day.

Though the abbot of Colchester was beatified as John Beche, his proper surname may have been Marshall, and his name in religion may have been Thomas. His birthplace and parentage are not known. He took his D.D. at Oxford in 1515 and for some years was abbot of St Werburgh's in Chester. In 1533 he was elected abbot of St John's, Colchester. Dom John Beche was a learned man, a friend of More and Fisher. He was interested in the new doctrines, and he and his community found it possible to take the Oath of Supremacy, but he was heard to speak against the executions of More and Fisher, and his words were reported to the king. In November 1538 commis-

extremity of the torture." He was offered a bishopric if he would abandon his allegiance to Rome.

After more than a year's imprisonment, Ralph Sherwin was brought to trial with Edmund Campion and others and convicted on the charge of entering the realm in order to raise a rebellion. He denied this, observing, "The plain reason of our standing here is religion, not treason." While awaiting death, Ralph wrote several letters to friends, including one to his uncle in Rouen, who had formerly been rector of Ingatestone. In it he says: "Innocency is my only comfort against all the forged villainy which is fathered upon my fellow priests and me. . . . God forgive all injustice, and if it be his blessed will to convert our persecutors, that they may become professors of his truth. . . . And so, my good old John, farewell."

On 1 December 1581 he was dragged to Tyburn on the same hurdle as Alexander Briant; he suffered immediately after Campion. On the scaffold he again protested his innocence of treason, professed the Catholic faith, and prayed for the queen. He died amid the open prayers of the crowd. He was thirty-one years old.

Ralph Sherwin was among the martyrs beatified in 1886 and was canonized as one of the Forty Martyrs of England and Wales on 25 October 1970. He is the proto-martyr of the English College at Rome.

See E. S. Keogh in *L.E.M.* 1, 2, pp. 358-96: earlier sources are listed on p. 396; Anstruther, 1, pp. 113-3, with portrait (copy of lost original) facing p. 199; also general sources as for Edmund Campion, especially *The Elizabethan Jesuits; Historiae Missionis Anglicanae Societatis Jesu, 1660, of Henry More*, trans. and ed. Francis Edwards (1951), pp. 128-9, 133-6, 173-4.

St Alexander Briant, *Martyr* (1556-81)

After the appearance of the publications of Fr Campion and Fr Persons the authorities made frantic efforts to capture the two Jesuits, and several other active Catholics were arrested. One of them was Alexander Briant, or Bryant, a young secular priest born in Somerset. During his time at Hart Hall, Oxford, he had renewed his allegiance to the Holy See. He went abroad to the seminary at Douai, was ordained, and returned to England, where he carried out a ministry in the West Country. When the Persons' house was searched he was in an adjoining house and so was arrested. His arrest took place on 28 April 1581. He was taken to the Counter prison, where it was determined to use whatever means were necessary to make him give information on the where-abouts of Fr Persons. After six days of almost complete starvation he was removed to the Tower of London, where needles were thrust under his finger-nails—he is the only martyr of whom this torture is recorded. When that was unsuccessful he was left in an underground cell for a week and then racked to the limit on two successive days. The rack-master, Norton, admitted that Briant was "racked more than any of the rest," and there was a public outcry, as a result of which Norton was imprisoned for a few days for cruelty.

Briant contrived to write a long letter from the Tower to the Jesuits in England in which he described his experiences on the rack: "I was without sense and feeling wellnigh of all grief and pain; and not so only, but as it were comforted, eased and refreshed of the griefs of torture bypast. . . . Whether this that I say be miraculous or no, God he knoweth; but true it is, and thereof my conscience is a witness before God." On the testimony of Norton (for what it is worth), Briant experienced great pain after the torture.

In the same letter he asked that he might be admitted to the Society of Jesus, even in his absence, having made a vow to offer himself if he should be released from jail, and he is in consequence numbered among the martyrs of the Society.

Alexander Briant was tried in Westminster Hall with Thomas Ford and others the day after Campion and Sherwin and on the same indictment. He came into court carrying a small crucifix drawn in charcoal on a piece of wooden trencher and with his head tonsured. In spite of his sufferings his appearance was still of "a serenity, innocency and amiability almost angelic." He suffered at Tyburn on 1 December 1581, after Edmund Campion and Ralph Sherwin. Like them, he was beatified in 1886 and canonized by Pope Paul VI as one of the Forty Martyrs of England and Wales in 1970.

Many of the publications noticed in connection with Edmund Campion have also some bearing on the story of his companion martyr. See especially *The Elizabethan Jesuits; Historiae Missionis Anglicanae Societatis Jesu, 1660, of Henry More*, trans. and ed. Francis Edwards (1951), pp. 129-33 and 135-6; *L.E.M.* 1, 2, pp. 397-423; Anstruther, 1, pp. 50-1.

Bd Richard Langley, *Martyr* (1586)

Richard Langley was probably born at Grimthorpe in East Yorkshire. He married Joan Beaumont of Mirfield, and they had a family of one son and four daughters. He was a wealthy man: his estates in East Yorkshire at Grimthorpe, Rathorpe, and Ousethorpe were extensive, and he provided hiding-places for Catholic priests after they were proscribed under the Elizabethan statute of 1571.

At Grimthorpe he constructed an underground hiding-place for the priests. This was betrayed to the authorities, and on 28 October 1586 a military detachment was sent to investigate. Langley and two priests were arrested: one was John Mush, the biographer of St Margaret Clitherow (25 Mar.).

Richard Langley was charged with harbouring priests in his mansions. He told his accusers that he would not deny the charge and added that if he had a hundred lives he would gladly sacrifice them all in so good a cause. He was hanged at York on 1 December 1586. Despite the representations of his friends, his body was refused honourable burial.

D.Cath.Biog., p. 671; *L.E.M.* 2, 2, pp. 259-64; *C.E.*, 8, p. 789; *B.D.E.C.*, 4, 131-3.

Bd Anuarite Nengapeta, *Martyr* (1964)

Anuarite's native country, formerly the Belgian Congo and now the Democratic Republic of Congo (but called Zaire from 1971 to the early 1990s), became independent in 1960. Preparation for independence was disastrously inadequate. Patrice Lumumba, the democratically elected prime minister, was overthrown only three months later, under Western pressure and with the collusion of a U.N. peace-keeping force; he was shortly afterwards assassinated. In the Cold War scenario he was widely seen by the "Eastern bloc" as a martyr to genuine independence from post-colonial manipulation who had tried to implement a genuinely socialist approach to the Congo's socio-economic problems. For the West, it was argued, keeping the country's rich mineral deposits within the capitalist sphere of influence took precedence over democratic rule for the people, as was demonstrated by Western support for General Mobutu when he took power in 1965. The Simbas, a rebel force loyal to the memory of Lumumba, tried to overthrow the government in 1964, with some support from Russia and China. The thrust of their rebellion was anti-Western, but there were many outbursts of violence in which Christians were a "symbolic" focus for attack, and Catholic priests, monks, and nuns were especially at risk because of their links with the Belgian missions, though in fact the Catholic Church had already begun to disengage from colonial structures before independence.

Sister Marie-Clementine Anuarite was a teacher, a young Congolese nun of the community of the Jamaa Takatifu, the Congregation of the Holy Family, at Bafwabakka (north-east of Kisangani—formerly Stanleyville—and fairly close to the Ugandan border). She had been baptized with her mother and sisters as a result of her father's posting to Palestine. She was much impressed by the story of the Martyrs of Uganda (3 June) in the 1880s. They were the proto-martyrs of Black Africa, and their canonization took place in 1964, when it must have been much discussed in the community. Soon after came the murder of their own Bishop Wittebols of Wamba (Anuarite's birthplace), and the danger to their own community became very real. But another side to the background to the events that followed was that in November 1964 the rebel headquarters in Stanleyville, Lumumba's home area, was seized by Prime Minister Moise Tshombe with large numbers of white mercenaries supported by Belgian partroopers airlifted in by the United States.

The Sisters were sitting down to lunch on 29 November 1964 when their compound was invaded by a lorry-load of Simba soldiers, who burst into the convent through doors and windows. The officer in charge told the Sisters not to be afraid: the Simbas had come to protect them from the Americans. The Sisters were told to pack their bags, and at four o'clock in the afternoon they boarded the lorry. They were forced to sit on the floor while the Simbas stood over them. The lorry stopped repeatedly at villages where the Simbas terrorized the people and looted whatever they could find. They became increasingly

17

drunken and menacing, sang bawdy songs, and threatened to rape the nuns. After a night spent in an abandoned mission station, the Sisters were forced into the vehicle again and taken on the road to Isiro. On the way they met the car of the colonel who was the commanding officer of the Simbas. The troops became excited and began to fire volleys of bullets into the air. The colonel, enraged to see one Sister holding her rosary, ordered all religious objects to be taken from them. Rosaries, crosses, and medals were thrown into the bush, and they were ordered to go back to Bafwabakka and to dress "like proper African women." The lorry took them on to the Simba headquarters at Isiro, where the Sisters were taken to a house, but young Anuarite was ordered to stay behind, as the colonel wanted her for the night. Mother Kasima, her superior, immediately said, "This girl has taken a vow of virginity before God. It is not possible." The colonel flew into a rage and hit Mother Kasima several times, but she held Anuarite and refused to let her go. Anuarite protested, "What you are asking is impossible. I cannot commit a sin. Kill me instead." She too was beaten, and her veil was torn off. She and Mother Kasima clung together and refused to be separated, even by force. Eventually they were allowed to rejoin the other Sisters. Later another colonel, who had been drinking heavily, tried to force Anuarite and another nun, Sister Bokuma, into his car, but they resisted, and he started to beat them both with the butt of his gun. Anuarite said again, "I don't want to commit this sin. If you want to, kill me," and then, "I forgive you, because you don't know what you are doing." Sister Bokuma's arm was broken, and Anuarite was beaten to the ground. Her last words were *Naivyo nilivyotaka*, which means something like "This is what I wanted." She accepted her martyrdom. The officer panicked and called other Simbas to kill her, saying that he was being attacked. Two of his henchmen came with knives and stabbed her many times. Then the officer drew his revolver and shot her through the heart.

The nuns took Anuarite's body into the house, and one, who was a nurse, set Sister Bokuma's arm. Their ordeal was not over, for Anuarite's killer came back several times and flew into a rage at the sight of the corpse. Another Simba tried to rape several of the Sisters, but they clung together and resisted, despite beatings and further menaces. In fear or superstition or both, the attackers finally left them alone, and the rest of the community was saved. Some days later they were freed by government forces.

In 1980 Anuarite's body was exhumed and ceremonially buried in a tomb in Isiro Cathedral, where it now rests. Pope John Paul II made his first visit to Zaire in that year and approved the setting up of her cause. On 15 August 1985 he visited Zaire again, and during a Solemn High Mass in Kinshasa, the capital, he announced her beatification. In a homily, he told the story of her martyrdom:

> When the hour of trial comes, this young religious faces it: her faith, her sense of commitment, the primary value she places on virginity, an intense prayer

life and the support of her community enable her to remain steadfast . . . It is the primary value of fidelity which led to her martyrdom. That is precisely what martyrdom means, "to be a witness."

Anuarite's beatification commemorates the witness of many other religious, Belgian and Congolese, who were loyal to their faith in a terrifying phase of their country's history.

Osservatore Romano, 9 Sept. 1985; James Fanning, *Clementine Anuarite*, Nairobi (1986); *N.S.B.*, 2 pp. 73-5. For the background see Ali A. Mazuri (ed.), *UNESCO General History of Africa, Vol. VIII—Africa since 1935* (1999), pp. 877-86; John D. Hargreaves, *Decolonization in Africa* (1996), pp. 190-7.

ST FRANCIS XAVIER (p.25)
Silver baptismal font on black field, for the many
conversions he made and Baptisms he performed

2

St Chromatius, *Bishop* (*c.* 407)

Chromatius was brought up in the city of Aquileia (near Trieste), which was probably his birthplace. He lived with his widowed mother, his brother, and unmarried sisters. After his ordination to the priesthood Chromatius took part in the Synod of Aquileia against Arianism in 381, baptized Rufinus (the translator of Eusebius) as a young adult, and in 388 was elected bishop of Aquileia. He became one of the most distinguished prelates of his time. He was a friend and correspondent of St Jerome (30 Sept.), who dedicated several of his works to him. At the same time he preserved his association with Rufinus and tried to act as peacemaker and moderator in the dispute over Origen's highly allegorical interpretation of the scriptures.

Chromatius was an energetic and valued supporter of St John Chrysostom (13 Sept.). He wrote to the emperor Honorius protesting against the persecution of Chrysostom, though his efforts were without effect. It was as a result of the encouragement of Chromatius that Rufinus undertook the translation of the *Ecclesiastical History* of Eusebius and other works; at his suggestion St Ambrose (7 Dec.) commented on the prophecy of Balaam; he helped St Heliodorus of Altinum (3 July) to finance St Jerome's translation of the Bible. He was himself a capable commentator on the holy scriptures.

Seventeen of his treatises on parts of St Matthew's Gospel are extant, as is a homily on the Beatitudes.

Propylaeum, p. 560; *D. Cath. Biog.*, p. 250; Bardenhewer, 3, pp. 548-9. The works attributed to Chromatius are printed in *P.L.*, 20, 247-436, but the state of the text is not satisfactory.

Bd John Ruysbroeck (1293-1381)

Jan van Ruysbroeck, Joannes Rusbruochius, or, as he is generally known in England, John Ruysbroeck, was born in Ruysbroeck, near Brussels, in 1293. In those days it was a small village, and John was of humble birth. Nothing is known of his father, and of his mother only her reputed goodness and her love for her son. At the age of eleven he went to live with an uncle, John Hinckaert, who was a minor canon of the collegiate church of St Gudula at Brussels, and attended schools in the city. Some years later his mother joined him there, living in a *béguinage*, and soon after her death John was ordained priest at the age of twenty-four.

Some time later Canon Hinckaert was deeply impressed by a sermon he heard in St Gudula's. He gave away all his spare goods and resolved to live a life of contemplation as far as that was compatible with his ecclesiastical duties. He was joined by a younger canon, Franco van Coudenberg, and by John.

In the spring of 1343 the three priests left Brussels. They were called to a complete dedication of themselves to God in a life of contemplation, and this was impossible in the city: many of the city clergy were debased and worldly, John had aroused hostility by his vigour against heresy, and Canon van Coudenberg had been in conflict with Duke John III of Brabant. With the duke's permission they took over the hermitage of Groenendael in the forest of Soignes, where they built a larger chapel and established themselves.

Life was not peaceful, even at Groenendael: the three did not belong to any established religious Order, so they had no protection against the criticism of neighbouring monks and of the chapter of St Gudule. It was also difficult to deal with the ducal hunt and its followers, who frequently demanded hospitality from them. By 1349, when two more canons had joined them, they formed themselves into a community of Canons Regular of St Augustine and made their vows before the bishop of Cambrai. In the following year Canon Hinckaert died. Franco van Coudenberg became the provost of the monastery, with John Ruysbroeck as prior. This was a good partnership—Franco had the administrative gifts to build up the life of the monastery, while John had great spirituality. He was docile, patient, obedient, fond of manual labour though rather clumsy, and perhaps a better subject than a superior.

John would spend hours in the forest surrounding the monastery, where no human distractions came between his ear and the voice of God. He made notes on waxed tablets and elaborated and arranged them in his cell. He wrote in the local Brabant dialect of Flemish so that his works might be read by laymen as well as clergy, and while some of his writings were translated into Latin in his own lifetime, they seem to have circulated slowly. It was not until a century later that his complete works were translated by the Carthusian monk Laurentius Surius and published in Cologne. They are difficult to classify; most of his major works are undated, and there has been considerable debate among scholars as to when particular works were written. He gave his books no titles, so that titles such as *The Book of the Kingdom of God's Lovers*, *The Book of The Sparkling Stone*, and *The Seven Degrees of the Ladder of Love* are only translations of titles originally used by early commentators in Brabant-Flemish or Latin.

Ruysbroeck's writings express a soaring faith, often in poetic form. Like other mystics of the period, such as Richard Rolle or Thomas à Kempis, he passes in inspiration from ordinary prose into a rhythmical cadence and sometimes into rhyme or alliteration. Yet he writes simply and often in a homely way about the great Christian truths. He writes directly out of his own experience as a contemplative, without concession to academic formulation or literary presentation. For example, he writes *in The Spiritual Marriage* of the nature of the Godhead:

> Simplicity and One-foldedness; inaccessible height and fathomless deep; incomprehensible breadth and eternal length; a dim silence, and a wild desert.... Now we may experience many wonders in that fathomless Godhead; but although, because of the coarseness of human intellect, when we would describe such things outwardly, we must use images, in truth that which is inwardly perceived and beheld is nought else but a Fathomless and Unconditioned Good.

His writing on the absolute nature of God, in whom he saw reconciled the antitheses of Eternity and Time, of Being and Becoming, of constant movement and utter stillness; and of the nature of the Trinity, which "ever worketh in a living differentiation" in "waves of endless love," was very different from the theology of the fourteenth-century Schoolmen but has a clear affinity with the work of other fourteenth-century mystics—Richard Rolle, Julian of Norwich, and Meister Eckhart.

Because of his disregard for academic formulation, and perhaps because he wrote in his local dialect, some commentators have speculated that John was illiterate or ignorant of Latin; but there is evidence in his writings that he was a competent philosopher and theologian, well read both in the works of the contemporary Scholastics and in those of earlier generations.

Ruysbroeck is one of the great contemplatives of the Middle Ages. His writing is crystal-clear, and its simplicity is deceptive: he is using inadequate words to describe experiences that lie beyond the intellect in the realm of pure spirit. His vision is personal and compelling. He is a poet rather than an expositor. His outstanding contribution is to make a link between medieval Scholasticism and Neoplatonism—a crucial step from the world of the Schoolmen toward the Renaissance.

If Ruysbroeck's writing had contained nothing original, the extraordinary influence he attained would be inexplicable. Perhaps the attraction of personal sanctity would be enough to account for the crowds that made pilgrimages to Groenendael, but he also had a strong influence on some outstanding scholars and ecclesiastics. Chief among them was Gerard Groote, founder of the Brothers of the Common Life, through whom John's teaching reached the school of Windesheim and Thomas à Kempis. It is significant that Windesheim became not Carthusian or Cistercian but Augustinian.

In the last few years of his life John was unable to leave the cell he shared with Provost Franco, who was even older than himself. He was physically feeble and nearly blind, but his spiritual vision was still clear. One night he dreamed that his mother came to him and said that God would call him before Advent. The next day he asked to be taken to the common infirmary, where, wasted by fever, he prepared for death with devotion and a steadfast mind.

Once a year, on the Second Sunday after Pentecost, the chapter of St Gudula's came in procession to Groenendael in honour of John Ruysbroeck. When the monastery was suppressed in 1783 his relics were transferred to Brussels, only to be lost in the French Revolution. Many attempts were made to secure his beatification. This might have come more quickly had he lived in the mainstream of Catholic tradition or had he written in Latin rather than in his native Flemish. His cult was finally confirmed in 1908 by Pope Pius X.

The standard Latin translation of Ruysbroeck's work is that of Laurentius Surius: *D. Joannis Rusbrochii Opera Omnia* (Cologne, 1552). A biography of Ruysbroeck in Latin appears from internal evidence to have been written some fifty years after his death. The author, Henry Pomerius (a Latinization of Bogaerts or van Bogaerde), had before him an earlier life by John van Schoonhoven which has since been lost. For the text of Pomerius and its limitations see *Anal. Boll.* 4 (1885), pp. 257-334. See also *Bibl. SS.*, 6, 880-95; C. S. Durrant, *A Link between Flemish Mystics and English Martyrs* (1925), pp. 3-14; S. Axters, *Spiritualité des Pays-Bas* (1948), trans. Donald Attwater (1954); D. Vincent Scully, *A Mediaeval Mystic* (1910); Evelyn Underhill, *Ruysbroeck* (1944); H. Blommerstijn, "Initiation into Love: John Ruusbroec," *Studies in Spirituality* 2 (1992), pp. 99-126; Guido de Baere, "Die Neue Ruusbroec-edition," *Studies in Spirituality* 2 (1992), pp. 267-87. For English translations of Ruysbroeck's work, see *The Seven Steps of the Ladder of Spiritual Love*, trans. F. Sherwood Taylor (1944); *The Adornment of Spiritual Marriage and The Sparkling Stone, etc.*, trans. C. A. Wynschenk, ed. Evelyn Underhill and J. M. Watkins (1916, rp. 1951); *The Spiritual Espousals*, trans. E. Colledge (1952); *John Ruusbroec: The Spiritual Espousals and Other Works*, intro. and trans. J. A. Wiseman, Classics of Western Spirituality (1985).

Bd Mary Angela Astorch, *Abbess* (1592-1665)

Sister Maria Angela Astorch was born in Barcelona on 1 September 1592 and was orphaned at the age of five, which brought on a sickness from which she nearly died. She was nursed back to life by Mother Angela María Serafina, foundress of the Capuchin convent in Barcelona, which she joined at the age of eleven. In 1609 the Capuchin nuns adopted the Rule of the Order of Poor Clares. Anglea Astorch was a member of their community in Barcelona when, at the age of twenty-five, she was sent to start another convent in Zaragoza, becoming novice-mistress there. She went on to found another convent in Murcia, where she spent the last twenty years of her life as abbess. She was a scholar, with a great love of the liturgy, and a spiritual director of distinction, with a gift for discerning the needs of individuals and helping them to find their own path in "keeping in step with God." She was beatified by Pope John Paul II on 23 May 1982.

Osservatore Romano, 14 June 1982; *N.S.B.* 1, p. 191; *D.N.H.*, 1, pp. 84-7, with portrait.

Bd Raphael Chylinsky (1694-1741)

Melchior Chylinsky was born in Poznan, Poland, the son of an aristocratic family. He had a devout upbringing and decided early to enter the religious life. He studied in his home town, and on 4 April 1714, at the age of twenty-one, he entered a Franciscan convent in Cracow. He was given the name Raphael in religion and was ordained priest in 1717, subsequently studying in Warsaw and Lagiewnicki, which is now a suburb of Lodz.

At this time Poland was exhausted after the Thirty Years' War, and both the kingdom and the Church were menaced by neighbouring powers—Sweden, Prussia, and the Lutheran German States to the north and west, Orthodox Russia to the east. The country was politically unstable under a weak king and an indifferent and demoralized nobility. There was extensive poverty and deprivation among the peasants and townspeople. Fr Raphael became known as a man of prayer who rallied his people and prayed God to free Poland from the invaders. He had a great devotion to sick and poor people, often giving them his own meagre food and his few clothes.

The period in which Fr Raphael carried out his ministry is known to historians as the "Dark Ages" of Poland. In 1734 Russia and Saxony invaded, and the War of the Polish Succession brought fresh misery—blockades, bombardments, battles, famine, civil disorder, epidemics. There was a major epidemic in Warsaw, and Fr Raphael rendered every service to the sick, nursing them and hearing the Confessions of the dying without thought for his own safety.

His own death took place on 2 December 1741, by which time he had inspired many by his example. The process for his beatification was started in August 1772 but stopped by the partition of Poland. It was not until 1949 that his cause went forward, and he was eventually beatified by Pope John Paul II on a visit to his native country on 9 June 1991. In his address the pope spoke of Fr Raphael's life as "a protest against the selfish spirit of his time, and the self-interest of the nobility," which demonstrated how, in the history of humankind and of nations, love was ultimately stronger than hate.

D.N.H., 3, pp. 255-7.

3

ST FRANCIS XAVIER (1506-52)

Francis Xavier was born in Spanish Navarre, at the castle of Xavier near Pamplona, in 1506. His first language was Basque. He was the youngest of a large family. At seventeen he went to the university of Paris where he was granted his licentiate in 1528. While he was in Paris he met another Spaniard of noble birth, Ignatius of Loyola (31 July), and although he did not at once accept his leadership, he was one of the band of seven, the first Jesuits, who vowed themselves to the service of God at Montmartre in 1534. They were to be spiritual soldiers, prepared to serve wherever they were called, and it was originally intended that their first mission would be to Palestine. The group received the priesthood at Venice in 1534 but had some difficulties in securing recognition.

In 1140 Ignatius appointed Francis Xavier to join Fr Simon Rodríguez on a mission to the East Indies. He found Fr Rodríguez in Lisbon staying in a hospital where he attended and instructed the sick and joined in his work. The two also catechized and instructed in the city, and Sundays and holidays were taken up in hearing Confessions at court. John had to stay in Lisbon for eight months. The king, John III, had a high regard for these religious. He kept them busy catechizing and instructing in the town and hearing Confessions at court. He was unwilling to let Francis go, but eventually he agreed and obtained documents from the pope in which Francis was appointed apostolic nuncio in the East.

Francis sailed on his thirty-fifth birthday, 7 April 1541. He refused gifts from the king, apart from some clothes and a few books, and would not take a servant, saying that "the best means to acquire true dignity is to wash one's own clothes and boil one's own pot, unbeholden to anyone." He had two companions in his journeys to the Indies, Fr Paul of Camerino, an Italian, and Francis Mansilhas, a Portuguese who was not yet in Orders.

Francis was accommodated on the flagship of a convoy which was carrying a new governor of the Indies to take up his post, but his companions were placed on another ship. The voyage turned out to be a very long one. They sailed south along the West African coast, round the Cape of Good Hope, and to Mozambique, where they wintered for two months, then up the African coast as far as Malindi, and across the Indian Ocean via Socotra. The admiral's vessel contained crew, passengers, soldiers, slaves, and convicts, all of whom Francis considered as committed to his care. Though suffering badly from seasickness he catechized, preached every Sunday before the mast, took care of the sick, and converted his cabin into an infirmary. Scurvy broke out, and the cramped conditions on the ship led to more sickness and ugly brawls. They did not reach Goa till 6 May 1542, after a voyage of thirteen months.

The Portuguese had been established in Goa since 1510, and there was a considerable Christian population, with churches, regular and secular clergy, and a bishop; but the sacraments were neglected, there were hardly any preachers and no clergy outside the walls of Goa, and the worst kinds of colonial abuses were practised. It was said that when slaves were flogged, their masters counted the blows on their rosaries. The debauched and avaricious behaviour of many of the Europeans, nominal Catholics whose behaviour was in direct opposition to the gospel they professed, could only alienate the local population. Francis began with a mission to the Indians. He would spend the morning working in the filthy prisons and the disease-ridden hospitals, then walk through the streets ringing a bell to summon the children and slaves to catechism. They gathered in crowds around him, and he taught them the Creed and the basic principles of Christian conduct. He offered Mass with the lepers every Sunday and preached in the open. For the instruction of the simple he set religious topics to verse to fit popular tunes, and this was so successful that his songs were soon being sung throughout Goa, in streets and houses, fields and workshops.

A particular problem was that of concubinage: there were very few Portuguese Catholic women in Goa, and Portuguese of all ranks took Indian concubines, often with little regard for their welfare or that of their children. Francis could not prevent the practice of concubinage by his appeals to Christian morality, but he taught the Portuguese that they must take responsibility for the women and children who were dependent on them.

After five months of work in Goa, Francis was told that on the Pearl Fishery Coast of India, which extends from Cape Comorin to the island of Manar, opposite Ceylon (now Sri Lanka), were people called the Paravas, who had been baptized in order to obtain the protection of the Portuguese against raiding Arabs but who knew nothing of the Faith and retained all their superstitions and vices. Francis went to the help of these people: in all, he made the long and dangerous journey thirteen times. He set himself to learn the Paravas' language, instructed and confirmed those who had already been baptized, and carried out a special mission to the children. In a long letter written to his Society on 15 January 1544, he described the great multitudes he baptized and how sometimes the fatigue of baptizing was so great that he could scarcely move his arms afterwards. The Paravas were a low-caste people. Francis had, predictably, little or no success among the Brahmins, the traditional priestly caste of Hindu religion, and was said to have converted only one; but his appeal to the poor was that he lived as they lived. His diet was rice and water; he slept on the floor in a simple hut. He returned to Goa to get help and came back to the Paravas with Francis Mansilhas, two Indian priests, and a lay catechist, whom he stationed in different centres. He wrote a series of revealing letters to Mansilhas, which illustrate very clearly his reactions to oppression and injustice. He described the sufferings of the local people at the hands of both Indians and Portuguese as "a permanent bruise on my soul."

Francis was able to extend his activities to Travancore. Here his achievements have been somewhat exaggerated by some writers. Christianity was not new to Travancore, where the Mar Thoma church, with its Syriac rites, had been established since early Christian times. The tradition was that it had been founded by St Thomas (3 July) in person. Village after village received him with joy. He made a journey on foot to the reputed shrine of St Thomas at Mylapore, where there was a small Portuguese settlement, and he called Mansilhas, by now ordained priest, to come and organize the converts. He himself was needed by the Paravas. A tribe from the north was attacking them—robbing, killing some, and carrying others off into slavery. Francis is said on one occasion to have held off the raiders, crucifix in hand.

Many incidents are related of him during his travels, especially of the gentle and courteous way in which he dealt with penitents. In 1545, from Cochin on the Malabar Coast, he sent a long and very outspoken letter to the king of Portugal giving an account of his mission. He spoke of the danger of those who had become members of the Church falling back into their former state, "scandalized and scared away by the many grievous injuries and vexations which they suffer—especially from your Highness's own servants. . . . For there is danger that when our Lord God calls your Highness to his judgment your Highness may hear angry words from him: 'Why did you not punish those who were your subjects, and who were enemies to me in India?'" He wrote in the highest terms of Don Miguel Vaz, vicar general of Goa, and asked the king to send him back to India with plenary powers after he had made his report in Lisbon. "As I expect to die in these Indian regions and never to see your Highness again in this life, I beg you, my lord, to help me with your prayers, so that we may meet again in the next world, where we shall certainly have more rest than here."

Francis set out in the spring of 1545 on the long and dangerous journey across the Indian Ocean to Malacca, where he spent four months. Malacca was then a large and prosperous city, captured by the duke of Albuquerque for the Portuguese from the Malays in 1511. It had all the disorder and vices of a frontier town, and Francis was able to establish reforms and to instruct many.

His movements during the next eighteen months are difficult to follow. He visited islands that he referred to in general as the Moluccas, not all of which are now identifiable. The Moluccas are the Spice Islands of what is now Indonesia, and Francis certainly visited Amboina and other places in which there were Portuguese merchants and settlements. In this mission he suffered much, but he wrote to St Ignatius:

> The dangers to which I am exposed and the tasks I undertake for God are springs of spiritual joy, so much so that these islands are the places in all the

world for a man to lose his sight by excess of weeping; but they are tears of joy. I do not remember ever to have tasted such interior delight, and these consolations take from me all sense of bodily hardships and of troubles from open enemies and not too trustworthy friends.

He returned to Malacca for four months. It was there that he first heard about Japan from Portuguese merchants and a fugitive Japanese named Anjiro. On his return to India he spent fifteen months in continual travel between centres in southern India and Ceylon. At the same time he began to prepare for a Japanese mission. No European had yet penetrated Japan, which was closed to all external influence. Francis wrote a final admonitory letter to King John III, saying, "Experience has taught me that your Highness has no power in India to spread the faith of Christ, while you have power to take away and enjoy all the country's temporal riches."

In April 1549 Francis set out, accompanied by a Jesuit priest, a lay brother, and three Japanese converts, of whom Anjiro, now baptized as Paul, was one. On the feast of the Assumption they landed at Kagoshima on Kyushu. Francis set himself to learn Japanese. So far from being gifted in languages, as has often been assumed, he seems to have found learning new languages very difficult. The belief that he was able to converse and hold disputations in Japanese is quite unfounded, but he made a translation of a simple account of Christian teaching, and this was recited to all who would listen. At the end of twelve months the mission had a hundred converts.

Leaving Paul in charge, Francis decided to push on further with his other companions and went by sea to Hirado, north of Nagasaki, where he was well received by the ruler and made a number of converts. At Yamaguchi in Honshu the missionaries were treated with scorn, and they pressed on to Miyako (Kyoto). It was nearly the end of December, and they suffered much on the road from heavy rains, snow, and difficult terrain. It was not till February that they reached Miyako—to find that they could not procure an audience with the local ruler without paying an impossibly large sum of money. Realizing that holy poverty did not have the appeal in Japan that he had found in India, Francis decided on different tactics. Well dressed, and with his companions as attendants, he presented himself before the ruler as the representative of the king of Portugal, giving him the letters and presents the authorities in India had provided for the Japanese emperor. These included a musical box, a pair of spectacles, and a clock. The ruler received the gifts with delight, gave Francis leave to teach, and provided an empty Buddhist monastery for a residence. With this protection Francis preached openly and baptized some two thousand people. It was his opinion that "among all unbelievers, no finer people will be found than the Japanese."

Leaving the Japanese Christians in the care of Fr Cosmas de Torres and Brother Fernández, Francis travelled back to India on a Portuguese ship. Among those on board was the traveller Fernáo Mendez Pinto, who left a full and amusing but highly fanciful account of Francis's activities and adventures in Funai, where he joined the ship. Francis found that good progress had been made in India, but there were also many difficulties and abuses, both among the missionaries and with the Portuguese authorities, and these needed his attention. These matters he dealt with lovingly and very firmly and thoroughly. At the end of four months he sailed eastward again.

He was awaited at Malacca by Diogo Pereira, whom the viceroy in India had appointed ambassador to the court of China; but at this point he ran into difficulties. The maritime authority in Malacca was Don Alvaro da Ataíde da Gama, a son of Vasco da Gama, who had a personal grudge against Diogo Pereira. He flatly refused to let Pereira sail either as an envoy or as a private trader. Nothing could move him, even when Francis informed him of the brief of Pope Paul III and his own status as papal nuncio. By offending a papal legate, Don Alvaro could have incurred excommunication, but Francis had unfortunately left the original document behind in Goa and was unable to prove his status. Eventually, after much argument and much delay, Alvaro conceded that Francis could sail for China in Diogo Pereira's ship, but without its owner. Francis therefore had no support from the civil power.

Francis could not go into China openly, for China was even more tightly closed to foreigners than Japan. He therefore sent his priest companion to Japan and eventually set sail for China with only his young Chinese interpreter, Antony (who had forgotten most of his Chinese). In the last week of August 1552 the convoy reached the desolate island of Shang-chwan, half a dozen miles off the coast of mainland China and about a hundred miles southwest of Hong Kong. From there Francis sent off letters, including one to Pereira saying, "If there is one man in the whole of this undertaking who deserves reward from divine Providence, it is undoubtedly you; and you will have the whole credit of it." Then he went on to tell of the arrangements he had made: he had with great difficulty induced a Chinese merchant to land him on the coast near Canton in return for payment, and he had bound himself by oath that nothing should ever make him confess the name of the man who set him ashore.

Francis Xavier's last days were confused. While waiting for his plans to mature, he fell ill, and when the Portuguese vessels had all sailed away save one, he was reduced to extreme want. In his last letter he wrote, "It is a long time since I felt so little inclined to go on living as I do now." He was taken aboard the one Portuguese vessel left in the area, but he found the motion of the ship hard to bear and was put ashore again with a high fever. He was left on the sands, exposed to a piercing north wind. A friendly Portuguese merchant took him into a hut where he was bled repeatedly, praying ceaselessly between spasms of delirium, but he became steadily weaker, attended only by the faithful Antony. On the morning of 3 December 1552 it was clear that he was dying. Antony put a lighted candle in his hand. Then "with the name of the Lord on his lips, he rendered his soul to his Creator and Lord with great repose and quietude." There were only four people at his burial, the Chinese Antony, a Portuguese, and two slaves. Antony wrote afterwards to give these details of Francis's death to Manuel Texeira, the saint's first biographer.

Francis was only forty-six years old. In his eleven years in the East he had opened up southern India, Ceylon, Malacca, and Japan to Christianity—and though his conversions in Japan bore the seeds of martyrdom, his memory would be preserved and his work bear fruit in many parts of east and south-east Asia. There are many examples of his humility and powers of spiritual and physical endurance. His life was spent in spreading the gospel and in mitigating the effects of a particularly harsh form of colonialism. He could rebuke kings and noblemen when necessary, and he showed a great tenderness for the poor and oppressed of any race.

His relics were taken to Malacca and then to Goa, where they are still enshrined in the church of the Good Jesus and carried in procession once every ten years in a crystal urn. Francis was canonized in 1622, at the same time as SS Ignatius of Loyola, Teresa of Avila (15 Oct.), and Philip Neri (26 May). Pope Pius X named him as patron of foreign missions and of all works for the spreading of Christianity.

The major source for the life of St Francis Xavier is the *Monumenta Xaveriana*, 2 vols. (1899-1912), published in Madrid. This is the critical edition of early materials, including the saint's own letters and a transcript of the depositions of witnesses in the process of beatification. Fr George Schurhammer, working in the archives in Lisbon and making use in Tokyo of Japanese sources previously unexplored, has been able to supplement and in some instances to correct this material. See his definitive edition of the *Letters*, 2 vols. (1943-4, with Fr J. Wicki), and his *Francis Xavier: His Life, His Times*, trans. M. J. Costello, 4 vols. (1973-82); also a number of important articles and monographs, most of which are to be found noticed in *Anal. Boll.*: see especially 40 (1922), pp. 171-8; 44 (1926), pp. 445-6; 46 (1928), pp. 455-6; 48 (1930), pp. 441-5; 50 (1932), pp. 453-4; 54 (1936), pp. 247-9; and 69 (1951), pp. 438-41. The notice in vol. 48 (1930) refers to Father Schurhammer's brochure, *Das kirchlichen Sprachproblem in der japanischen Jesuitenmission* (1928). Lives by Edith A. Stewart (1917), with translations from letters by David Macdonald; James Brodrick, S.J., (1952).

There is a statue of Francis at Malacca, looking out to sea, set by the ruins of the hill church where his body rested on its journey back to Goa. A famous painting by Rubens in Vienna dates from about the time of his canonization, as does one by Van Dyck. Two altarpieces in Rome showing his death date from the 1670s: in the Gesù, by Maratta (which has the wrong type of Indian—American—in the background), and in Sant'Andrea al Quirinale, by Baciccia.

St Lucius (? Second Century)

In the earliest part of the *Liber Pontificalis*, compiled about the year 530, it is stated under the name of Pope St Eleutherius (*c.* 174-89) that "he received a letter from Lucius, a British king, to the effect that he might be made a Christian by his order"—*i.e.*, asking that the pope would send missionaries.

This statement was copied by Bede into his *Chronicon* in almost the same words. In his *Ecclesiastical History*, he writes:

> In the year of our Lord's incarnation 156, Marcus Antoninus Verus [*i.e.* Marcus Aurelius], the fourteenth from Augustus, was made emperor together with his brother Aurelius Commodus [*i.e.* Lucius Verus]. In their time, while the holy man Eleuther presided over the Roman church, Lucius, King of Britain, sent a letter to him asking that by his mandate he might be made a Christian. He soon obtained his religious request, and the Britons kept the faith as they had received it, pure and in its fullness, in peace and quietness until the time of the Emperor Diocletian.

Bede makes a third reference to the conversion of Lucius in the recapitulation at the end of the *Ecclesiastical History*, though here he dates it in the year 167. The dates are not necessarily incompatible if one allows for the acceptance of the request, the sending of a mission and the public recognition of the Faith by the king and his people.

It is certainly possible that a British chief or local king (not, at this early date, a king of Britain) should wish to be a Christian and should send to Rome for this purpose. However, a mission of Pope Eleutherius to Britain is not mentioned by Gildas, Gregory the Great, Augustine of Canterbury, or any other authority. Bede's word and his source, the *Liber Pontificalis*, are the only testimonies.

It has been argued that the story of Lucius was deliberately invented to demonstrate the Roman origin of the Church in Britain in the face of claims from the Northumbrian bishops prior to the Synod of Whitby (663/4); but in Rome the story appears before these dissensions began, and in England it is first heard of from Bede nearly two hundred years after they were resolved. There is no evidence that the Lucius story was used in controversy to support the Roman claim to Christianize Britain until after the Reformation, and these later claims tend to confuse the issue.

An ingenious explanation has been put forward by Adolf Harnack: he points out that only one king and kingdom is known to have accepted the Christian faith by the end of the second century. The king was Abgar IX of Edessa, who is known to have become a Christian about the time that Eleutherius was pope. The apostles Thaddeus and Jude carried out a mission to Edessa and were buried there. King Abgar's full name was Lucius Aelius Septimius Megas Abgarus bar Ma'nu, and the fortress of Edessa is found Latinized in ancient documents as Britum Edessenorum. In copying a record of the conversion of Lucius Abgar, "Hic accepit epistulam a Lucio in Britia rege," the transcriber may have misread the latter phrase as "a Lucio in *Britannio* rege." Canon Dixon, who accepts Harnack's version, comments that the three extra letters involved in substituting "Britannia" for "Britio" were destined, among other things, to provide Britain with an extra king and the Church with a nonexistent saint.

31

The original fairly simple story has been considerably embroidered. The *Historia Brittonum* re-told the story in the ninth century, Celticizing Lucius into *Lleufer Mawr* ("Great Splendour") and calling the pope "Eucharistus." The *Liber Landavensis* gives the names of the envoys sent by Lucius as Elvinus and Meduinus. They became Elfan and Medwy in the Welsh version. An early editor of William of Malmesbury gives the names of the missionaries sent as Faganus and Deruvianus. In the twelfth century Geoffrey of Monmouth, whose imagination was stronger than his history, described in detail how the whole country was converted to the Faith, and the *flamens* and *archflamens*, priests of the Roman gods, were replaced by Christian bishops and archbishops, the latter based on London, York, and Llandaff. Rudbourne, a fifteenth-century historian of Winchester Cathedral, attributed its foundation to Lucius. John Stow, in his survey of sixteenth-century London, writes of St Peter's in Cornhill:

> There remaineth in this church a table whereon it is written, I know not by what authority, but of a late hand, that king Lucius founded the same church to be an archbishop's see metropolitan and chief church in his kingdom, and that it so endured the space of four hundred years until the coming of Augustine the monk.

Medwy and Ffagan are church dedications in the Llandaff area, and St Fagan's is the name of a railway station beyond Cardiff. It appears that these names of church-founders have become attached to the Lucius story but that they do not form part of it. Other legends such as the legend of the church of Chur in the Grisons that Lucius of Britain was a missionary, a bishop, and a martyr and the Swiss story that he was baptized by St Timothy (26 Jan.) appear to have no foundation.

Bede, *H.E.*, 1, 4; *Lib.Pont.*, pp. 222 ff.; Geoffrey of Monmouth, *Hist. of the Kings of Britain*, 4, 19; review by A. H. Mathew of Adolf Harnack's *Der Brief des britischen Königs Lucius an den Papst Eleutherius*, *E.H.R.* 22 (1907), pp. 767-70; A. Harnack's paper in the *Sitzungsberichte* of the Berlin Academy for 1904, pp. 906-16; Haddan and Stubbs, 1, pp. 25-6; H. Leclercq in *D.A.C.L.*, 9, 2661-3; Stanton, p. 580.

St Cassian of Tangier, *Martyr* (? 298)

The tradition is that St Marcellus the Centurion (formerly 30 Oct.) was tried before Aurelius Agricolan at Tangier and that the proceedings were being taken down by a scribe named Cassian. When Cassian heard Agricolan sentence Marcellus to death he dashed his stylus and tablets to the ground in protest. Agricolan jumped up, trembling at this defiance, and demanded an explanation. Cassian said that the sentence was unjust, and Agricolan ordered him to be at once removed and cast into prison. Subsequently he was tried, made almost the same replies and statements as Marcellus had made, and was martyred in the same way.

The account given in Ruinart is almost certainly not a verbatim report, and there is some doubt as to whether Cassian was actually associated with St Marcellus; but a martyr named Cassian was certainly honoured at Tangier as early as the fourth century. Prudentius wrote a hymn commemorating his martyrdom. This may be an archetypal account: the situation in which a clerk to a military court, himself of Christian sympathies, found the strength to join the accused in witness may have occurred on a number of occasions, and the substance of the account may be accepted.

Ruinart, pp. 344-5: the hymn by Prudentius is given on pp. 553-5. See also *Anal.Boll.* 41 (1923), pp. 276-8 (in an account of the martyrdom of St Marcellus), and 64 (1946), pp. 281-2; *Propylaeum*, p. 561; *C.M.H.*, pp. 630, 634; *D.A.C.L.*, 11, 1140; H. Leclercq, *Les Martyrs*, (1903), 2, pp. 274-81; *D.Cath.Biog.*, p. 221.

St Birinus, *Bishop* (? 650)

Birinus (Birin, Berin) was possibly a Lombard, a Benedictine monk sent from Rome by Pope Honorius I on a mission to the island of Britain. On his way there he was consecrated by Asterius, who was bishop of Genoa, according to Bede. He was told to "scatter the seeds of the holy faith in the remotest regions of England where no teacher had been before."

It is not clear why the pope found it necessary to send a consecrated bishop from Italy on this mission, independently of the church structure already set up from Canterbury. There is no record of any contact between Birinus and Canterbury. The *Anglo-Saxon Chronicle* calls him "the Romish bishop," which may indicate that his presence was somewhat unwelcome to the English hierarchy.

When Birinus arrived in Wessex he found the people so ignorant of the Faith that he decided to remain there and teach them. After an itinerant mission in Wessex he converted Cynegils, king of the West Saxons, and baptized him and his family. He was given Dorchester (Oxfordshire)—then a flourishing Romano-British town of some importance and in a heavily populated area—as his see.

His apostolate lasted fifteen years. During this time he built many churches, though it is now difficult to establish his connection with those surviving in the area from this period: the church at Wing (Buckinghamshire) is the most likely to have been his foundation. In his later years Birinus dedicated a church at Winchester, a city of growing importance, which was to become the royal capital by the Middle Ages.

He died in or about 650. He was succeeded by Egelbert from Gaul, but there is no record of Wessex bishops at Dorchester after 660. The town began to decline, the district was absorbed into Mercia, and in the ninth century it became a Mercian see.

Hedda, bishop of Winchester (7 July), translated the relics of Birinus to Winchester about 690. There they remained, though they were moved to fresh shrines by Ethelwold (1 Aug.) in 980 and Henry of Blois in 1150. In the early thirteenth century the Austin Canons of Dorchester claimed to possess the relics; Archbishop Stephen Langton presided over an inquiry into the claim, but the results were inconclusive. By the early fourteenth century a shrine of fine workmanship had been erected in Dorchester, and pilgrims visited both shrines. The Dorchester shrine has recently been restored.

Birinus' feast was not in the Sarum calendar, though it was kept in such centres as Winchester, Dorchester, and Abingdon. The failure to develop a wider cult was probably due to the declining importance of Dorchester, which became no more than a village. Berinsfield, a small village near Dorchester, still bears his name, as does Berin's Hill, where he was reputedly bitten by an adder.

The earliest evidence for the cult occurs in a Winchester calendar of the late ninth century. In the late eleventh and early twelfth centuries, Goscelin, Henry of Avranches, and others wrote accounts of his life. His feast was added to the Roman Martyrology in the late sixteenth century.

For the manuscript Lives, none of which is older than the eleventh century, consult T. D. Hardy, *Catalogue of Materials, History of Great Britain and Ireland* (R.S., 26), 1, pp. 235-9. Bede, *H.E.*, 3, 7, and 4, 12; *A.S.C.* for 635 and 665; *Anal.Boll.* 53 (1934), pp. 417; 107 (1989), pp. 129-59; 112 (1994), pp. 309-38. See also John E. Field, *Saint Berin of Wessex* (1902); T. Varley, *St Birinus and Wessex* (1934); *N.L.A.*, 1, pp. 118-22; *O.D.S.*, pp. 55-6; *D.N.B.*, 2, pp. 542-3; *D.H.G.E.*, 8, 1530-1; Stanton, pp. 581-2; C. J. Wall, *The Shrines of British Saints* (1905), p. 120.

Bd Edward Coleman, *Martyr* (1678)

Edward Coleman was the first victim of the public agitation stirred up by Titus Oates in 1678. Oates, a man of ill reputation who had been expelled from the Jesuit College at Saint-Omer, stopped King Charles II, who was on his way to walk in St James's Park, in August, to tell him of a plot to assassinate him and to put his brother, the duke of York, on the throne. Oates alleged that the Catholics in England, the Jesuits, and the French government were all involved. The king might have shrugged these accusations aside had it not been for the fact that they directly concerned the royal household. Oates named the queen's physician, Sir George Wakefield, and the duchess of York's secretary, Edward Coleman, as the leaders. The queen, Catherine of Braganza, was a Catholic princess from Portugal. The duke of York, later James II, was unpopular and a Catholic, and his duchess, Mary of Modena, was a Catholic from Italy.

Oates was allowed to make depositions before the Privy Council, at which the king questioned him personally. His evidence was muddled and contradictory. The matter might have rested there had it not been for the sudden death of a Westminster magistrate, Sir Edmund Berry Godfrey. Before the Privy Council hearing, perhaps anticipating that he would not be taken seriously, Oates had made depositions before Sir Edmund. When in October Sir Edmund was found dead in a ditch, face down and transfixed with his own sword, the

jury returned a verdict of "wilful murder" against a person or persons unknown.

How and why Sir Edmund died is still a mystery. One theory is that he died
of natural causes, and that an attempt was made to make it seem like murder in
order to inflame feeling against the Catholics. Continuing public and parlia-
mentary suspicion of the Catholic community suddenly flared to the surface,
and all Catholics were suspected of treasonable activity. The king and the
Privy Council were thought to be trying to hush up the affair because royal
persons were involved, and there was widespread panic and alarm. Even corresponding with Catholics on the Continent was taken as evidence of complicity
in the non-existent plot. All Catholics were ordered ten miles out of London,
and some were arrested and tried for treason.

Edward Coleman's trial was conducted in November—a month when people
recalled the events of the Gunpowder Plot against Parliament in the time of
the king's grandfather, James I. There was evidence that Coleman had corresponded with people at the French court (which might be expected of the
duchess of York's secretary), and though Titus Oates and his companions had
obviously manufactured their evidence, Coleman was found guilty of corresponding with a foreign power. He died at Tyburn on 3 December 1678, the
first of some forty-five victims of perjury, maintaining his innocence.

He was beatified by Pope Pius XI in 1929.

M.M.P., pp. 515-8; George Clark, *Oxford History of England: The Later Stuarts* (1955), pp.
92-5.

4

ST JOHN DAMASCENE, *Doctor* (*c.* 657-749)

To be born into a Christian family in Damascus in the second half of the seventh century was to be born into religious conflict, for the powerful desert creed of Islam was gaining in strength among the Arab races. John was born only five years after the death of Mohammed, and Damascus was a Muslim city. Many other beliefs circulated in the Middle East. They came from classical Greece, from Persia, from Egypt, and there was also a rich variety of Christian heresies. Even within the Church the Romano-Greek tradition in which John was educated faced fierce attack from the Iconoclasts, a Christian sect who, under the Byzantine emperor Leo the Isaurian, burned books and smashed images, destroying cherished traditions and aids to devotion (see Pope Gregory III; 10 Dec.). It was against these ideological pressures that John hammered out his faith.

Damascus had fallen to the Arabs in 635, but there was a sizeable Greek population, and some Greek officials remained in posts demanding technical skill or specialist knowledge. One of them was probably John's grandfather, Mansur. John's father, Sergius, known as Sarjem ben Mansur, succeeded him. His post at the court of the caliph involved the control of revenue. He is sometimes described as a tax-collector or the head of the revenue department, but the Arabic term of "grand vizier" may be more appropriate. The post seems to have been hereditary, for John took it over in his turn.

Christians were tolerated in Damascus. Muslims regarded Christ as a prophet, though they thought Mohammed a greater one. The Christians had to pay a poll tax but were otherwise free to worship as they pleased. John was baptized and given a classical Christian education. He had as a tutor a monk named Cosmas, whom the Arabs had brought back from Sicily as a captive. His father had to pay a great price for Cosmas, who was said to know grammar and logic and to rival Pythagoras in arithmetic and Euclid in geometry. He taught John all the sciences and excelled in the teaching of theology.

In spite of his theological training John does not seem at first to have contemplated any career except that of service at the court of the caliph. He was able to live a Christian life at court, and he was respected there for his competence, his fairness, and his humility; but after he had held this responsible office for some years his position became untenable. A new caliph, Abdul Malek, was hostile to Christians. They were required to keep accounts in Arabic, and new restrictions were placed on them. While they had formerly been able to share the basilica of St John the Baptist with the Muslims, they were now forbidden to use it. John resigned about the year 700, distributing his wealth to relatives, to the Church, and to the poor, and went to join the Great *Laura* of St Sabas (5 Dec.), near Jerusalem. A *laura* was a monastery in which the monks lived in separate huts or cells, grouped round the church, with a maximum of solitude. It gave him the peace he required for writing. Jerusalem was central to his faith: it was also outside the Roman Empire, so he was able to write without fear of persecution from the eastern emperor.

John's closest associate was a poet and singer who bore the same name as his tutor, Cosmas. In some accounts young Cosmas is described as John's adopted brother. The two were certainly monks together at Mar Saba, where they occupied their time in writing books and composing hymns. The other monks complained about their activities: they disliked theological controversy and objected to their hymn-singing.

Their work was better appreciated by the patriarch of Jerusalem, John V, who thought they should leave the *laura*. He made Cosmas bishop of Majuma and ordained John priest, bringing him into the city of Jerusalem. Cosmas reputedly made an excellent bishop; but John, who had given up secular administration, had no taste for ecclesiastical administration and soon returned to his theological work in the monastery. His writing in defence of icons became widely known and earned him the hatred of the persecuting emperors. If the Iconoclasts never succeeded in injuring him, this was only because he never crossed the frontier into the Roman Empire. So we have the curious situation of a great Christian writer who was able to defend his faith and attack heresy only because he lived under the protection of a Muslim ruler. This did not guarantee his safety: the Muslims were equally opposed to any picture or image of a living creature, and John attacked Islam as forcibly as he attacked Iconoclasm. He never lacked intellectual or physical courage.

We know relatively little about his life, which was lived wholly in Mar Saba apart from preaching engagements and consultations with bishops and theologians. Even the chronology is uncertain, but he is known to have lived to a great age, even if he did not reach the one hundred and four years ascribed to him by an Arabic menology. His written output in this long life was prodigious. It covered doctrine, worship, exegesis, ethics, homiletics, liturgiology, and poetry. It was based on solid scholarship and a very wide knowledge of patristic literature.

Of immediate importance to the Church of his own day were John Damascene's three treatises against the Iconoclasts. He insisted that the saints, members of the Church Triumphant, were to be respected, their pictures and statues cherished, their lives recorded and kept in mind, their cults encouraged. He saw Iconoclasm as a great evil, destroying precious Christian traditions relating to Christ, the Virgin Mary, and the saints. He argued from a sacramental view: pictures and images were the means through which the Holy

Trinity was worshipped and not ends in themselves. Matter was not evil and opposed to spirit; it was the means through which the spirit could find expression:

> Was not the thrice happy and thrice blessed wood of the Cross matter? Was not the sacred and holy mountain of Calvary matter? What of the life-giving rock, the Holy Sepulchre, the source of our resurrection: was it not matter? Is not the most holy book of the Gospels matter? Is not the blessed table matter which gives us the Bread of Life? And before all these things, is not the body and blood of our Lord matter? Do not despise matter, for it is not despicable. Nothing is that which God has made.

His main dogmatic work was *The Fount of Knowledge*, which is generally held to be the title of three major and related works. Part I is the *Dialectica*, a philosophical preparation for faith in sixty-eight chapters. True to his classical Greek education, John starts from a consideration of being and substance, of genus and species, of likes and differences, of potential and actual, of stasis and motion. This clears the ground for his analysis of heresies in Part II. Here he deals at length with the Greek philosophies, such as those of the Pythagoreans, the Platonists, the Stoics, and the Epicureans; with Jewish beliefs, including those of the scribes, the Pharisees, and the Sadducees; with the Essenes and the Gnostics and the Manichees; with Christian heresies, such as those of the Arians, the Nestorians, the Monothelites, and the Eutychians. In all, he identifies a hundred heresies, saying that this is a relatively small selection of those that exist, but "all the rest come from them." He then turns his attention to Islam and dismisses it in a few pages as a distortion of the Christian message. He ends with a meditation on the Trinity:

> Think of the Father as a spring of life begetting the Son like a river and the Holy Ghost like a sea, for the spring and the river and the sea are all one nature. Think of the Father as a root, and of the Son as a branch and of the Spirit as a fruit, for the substance in these three is one. The Father is a sun with the Son as rays and the Holy Ghost as heat. The Holy Trinity transcends by far every similitude and figure.

Part III is his most celebrated work, *De Fide Orthodoxa*, a hundred chapters dealing with the nature of God, the Creation, the nature of the universe, the divinity and humanity of Christ, the purpose and function of the Church, and the Second Coming. John drew on many patristic writers, sometimes appropriating whole chapters or sections from other works; since he did not indicate his sources, he has been accused of plagiarism by some later scholars who have spent much time in identifying the originals. This, however, was a perfectly acceptable practice in his day, and his reading was so wide and so well integrated that his own strong faith enabled him to make a synthesis of some very disparate material. He shows a very clear vision of God and his universe, centred on the life of the Church. He writes: "He who seeks God continually will find him; for God is in everything." In God's world love is the basic principle and the source of all virtue. It grows through the maintenance of Christian traditions:

> Order is good; the breakdown of order is evil . . . the natural order is obedience to the Creator: disobedience is chaos. . . . We must submit humbly to God as our Creator, and conform to the Creator's laws.

Christ left the Church as his body in the world, and true peace can be found only through the Church:

> Nothing is greater than the peace of the Church. The law and the prophets came to make it possible. For this, God was made man. This is what Christ came to announce; this he gave to his disciples before his Passion, and after his Resurrection; going up into the heavens in the flesh, he descended without flesh; he left his peace to his disciples, and through them to the Church. This peace is to live according to what is good.

John had a particular devotion to the Virgin Mary, saying that she "has captivated my spirit . . . day and night I see her in my imagination. It is she, the Mother of Virtue, who gives me eloquence." His Marian sermons, particularly three homilies for 15 August preached on the reputed site of Mary's Dormition in Jerusalem, are widely known.

John is also renowned as a poet and hymnologist. At least eight of the *Canones*, or poems celebrating the principal feasts of Our Lord, are thought to be authentically his, and a number of the hymns in the *Octoechos* bear the marks of his authorship.

John died at Mar Saba in or about the year 749. He had certainly died by the time the Iconoclastic council, held at the Palace of Hiera near Constantinople, declared him to be anathema in 753, describing him as "the man of evil name and Saracen sentiments . . . the worshipper of images and writer of falsehood . . . the insulter of Christ and traitor to the Empire." But John's writing survived Iconoclasm and many other attacks on the central tenets of the Faith. The historian Theophanes says that he was named *Chrysorrhoas* or "golden-flowing" because of the eloquence and grace of his writing.

John Damascene was not a creative writer; but his aim was not to invent something new. It was to take all the accumulated material of some five centuries of Christian writing and to sift and evaluate it in the light of the Gospels. The Byzantine world in which he lived did not value originality. The Eastern Church, beset by heresy and attacks from Islam, Zoroastrianism, and other Eastern creeds, needed a firm basis of belief, and that John provided in a range of works remarkable for their clarity of expression, their width of knowledge, and their depth of theological understanding.

His work bears comparison in these respects with that of Thomas Aquinas (28 Jan.), who similarly welded philosophy, theology, and poetry into a doctrinal unity to the glory of God and the edification of the Church. Unlike Aquinas,

John Damascene had no disciples, and no school of theological thought developed his ideas. This is not a reflection on the quality of his work; it reflects rather the different scholastic traditions of the Byzantine Church and the increasing marginality of those traditions to the Church in the West. Arabic, Armenian, and Georgian literature were certainly enriched by translations from his works, but it took a very long time for his contribution to be appreciated in the West. *De Fide Orthodoxa* was not even translated into Latin until 1150, and the first translation was a very poor one. Most of his other writings were not published in the West until the sixteenth century, and his complete works were not available until the eighteenth century.

John Damascene was finally recognized as a Doctor of the Church by a proclamation of Pope Leo XIII in 1890.

A Life by John, patriarch of Jerusalem, apparently written in the tenth century, is in *P.G.*, 94, 429-90. Fr M. Jugie has a full and detailed analysis of John Damascene's writings and doctrine in *D.T.C.*, 8, 693-751, and two papers in *Echos d'Orient*: "La vie de S Jean Damascène" in 23 (1924), 137-61, and "Une nouvelle Écrit de saint Jean Damascène" in 28 (1929), 35-41, which explains the complexities of some obscure and fragmented Greek manuscripts. Lives by J. H. Lupton (1883); M. Fortescue, *The Greek Fathers* (1908), pp. 202-48; J. Nasrallah (1950). See also *Synax. Const.*, p. 278; *Bibl.SS.*, 6, 732-40. Works in *P.G.*, 94-6, and critical ed. by B. Kotter in *Patristiche Texte und Studien*, (1969); Eng. trans. of *De Fide Orthodoxa* by S. D. F. Salmond, N.P.N.F., 9 (1899), and of the *Apologia in Defence of Holy Images* by M. H. Allies (1898).

St Fare, *Abbess* (657)

Fare, or Burgundofara, was the daughter of Agneric, a wealthy nobleman at the court of the Merovingian king Theodobert II, and sister of St Faro of Meaux (28 Oct.) and St Chainoaldus, or Cagnoald, of Laon (23 Nov.). She was born at Poincy, near Meaux, and soon after her birth was blessed and dedicated to God by St Columbanus (22 Nov.), the great Irish missionary monk who travelled to Gaul and founded the monasteries of Annegray, Luxeuil, and Fontes. Faro was chancellor at the court of King Dagobert I but later became a priest in the diocese of Meaux and bishop about the year 628. Chainoaldus became a monk in Luxeuil and followed Columbanus into his Italian exile after his disagreement with Theoderic II in 610. He assisted Columbanus in the foundation of the monastery of Bobbio, later becoming bishop of Laon.

Fare, like her brothers, was determined to become a religious, but her father wished her to make a political marriage to his advantage. During this battle of wills she became seriously ill. Columban's successor at Luxeuil eventually persuaded Agneric that her illness was caused by his insistence on her marriage. Agneric promised to allow her to enter a religious Order, and she recovered. Though he changed his mind at least once, he finally respected her wishes. He built and endowed a monastery for her. This was a double monastery of monks and nuns, following a Rule that was primarily Benedictine but owed something to the austerity of St Columbanus.

Later Fare's monastery became the famous Benedictine house of Faremoûtier-en-Brie. Fare served as abbess for thirty-seven years, and a number of English nuns were trained there under her guidance.

Among them were St Sethrida and St Ethelburga, the step-daughter and daughter of king Anna of the East Angles (both 7 July). Sethrida later became abbess of Fare's monastery, and Ethelburga followed her. Another English nun was Ercongota, daughter of St Sexburga (6 July) and Anna's grand-daughter, whom Bede describes as "a nun of outstanding virtue." He says that she "served God in a convent in Gaul founded by the noble Abbess Fara at a place called Brie, for as yet there were few monasteries built in England." Girls of noble birth were sent to Brie and other famous monasteries for their education and, if they so desired, "to be betrothed to their heavenly Bridegroom."

Bede, *H.E.*, 3, 8; *M.G.H.*, *Scriptores Rer. Merov.*, 4, contains a Life by Abbot Jonas of Bobbio; *Bibl.SS.*, 3, 611-2.

St Sigiramnus, *Abbot* (? 655)

Sigiramnus, or Cyran, was a member of a noble Frankish family from Berri and became cupbearer to Clotaire II. Though he felt drawn to the contemplative life, his father, count of Bourges and later bishop of Tours, wished him to marry the daughter of a wealthy nobleman. Sigiramnus refused, left the court, and received the tonsure at the church of St Martin at Tours. He remained vehemently opposed to a life of wealth and public position. After his father died he distributed his goods and money so freely to the poor that he was put under restraint as a lunatic for a time by a local official. On his release he continued to practise holy poverty. On one occasion, when he travelled to Rome in the company of an Irish bishop named Flavius, he crossed the diocese of Tours during the harvest season. He was "seized with compassion at the sight of the peasants covered with dust and sweat," according to a local account, and he insisted on doing a day's work with the peasants and serfs before gathering them in the evening to hear the word of God.

On his return from Rome the king gave him an estate at Méobecq, in the forest of Brenne, with all the rights, honours, land, rents, and taxes pertaining to it. There Sigiramnus had wooden huts constructed while a monastery and a church were built, and other noblemen came to join him. Later he founded another monastery on the royal estate of Longoretum (Lonrey), where he lived as abbot. Several notable stories are told of his sympathy with the oppressed peasants and with petty criminals.

The abbey at Lonrey, which later took the name of Saint-Cyran-du-Jambot, was dissolved in 1712. Jean Duvergier de Hauranne, one of the leaders of the Jansenists, took his title "Abbé de Saint-Cyran" from this monastery.

The relics of Sigiramnus and other saints that had been kept at the abbey were preserved through the French Revolution, and in 1860 the empress Eugénie presented the church of Saint-Michel in Brenne with a magnificent reliquary to encase them.

There is a Latin Life of St Sigiramnus, apparently written in the ninth or tenth century, but compiled, so the author insists, from an earlier text, which had become almost illegible through age. See *Anal.Boll.* 3 (1884), pp. 378-407; *M.G.H., Scriptores rer. Merov.*, 4., pp. 603-25. P.B., pp. 77-8, includes an account from the *Pieuses légendes du Berri.*

St Anno, *Bishop* (1010-75)

Anno, the son of a minor Swabian nobleman, was educated at the episcopal school of Bamberg. There he developed in learning, eloquence, and manners, and he came to the notice of the emperor Henry III, who made him one of his chaplains. In 1056, when he was forty-six years old, he was appointed to be archbishop of Cologne and chancellor of the Holy Roman Empire, with many secular responsibilities and duties.

This was a turbulent period in both political and ecclesiastical affairs, and Anno's eighteen years as archbishop were difficult ones. The citizens of Cologne resisted his appointment because they did not think he was sufficiently well born to rule over them. He became for a time regent and guardian for the young emperor, Henry IV, but Henry disliked him and, once he attained his majority, kept Anno out of public affairs. Though Anno led the German bishops in support of Pope Alexander II against the antipope Cadalus of Parma, Pope Alexander doubted his loyalty. He was summoned to Rome, accused of secret contacts with Cadalus, and later of simony. Like many bishops of the time he was inclined to give benefices freely to his relatives and supporters. His greatest problems came when he nominated his nephew, Conrad, as bishop of Trier. The people of Trier had a canonical right to elect their own bishop, and when Anno sent Conrad in with an armed guard there was resistance. Conrad was imprisoned and subsequently murdered.

Despite a certain political unwisdom, Anno was a conscientious and thorough archbishop who never allowed secular duties and activities to lead him to neglect the welfare of his diocese. He rigorously reformed the monasteries and established new ones. He rebuilt or enlarged a number of churches. He upheld standards in public morals, and he distributed large sums in alms. He never succeeded in overcoming the opposition of Cologne, which caused him much regret in his later years. At last he retired to the abbey of Siegburg, which he had founded, and spent the last twelve months of his life there in rigorous penance.

Most of the events of Anno's life belong to the troubled political history of his age. He was canonized (*c.* 1136) for his reforming energy in his diocese and for the austerity of his private life.

A long but unsatisfactory Life of St Anno compiled by a monk of Siegberg in the twelfth century has been edited with useful annotations by R. Kôpke in *M.G.H., Scriptores*, 9, pp. 463-514. The text in *P.L.*, 143, 1517-86, is also somewhat inadequate. The early German metrical Life known as the *Annolied*, is in *M.G.H., Scriptores*, 11, pp. 462-4. It is interesting as an example of Middle High German in the early twelfth century but is of no value as a historical source. See also *D.H.G.E.*, 3, 395-6; *N.C.E.*, 1, p. 562.

St Osmund, *Bishop* (1099)

A late-fifteenth-century document states that Osmund was the son of Henry, count of Séez, and Isabella, a half-sister of William the Conqueror. He came to England with the Normans and replaced Herfast as chancellor in 1072. In 1078 William nominated him bishop of Salisbury, and he was consecrated by Archbishop Lanfranc of Canterbury. Osmund's predecessor, Herman, had begun the building of a cathedral on the site known as Old Sarum. This was finished under Osmund and consecrated in 1092. Five days later it was struck by lightning and badly damaged. There is no record of what Normans and Saxons respectively made of this event. The damage was repaired, and the foundations of Osmund's church are still clearly marked on the hill, which is now a children's playground.

Osmund constituted a cathedral chapter on the Norman model, with a clergy school presided over by the chancellor, canons bound to residence, and the choral celebration of the divine office. Osmund was one of the royal commissioners for the Domesday survey and is thought to have been responsible for the surveys of Derby, Nottingham, Huntingdon, Lincoln, York, and parts of Lancashire and Westmoreland. He was one of the principal ecclesiastical lords present at Old Sarum in 1086, when the barons did homage to William and the Domesday Book was presented.

Osmund took charge of the building of the cathedral at Sarum and of the foundation and endowment of a regular body of cathedral clergy on the Norman model. His name is commonly associated with the "Sarum use." In his time, and for long after, many dioceses had their own liturgical uses—variations from that of Rome. The liturgical books of the church of Salisbury were in a state of considerable confusion. Osmund reduced them to order and drew up regulations for the celebration of Mass and the divine office and the administration of the sacraments uniformly throughout his diocese. Within a hundred years these revised offices, described as "according to the use of the Distinguished and Noble Church of Sarum," had been adopted in most of the English and Welsh dioceses. They were introduced into Ireland in 1172 and into Scotland about 1250. They remained the ordinary use in England until after the reign of Queen Mary, when they were gradually superseded by the reformed Roman rite of Pope Pius V. This change was made at the Douai College in 1577. There was some talk of reviving the Sarum use after the re-establishment of the ordinary hierarchy in England in 1850. At the present day, the Mass and Offices of the Dominicans most closely resemble the Sarum use, and the distinctive customs of the English Catholic marriage service are a survival from the Sarum *rituale*.

For this major work of liturgical revision, a considerable collation of documents was necessary, and Osmund collected together a very large library at his cathedral. He is said to have written a Life of St Aldhelm (23 May), a distant predecessor in the ecclesiastical government of west Wessex, for whose memory he had a great reverence: he assisted in the enshrining of his relics at Malmesbury.

Osmund seems to have spent much of his time quietly in his cathedral city, where he liked to copy and bind books in the library. William of Malmesbury praises his high personal standards and remarks that he was neither ambitious nor avaricious, the besetting temptations of great prelates in those days. He was known for his rigour and severity in dealing with penitents but was no harder to others than he was to himself. He died on the night of 3-4 December 1099 and was buried in his cathedral.

His relics were transferred from Old Sarum to the Lady Chapel in the new Salisbury Cathedral, and despite the destruction of the shrine in Henry VIII's reign, a slab from his tomb, inscribed with the date MXCIX, still lies in one of the bays of the cathedral nave.

Though Richard Poore, bishop of Salisbury, petitioned for Osmund's canonization in 1228, it was not till 1457 that it took place—the last canonization of a saint from England before St Thomas More and St John Fisher (both 22 June) in 1935.

There is no early Life of St Osmund, though a fragment of biography appears to be preserved in MS. Cotton, F. III, at the British Museum. The main details of the saint's life come from the monk-chroniclers: William of Malmesbury, *Gesta Pontificum* (R.S., 52), pp. 98, 424, 428; *Gesta Regum* (R.S., 90), pp. 372, 375; Eadmer, *Historia novarum*, trans. G. Bosanquet as *Eadmer's History of Recent Events in England* (1964), pp. 72, 82. See also Wilts. Record Society, *The Canonization of Saint Osmund from the ms. records in the muniment room of Salisbury Cathedral*, ed. A. R. Malden (1901); W. H. Frere (ed.) *Antiphonale Sarisburiense*, 2 vols. (1896 and 1901); W. H. R. Jones, *Vetus Registrum Sarisberiense, alias dictum S. Osmundii episcopi*, 2 vols. (1883-4); William Worcestre, pp. 53, 89, 157; *D.N.B.*, 14, pp. 1207-9; Stanton, pp. 583-4; W. J. Torrance, *St Osmund of Salisbury* (1920, rp. 1941); J. C. Wall, *The Shrines of British Saints* (1905), pp. 122-5.

St Bernard of Parma, *Bishop* (1133)

Bernard was a member of the great Uberti family at Florence and gave up a life of power and luxury to become a monk with the Vallombrosans, an austere community founded not long before by St John Gualbert (12 July). In time Bernard became the abbot of the monastery of San Salvio, then abbot general of the whole Order. Bd Urban II (29 July) created him a cardinal and entrusted him with duties as papal legate. Parma at this time was seriously disturbed by schisms—first by Bishop Cadalus, who set himself up as an antipope, then by other bishops who supported another antipope, Guibert of Ravenna. In the midst of these disorders Bernard was appointed bishop of Parma and consecrated by Pope Paschal II. He was a zealous supporter of the true pope and of the reforms of Gregory VII. He was particularly opposed to simony, which was widespread in his diocese. In 1104 he was driven from his see by supporters of the antipope Maginulf, who apprehended him at the altar. He was in exile for two years.

At a time when many bishops not only accepted but sought temporal power, Bernard actually resigned the temporal power of his predecessors in the see of Parma. He never forgot, or allowed others to forget, that he had been trained as a monk in a school of great austerity; and so far as was compatible with his duties, he retained all his monastic observances. When in 1127 the leaders of the Hohenstaufens proclaimed Conrad as Holy Roman Emperor-elect against Lothair II, Bernard protested and was again driven into exile. Lothair came to Rome to be crowned in 1133, and Bernard died in Parma in the same year on December 4. His monument is in the choir of Parma Cathedral.

In the supplement to *M.G.H.*, 30, 2, pp. 1314-27, the two more important Latin Lives of St Bernard of Parma, formerly printed in the *Chronica Parmensia*, have been re-edited by P. E. Schramm from better texts. A biography on popular lines is that of M. Ercolani, *S. Bernardo degli Uberti* (1933). Of the older biographies, the best is that of I. Affo (1788). See also *Propylaeum*, p. 566; commentaries in *Anal. Boll.* 48 (1930), p. 414; *Dict.Sp.*, 1, 1512 n. 14; *D.H.G.E.*, 8, 718-21; *Saints in Italy*, p. 69.

Bd Peter of Siena (1289)

Peter Tecelano was a citizen of Siena and a comb-maker by trade. He and his wife had a very happy marriage, but they were childless. When she died he was left alone. Peter joined the Third Order of St Francis, determining to devote to others the time and money that were no longer required for his household. His life as a craftsman was simple and uneventful: he worked hard and for long hours, and at night he would go to a church to pray and meditate on the life and work of St Francis. When he wanted to be closer to his religious "family," the guardian of the Friars Minor gave him permission to live in a cell adjoining their infirmary, where he carried on his business almost to the end of his life. He used frequently to visit the sick in the hospital of Our Lady della Scala, and he had a strong sense of his public as well as his private duties as a citizen. Once, when he had been deliberately passed over in the collection of a war-tax, he assessed himself and insisted on paying what seemed to him to be due.

Peter attained a high degree of contemplative prayer and received spiritual graces, which became known to many. His opinion and advice were valued by priests and theologians as much as by his fellow-craftsmen, but not at all by himself: "You are raising too much wind for this poor dust," he said to one who praised him. Among his chief faults in his own opinion was talkativeness, and it took him fourteen years of hard work to reduce it and to build up the habit of silence at which he aimed. He lived to a very advanced age. After his death he was buried in the Franciscan church at Siena, and pilgrims came from all over Italy to visit his tomb. He is thought to be the original of Dante's

"Pier Pettinaio," the *commercio de pettini*, or comb-seller, found at his holy prayers in the *Purgatorio*.

Peter's cult was approved in 1802.

Dante, *Purgatorio*, canto 13, line 128. There is a Life by Peter of Monterone, said to have been a contemporary, written in Italian and published in 1529. Wadding, 5, pp. 243-8; *Auréole Séraphique*, 1, pp. 456-63; *F.B.S.*, p. 925. See also F. Schevill, *Siena: The History of a Mediaeval Commune* (1964), pp. 254-5.

BB Francis Galvez, Simon Yempo, and Jerome de Angelis, *Martyrs* (1623)

Francis was born in Spain—in Utiel, near Valencia—in 1567. He joined the Friars Minor of the Observance in Valencia in 1591 at the age of twenty-four. He was sent first to Manila and then, as a member of a mission, to Japan. After the death of St Francis Xavier (3 Dec.) in 1551 other missions had extended his work in East and South-East Asia. In this period, while the work of the Inquisition was at its height in Spain, it was held as an article of fundamental belief that all those who died unbaptized—even if they had never encountered the Faith—were damned. Missionaries therefore felt it a duty to proselytize, even in conditions of extreme personal danger.

The danger in Japan appears to have been localized and intermittent at this time. Local Japanese warlords were largely independent of central control: the traditional imperial rule of the medieval period was not re-established till 1868. This meant that the missionaries' reception, like Francis Xavier's, varied. In some areas they were liable to be killed or driven out. In others they were allowed to set up churches, but there was always the risk of a sudden outbreak of violence against foreign influence.

In one period of persecution, Francis Galvez was forced to return to Manila for a time. Reports say that he "blackened his face" so that he could pass as a Japanese in order to gain entry to Japan again. The arrival of someone who looked like a Black African in early-seventeenth-century Japan would of course have aroused immediate and acute suspicion. Presumably this account goes back to the days when very few people in Europe had actually seen Japanese or appreciated that they did not look like Africans. Perhaps this helps us to understand the extent to which the early missionaries were venturing into the unknown. They had no understanding of Eastern peoples, nor of Eastern religions or cultures: only the determination to save souls.

Francis continued his ministry with courage and fervour until he was apprehended by the authorities. In 1614, when Japan cut itself off completely from the rest of the world, all missionaries were expelled. They were evacuated in four ships which left Nagasaki in November of that year, three for Macao and one for Manila. All religious houses were confiscated, churches were destroyed or desecrated, and searches were carried out for hidden missionaries; but priests continued to minister in hiding, with the loyal and courageous support of Japanese Catholics, and there were many martyrdoms.

Simon Yempo, a Buddhist monk who became a Catholic and a lay catechist, was captured with Francis Galvez. They were both martyred by burning at Yeddo in 1623. In the same year Jerome de Angelis, a Jesuit monk, was martyred at Tokyo. All three were beatified in 1867.

N.C.E., 7, pp. 838–45; *N.D.S.*, pp. 116, 291, 156; *D.Cath.Biog.*, p. 459; A. Valigno, *Les Jésuites au Japon: relation missionaire* (1583, rp.1990); C. M. Cadell, *The Cross in Japan* (1904); O. Carey, *Christianity in Japan* (1976). See also the general entry on the Martyrs of Japan, 6 February.

Bd Adolf Kolping (1813-65)

Adolf Kolping was the son of a shepherd, born at Kerpen near Cologne on 8 December 1813. Industrialization had begun: rural occupations were declining, and having no formal education, he found work in a shoe factory, where the work was repetitive and the hours were long. For some years he worked twelve hours a day and then studied at night. He was twenty-four when he graduated from high school, and he went on to study at Munich and Bonn before being ordained at Cologne in 1845. His experience as a factory worker and his long period of poverty gave him a great sympathy with young workers in industry, and he joined an organization for young Catholic men founded by a teacher, Johann Gregor Bruner. He soon became its president and was known as "the father of the journeymen," or artisans.

At this time industrial workers were often subject to exploitation, and many young artisans, brought up in villages, were lost and rootless in the rapidly-growing cities. Adolf Kolping understood their problems. He was transferred to the staff of Cologne Cathedral to carry out an industrial mission. He taught the value of labour in the framework of a philosophy very different from that of his contemporary, Karl Marx: the labourer was worthy of his hire, but he had a responsibility to work efficiently and well in return. He taught the dignity of man and the dignity of work. The members of his "Kolping Families" were encouraged to better themselves, as he had, by education. This drew a response from good employers, who increasingly needed a skilled and educated workforce.

By the time he died in 1865, there were twenty-six thousand members of "Kolping Families" in many countries. "Kolping Houses" provided adult education programmes with an emphasis on the Christian response to work and to family life, as well as hostel accommodation. While the movement has been most successful in the industrial areas of the Rhine, from the Netherlands through Germany to Switzerland, it has also spread to the United States, to Argentina, to Australia, and to India. Today, there are some 420,000 members in forty countries. At his beatification on 27 October 1991 Pope John Paul II stressed Kolping's contribution to Catholic social thought, calling him "the precursor of the great social encyclicals."

Lives by T. Braner (1935); S. G. Schóffer and J. Dahl, *Adolf Kolping der Geselenvater: Ein Lebensbild*, 8th ed. (1961); J. Nattermann, *Adolf Kolping als Sozialpédagoge* (1926); *N.C.E.*, 8, pp. 247-8; *L.D.H.* p. 323; *D.N.H.*, 3, pp. 269-76.

Bd John Calabria, *Founder* (1873-1954)

Born in a garret in the back streets of Verona, John Calabria knew poverty and hardship as a boy. His father died when he was twelve years old, and only the Church provided him with an education. He studied at a seminary and had no ambition for ecclesiastical preferment. He did his military service and, having no taste for war, volunteered for the most dangerous job available: nursing patients with typhus in the military hospital. After that he became a secular priest and devoted his life to the poor of his parishes. He founded an orphanage for neglected or abandoned children and homes for the aged and sick. He set up the Congregation of the Poor Servants of the Divine Providence, consisting of priests or brothers, and a corresponding Order for women. Later he founded a lay Order—the Family of Extern Friars—to work in poor districts.

John Calabria's work was characterized by a clear and shining faith. His prayer life was intense, and he is said to have suffered the pains of the cross. His trust in God was immediate and total: he was fond of quoting Matthew 6: "That is why I am telling you not to worry about your life and what you are to eat, nor about your body and how you are to clothe it. Surely life means more than food, and the body more than clothing!"

Born poor, he worked for the poor all his life and despised material possessions. He was beatified on 17 April 1988. Pope John Paul II commended his ecumenical approach to his work and his deep sense of Christian unity.

N.S.B. 1, pp. 163-5; *D.N.H.*, 3, pp. 12-7, with photograph.

5

ST SABAS, *Abbot* (439-532)

Sabas is one of the outstanding figures of early monasticism, and his feast on 5 December is kept throughout the Church in both the Eastern and Western traditions, though in the 1969 revision to the Calendar of the Latin rite he has lost his rank of "commemoration." He was born at Mutalaska in Cappadocia, the son of an army officer. In his parents' absence, disputes between relatives responsible for caring for him and administering the family estate drove him into a monastery near Mutalaska at the age of eight, and, though the family disputes were settled, he felt a strong vocation to the monastic life. He was sent to Jerusalem at the age of eighteen to learn from the example of the solitaries of that country, but the abbot, St Euthymius (20 Jan.), judged him to be too young to lead a completely solitary life and recommended him to his own monastery.

Sabas was known as a very hard worker. He would help his brothers in the heavier work, chopping all the wood and fetching water for the house. When he was thirty years of age the abbot gave him leave to spend five days a week in a remote cave. He spent them in prayer and manual labour, taking bundles of palm fronds with him every Sunday evening and setting himself a task of making ten baskets a day. He returned every Friday with fifty woven baskets.

On one occasion he was sent with a companion on business to Alexandria. There Sabas met his parents, who pleaded with him to give up the monastic life and take up his father's profession. When he refused they asked him at least to accept money, but he would take only three pieces of gold, which he gave to his abbot on his return.

After Euthymius died Sabas retired deeper into the desert in the direction of Jericho and spent four years alone in the wilderness. He lived on wild herbs and water from the brook Cedron until the local people began to bring him simple offerings of bread, cheese, and dates. Many people came to him asking him to found a new community, and eventually he consented to found a *laura* (see St John Damascene, 4 Dec.), where he and his companions could live a semi-eremitical life. The number of his disciples grew to 150. There was no priest in the community, because Sabas thought that no religious man could think himself worthy to enter the priesthood.

Eventually some of the monks asked Sallust, patriarch of Jerusalem, to intervene, and in 491 he insisted that Sabas should be ordained. He was then fifty-three years old. Some of his monks also complained that he was often absent from the *laura*. Like Abbot Euthymius, he spent much time in solitude and made a practice of spending Lent alone. Sixty monks withdrew and set up a separate *laura* some miles away. When Sabas heard that they had run into difficulties he sent them supplies and repaired their church.

The reputation Sabas acquired for holiness brought people from remote countries to his *laura*, and among the monks were Egyptians and Armenians for whom special arrangements had to be made so that they could celebrate the offices in their own languages. After the death of his father, his mother came to Palestine and served God under his direction. She provided the money for two buildings, a hostel for strangers and a hospital for the sick, as well as for another hospital in Jericho and a new monastery near the *laura*.

The patriarch of Jerusalem appointed Sabas in 493 as archimandrite over all the monks of Palestine who lived the eremitical life in separate cells. St Theodosius the Cenobiarch (11 Jan.) was appointed to a similar position over the monks who lived in community. In 511 Sabas was sent by Patriarch Elias of Jerusalem with other abbots on a delegation to the emperor Anastasius in Constantinople. When the delegation arrived, the members were admitted to the palace—all but Sabas. The officer at the gate thought he was a beggar and turned him away. Sabas withdrew, saying nothing. When the emperor had read the patriarch's letter, which included a strong commendation of Sabas, he asked where he was. The saint was found in a corner, saying his prayers.

Though Sabas spent the winter in Constantinople and often visited the emperor to argue against the Monophysite heresy, the patriarch Elias was banished from Jerusalem and lived in exile at Aïla (Eilat) on the Red Sea. Sabas was with him when he died. Afterwards he went on a mission through Caesarea, Scythopolis, and other districts, preaching and opposing heresy.

In his ninety-first year he went again to Constantinople at the request of Patriarch Peter to make representations concerning the Samaritan revolt and its violent repression by the imperial forces. The emperor Justinian received him with honour and offered to endow his monasteries. Sabas thanked him but said that the monks had no need of such endowments as long as they served God. He asked instead that the people of Palestine should not be taxed so heavily, that the Emperor should build a hostel at Jerusalem for pilgrims and a fortress for the protection of monks and hermits against raiders, and that there should be further measures to settle the problem of the Samaritans. All these requests were granted.

Very soon after his return to his *laura*, Sabas became ill. The patriarch had him taken to a nearby church, where he personally tended his needs. Sabas suffered a great deal but bore his sufferings with patience and resignation. When he was dying he begged to be taken back to his *laura*, where he appointed his successor, gave him instructions, and lay for four days in perfect silence, concerning himself with God alone. He died in the evening of 5 December 532, at the age of ninety-four.

His chief monastery, called after him Mar Saba and sometimes distinguished as the Great *Laura*, still exists in a gorge of the Cedron, ten miles south-east of Jerusalem in the desert. Among its monks were St John Damascene (4 Dec.) and St John the Silent (13 May). After a period of ruin, the monastery was restored by the Russian government in 1840 and is now inhabited by monks of the Eastern Orthodox Church. The relics of St Sabas were returned to the monastery in 1965 by Pope Paul VI.

The Life of St Sabas, written in Greek by Cyril of Scythopolis, is one of the most famous of hagiographical documents: see E. Schwarz (ed.), *Kyrillos von Skythopolis* (1939) for full text. There is an English version in de Villegas, pp. 463-6. See also P.B., pp. 67-77; *D. Cath. Biog.*, p. 1017; *Bibl.SS.* 11, 533-5. An exhaustive account of Sabas and his monastery was published in Greek by J. Phokylides at Alexandria in 1927. On the return of the relics see E. Salem in *Eastern Churches Review* 1 (1966), pp. 41-6.

St Crispina, *Martyr* (304)

St Augustine (28 Aug.) frequently mentions Crispina as a martyr well known in North Africa in his time. He tells us that she was a woman of rank, a native of Thagara in Numidia, married, with several children, and worthy of estimation with such famous martyrs as St Agnes (21 Jan.) and St Thecla (23 Sept.). The account of her trial is probably not an exact transcript of her cross-examination: no doubt later telling made the statements sharper and elaborated some of the arguments, producing a rather stilted dialogue, but it does give a very clear impression of a courageous and articulate woman testifying to her faith.

Crispina was brought before the proconsul Anulinus at Theveste during the persecution of Diocletian charged with ignoring the imperial commands. Anulinus asked, "Have you understood the meaning of the decree?" to which Crispina replied, "I do not know what that decree is."

ANULINUS: It is that you should sacrifice to all our gods for the welfare of the emperors, according to the law given by our lords Diocletian and Maximilian, the pious Augusti, and Constantius, the most illustrious Caesar.
CRISPINA: I will never sacrifice to any but the one God, and to our Lord Jesus Christ his son, who was born and suffered for us.
ANULINUS: Give up this superstition, and bow your head before our sacred gods.
CRISPINA: I worship my God every day, and I know no other.
ANULINUS: You are obstinate and disrespectful and you will bring upon yourself the severity of the law.
CRISPINA: If necessary I will suffer for the faith I hold.
ANULINUS: Are you so vain a creature that you will not put away your folly and worship the sacred deities?
CRISPINA: I worship my God every day, and I know no other.
ANULINUS: I put the sacred edict before you for your observance.

CRISPINA: I observe an edict, but it is that of my Lord Jesus Christ.

ANULINUS: You will lose your head if you do not obey the emperor's commands. All Africa has submitted to them and you will be made to do the same.

CRISPINA: I will sacrifice to the Lord who made the heavens and the earth, the sea and all things that are in them. But I will never be forced to sacrifice to evil spirits.

ANULINUS: Then you will not accept those gods to whom you must give honour if you are to save your life?

CRISPINA: That is no true religion that forces the unwilling.

ANULINUS: But will you not comply, and with bent head offer a little incense in the sacred temples?

CRISPINA: I have never done such a thing since I was born, and I will not do it so long as I live.

ANULINUS: Do it, however, just to escape the penalty of the law.

CRISPINA: I do not fear what you threaten, but I fear the God who is in heaven. If I defy him then shall I be sacrilegious, and he will cast me off, and I will not be found in the day that he comes.

ANULINUS: You cannot be sacrilegious if you obey the law.

CRISPINA: Would you have me sacrilegious before God so that I may not be so before the emperors? No, indeed! God is great and almighty. He made the sea and the green plants and the dry land. How can I consider men, the work of his hands, before himself?

ANULINUS: Profess the Roman religion of our lords the unconquerable emperors, as we ourselves observe it.

CRISPINA: I know only one God. Those gods of yours are stones, things carved by the hands of men.

ANULINUS: You utter blasphemy. That is not the way to look after your own safety.

Then Anulinus ordered her hair to be cut off and her head shaved, exposing her to the derision of the mob, and when she still remained firm asked her: "Do you want to live? Or to die in agony like your fellows Maxima, Donatilla and Secunda?"

CRISPINA: If I wanted to die and abandon my soul to loss and endless fire, I should treat your demons in the way you wish.

ANULINUS: I will have you beheaded if you persist in mocking at our venerable gods.

CRISPINA: Thank God for that. I should certainly lose my head if I took to worshipping them.

ANULINUS: Then do you persist in your folly?

CRISPINA: My God, who was and who is, willed that I be born. He brought me to salvation through the waters of baptism. And he is with me to stay my soul from committing the sacrilege that you require.

ANULINUS: Can we endure this impious Crispina any longer?

The proconsul then ordered the proceedings to be read over aloud, and he sentenced Crispina to death by the sword, at which she exclaimed, "Praise to God, who has looked down and delivered me out of your hands!" She was executed at Theveste on 5 December 304, probably with a group of other martyrs. There was a great basilica at Theveste (now Tabessa) which may have contained her shrine.

Crispina's name occurs in the *Hieronymianum*, p. 406; Ruinart, pp. 476-9: see Delehaye's comments on the text in *Les passions des martyrs . . .* (1921), pp. 110-4; also Leclerc, *Les Martyrs*, 2 (1903), pp. 287-90; H. Musurillo, *The Acts of the Christian Martyrs* (1972), pp. 302-9.

St Sola (794)

Sola was an Englishman who followed St Boniface (5 June) into Germany, became his disciple, and was ordained priest by him. Called to a solitary life, he retired on the advice of Boniface to a lonely place at Fulda. Later he moved to the banks of the river Altmuhl, near Eichstätt. He passed his days in a little cell in penance and prayer. After the death of Boniface, St Willibald (7 June, but 7 July in future editions) and St Winebald (18 Dec.) asked him to make his cell the religious centre of the surrounding country. He was given a piece of land, and the abbey of Solnhofen, which was a dependency of Fulda, was erected on it. Sola died on 3 December 794, and a chapel was built where his oratory had stood. His name is still preserved in that of the village of Solnhofen, to the west of Eichstätt.

The Life of St Sola was written in 835, forty years after his death, by Ermanrich, a monk of Ellwagen, who obtained his information from a servant of the saint and other surviving contemporaries. The Latin of this biography was revised in the following year by Master Roland. For texts see *M.G.H., Scriptores*, 15, 1, pp. 151-63; *AA.SS.OSB.*, Saec. 3, pp. 242-59. See also Stanton, p. 582; *D.Cath.Biog.*, p. 1069.

St Christina of Markyate (c.1097-1161)

The first part of the Life of Christina (or Theodora) of Markyate is the familiar story of a girl who had a religious vocation but whose parents were determined that she should make an advantageous marriage. What is remarkable in her case is the strength of her response in the face of ecclesiastical as well as parental opposition.

Christina came of a noble Saxon family in Huntingdonshire. Nearly half a century after the Norman Conquest, invading Normans and conquered Saxons were coming to terms. Christina's father, Aitti, was a rich and influential guild merchant. Apparently he and her mother, Beatrice, were at least conventionally pious, for in 1112, when she was about sixteen years old, they took her to St Alban's Abbey, to visit the shrine of the martyr.

When the girl had looked carefully at the place and observed the religious bearing of the monks who dwelt there, she declared how fortunate the inmates were and expressed a wish to share in their fellowship. At length, as her parents were leaving the monastery, she made a sign of the cross with one of her fingernails on the door as a token that she had placed her affection there.

She made a private vow of virginity. Apparently there were no witnesses, and before she could dedicate herself publicly her parents arranged a marriage for her to a young Saxon nobleman named Burhtred. Christina was forced to go through a marriage ceremony against her will, but she refused to consummate the union. Flattery, "grand promises," threats, and even beatings did not change her mind. Her parents took her before the prior of St Mary's, Huntingdon, saying that she was making them "the laughing stock of our neighbours, a mockery and derision to those who are round about." The prior preached the sanctity of marriage. Christina answered him with spirit, until he despaired of changing her mind and suggested that she should be brought before the bishop of Lincoln, who was coming into residence at a nearby estate.

The question was a difficult one in ecclesiastical law: marriage is a sacrament of the Church, but a commitment to celibacy, if proved, is an obstacle to marriage. The prior went to consult Bishop Robert Bloet of Lincoln accompanied by "the most noble citizens of the town, who thought that, as the marriage had already been performed, the bishop would immediately order the betrothed woman to submit to the authority of her husband." By this time Christina's determined stand had become a matter of public concern in Huntingdon: she had refused to accept the authority of her father, her husband, and the prior, and the outraged nobles can have expected only one answer.

Surprisingly, the bishop disagreed, saying that "there is no bishop under heaven who could force her into marriage, if according to her vow she wishes to keep herself for God." But later, it is said under pressure and after being handsomely bribed, he reversed his judgment. Christina, desperate and still imprisoned in her father's house, managed to contact a hermit named Eadwin, who heard her story and agreed to help her.

The practice was for hermits to spend two years in a monastery before being allowed to live a solitary life. They owed allegiance to their abbots but not to secular bishops, and Eadwin seems to have been free to make his own decisions. It was clear to him that Christina could not find safety in the Huntingdon district, for "the whole of that district for miles around was full of her relatives"; but he had an elderly relative named Roger who was a hermit of St Alban's Abbey and lived at Markyate, a few miles to the north of the city. He went to see Roger and asked him to take Christina into his care. Roger rejected the proposal angrily, saying that it was not his purpose to dissolve marriages.

Eadwin was so convinced of the justice of Christina's cause that he explored several other temporary hiding places for her and then took the only ecclesiastical action possible: he appealed to the archbishop of Canterbury. He secured a private interview with the archbishop and told Christina's story. The archbishop, Ralph d'Escures, "a man deeply versed in both the divine and civil law, as a man in his position should be, and acceptable to all for his piety," decided in Christina's favour, telling Eadwin to "hasten away and sustain the precious dove of God."

Christina chose to go to an anchoress named Alfwen at Flamstead, not far from Roger's hermitage. She escaped from her father's house and rode the thirty miles to Flamstead on horseback, in fear of capture. It took six hours. She was joyfully welcomed by Alfwen, given the habit, and hidden in a small dark room. She "remained carefully concealed there for a long time, finding great joy in Christ." Though her parents and Burhtred scoured the country-side they failed to find her, and after two years (perhaps when Alfwen died) Roger, recognizing the strength of her vocation, agreed to care for her. She continued to live in hiding and suffered many privations and illnesses, but she was sustained by visions of the Queen of Heaven. At last Burhtred came to the hermitage, accompanied by his two brothers, one a canon and the other a layman, and the marriage was solemnly renounced in the presence of Roger and five other hermits who lived in the locality. In 1122 both her betrothal and her marriage were formally annulled by Thurstan, archbishop of York, on the grounds that she had made a vow of virginity, she had been forced into mar-riage under duress, and the marriage was unconsummated.

After Roger's death Christina had to leave Markyate for a time because of the continued antagonism of Bishop Robert Bloet, but she was able to return after his death in 1123, and she remained there peacefully in the hermitage for the rest of her life. Her brother Gregory became a monk of St Alban's Abbey, and the abbey was her spiritual centre. Other young women vowed to virginity came to stay with her, and the house at Markyate became a regular priory of nuns. Archbishop Thurstan was so impressed by her holiness of life and her management of the priory that in 1130 he asked her to become abbess of his nunnery of St Clement at York. The great foundations of Fontrevault and Marcigny also asked her to join them, but she was persuaded by Abbot Geoffrey of St Alban's to remain at Markyate. She had a considerable influence on Geoffrey, leading him to follow a life of prayer, solitude, and poverty rather than being ambitious for ecclesiastical preferment.

Christina seems to have been a tranquil and composed woman who was not given to excessive mortification. She was a skilled needlewoman and embroi-dered a present of mitres and sandals for the English pope, Adrian IV, who had been educated at St Alban's Abbey. She probably owned the sumptuous and magnificently illustrated St Alban's Psalter, which Holdsworth argues had been made for her: it contains references to her father, her mother, her broth-ers Gregory and Simon, and her sister Margaret; and there are specific refer-ences to women saints who rejected marriage for the religious life.

There are some traces of a cult. There was a feast at St Albans, city of Christina's companions Roger and Sigar, on 5 December, and a Christina is mentioned on the same day in some Parisian calendars and in the English martyrology of 1608. Among other saints on the rood-screen of the church at Gately in Norfolk is a *puella de Ridibowne*—probably Christina, since the village of Redbourn is close to Flamstead and Markyate on the old Roman road from St Albans to Dunstable. She is not included in the new draft Roman Martyrology, but her story is worth retaining here as that of a determined as well as holy woman.

The Life of Christina of Markyate by a monk of St Alban's is in MS. Cotton Tiberius E.1, vol. 2. Nicholas Roscarrock (1549-1634) was the first to record the provenance of the manuscript in his *Lives of the English Saints*. It is now published in C. H. Talbot's version (trans. and intro. 1959). See also O. Pächt, *The St Alban's Psalter* (1960); *N.L.A.*, 2, pp. 532-7; P. Grosjean in *Anal.Boll.* 77 (1960),pp. 197-206; C. J. Holdsworth in Derek Baker (ed.), *Mediaeval Women* (1978), pp. 185-204.

Bd Bartholomew of Mantua (1495)

Bartholomew Fanti was a Carmelite friar of Mantua. He was born in that city in 1443 and joined the Order when he was seventeen years old. After his ordination he became a preacher of great power, with a special devotion to the Blessed Sacrament. He was known as a healer and used oil from the lamp burning before the tabernacle as a means of healing.

In Mantua he instituted a branch of the Confraternity of our Lady of Mount Carmel for laypeople and drew up the statutes and devotional exercises himself. His Rule, expounded in twelve short chapters, is simple and clear and fully in the Carmelite tradition. He also instituted a record of the main events in the history of the confraternity.

Bartholomew is said to have been the novice-master of the Carmelite poet Bd Baptist Spagnuolo (20 Mar.), who was six times elected vicar general of the friars at Mantua and eventually became prior general of the Order, but this now seems unlikely. Baptist Spagnuolo spent his year of probation at Ferrara, not at Mantua, and Bartholomew is not thought to have held the office of novice-master. However, Spagnuolo speaks of Bartholomew as a "most holy guide and spiritual master." Bartholomew's cult was confirmed by Pope Pius X in 1909.

There is a Life, transcribed in the second half of the sixteenth century by the English Carmelite John Bale, in MS. 73 of the Bodleian Library at Oxford. See also L. Saggi, *Saints of Carmel*, trans. G. N. Pausback (1972), pp. 61-2; C. de Villiers, *Bibliotheca Carmelitana*, 1, p.243; Rafael María López-Melús, *Los Santos Carmelitas* (1909), pp. 38-9.

St John Almond, *Martyr* (1612)

John Almond was a Lancashire man, born at Allerton near Liverpool. After studying at the English College at Reims he was sent to Rome, where he completed his training with a brilliant disputation praised by Cardinal Baronius, who presided. He was ordained and four years later was sent on the English mission.

After ten years' work, including one period of imprisonment, he was re-arrested in March 1612 and examined by Dr John King, the bishop of London. He defended himself with vigour, refusing to sign the Oath of Allegiance in the form in which it was tendered but offering to swear that he bore in his heart "so much allegiance to King James (whom I pray God to bless now and ever-more) as he, or any Christian king, could expect by the law of nature, the law of God, or the positive law of the true Church, be it which it will, ours or yours."

John Almond was committed to Newgate. Nine months later he was tried for high treason as a seminary priest and sentenced to death. He was drawn to Tyburn on 5 December 1612 and, after addressing the crowd, publicly an-swered the objections put to him. He then emptied his pockets and threw three or four pounds in silver to the crowd, complaining that the keeper at Newgate had not left him much. "One hour overtaketh another," he said,

> and though never so long, at last cometh death. And yet not death; for death is the gate of life unto us whereby we enter into everlasting blessedness. And life is death to those who do not provide for death, for they are ever tossed and troubled with vexations, miseries and wickedness. To use this life well is the pathway through death to everlasting life.

He asked for a handkerchief from the crowd to cover his face, and died with the name of Jesus on his lips. He was canonized as one of the Forty Martyrs of England and Wales by Pope Paul VI on 25 October 1970.

J. H. Pollen, *Acts of the English Martyrs* (1891), pp. 170-94; Stanton, pp. 586-7; Bede Camm, *Forgotten Shrines* (1910), pp. 164, 357, 378; Anstruther,1, p. 6.

Bd Nicholas Stenson, *Bishop* (1638-86)

Nicholas (Niels) Stenson was born in Copenhagen, the son of a goldsmith. He studied at Copenhagen and at Leyden and became a doctor of medicine and an eminent scientific scholar. In the second half of the seventeenth century, when the first great discoveries of modern science were being made, he pioneered in several different fields—anatomy, physiology, crystallography, geology, and paleontology. To him are attributed several ideas that are now fundamental to the study of geology: for instance, that fossils are the petrified remains of living organisms, and that rocks tend to occur in layers from which their geological history can be deduced. In medical practice he made new discoveries about the operation of the glandular system.

In 1667 he was working in a hospital in Florence, and his search for truth led him to become a Catholic. When he returned to Denmark he was debarred from being appointed a professor in the university of Copenhagen, which was exclusively Lutheran, but his work was recognized by his appointment as "Royal

Anatomist." He was ordained priest in 1675 and appointed vicar apostolic of Hanover. Later he became suffragan bishop of Münster, with episcopal oversight of Catholics in northern Germany and Scandinavia. His remains were interred in the basilica of San Lorenzo, Florence, and he was beatified by Pope John Paul II on 23 October 1988.

W. Plenkers, *Der Dane Niels Stenson* (1884); *D. Cath. Biog.*, pp. 1079-80. *N.S.B.*, 1, pp. 197-201; *D.N.H.*, 3, pp. 86-95. The *Dansk Biografisk Leksicon* has a long entry (cc. 1485-93) and an extensive bibliography.

There is an oil portrait (artist unknown) in the Uffizzi Gallery in Florence.

Bd Philip Rinaldi (1856-1931)

Filippo Rinaldi was born in Lu Monferrato in northern Italy. He attended the Salesian College at Mirabello, where he was taught by St John Bosco (31 Jan.), founder of the Salesian Congregation, and he subsequently studied in Turin. He entered the novitiate of the Order in Turin and was ordained priest on 23 December 1882. He worked closely with Don Bosco, learning much from him of the principles of the new educational movement, establishing general schools, trade schools, and agricultural schools. When Don Bosco died, Philip was sent to Spain as provincial of the Order. There he was highly regarded for his spirituality and his administrative gifts. In 1901 Don Bosco's successor, Bd Michael Rua (6 Apr.) called him back to Turin as his own deputy, and in 1922 he became superior of the Order.

Philip earned a great reputation as a teacher and trainer and did much to build up the work of the Order. He also supported and developed an Order for women, the Order of Our Lady Help of Christians, and is said to have had an intuitive understanding of the problems women faced in the religious life. He had a great love of the Church, promoted church organizations for social work, and directed the Salesians to missions in Asia and the Far East in response to an appeal from Pope Pius XI. He died in Turin in 1931 and was beatified by Pope John Paul II on 29 April 1990.

D.N.H., 3, pp. 185-8; *N.D.S.*, p. 258.

6

ST NICHOLAS, *Bishop* (Fourth Century)

St Nicholas has been greatly venerated through the ages, and many altars and churches have been dedicated in his memory. He is said to have been born at Patara in Lycia, a province of Asia Minor. Myra, the capital of the province, was an episcopal see, and Nicholas was chosen bishop. He was renowned for his great piety and zeal. The Greek histories of his life agree that he suffered imprisonment for the Faith in the latter part of the persecutions introduced by Diocletian and that he was present at the Council of Nicaea, where he condemned Arianism. He is thought to have died at Myra and to have been buried in his cathedral.

All that is known for certain is that Nicholas was bishop of Myra and that his alleged relics, stolen by Italian merchants in 1087, now rest at Bari. Though there are many accounts of his life and work, the earliest was written some five hundred years after his death. This is the work of St Methodius (14 June), patriarch of Constantinople, who died in 847. Methodius tells his readers that "up to the present, the life of this distinguished shepherd has been unknown to the majority of the faithful."

A vast amount of literature, critical and expository, has grown up around relatively late biographical sources. The universal popularity of St Nicholas—patron saint of Russia, Greece, Apulia, Sicily, and Lorraine, and of many cities and dioceses, and the origin of "Santa Claus" (from the Dutch "Sint Niklaas")—requires that the traditions should be stated.

His parents are said to have died when he was young, leaving him wealthy, and he determined to devote his inheritance to works of charity. On one occasion, he heard of a fellow-citizen of Patara who had lost all his money and whose daughters, unable to find husbands, were to be given over to prostitution. According to the legend, Nicholas three times threw a bag of gold through the open window of the man's house—one for each daughter. On the third occasion he was recognized as the benefactor. A painting by Crivelli (d. 1494) shows him standing at the window, the father receiving the bags of gold, and the three daughters lying in bed. This story had by then been current for over a thousand years, and it may have generated the absurd story of three children, killed and pickled in a brine-tub by an innkeeper, whom the saint was said miraculously to have brought to life: the purses of gold in older paintings may have been mistaken for the heads of children. The legend is also said to be the origin of the pawnbroker's three golden balls, which were adopted from the coat of arms of the Medici family.

After his election as bishop of Myra, Nicholas was imprisoned during the persecutions, but Methodius says that he was set free and returned to Myra after the accession of Constantine. He says nothing about Nicholas' presence at the Council of Nicaea in 325, but other sources suggest that he was there and that it was a stormy meeting. He is said to have actually struck Arius and to have been temporarily deprived of his office and imprisoned for doing so. He preached tirelessly against Arianism, which denied that the Son was co-eternal with the Father. He also opposed paganism wherever he found it, and he had a great love of justice. He intervened with governors and even with the emperor Constantine to save unjustly condemned men.

The accounts are unanimous that St Nicholas died and was buried in his episcopal city of Myra and that by the time of Justinian there was a basilica built in his honour at Constantinople. An anonymous Greek wrote in the tenth century:

> Wherever there are people, in the country and the town, in the villages, in the isles, in the furthest parts of the earth, his name is revered and churches are built in his honour. Images of him are set up, panegyrics preached, and festivals celebrated. All Christians, young and old, men and women, boys and girls, reverence his memory and call upon his protection. And his favours, which know no limit of time and continue from age to age, are poured out over all the earth: the Scythians know them, as do the Indians and the barbarians, the Africans as well as the Italians.

When Myra and its great shrine were finally taken over by the Saracens, there was competition among Italian cities to claim the relics of St Nicholas. Bari and Venice were the main contenders, and eventually Bari was successful: Nicholas was the patron saint of Apulia, and there were large Greek colonies in the area. The relics were secretly carried off without the knowledge of the Greek custodians and their Muslim masters and transported to Bari, where a new church was built to contain the shrine. Pope Urban II was present at the enshrining. Since then it has attracted pilgrims from all over the world.

St Nicholas is the patron saint of several classes of people, including sailors in the East and children in the West. Sailors in the Aegean and Ionian seas had their "star of St Nicholas" and wished each other a good voyage with the phrase "May St Nicholas hold the tiller." The legend of the three children gave rise to his patronage of children, as well as various observances ecclesiastical and secular, such as the boy-bishop and the giving of presents at Christmas. This is not an old Catholic custom. It seems to have originated among the Protestants of the Low Countries and to have been taken to America by the Dutch immigrants of New Amsterdam. In the Netherlands presents are still given on his feast-day.

In England there are some four hundred churches dedicated to St Nicholas. He was an extremely popular figure in medieval drama (a tradition continued by Benjamin Britten's *Saint Nicholas*). Prayers to him were composed by Anselm

(7 Apr.) and Godric (21 May). He has an important place in the Byzantine liturgical tradition.

P.G., 116, 317-56; G. Anrich, *Hagios Nikolaos . . . in der griechischen Kirche*, 2 vols. (1917), contains all the Greek texts of any interest, better edited than in Migne, and with a full introduction and notes. See also K. Meisen, *Nikolauskult und Nikolausbrauch im Abendlande* (1931), with many pictorial illustrations; commentary in *Anal.Boll.* 12 (1893), pp. 459, and 45 (1932), pp. 178-81. Modern studies by E. Crozier, *The Life and Legends of St Nicholas* (1949); A. D. de Groot, *St Nicholas: a psycho-analytic study of his history and myth* (Eng. trans., 1951). For legends, see *Golden Legend*, 1, pp. 21-6; Karl Young, *The Drama of the Mediaeval Church* (1933).

There are two important iconographical sources of his life, both dating from the twelfth century: on the font at Winchester Cathedral, and on a finely-carved ivory crozier-head in the Victoria and Albert Museum. Other examples include a fine late medieval window at North Moreton (Oxon.) entirely devoted to his life, and windows in the Jerusalem Chamber in Westminster, at Great Malvern, and at Hillesden (Bucks.). There are stained-glass cycles of his life at Chartres, Le Mans, and Tours, and magnificent frescoes, particularly those at Santa Maria Antiqua, Rome (eighth century), St Sophia, Istanbul (tenth century), and St Mark's, Venice and Monreale, Sicily (both twelfth century). There is a painting in the Vatican by Gentile da Fabriano of St Nicholas saving a ship at sea, also shown on a *predella* by Fra Angelico in the Vatican Museum, together with the story of the three girls and the "miracle" of the three boys. These also form part of an altarpiece by Gerard David in the National Gallery of Scotland in Edinburgh. The Crivelli painting of the merchant, his daughters, and the three purses of gold is in the Sainsbury Wing of the National Gallery in London.

SS Dionysia, Majoricus, and Companions, *Martyrs* (484)

In the year 484 the Arian king in North Africa, Huneric, banished the Catholic bishops from their African sees and began a violent persecution of orthodox Christians. Among those martyred were a woman named Dionysia and her young son Majoricus, her sister Dativa, her cousin Emilian, and at least three others.

With them are commemorated on the following day St Servus, who was killed at Thurbobo, and other martyrs, including a young mother named Victoria, who suffered at Cucusa.

The only reference to these martyrs comes from the *Historia persecutionis provinciae Africanae*, written by Victor, bishop of Vita, who was a contemporary: see *M.G.H., Auctores Antiquissimi*, 3, part 1, pp. 45-6.

St Abraham of Kratia, *Bishop* (474-558)

The Lives of the saints give many examples of people who had offices of responsibility thrust upon them against their wishes and chose a solitary life when they could, seeking quiet for contemplation. The tradition is particularly strong in the Eastern Church. Abraham, bishop of Kratia, followed this path. He was born at Emesa in Syria and became a monk there. When he was eighteen the community was broken up by raiding nomads, and he fled with his spiritual counsellor to Constantinople. Here they found a home in a monastery where the older monk became abbot and Abraham procurator. When he was only twenty-six he was so well regarded that he was elected abbot of Kratia in Bithynia.

After ten years he went away secretly into Palestine, but his bishop found him and forced him to return to his duties. Soon afterwards he himself was made bishop of Kratia, and he fulfilled that office conscientiously for thirteen years. Then he again left and found refuge in a monastery at the Tower of Eudokia. Here he led a most rigorous life of prayer for some twenty years. He died about 558 without being recalled to his diocese. He was the most noted of the bishops who occupied the see of Kratia, from its foundation in the third century to its abolition in the twelfth, and is retained here, although not in the new Roman Martyrology.

The original Greek text of the Life of Abraham and six other saints by Cyril of Skythopolis, a contemporary, has been edited by H. Gregoire in the *Revue de l'Instruction publique en Belgique* 49 (1906), pp. 281-96; by K. Koikylides in the Greek periodical *Nea Sion* 4 (1906), July supp. pp. 1-7; E .Schwartz in *Kyrillos von Skythopolis* (1939). These editions are founded on a single manuscript in the monastery of Mount Sinai, which is unfortunately defective at the end, though an ancient Arabic version has preserved it complete. See P. Peeters, *Anal.Boll.* 24 (1905), pp. 349-56, and 26 (1907), pp. 122-5. The notice in no. 24 contains a Latin translation from the Arabic. An English translation is now available in R. M. Price (ed.), *Cyril of Scythopolis: Lives of the Monks of Palestine* (1991).

Bd Peter Pascual, *Bishop and Martyr* (1227-1300)

The Valencian family of Pascual, or Pascuález (Latinized as Paschasius), is said to have given the Church six martyrs, of whom Peter was the last. He was tutored by a priest from Narbonne with a doctorate of divinity from Paris, whom his parents had ransomed from the Moors. Peter went with his tutor to Paris and himself took the degree of doctor. He then returned to Valencia and received Holy Orders at the age of twenty-four. He taught theology at Barcelona until James I of Aragon chose him as tutor to his son Sancho. Subsequently he was appointed administrator of the diocese of Toledo and then titular bishop of Granada, which was in the hands of the Moors. In 1296 he was appointed bishop of Jaén, which was also under Moorish domination.

In this period, soon after the collapse of the Eighth Crusade, the Holy Land was left in Muslim hands, and the Moors controlled most of Spain. In spite of the dangers Bishop Peter ransomed captives, instructed and comforted Christians, brought many back to the Church, and even preached to the Moors. He was seized while on a visitation, carried off to Granada, and imprisoned in a dungeon. Orders were given that no one should be allowed to speak to him. He received money for his ransom, but with it he bought the freedom of others whom he thought were in danger of apostasy. In spite of solitary confinement he found means to write a treatise against Islam. This was circulated, provoking the Islamic authorities to plan his death.

Peter is thought to have died from the hardships of his captivity, though there is a tradition that he was killed in prison. In 1673 Pope Clement X confirmed his cult. He is referred to as *Beatus* in the Roman Martyrology, though commonly called Saint.

The best materials are those published by Fr Fidel Fita in the *Boletín* of the Historical Academy of Madrid 20 (1892), pp. 32-61; cf. 41 (1902), pp. 345-7. For the general reader of Spanish, the most thorough discussion of the problems involved is that of R. Rodríguez de Gálvez, *San Pedro Pascual, obispo de Jaén y Mártir* (1900). See also the *Estudios Críticos* of the same author. In these, it is satisfactorily established that Bishop Peter was not a member of the Mercedarian Order and that he was not executed. A bulky work supporting the Mercedarian contentions, *Vida de San Pedro Pascual*, has been published by P. Armengol Valenzuela (1901), but the Bollandist reviewers find it unconvincing. See *Anal. Boll.* 20 (1901), pp. 233-4.

ST NICHOLAS (p. 59)
Three gold roundels on blue field, for the three purses of gold
he threw secretly into a poor family's house

ST AMBROSE (over page)
Gold beehive (for eloquence), silver scourges (for strict
discipline as bishop), on blue field

7

ST AMBROSE, *Bishop and Doctor* (*c.* 340-397)

Ambrose was born in Trier when his father was prefect of Gaul. After his father's death his mother returned with her children to Rome, and Ambrose owed much to her and to his sister, St Marcellina (17 July). He learned Greek, became a good poet and orator, and went on to practise as a highly successful advocate. The emperor Valentinian made him governor of Liguria and Aemilia, with full consular rank and residence at Milan, before he was forty years old.

At this time the Church was divided by controversy over the Arian heresy— the belief that Christ was created by God the Father as a means for the salvation of the world but was not of the nature of God himself. Auxentius, bishop of Milan, was an Arian, and on his death in 374 the city was divided by party strife about who should replace him. The two parties could not agree on a candidate, and there was street fighting. Ambrose went to the church and made a speech to the people, exhorting them to make their choice in the spirit of peace. During this speech, a voice, said to be that of a child, cried, "Ambrose for bishop!" and the whole assembly took up the cry. Catholics and Arians unanimously proclaimed him bishop of Milan. Ambrose was astonished—though he had become a professed Christian he was not yet baptized, and he had no ambitions in the Church.

Given his capacity to reconcile the two opposing factions and his popular support, the bishops of the province ratified the election. Though Ambrose pleaded his unsuitability, the emperor Valentinian commented that it gave him the greatest pleasure that he had chosen a governor who was fit for the episcopal office, and within a week Ambrose was baptized and consecrated.

Ambrose resolved to break all the ties that held him to the world. He gave his personal property to the poor and his lands and estates to the Church, keeping only an income for the use of his sister Marcellina. He was acutely conscious of his lack of knowledge of theology and at once began to study the scriptures and the work of the Fathers of the Church, particularly Origen and St Basil the Great (2 Jan.). For these studies, he put himself under the instruction of St Simplician (13 Aug.), a learned priest who was his beloved friend and respected teacher. His personal life was one of simplicity and hard work: he excused himself from going to banquets and entertained others with decent frugality. Every day he offered Mass for his people, and he devoted himself entirely to the service of his flock, any member of which could see and speak with him at any time, so that his people loved and admired him. It was his rule, in order to avoid controversy, never to take part in arrangements for marriages, which were often largely concerned with settlements of property; never to persuade anyone to serve in the army; and never to recommend anyone for a place at court. St Augustine of Hippo (28 Aug.), when he came to visit him, found him overwhelmed with work and constant callers. On one occasion Augustine, unable to gain his attention, left the room without explanation. When he returned some time later Ambrose had not even noticed his absence.

Ambrose in his discourses frequently spoke in praise of the state of virginity undertaken by women for God's sake, and he had many consecrated virgins under his direction. At the request of Marcellina he collected his sermons on the subject, making thereby a famous treatise, *De Virginibus*. Mothers tried to keep their daughters away from church when he was preaching lest they were turned against marriage, and he was charged with trying to depopulate the empire; but he maintained that war, not the practice of virginity, was the destroyer of the human race.

The Goths invaded Roman territories in the East, and the emperor Gratian determined to lead an army to help his uncle, Valens. Since Valens was an Arian, Gratian asked St Ambrose for instruction to protect him against that heresy. Ambrose accordingly wrote *To Gratian, concerning the Faith*, a treatise he later expanded. As the Goths swept along the Adriatic and across Greece he spent all the money he could raise in ransoming captives and melted down gold vessels belonging to the Church to raise more. The Arians accused him of sacrilege, but he replied that it was more expedient to save the souls of men than to save gold. "If the Church possesses gold, it is in order to use it for the needy, not to keep it." After the murder of Gratian in 383 the empress Justina implored Ambrose to plead with the usurper Maximus so that he would not attack her son, Valentinian II. Ambrose went to Trier and persuaded Maximus to confine his claims to Gaul, Spain, and Britain. This is said to be the first time that a Christian priest was called on to intervene in matters of high politics: Ambrose did so in order to vindicate right and order against a usurper in arms.

At this time certain senators in Rome were trying to restore the cult of the goddess of Victory. Their leader was Quintus Aurelius Symmachus, a scholar and a skilled orator, who drew up a petition asking Valentinian to re-establish the altar of Victory in the senate-house: he ascribed the victories and prosperity of ancient Rome to worship at this altar. The petition was a covert attack on Christianity. Ambrose wrote to Valentinian asking for a copy and then drew up his own reply. This ridiculed the suggestion that what was achieved by military valour was due to the entrails of sacrificed cattle and exhorted Romans to change with a changing world. He appealed to Symmachus and his friends to learn the mysteries of nature from God who created it. He ended with a parable of progress and development in the world. Both documents, that of Symmachus and that of Ambrose, were read before Valentinian in council.

Then the emperor gave what was, in the circumstances of this heated discussion about the old and the new, a deft and plausible judgment: he said that his father had not removed the altar to Victory, nor had he put it back. He therefore proposed to maintain tradition by doing nothing. The movement for the worship of Victory failed, not on the grounds that it was too old, but because the emperor represented it as an unjustified innovation.

Although Ambrose had helped the empress Justina by securing peace with Maximus, she supported the Arians. Shortly before Easter 383 she induced Valentinian to demand the Portian basilica, now called St Victor's, outside Milan, for the use of the Arians, including herself and many officers at court. Ambrose refused. Valentinian then demanded the new basilica of the Apostles, and Ambrose refused again. Officers of the court were sent to take possession of the basilica, and the citizens, enraged, seized an Arian priest. Ambrose would suffer no blood to be shed and sent out priests and deacons to rescue him. Throughout the ensuing troubles Ambrose, though assured of the support of the crowds and much of the army, was careful to do nothing that would provoke violence or endanger the position of the emperor or his mother. He was resolute in his refusal to give up the churches but would not officiate in either for fear of creating a disturbance.

Ambrose wrote an account of these events to Marcellina and added that he foresaw even greater trouble. An imperial chamberlain had said to him, "You despise Valentinian. I will cut off your head," to which Ambrose replied, "May God permit it. Then I shall suffer as a bishop should, and you will act according to your kind!"

In January 386 a law was passed authorizing the religious assemblies of the Arians and in effect proscribing those of the Catholics. It forbade anyone, under pain of death, to oppose Arian assemblies or to obstruct their taking over churches. Ambrose disregarded the law and refused to give up a single church: "I have said what a bishop ought to say; let the emperor do what an emperor ought to do. Naboth would not give up the inheritance of his ancestors, and shall I give up that of Jesus Christ?" On Palm Sunday he preached about not giving up the churches; fearing for his life, the people barricaded themselves in the basilica with their pastor. The imperial troops surrounded the place to starve them out, but on Easter Day they were still there. To occupy their time Ambrose taught them psalms and hymns composed by himself, which, at his direction, they sang in two choirs, singing alternate stanzas. Ambrose told his congregation all that had happened between him and Valentinian in the past year and summed up the principle at stake: "The emperor is in the Church, not over it."

Meanwhile Maximus, using Valentinian's persecution of the Catholics as an excuse, invaded Italy. Justina and Valentinian fled to Greece and threw themselves on the mercy of Theodosius the Great, the eastern emperor. Theodosius defeated and executed Maximus, restored Valentinian, and stayed for a time in

Milan, inducing Valentinian to abandon Arianism and to have respect for Ambrose. However, this support did not prevent Ambrose from confronting Theodosius on at least two major occasions. The first of these concerned a situation in Kallinikum in Mesopotamia, where zealot Christians pulled down a Jewish synagogue. Theodosius, anxious to secure religious toleration, ordered them to rebuild it. Ambrose supported the zealots, arguing that no Christian bishop could pay for the erection of a building to be used for what he considered to be false worship. Though this may now seem a highly intolerant attitude, it is necessary to recall that he was defending a Church riven with conflict and fighting for its existence against unorthodox and heretical beliefs. In a dramatic gesture he confronted the emperor in church, refusing to proceed with the Mass until the emperor unwillingly gave way.

The second confrontation followed the infamous massacre at Thessalonica (Salonika) in 390 of some seven thousand men, women, and children in reprisal for the death of a governor, with no attempt to distinguish the innocent from the guilty. Ambrose consulted with his fellow-bishops and held Theodosius personally responsible. He wrote to the emperor, exhorting him to public penance and saying that he neither could nor would receive his offering at the altar nor celebrate the Eucharist until that obligation was satisfied. Again, the emperor gave way.

Theodosius died in 393. In his funeral oration Ambrose spoke eloquently of his love for the dead emperor, praising him for his humility: "He stripped himself of every sign of royalty and bewailed his sin openly in church. He, an emperor, was not ashamed to do the public penance which lesser individuals shrink from, and to the end of his life he never ceased to grieve for his error." Ambrose was unimpressed by wealth or position. He demonstrated that Christian morality applied to emperors as to other believers.

Ambrose survived Theodosius by only two years, and one of his last treatises was "On the Goodness of Death." When he fell sick he foretold his own death but said that he would live till Easter. He continued his usual studies and began to expound the forty-third psalm, but he never completed the exposition. On the day of his death he lay with his hands extended in the form of a cross for several hours, moving his lips in constant prayer. His friend Honoratus of Vercelli, who was in a nearby room, seemed to hear a voice telling him to go quickly to Ambrose's side. He did so, administered the Last Rites, and soon Ambrose was dead. It was Good Friday, 4 April 397, and he was about fifty-seven years old. He was buried on Easter Day, and his relics rest under the high altar of his basilica in Milan, where they were buried in 845.

Ambrose's written works, mostly in the form of homiletics, were numerous. The Breviary hymn *Aeterne rerum conditor* is certainly his, and other hymns are ascribed to him. As the Roman Empire declined in the West, these works gave Latin a new lease on life as the universal language of the Church. He wrote of himself:

I do not . . . claim for myself the glory of the apostles . . . nor the grace of the prophets, nor the virtue of the evangelists, nor the cautious care of the pastors. I only desire to attain to that care and diligence in the sacred writings which the Apostle [Paul] has placed last among the duties of the saints; and this very thing I desire, so that, in the endeavour to teach, I may be able to learn.

His cult is ancient and well established. In art, he is often represented in episcopal vestments with the emblem of a scourge, symbolizing the penance he imposed on the emperor, or else with a beehive: a swarm of bees, symbolizing his future eloquence, is said to have settled on him when he was a child. He is the patron saint of stonemasons, since many of these in the Middle Ages were from Lombardy, of which Milan is the principal city. The church of Sant'Ambrogio in Milan, erected in the ninth century on the site of one the saint founded, contains his relics under the high altar and his archiepiscopal throne. In England there were no ancient dedications, but there are images of him as one of the four Latin Doctors of the Church, with SS Augustine (28 Aug.), Jerome (30 Sept.) and Gregory (3 Sept.).

Ambrose actually died in April, but 7 December is his memorial in the revised universal Calendar, being the date of his consecration.

Contemporary materials for Ambrose's life in *P.L.*, 14, 65-114; Life by Paulinus, trans. F. R. Hoare, in *The Western Fathers* (1954); J. R. Palanque, *S. Ambroise et l'empire romain* (1933); F. H. Dudden, *The Life and Times of St Ambrose* (1935). Both Palanque and Dudden contain full bibliographies. See also commentary in *Anal. Boll.* 55 (1937), pp. 116-7. Works in *P.L.*, 14-17, and Eng. trans. in N.P.N.F., 10. Poems, with Eng. trans., in Helen Waddell, *More Latin Lyrics*, ed. Dame Felicitas Corrigan (1978), pp. 70-1. See also H. Spitzmüller, *Poésie Latine Chrétienne du Moyen Âge* (1971), pp. 39-54.

The many paintings depicting St Ambrose include one in a triptych in the FitzWilliam Museum, Cambridge, one by Michael Pacher in the Alte Pinakotek, Munich; and frescoes in the churches of St Francis, Assisi, and San Miniato, Florence. The earliest representation is a fifth-century mosaic, which shows him without a halo, in the surviving portion of Sant'Ambrogio. In the same church the Golden Altar by Wolvinius (*c*. 824-59) shows scenes from his life. In England he is shown with a book and crozier on a painted screen at Ashton in Devon; as a bishop holding an open book and a scourge in the Henry VII Chapel of Westminster Abbey; in glass at All Souls' College, Oxford, reading from a book held by an angel; and at Fairford in Gloucestershire, holding a pastoral staff. See E. Tasker, *Encyclopedia of Medieval Church Art* (1993), pp. 110-1.

St Sabinus and Companions, *Martyrs* (? 303)

A martyr named Sabinus was buried a short distance from Spoleto but is claimed by several Italian cities. St Gregory the Great (3 Sept.) speaks of a chapel built in his honour near Fermo, for which he asks for relics of the martyr from Chrysanthus, bishop of Spoleto.

For the rest we are dependent on tradition in the story of his passion, which goes back no earlier than the fifth or sixth century. It is said that Sabinus was a bishop and that he and several of his clergy were arrested during the persecution of Diocletian. When Venustian, the governor of Etruria, ordered him to worship a small statute of Jupiter he threw it contemptuously to the ground and broke it. For this, his hands were cut off. His two deacons, Marcellus and Exsuperantius, who had also made a confession of faith, were scourged and racked, and both died under torture. Their bodies were buried at Assisi.

Sabinus was taken back to prison, where he healed a blind boy, and other prisoners asked to be baptized. The governor, who had an affliction of the eyes, was healed and also converted together with his wife and children, and they died for their faith. Sabinus was executed at Spoleto and was buried a mile from the city.

Sabinus of Spoleto should be distinguished from St Sabinus, bishop of Piacenza (17 Jan.), who was a contemporary of St Ambrose of Milan (above).

The Passion of Sabinus of Spoleto was first published in Baluze-Mansi 1, pp. 12-4. See also H. Delehaye, *Origine du culte des martyrs*, p. 317; Duchesne, *Fastes*, 1, pp. 253-4; Quentin, p. 43; *D.Cath.Biog.*, p. 1018.

St Buithe, *Abbot* (521)

Traditions differ as to whether Buithe (Buite, Boethius) was born in Scotland or Ireland. The Scottish tradition is that he visited the Scottish Lowlands, preached to the Picts, and restored a Pictish king to life by his prayers. Kirkbuddo (Castrum Butthi) may derive its name from him. The Irish tradition is that he was born in Co. Louth and that his father's name was Bronach. He is said to have gone to Italy and studied under Tilianus, but this seems to be a transcriber's error: it is more probable that he went to Wales (*Walia* rather than *Italia*) and studied under St Teilo (9 Feb.). He then went back to Ireland and founded the monastery of Monasterboice, north of Drogheda, near his home. This was one of the earliest of the Irish foundations, and there is a record of the abbots of Monasterboice from 759 to 1122, but of Buithe, two and a half centuries before the record began, we know little apart from his name, the date of his death, and the link with Monasterboice. He has no modern cult and so is not included in the new Roman Martyrology.

Plummer, *V.S.H.*, 1, pp. xxxiv-xxxvi, 87-92; *Irish Saints*, pp. 48-50; H. M. Roe, *Monasterboice and its Monuments*, Co. Louth Archaeological and Historical Society (1981). *D.H.G.E.*, 10, 1099, includes a bibliography.

At Monasterboice there are two Celtic high crosses standing and fragments of two others on site, while two other fragments are in the National Museum in Dublin, but these probably date from the ninth or tenth century. Of the two standing crosses, one is over twenty-one feet high; both are carved with biblical scenes, including the crucifixion and the last judgment. See P. Harbison, *The High Crosses of Ireland* (1992), 1, pp. 139-53 and 367-73.

St Josepha Rossello, *Foundress* (1811-80)

Dr P. D. Sessa, one of the biographers of St Josepha, points out that, so far as is known, her life was not marked by visions, heavenly voices, or other marvels; yet it was nothing short of miraculous that the three Sisters with which her

Congregation began increased in a few years to over a hundred and her first house became the motherhouse of sixty-eight others during her life-time.

She was born in 1811 at Albisola Marina, a small town on the Ligurian coast of Italy, the fourth child in a family of nine. Her father, Bartolomeo Rossello, was a potter by trade, and he and his wife, Maria Dedone, named the child Benedetta. She was lively and intelligent and something of a leader among the other children. On one occasion, when she was about nine, the people of Albisola went on pilgrimage to the shrine of Our Lady of Mercy at Savona, leaving the children at home. In her parents' absence Benedetta organized a pilgrimage of her own, leading both boys and girls in procession to pray at the local sanctuary of Our Lady of Mercy. On the way back they sang hymns, and the sacristan, thinking that he heard the adult pilgrims returning from Savona, ordered the church bells to be rung.

Benedetta was sensitive to the beauty of created things and felt close to St Francis of Assisi (4 Oct.). When she was sixteen she was received into the Third Order of Franciscans and came under the spiritual guidance of a Capuchin friar, Fr Angelo of Savona. For a time she wished to become a solitary, but her director dissuaded her, and when she was nineteen she took service with the Monleone family in Savona. "The hands are made for work, and the heart for God," she said, and her work for the next seven years was to look after Signor Monleone, who was an invalid. The money she earned went to her family, who were poor. She could have stayed in the comfortable home of the Monleones for the rest of her life, but when her patient died her desire to "leave the world" revived more strongly than ever.

At this time the bishop of Savona was Mgr Agostino de Mari; he was very perturbed by the dangers that faced many girls and young women in the city and wanted to start some work on their behalf. Benedetta Rossello heard about this; she had already been refused by one convent for lack of a dowry, so she called on the bishop and offered her services. He was impressed by her appearance and manner and accepted her offer. On 10 August 1837 Benedetta, her cousins Angela and Dominica Pescio, and a fourth young woman named Paolina Barla took up their residence in a shabby house called the Commenda in Savona. They called themselves the Daughters of Our Lady of Mercy, and Benedetta took the names Mary Josepha. Their endowment was a little furniture, a straw mattress apiece, a sack of potatoes and a few lire, with a crucifix and a statue of Our Lady. Their work was to instruct poor girls, especially in the Faith, and later to open hostels, schools, and hospitals.

The Congregation was formally inaugurated in October of the same year. The first superior was Sister Angela, but three years later Sister Josepha was elected superior, and she remained in that office for the rest of her life. The community outgrew its first quarters and moved into a rented mansion which became the motherhouse, the core of a huge group of buildings. One of Mother Josepha's early difficulties was the death of her supporter Bishop de Mari: the vicar capitular was hostile to the community, but fortunately the new bishop, when he was appointed after a considerable delay, proved to be of Mgr de Mari's mind. He approved the Rule of the Congregation in 1840, when it numbered thirty-five members. It had already sent out its first colony to work in the municipal schools and hospital in Varazze, and from then on it spread to many other places in Italy. There were difficulties: sometimes the Sisters faced opposition. Mother Josepha's health broke down, and the bishop had to insist that she should go away to recuperate. There were also money problems, but these were eased by two unexpected legacies, one from Josepha's old friend and employer, Signora Monleone.

Mgr de Mari had wanted to establish rescue homes for girls in difficulties, and Josepha tried to develop this work. A first experiment at Genoa failed, but she eventually succeeded in establishing three homes, which she called Houses of Divine Providence. One of them was in her own birthplace, Albisola. It was housed in the former home of Ferdinand Isola, a Franciscan martyred by the Turks at Scutari in 1648.

It was said of Mother Josepha that whenever she had five pounds in her pocket she found something new to do. One of her new enterprises was a House of Clerics to foster and assist vocations to the priesthood. Her energy and foresight were too much for many of the clergy, who strongly opposed this innovation, but she succeeded in winning over the bishop, Mgr Cerutti. He and his successor, Mgr Boraggini, actively encouraged it. Then in 1875 came the first foundation in South America, when a company of the Daughters of Our Lady of Mercy, with the blessing and commendation of St John Bosco (31 Jan.), left for Buenos Aires. Soon schools, hospitals, rescue-homes, and other works were developing on the American continent.

In her later years Mother Josepha combined great energy with great humility. The foundress of numerous convents and charitable establishments was never more herself than when she was sweeping the floor, polishing the tables, or washing the dishes. When she was sixty-four a life of toil began to tell: she developed a weak heart and lost the use of her legs, so that she could only oversee the work of others and no longer take an active part in it herself. This depressed her, and she went through a period of great spiritual trial in which she was beset by many scruples and convinced of her own sinfulness. Her faith remained firm: "Cling to Jesus," she repeated over and over again to her community. "There are God, the soul, eternity: the rest is nothing." Josepha Rossello died, peacefully and with humble confidence, on 7 December 1880 at the age of sixty-nine. Her canonization by Pope Pius XII took place in 1949.

Lives by F. Martinengo (1910); F. Noberasco (1921); L. Traverso (1934); P. S. Delfino (1938); A. Oddone (1939, rp. 1949); *D. Cath. Biog.*, p. 1007; *F.B.S.*, pp. 916-8. *Bibl.SS.*, 8, pp. 1070-2. As a tertiary of their Order, Josepha is included among the Franciscan saints.

8

THE IMMACULATE CONCEPTION OF THE
BLESSED VIRGIN MARY

By the papal Bull *Ineffabilis Deus* of 8 December 1854, Pope Pius IX pronounced it to be "a doctrine revealed by God and therefore to be believed firmly and constantly by all the faithful that the Blessed Virgin Mary, in the first instant of her conception, was, by a unique grace and privilege of Almighty God in view of the merits of Jesus Christ, the Saviour of the human race, preserved exempt from all stain of original sin." The stain of original sin was not removed but excluded from her soul.

For many centuries before this solemn definition, the doctrine had been widely believed in the Church, but it was not "of faith": it had much the same position as the doctrine of the Assumption of Our Lady had until 1950. Since Pius IX's ruling in 1854, every Catholic is bound to believe the doctrine of the Immaculate Conception.

A liturgical feast commemorating the conception of our Lady seems to have been celebrated originally in Palestine; but the expression "Conception of Mary" did not apply to that feast: it was taken to mean the conception of Our Lord by the power of the Holy Spirit, and the conception of Our Lady herself was referred to as "the Conception of St Anne." The feast has maintained this name in the East, and Eastern Catholics call it officially "The Child-begetting of the holy Anne, mother of the Mother of God."

The idea that Mary was the "new Eve," free from the taint of sin, is to be found in the works of some of the early Fathers of the Church, notably those of St Justin Martyr (14 Apr.), St Irenaeus (28 June), and St John Damascene (4 Dec.). The feast seems to have been imported into Italy from Constantinople in the ninth century, still called the Conception of St Anne. The first clear evidence of a feast of the Conception of Our Lady, and under that name, in the West, comes from England, at Winchester, Canterbury, and Exeter just before the Norman Conquest. This was identified with 8 December. Since 9 December was the day assigned to the feast in Jerusalem, Constantinople, and Naples, the probability is that it came from the East.

In England, again as in the East, the observance began in monasteries, and the first two mentions are found in the abbey called New Minster at Winchester. It met with opposition as an innovation, but Eadmer of Canterbury wrote an important treatise on Our Lady's conception when St Anselm (21 Apr.) was archbishop of Canterbury. The archbishop's nephew, another Anselm, introduced the feast of the Conception into his own abbey at Bury St Edmunds. It was soon taken up by St Alban's, Reading, Gloucester, and other monastic communities. Some monks of Westminster, where the prior, Osbert of Clare, favoured the feast, challenged its lawfulness, but it was approved by a synod in London in 1129. At the same time, the feast began to spread in Normandy, though whether it was brought there from England or from the Norman kingdom of Sicily is not clear.

The adoption of the feast in the cathedral church of Lyons, about the year 1140, was the occasion of a protest by St Bernard of Clairvaux (20 Aug.), which precipitated a theological controversy lasting three hundred years. St Thomas Aquinas (28 Jan.) also opposed the feast, as did the Dominicans, but the whole Order of Friars Minor adopted it in 1263. The point at issue was at what moment the sanctification of Mary took place; but though controversy continued, the observance of the feast of the Conception of Our Lady steadily progressed. In 1476 Pope Sixtus IV approved the feast with its own Mass and Office, though this was still a celebration of the conception of the immaculate Virgin Mary rather than of the Immaculate Conception as now understood.

Alonso de Villegas, cardinal of Segovia, produced a defence of the full doctrine of the Immaculate Conception in 1623, arguing that there were good reasons why this had not been revealed to the Church in earlier times:

. . . the saying that the mother of God was conceived without sin was hidden and secret many yeares; which was a thing not without cause. The reason might be this: that the common people were so devote to her, that if it had bene published and affirmed in former times when things were not so well declared, and when they which had erred could not so well have bene instructed and reformed . . . it might have been that the B. Virgin should have bene adored for God. To avoid this inconvenience, it seemeth good reason, this secret should be kept close. At this present time, the Church hath opened this secret in giving leave that we may hold and believe the glorious Virgin was conceived without sinne.

At the Council of Trent (1545-63) it was explicitly declared that a decree on original sin did not apply to the Blessed Virgin Mary. In 1661 Pope Alexander VII declared that the feast celebrated the immunity of Our Lady from original sin in the first moment of the creation of her soul and its infusion into her body. In 1708 Pope Clement XI imposed the festival on the whole Western Church as a feast-day of obligation. By that time it was being observed not only by the Franciscans but by Carmelites, Jesuits, and many Dominicans. The acceptance of the dogma can therefore be seen as the culmination of a long process in the development of doctrine.

After the solemn definition in 1854 the name of the feast was altered to the Immaculate Conception of the Blessed Virgin Mary, and nine years later a new

Mass and Office were prescribed. Since then, the feast has become an increasingly popular aspect of Marian devotion. Of the eighteen Catholic dioceses of England and Wales, ten have Our Lady as conceived sinless for their principal patron, and she was declared patroness of the United States under this title by the First Council of Baltimore eight years before the definition. Hundreds of churches have a similar dedication. The object of the Church's devotion is to honour the Blessed Virgin rather than to prescribe, in the manner of the medieval Schoolmen, the precise time at which her sanctification took place.

The date for the feast has been fixed nine months before the Birthday of our Lady, which is observed on 8 September. Why this date was selected for the birthday is not known. The Anglican Church keeps the feast of the Conception of the Blessed Virgin Mary on 8 December according to the Book of Common Prayer, but this is omitted in the Calendar for the Alternative Service Book. Eastern Catholics still keep the feast on 9 December. Eastern Orthodox Churches have no official teaching about the doctrine: some theologians have repudiated it, while others have taught it. The original Russian sect of Old Believers is said to have professed it formally.

There is an immense literature connected with the doctrine of the Immaculate Conception and with its liturgical celebration. Perhaps the fullest account is given by Frs le Bachelet and Jugie in *D.T.C.*, 7, which runs to over 350 columns, including an extensive bibliography. See also H. Thurston in *The Month* (1904), May, June, July, and December, with E. Bishop's criticisms in the *Bosworth Psalter*, pp. 43-51, and *Liturgica historica*, pp. 238-59. On the entry in early Irish calendars see Fr Grosjean's very important note in *Anal.Boll.* 61 (1943), pp. 91-5, where he shows that these entries got into certain manuscripts through a copyist's error. On the feast in the Eastern Catholic Church see *Bessarione*, September and December 1904. For the origin of the Western feast see S. J. P. van Dijk in the *Dublin Review*, 3d and 4th quarters, 1954. Eadmer's treatise is critically edited by Slater and Thompson in *Eadmeri Tractatus de Conceptione Sanctae Mariae* (1904). See also de Villegas, pp. 511-25; M. Jugie, *L'Immaculée Conception dans L'Écriture sainte* (1952); *Vatican Council II*, ed. A. Flannery (1977), pp. 413 ff.; *The Catechism of the Catholic Church* (1994), nn. 491-2 (page nos. vary in different editions).

St Eutychian, *Pope* (283)

Very little that is historically reliable appears to be known of this pope. The *Liber Pontificalis* says that he came from Tuscany and succeeded Pope Felix I in the year 275. Though he was classified as a martyr in the Roman Martyrology and is said to have buried 342 martyrs with his own hands, both traditions are unlikely, as there was no persecution of Christians in his time. His pontificate came in the period of peace between the persecutions of Valerian (253-60) and those of Diocletian (284-305). Records were probably destroyed in the latter period.

In the fourth-century Liberian catalogue Eutychian is listed among the bishops, not among the martyrs. The decretals which bear his name are said to be spurious. He died on 8 December 283 according to the *Depositio episcoporum*, and this date, rather than the 7th, is accepted in the new Roman Martyrology. He was the last pope to be interred in the catacomb of Callistus. Fragments of an epitaph bearing his name were identified in the nineteenth century by the archaeologist G. B. de Rossi.

Lib.Pont., 1, pp. 159-60; Jaffé, 1, pp. 24-5; *D.H.G.E.*, 16, 91-2; *D.C.B.*, p. 357; *O.D.P.*, pp.23-4; *Bibl.SS.*, 5, 317-9.

St Budoc, *Abbot* (Sixth Century)

St Budoc (Budock, Buoc, or Beuzec) is a Celtic saint, variously described as a Welshman, an Irishman, or a Breton. He is the patron saint of Budock and Budoc Vean in Cornwall and of St Budeaux in Devon. Budoc was also honoured at Steynton in Pembrokeshire (Dyfed) and in an Oxford church near the castle, probably of pre-Conquest date.

Budoc is venerated in Brittany. The ninth-century Life of Winwaloe (3 Mar.) describes him as a teacher living on the island of Laurea. The Life of Maglorius (24 Oct.), written about 900, and the eleventh-century *Chronicle of Dol* refer to him as abbot of Youghal and Maglorius' successor as archbishop of Dol. He is the local saint of Plourin, where his relics are venerated. There is a cult without place names at Dol, and there are place names without a cult in Cornouaille.

Budoc is traditionally associated with St Mawes (18 Nov.). In Cornwall, Budock Water and St Mawes are towns on opposite sides of Falmouth harbour; in Brittany, St Mawes was abbot of an island monastery, and Budoc's monastery stood close to it. The main centres of the cult (or cults) are all close to the coast.

Most of the extravagant legends that surround Budoc's name, such as the story of his birth in a barrel at sea, come from the Chronicle of Saint-Brieuc, compiled sometime before 1420, and seem to be derived from Greek mythology. There may have been one Budoc or two—or even more; but there is a very strong tradition of a holy abbot, teacher, and bishop of this name on both sides of the sea route from south-west England to Brittany.

G. H. Doble, *The Saints of Cornwall*, 3 (1964 ed.), 3-14. D. Attwater (ed.), *Saint Budock*, no. 3 in Cornish Saints Series (rp. 1960), is based on Doble's account but omits some local historical and antiquarian material. See also P.B., pp. 166-7, from the *Saints de Bretagne*; *O.D.S.*, p. 74; *S.B.I.*, p. 150; *Dictionnaire des saints Bretons* (1979), pp. 61-3.

St Romaric, *Abbot* (653)

St Amatus (the Abbot; 13 Sept.) tells how he brought about the conversion of a Merovingian nobleman named Romaric, or Remiré. His father's death and the loss of his lands when young had turned Romaric into a homeless wanderer, but before he met Amatus he had become a person of distinction at the court of Clotaire II, with considerable property and a number of serfs. On conversion he set the serfs free, and when he entered the monastery at Luxeuil several of them presented themselves to the abbot, asking to be admitted with him.

In or about 620 Amatus and Romaric left Luxeuil to found another monastery on Romaric's former estate at Habendum in the Vosges. The circumstances are obscure, but it seems that Romaric wanted to found a religious house for women at a time when these were comparatively rare. He had at one time been married, and he had three daughters, two of whom wished to enter the religious life. At Habendum (later to be known as Remiremont) a monastery was established for women as well as one for men, and the two girls took the veil there. Amatus was the first abbot, but he soon retired to a hermitage, visiting the communities only on Sundays to expound scripture and give counsel. His duties devolved upon Romaric, who ruled the communities of monks and nuns from day to day and became abbot when Amatus died. The size of the communities (there were said to be six hundred nuns in addition to the monks) enabled the *laus perennis* to be sung, seven choirs taking it in turns to sing the divine office without intermission. Among the early members of the Congregation was a friend of Romaric, Bishop Arnulf of Metz (18 July), who in about 629 came to end his days in a nearby hermitage.

Romaric's rule lasted for thirty years in all. Shortly before his death he was disturbed to hear that nobles were planning to exclude the young prince Dagobert (24 Dec.) from the Austrasian throne. Old and sick as he was, he made his way to Metz to protest. The nobles treated him with courtesy and escorted him part of the way back to his monastery, where he died only three days later. Dagobert escaped to Ireland and was not immediately restored, but he did regain his throne some twenty years later.

In 1051 a solemn enshrining of Romaric's relics was authorized by Pope Leo IX (19 Apr.), who was a benefactor of Remiremont. The present town of that name marks the site to which the nuns' monastery was removed at the beginning of the tenth century. The monks' monastery continued on the hill above until the time of the French Revolution.

Critical edition of Life in *M.G.H., Scriptores rer. Merov.*, 4, pp. 221-5. See also de Villegas, pp. 511-25; P.B., pp. 131-6, from the *Vie des saints de Franche-Comté*; *D.Cath.Biog.*, p. 1003.

St Galgano (*c.* 1140-81)

Born at Chiusdino, near Siena, of a noble family, Galgano gave himself up to pleasure as a young man, but after experiencing visions of the archangel Michael he became a hermit. He built a cell on a steep mountain near a monastic community founded by St William of Mavalla (10 Feb.) at Monte Siepi. Disciples joined him there but after a time he became worried that ruling a community was not his true vocation. He visited Pope Alexander III in 1181 to discuss the problem but did not live long enough to solve it.

After his death a round church was built over his tomb, where pilgrims came in large numbers. A papal commission of inquiry was set up in 1183, and it is probable that Galgano was canonized in 1190. In that year Cistercian monks took over Monte Siepi at the request of Hugh, bishop of Volterra, but most of Galgano's monks left, scattered over Tuscany, and became Augustinian hermits.

By 1220 a large Cistercian monastery had been built in front of Galgano's hermitage. The Cistercians claimed him as a Cistercian saint. His cult was strongly supported in Siena and Volterra. His relics are preserved in the baptistery of St John Lateran in Rome.

R. Arbesmann, "The three earliest Vitae of S Galganus," in *Didascaliae: Studies in honour of A. M. Albareda* (1961), pp. 3-37; *D.H.G.E.*, 19, 767-8; *Bibl.SS.*, 6, 1-6; *Saints in Italy*, pp. 189-90.

There is a picture of him by Segno in the Opera del Duomo at Siena, and three small pictures of scenes from his life hang in the civic museum at Pisa. The ruins of his hermitage can still be seen.

Bd Narcisa de Jesús Martillo Morán (1837-69)

Narcisa was born at Nobol in Ecuador. Her parents, Pedro Martillo Mosquera and Josefina Morán, worked as farm labourers, and both died when she was very young. She moved to Guayaquil, a large town on the coast, where she lived for more than fifteen years, supporting herself as a manual worker and devoting her life to prayer and care for her neighbours. Early in 1868 she moved to Lima, the capital of Peru, where she lodged in the hostel of the Lay Brothers of St Dominic.

She saw the way to sanctity as through the wisdom of the cross and sought her own crucifixion in poverty and humility. She dedicated eight hours a day to prayer in silence and solitude and frequently spent four hours of the night in penanace, wearing a crown of thorns and supending herself from a cross. She offered her penances to God as a sacrifice for the salvation of mankind, seeking no kind of public recognition or religious status. Her spiritual life was hidden from the world, though witnesses testified to having seen her in a state of ecstasy on a number of occasions.

She died at the age of thirty-seven on 8 December 1869. Her body was translated to Guayaquil in 1955 and subsequently to her place of birth, and she was beatified by Pope John Paul II on 25 October 1993. The pope stressed her close union with God and, because she had moved from country to city, held her up as a model to the many peasant women of Latin America forced to do the same in search of work and sustenance, though their lives might be considered sufficient crucifixion. Locally, her feast-day is celebrated on 30 August.

A.A.S. 85, 7-12 (July-Dec. 1993), p. 665. There is a conventional image of her on the Internet at http://www.aciprensa.com/santecua.htm.

9

The Seven Martyrs of Samosata (? 297 or 308)

Hipparchus (Hyperechius or Hypericus) and Philotheus, magistrates of
Samosata, were commanded to take part in three days of public sacrifices to the
gods. Five young patrician friends, James, Paregrus, Abibus, Romanus, and
Lollian, coming to visit them, found them praying before an image of the cross
and asked why, when the emperor had commanded everyone to prayer at the
temple of Fortune, they were praying at home. They answered that they worshipped the Maker of the world and that they had been brought to the Faith by
a Christian priest. "We therefore find it unlawful to stir out of doors during
these three days, for we abhor the smell of the offerings with which the whole
city reeks." After much discussion the visitors asked to become Christians, and
a messenger was sent for the priest, who baptized them and celebrated Mass.

On the third day of the festival the emperor inquired whether the magistrates had all performed the duty of public sacrifice. He was told that Hipparchus
and Philotheus had absented themselves from public worship for three years,
so he ordered that they should be brought before him. When they came he
asked why they scorned both him and the gods. Hipparchus replied that he
was embarrassed to hear wood and stone called gods. The emperor commanded
that Hipparchus, the elder of the two, should receive fifty stripes and promised
to make Philotheus praetor if he worshipped the gods. Philotheus replied that
honours on such terms would be ignominy. The emperor commanded that
they should both be put in irons and that the five younger men should be
apprehended. They too refused to sacrifice, and each was placed in solitary
confinement.

When the festivities were over all seven were brought out and stretched on
the rack, and each was given twenty stripes. Then they were carried back to
their prison, with orders that no one should be allowed to see them or help
them and that they should be given just enough bread to keep them alive. They
were left in this state for over two months. They were brought out again before
the emperor looking more like corpses than living men. When they were again
invited to sacrifice they asked him not to draw them away from the way to
salvation which Jesus Christ had opened to them. The emperor replied with
fury, "You seek death! Your desire is granted, that you may cease to insult the
gods." He commanded that they should be crucified. A group of other magistrates tried to secure a delay, asking that sentence might be suspended while
Hipparchus and Philotheus settled the public affairs with which they had been

entrusted before their imprisonment and the younger men had time to make their wills. The emperor agreed. When the seven had been brought out to the porch of the circus the magistrates asked a blessing on themselves and the city. The martyrs gave their blessing and addressed the people who had assembled.

Then the emperor ordered seven crosses to be set up near the gate of the city. The martyrs were fastened to their crosses. At noon several women came out and bribed the guards to let them sponge their faces and wipe away the blood. Hipparchus died quickly. James, Romanus, and Lollius died the next day, but Philotheus, Abibus, and Paregrus were still alive when they were taken down, and they were killed by the soldiers. It was ordered that their bodies should be thrown into the river, but a Christian named Bassus bought their bodies from the guards and buried them by night.

These martyrs were commemorated on 29 January in the Byzantine Church, and among the Armenians in October.

This Syriac *passio* was first printed, with a Latin translation, by S. E. Assemani in his *Acta sanctorum martyrum orientalium*, 2, pp. 127-47. Another edition of the Syriac text is that of Bedjan in vol. 4 of his *Acta martyrum et sanctorum*. A translation of the document in French will be found in H. Leclercq, *Les Martyrs*, 2, (1903), pp. 391-403. In *D.C.B.*, 3, p. 85, Dr G. T. Stokes points out that the description of the Baptism of the five young men contains points of considerable liturgical interest, and he raises the question of the date and the emperor concerned, who could have been either Galerius or Maximinus.

St Leocadia, *Martyr* (? 304)

The accounts of Leocadia's passion state that she was a young noblewoman of Toledo who was tortured and imprisoned during the persecution of Diocletian by the governor, Dacian. She was in prison when she heard of the passion of St Eulalia (12 Feb.) and prayed that she might be similarly worthy to die for Christ. She died in prison as a result of her sufferings.

St Ildephonsus (23 Jan.), who was a seventh-century archbishop of Toledo, is said to have had a vision or a dream in which Leocadia arose out of her tomb to thank him, in the name of the Queen of Heaven, for writing the treatise *De virginitate Sanctae Mariae*. Leocadia's cult was clearly well established in his lifetime.

She is the principal patroness of Toledo, and three old churches in the city are dedicated under her name, on what are reputed to be the sites of her home, her prison, and her burial place.

P.L., 115, 1269-72. Leocadia's name occurs in the *Hieronymianum* on 13 December. See Delehaye's commentary, p. 646, and also his *Origines du culte des martyrs*, p. 369, with the references there indicated. The passion of Leocadia printed in *España Sagrada*, 6, pp. 315-7, and in *La Fuente, Hist. eccl. de España*, 1 (1873), pp. 335-7, is late and untrustworthy: cf *Anal.Boll.* 17 (1898), p. 119; *Bibl.SS.*, 7, 1187.

A fifteenth-century statue commemorates her in the church of Cristo de la Vega, Toledo, and there is a seventeenth-century statue in the cathedral at Córdoba.

St Gorgonia (372)

Gorgonia was the elder sister of Gregory Nazanzien (2 Jan.) and of Caesarius of Nazianzen (25 Feb.), who became a distinguished physician. They were the children of a bishop in Cappadocia. Both Gorgonia and Caesarius are known largely through the orations preached at their funerals by their brother Gregory.

Gorgonia married and had three children. She loved the services of the Church, tended the church building, and lived in a sober and God-fearing style. In this period it was often the custom to delay Baptism until quite late in life: Caesarius remained a catechumen until a few months before his death and was baptized only after a narrow escape in an earthquake. Gorgonia did not receive Baptism until she was past middle age, when she was baptized with her husband, children, and grandchildren at what must have been a celebration of a close and loving family life.

Gregory praised her lack of feminine vanity: "She whom we are praising was unadorned, and the absence of ornament was, to her, beauty." He used the occasion as an opportunity to preach against the cosmetics, jewels, and elaborate hairstyles of the fashionable women of his day: "Pigments and pencillings ... she left to women of the stage and of the streets." She devoted her energies to helping those less fortunate than herself, becoming "eyes to the blind, feet to the lame and a mother to the orphan."

P.G., 35, 789-817, contains St Gregory's oration on his sister. N.P.N.F., 7, pp. 238-45, has an English version.

Bd Liborius Wagner, *Martyr* (1593-1631)

When Liborius Wagner was born in Mülhausen in south-west Germany the area was torn with religious conflict. Lutheranism had made great headway, but Catholics such as Peter Canisius (21 Dec.) had rallied his co-religionists with new writings and powerful preaching. Liborius was born into a practising Lutheran family, but at the age of twenty-eight he left his family to become a Catholic. He studied at Strasbourg and was ordained priest in 1625.

In the same year he was sent back to Germany to work in a difficult parish at Altenmünster, in the diocese of Würtemburg. He had a reputation for being devoted to the people of the district, both Catholic and Lutheran, and for defending their rights. He worked there for six years, until the district was invaded by the Swedish army of Charles X in a Protestant crusade. Fr Liborius was betrayed by some Lutherans in his own parish and arrested. He was offered inducements, threatened, beaten, and eventually condemned to death, but his reply was, "I live, suffer, and die as a Catholic, loyal to the Pope."

He died on 9 December 1631. According to one account he was crucified and burned to death on a cross, but others say that he was murdered by the son of a Lutheran preacher. He was thirty-nine years old. At his beatification on 24 March 1974 Pope Paul VI cited him as a model of ecumenism and Christian unity.

N.S.B., 1, p. 113; *N.D.S.*, p. 194.

St Peter Fourier, *Founder* (1565-1640)

Pierre Fourier was born at Mirecourt in Lorraine. At the age of fifteen he was sent to the university directed by the Jesuits at Pont-à-Mousson. He completed his course of studies and when he was twenty joined the Canons Regular of St Augustine at Chaumousey. In 1589 he was ordained priest. It was not until some months later that he sufficiently overcame his sense of unworthiness to say his first Mass.

His abbot sent him back to the university for further theological study. He remained there for some years and completed his doctorate. When he was recalled to his monastery he was appointed procurator and vicar of the abbey parish. It was a difficult task, because the observance of the abbey was poor and his attempts to improve it met with opposition and ridicule. In 1597 he was offered one of the three other parishes served by the Canons, and he deliberately chose Mattaincourt as the most difficult of the three. He set out on a mission to the mountain villages of the area, and according to a companion:

> He travelled on foot, dressed in a coarse robe with a large breviary under his arm, and although poor and without even the means of supporting an ordinary priest, he paid the expenses of his travels, which lasted two months. . . . He would receive nothing from the villagers; he slept on the floor or the ground or on a bench, as he used to do at home . . . and he endured all without complaining, his one satisfaction being to labour for souls.

Peter never forgot that he was a Canon Regular and always lived with an austerity, poverty, and simplicity befitting the monastic life. Although his father had become wealthy and acquired a title under the patronage of a grand duchess of Tuscany, he never sought favours and did not claim the title for himself. He never refused alms or advice, whether spiritual or temporal, to the needy and he showed a remarkable charity for his time, even to Huguenots. On one occasion his companions complained that a Huguenot blacksmith working opposite the church had deliberately made a great noise with blows on his anvil while Peter was celebrating Mass. Peter brushed the complaint aside, saying that the blacksmith probably acted in ignorance.

After much prayer and consideration he decided that the main need of the parish was the education of the children and that this should be free. His first attempt at educating the boys was a failure, but he recruited four women volunteers, Alix Le Clercq, Ganthe André, and Joan and Isabel de Louvroir. He tested them, placed them for training in the House of Canonesses of Poussey in 1598, and eventually helped them to open a free school for girls at Mattaincourt, where he continued to train the teachers daily. He saw that the girls were given what would now be called a business training: they learned how to draw up invoices and receipts, were given practice in composition and writing letters, and were taught to speak correctly. The new Institute of nuns received papal approval in 1616 as the Canonesses Regular of St Augustine of the Congregation of Our Lady. In 1628 Pope Urban VIII allowed the nuns to take a fourth vow binding themselves to the free education of children. Peter Fourier's chief partner, Alix Le Clercq, was beatified as co-foundress in 1947.

Monastic life was at a low ebb in Lorraine at this time. In 1662 the bishop of Toul appointed Peter as visitor apostolic of his Order, with the charge of re-establishing discipline and uniting the houses of the Order into one reformed Congregation. His mission met with opposition, but in the following year the abbot of Lunéville handed over his monastery to Peter and a handful of re-formed Canons. By 1629 observance was re-established, and the Canons Regular of Lorraine were formed into the Congregation of Our Saviour. Much against his will, Peter Fourier was elected superior general in 1632.

It was his hope that the reformed Canons could take up the educational work with boys which he had failed to establish at Mattaincourt. Though he had representations made in Rome, this proposal was not accepted; but the Canons were able to do other kinds of educational work, and when the Jesuits were suppressed in the eighteenth century those of Lorraine handed over their colleges to the Canons Regular.

Peter Fourier was loyal to the House of Lorraine, though he was prepared to remind the duke of his duty. On one occasion his fellow-religious heard his voice raised in a conversation with Duke François in the next room:

"Your Highness will not do that."

"Yes, I shall do it. Why? Who will prevent me?"

"I, for it is not the will of God, and I forbid it."

When he was required to take the Oath of Allegiance to the French king, Louis XIII, he refused and fled to Gray in Franche-Comté. He spent the last four years of his life in exile as chaplain of a convent and teaching in a free school he established there. He died on 9 December 1640 and was canonized in 1897.

Vita P. Forerii (1730); J. Bedel, *La vie du très révérend père Fourier, dit vulgairement le Père de Mattaincourt* (1869 ed.); Fr Bedel was Peter Fourier's disciple and companion. Other Lives by E. de Bazelaire (1846; trans. and ed. G. W., 1850); A. Allaria (1898); L. Pingaud, trans. C. W. W. (1905); J. Renault (1919); B. O. W., in The Saints series (1913); and B. Berthem-Bontoux (1949). *Bibl.SS.*, 10, 828-37.

Bd Bernard Silvestrelli (1831-1911)

Cesare Silvestrelli was born in Rome on 7 November 1831. He entered the Passionist novitiate in 1854. He may have been initially uncertain about his commitment to the Order, as he did not take his first vows till 1857, when he received the names Bernard Mary of Jesus in religion. Once he had made his decision, he was wholeheartedly committed to it. He became superior general in 1878 for a period of ten years and was elected again in 1893, holding the office till 1907.

Little is known about him outside the Order. He had the reputation of being a model priest with a deep spiritual life, and he inspired great affection and loyalty in his brother monks. One of his favourite texts came from Hebrews 4:15: "For it is not as if we had a high priest who is incapable of feeling our weaknesses with us; but we have one who has been tempted in every way that we are, though he is without sin."

Fr Bernard was beatified by Pope John Paul II on 2 October 1988.

N.S.B. 2, pp. 190-1; *N.D.S.*, p. 51.

10

St Gregory III, *Pope* (741)

Among the clergy at the funeral of Pope Gregory II (11 Feb.) in the year 731 was the cardinal priest of the basilica of St Mark—a Syrian who was so well known for his holiness, learning, and ability that the people spontaneously carried him off from the procession and elected him by acclamation to the vacant see: he became pope as Gregory III. He was the last pope to have his election confirmed by the exarch of Ravenna in the name of the Byzantine emperor, but neither this ratification of his election nor his Syrian origin was sufficient to prevent conflict with the Byzantine emperor Leo III. As Islamic pressure increased in Asia Minor the strains between Rome and Constantinople had become acute.

One cause of strain was the different forms taken by pictures and statues and the significance attached to them. In the Eastern Church representations were more prolific, more symbolic, and often took forms in which they might be confused with oriental or classical Greek images. The pictures or statues themselves tended to become objects of adoration. In order to rid their faith of non-Christian associations and superstitions—and perhaps influenced by the fact that Islam allowed no pictorial representation at all—the Iconoclasts in Constantinople began to attack *Iconodulia*, or "Christian Idolatry."

Leo the Isaurian was an Army commander who had seized power in Constantinople after defending the city against an Arab attack. In the philistine hands of his military commanders Iconoclasm became persecution. According to Theophanes, the schools of arts and theology in Constantinople were closed, and "the burning of the books" began. Pictures and statues were smashed. In 726 the image of Christ over the gate of the imperial palace in Constantinople, greatly venerated by the people of the city, was demolished by a party of workmen and soldiers. There were riots in protest, and there may have been some bloodshed, though George the Monk's unsupported story of the burning of the professors is probably a partisan account. In 730 Leo forbade the veneration of all holy images.

In Rome, where the artistic traditions were very different, these developments were viewed with great alarm. Pope Gregory sent a priest with a message of protest to the emperor, but the priest was deterred and returned to Rome without delivering the message. Successive envoys were despatched, but they were seized by Leo's imperial officers and banished.

Gregory then summoned a synod in Rome, where bishops, clergy, and nobility approved the excommunication of anyone condemning the veneration of images or destroying them. The emperor, outraged, decided to use force: he sent an armed fleet to capture the pope and convey him to Constantinople. The ships were lost in a storm, so he took further action by seizing the papal estates in Calabria and Sicily and recognizing the jurisdiction of the patriarch of Constantinople over eastern Illyricum. This was a serious financial blow to the papacy and the first major step to schism between Rome and Constantinople.

The exarch had presented Pope Gregory with six magnificent onyx columns: Gregory had them set before the altar above St Peter's tomb, with images of Christ and the saints and lamps burning around them—a silent protest against Iconoclasm. Five of the columns are still in St Peter's, though one has been lost. Gregory rebuilt and decorated a number of churches and beautified Rome with magnificent images to reinforce his opposition to the Byzantine emperor. He built an oratory in St Peter's and ordered special prayers to be recited: fragments of inscriptions may still be seen in the crypt of the Vatican basilica.

The writer of the *Liber Pontificalis*, who is concerned primarily with material and liturgical developments in Rome, has little to say about Pope Gregory's other preoccupations. Losing power in the East, Gregory turned his attention to missionary work and church organization in the West. He appointed St Boniface (5 June) archbishop in Germany and gave full backing to his work, sending the English monk St Willibald (7 June in this edition; 7 July in future editions) to assist him. A decision with less happy consequences was the recognition of Egbert as archbishop of York in 735. The pope gave him rights in the north of England equivalent to those of the archbishop of Canterbury in the south; but when Tatwine of Canterbury visited, he appointed him his vicar for the whole of England—thus setting the conditions for the long conflict between the two English provinces that was to reach crisis point in the martyrdom of Thomas Becket (29 Dec.) in 1170.

Shortly before the end of Pope Gregory's life the Lombards threatened Rome, and he sent a famous appeal to Charles Martel and the Franks of the West rather than to the emperor in the East; but on 22 October 741 Charles Martel died, and Gregory died only a few weeks later, on 10 December. "He was," says the *Liber Pontificalis*, "a man of deep humility and true wisdom. He had a good knowledge of the Sacred Scriptures and knew the psalms by heart. He was a polished and successful preacher, skilled in both Latin and Greek, and a stout upholder of the Catholic Faith: a lover of poverty and the poor, a protector of the widowed and orphaned, a friend to monks and nuns."

Jaffé, 1, pp. 257-62; *Lib.Pont.*, 1, pp. 415-25; Mann, 1, part 2, pp. 204-24; *P.L.*, 89, 557-98; G. Every, *The Byzantine Patriarchate*, 451-1204 (1947), chs. 7 and 8, "Iconodulia" and "Iconoclasm," pp. 99-111.

Bd Jerome Ranuzzi (1455)

Jerome Ranuzzi was a scholar and a contemplative, born near the end of the fourteenth century at Sant'Angelo in Vado, a small town near Urbino. Vado was one of the first places to have a convent of Servite nuns, and before he was twenty Jerome took the habit of the Servite friars. After his profession he was sent to the university of Bologna, where he took his doctorate in theology and was later ordained priest. He was employed as a teacher in various Servite houses of study in Italy.

After some years he was given permission to retire for a time to the priory in his native town, and there he developed a reputation as a wise counsellor. Frederick of Montefeltro, duke of Urbino, asked the Servite authorities for his services as a theologian and personal adviser. Although Jerome did not want to enter court life, he was constrained by obedience to accept the post. It is not known how long he remained at Frederick's court, but he conducted negotiations with the Holy See and other matters of State to the duke's satisfaction. Eventually he was allowed to go back to Sant'Angelo, where he lived a life of solitude and prayer.

Jerome died suddenly in 1455, and the devotion of the people was so great that his body, instead of being buried in the graveyard, was enshrined above an altar in the church of the Servites in Sant'Angelo. His cult was confirmed by Pope Pius VI in 1775.

Some Servite writers are said to have confused this Jerome with another Servite named Jerome who lived rather earlier and died in another part of Italy. Consequently, there is only limited information that can be confidently attributed to the life of Jerome Ranuzzi.

A. Giani, *Annalium Sacri Ordinis Servorum*, 1 (1719), pp. 491-2; B. M. Sporr, *Lebensbilder aus dem Serviten-Orden* (1892), pp. 615-20; *Nota Bibliografica of the Order of the Friar Servants of Mary* (1982), pp. 11-43; A. Serra in *Bibl.SS.*, 11, 47-50; *D.Cath.Biog.*, p. 974; J. M. Chamberlain, *Servants of Mary* (1988), pp. 38-9.

The London Martyrs of 1591

Under this title are celebrated the lives of seven martyrs who died in London on 10 December 1591 following a royal proclamation leading to a stricter enforcement of the laws against Catholics: St Edmund Gennings, St Polidore Plasden, St Swithin Wells, Bd John Mason, Bd Sidney Hodgson, St Eustace White, and Bd Brian Lacey.

Edmund Gennings, or Genyngs, alias Ironmonger, born in Lichfield in 1567, was the principal priest concerned. He studied at Reims, was ordained at Soissons, and was sent to England on 9 April 1590, landing at Whitby. He was estranged from his family because of his faith. He made his way to Lichfield, only to find that his parents had died, and then went to London to seek his brother John, who was an ardent Puritan. John warned him that if, as he suspected, he had become a priest, he would bring death upon himself and discredit his friends. Edmund went into the country for some months, but in the autumn of 1591 he was back in London, where he celebrated Mass at the house of an elderly schoolmaster, Swithin Wells, and his wife, Margaret. During the celebration the notorious Topcliffe the priest-catcher arrived with his officers. The men in the congregation kept them at bay until Mass was finished; then Edmund Gennings and Polidore Plasden, also a priest, were arrested, together with Mr and Mrs Wells and two laymen, John Mason and Sidney Hodgson, who were all accused of helping them.

All six were sentenced to death. Edmund Gennings was hanged, drawn, and quartered and Swithin Wells hanged, at Gray's Inn Fields, close by the Wells' house. Polidore Plasden and the two laymen were executed with equal barbarity at Tyburn, together with Eustace White and Brian Lacey. Mrs Wells was sentenced to death with her husband, but reprieved. She died in prison eleven years later.

Eustace White was a priest from Louth in Lincolnshire. Like Edmund Gennings, he was estranged from his family. At his conversion his father had deliberately cursed him. He was betrayed during his apostolate in the west of England by a Blandford lawyer to whom he talked too freely of religion, taken to London, and treated with extreme cruelty in Bridewell. He was chained, half-starved, and tortured by Topcliffe seven times to make him reveal the names of those who had helped him or in whose houses he had celebrated Mass.

Brian Lacey was also a priest from Louth in Lincolnshire. He was betrayed by his own brother. Edmund Gennings' brother, John, his only surviving relative, maintained at the time of Edmund's death that he "rather rejoiced than any way bewailed the untimely and bloody end of his nearest kinsman," but ten days later he underwent a remarkable conversion. He became a Catholic, a Friar Minor, and the minister of the English Franciscan province. In 1619-21 he founded the convent of English Tertiary Sisters at Brussels, which later moved to Taunton.

All seven martyrs were beatified in 1929, when the cause of Mrs Wells was postponed for further evidence. The canonization of Edmund Gennings, Polidore Plasden, Swithin Wells, and Eustace White took place on 25 October 1970, and they rank among the Forty Martyrs of England and Wales.

A Life of Edmund Gennings, written by his brother John, was printed at Saint-Omer in 1614. Further sources on this group of martyrs will be found in the publications of the Catholic Record Society, 5, (1908) *passim*: see especially pp. 131ff., pp. 204ff. See also Bede Camm, *Nine Martyr Monks* (1931 reprint), pp. 60-72; J. H. Pollen, *Acts of the English Martyrs* (1891), pp. 98-126; Anstruther, pp. 128-9, 278-9, 377-8.

St John Roberts and Bd Thomas Somers, *Martyrs* (1610)

John Roberts was a Benedictine monk, born in Wales, and a member of the Benedictine monastery at Valladolid in Spain. Thomas Somers was a secular priest from Westmoreland. Though their apostolates were very different, they were charged together, sentenced together, and martyred together at Tyburn after a memorable joint witness.

The village of Trawsfynedd, where John Roberts was born in 1577, lies some miles north of Dolgellau, in mid-Wales. His family and the exact place of his birth are uncertain, but he seems to have been of ancient stock on both sides. He received his early education from an aged priest, and, though brought up nominally a Protestant, he was, as he himself said, always a Catholic at heart. When he was nineteen he went to St John's College at Oxford, where William Laud was still in residence, and Roberts shared the rooms of John Jones of Llanfrynach, afterwards well known as Fr Leander-of-St Martin, O.S.B. He was evidently seeking his vocation: he did not finish his course at Oxford, probably because he was unwilling to take the Oath of Supremacy. At some point he spent a few weeks at Furnivall's Inn as a law student. He taught in a grammar school for a time and sent students to Douai. Early in 1598 he went to Douai himself. In June he was formally received into the Catholic Church at Notre-Dame-de-Paris by Canon Louis Godebert. He then went to the English College at Valladolid before receiving the Benedictine habit at the royal monastery of San Benito in Valladolid. His name in religion was Brother John of Merioneth. His old friend John Jones soon joined him, and they were professed together with six others from the English College before the end of 1560 at the monastery of St Martin at Compostela.

The Spanish Benedictines were bound by perpetual enclosure, so it seemed unlikely that they would be able to take part in the English mission; but on 27 February 1601, Bd Mark Barkworth (27 Feb.), who had been the originator and leader of the Benedictine movement among the English students at Valladolid, was martyred at Tyburn. Petitions were presented to the pope asking that the English monks might be allowed to go on the mission, and on 5 December 1602 Pope Clement VIII granted permission to the English monks of both the Valladolid and Cassinese Congregations. Three weeks later, on the feast of St Stephen, the first martyr, Fr Roberts set out, accompanied by Fr Augustine Bradshaw. It took the two monks three months to reach London, and although they came disguised in plumed hats and doublets and wearing swords, they were soon arrested and deported.

The history of John Roberts' witness is one of repeated arrest, imprisonment, release, and exile. Within a few weeks he returned to London, where there was an epidemic. Some thirty thousand people are thought to have died during its first and worst year, and all the early writers who refer to John Roberts (or Wilson, which was his alias) mention his work for the sick with admiration. He was known as "the parish priest of London" and made many converts. In the spring of 1604 he was arrested on the point of embarking for the Continent, but his captors failed to identify him as a priest, perhaps because he still looked very young, and he was released again. He continued his labours till 5 November 1605, when there was a round-up of Catholics on discovery of the Gunpowder Plot. He was arrested in the house of the wife of Thomas Percy, one of the conspirators. On this occasion he was kept in the Gatehouse prison at Westminster, within the precincts of the abbey. Eventually it was established that Mrs Percy was his landlady. Her house was his normal lodging when he was in London. Thomas Percy had left his wife some months before, so that she was not in any way implicated in the conspiracy. As a result of the intervention of the French ambassador Fr John was released and banished.

This time he remained abroad for over a year, taking a principal part in the foundation, with Fr Augustine Bradshaw, of the monastery for the English monks of the Valladolid Congregation at Douai. This became the headquarters of the English Congregation and is now St Gregory's Abbey at Downside. At the end of 1607 he came back to England and, for the fourth time, "fell into the hands of the priest-catchers." He was examined and refused to take the Oath of Allegiance, even in a shortened form. He escaped from the Gatehouse and was at large for some time in conditions of great secrecy but was again apprehended. Again the French ambassador came to the rescue, and again John was banished. He went to Spain and then to St Gregory's at Douai.

When there was a renewed outbreak of plague in England he came back for the last time, early in 1610. By this time alarm over the Gunpowder Plot had resulted in a new wave of severe measures against Catholics: on 2 June a proclamation from Parliament was issued requiring all Catholics to leave England within four weeks and enjoining bishops, justices, and other officials to be diligent in administering the oath. Fr John may have been arrested and have escaped in July, but this is not certain. In December he was arrested for the last time. It was the first Sunday in Advent, and he was just ending Mass at a house in Holborn with five other priests. He was about to recite the Prologue to St John's Gospel when the officers broke in. The altar was hastily dismantled, the lights extinguished, and the priests hidden in a cellar. There they were discovered and, still in their vestments, were dragged through the streets to Newgate.

The trial was a notable occasion. John Roberts was arraigned together with Thomas Somers, a secular priest who had probably been present at the Mass, before Lord Chief Justice Coke, the bishop of London, and others. They were charged with their priesthood under 27 Eliz. c. 2, the Act which enjoined all Jesuits, seminary priests, and other priests to leave the country within forty days, on pain of death for high treason. They both refused the Oath of Allegiance, and Fr John stated under examination that he was a priest and a monk who had come into the country "to work for the salvation of souls, and would continue to do so were I to live longer." George Abbot, the bishop of London, called him a disturber and a seducer of the people, to which Fr John replied that if he were so, "then were our ancestors deceived by blessed St Augustine, the apostle of the English, who was sent here by the pope of Rome, St Gregory the Great. . . . I am sent here by the same Apostolic See that sent him before me." When ordered to be silent, he made a spirited attack on the clergy who subscribed to the Elizabethan settlement:

> I must speak, as my mission is from heaven. St Matthew says in chapter 28 "Go ye and teach all nations, baptizing them and teaching them to observe all things whatsoever I have commanded you." Your ministers do not do this, because they do not fulfil in their lives and actions the command of Christ. They do not administer the sacrament of penance or of extreme unction. I do. And withal I teach obedience to princes as a matter of conscience, against the false doctrine of Luther and his companions. All this I can prove to you.

He rebuked the bishop for sitting with civil judges in the trial of a capital cause, and appealed to the bench to decide the case themselves lest the jury, simple and ignorant men who would not understand the issues, should be guilty of his blood and that of his fellow-prisoner. The appeal was disregarded and they were both found guilty and condemned to death.

The next day a Spanish lady, Doña Luisa de Carvajal, who had come to England to assist the priests, bribed the jailer of Newgate to transfer the two from the condemned cell to the company of other Catholic prisoners, and a remarkable scene ensued. Twenty Catholics sat down together for supper. Doña Luisa headed the table, with John Roberts to her right and Thomas Somers to her left. Both were full of joy, and Fr John had a scruple of conscience. During supper he asked Doña Luisa whether his "great glee" might not be disedifying to others: should he retire into a corner and give himself up to prayer? Doña Luisa told him that he could not be better employed than in letting them all see with what cheerful courage he prepared to die for Christ. After supper she washed the feet of the martyrs, an act of homage which greatly angered the king (James I) when it was reported to him.

On the following morning they were handed over to the sheriff of Middlesex, drawn on hurdles to Tyburn, and there hanged with sixteen other condemned men. The martyrs were allowed to hang until they were dead because of the great sympathy shown by the crowd. Afterwards their heads were displayed on London Bridge and their bodies buried at Tyburn, from where their remains were recovered by Bd Maurus Scott and Doña Luisa. John Roberts was thirty-three years old at the time of his death. His relics have disappeared in revolutionary upheavals, but some relics of Thomas Somers are now at Downside Abbey.

John Roberts and Thomas Somers were both beatified in 1929; John Roberts was canonized as one of the Forty Martyrs of England and Wales (25 Oct.) in 1970.

A full biography of John Roberts, *A Benedictine Martyr in England*, was published by Dom Bede Camm in 1897, and this includes an exhaustive list of the sources. See also J. H. Pollen, *Acts of the English Martyrs* (1891), pp. 143-70; Stanton, pp. 593-5; T. P. Ellis, *Catholic Martyrs of Wales*, 1535-1680 (1933), pp. 79-91, and *The Welsh Benedictines of the Terror* (1936), *passim*, especially pp. 43-54, 76-104; Bede Camm, *Nine Martyr Monks* (1931), pp. 107-70. An appendix deals with relics and sources. For the relics of both martyrs see Bede Camm, *Forgotten Shrines* (1910), pp. 355-6, 373, 378. For Thomas Somers see *M.M.P.*, pp. 321-3.

ST JOHN OF THE CROSS (p. 121, below)
White top half of cross, for his purity in faith; red lower half,
for his witness under persecution. Black top field for his Jesuit training,
divided light and dark brown lower field for Carmelite habit

11

ST DAMASUS I, *Pope* (384)

Damasus is said to have been a Spaniard, but he was probably born in Rome.
His father was a priest in the church of San Lorenzo in Rome, according to
inscriptions. Damasus became deacon in the same church. When Pope Liberius
died in 366, Damasus, who was then about sixty years old, was chosen Bishop
of Rome. According to the *Liber Pontificalis*, "a council of *sacerdotes* was held,
and they confirmed Damasus because he was the stronger and had the greater
number of supporters: that is how Damasus was confirmed." A minority group
chose another candidate, Ursinus or Ursicinus, who was irregularly consecrated and whom they supported with great violence and some bloodshed.
They were put down with even greater force by the civil power, and Damasus
was personally accused of hiring mercenaries who carried out a three-day massacre. The charioteers are said to have supported him, and the grave-diggers
came out of the catacombs with their spades as weapons. About 150 people
were killed in all.

The emperor Valentinian banished Ursinus, but he continued to make alle-
gations against Damasus, and the bishops, appalled by the ferocity of the massacre, were not enthusiastic in their support of the new pope. Damasus called a
synod in September 368 and asked them to condemn Ursinus, but they replied
that they had not come together to condemn anyone unheard. Ursinus made a
variety of accusations against Damasus, including one of adultery, and greatly
weakened his moral authority. As late as 378 Damasus had to clear himself of
charges before the prefect of Rome and again before a synod.

Damasus is said to have lived in great pomp and magnificence. St Jerome (30
Sept.), who was his secretary for a time, reports that one pagan senator said to
Damasus, "Make me Bishop of Rome, and I will be a Christian tomorrow."
His entertainments were opulent and rivalled those of the imperial court. His
Christian critics said that he was a worldly man with social ambitions; but it
could be argued that his success with the great families of Rome helped to
promote Christianity as the accepted religion of the empire at a crucial period.
In 380 he saw the end of the public worship of the old Roman gods. The
emperor Gratian in the West and the emperor Theodosius in the East proclaimed Christianity, as professed by the bishops of Rome and Alexandria, to
be the religion of the Roman power. On the petition of the Christian senators,
supported by Damasus, Gratian sanctioned the removal of the altar of Victory
from the senate-house and resigned the title of *pontifex maximus*.

From that time on the papacy became increasingly identified with Roman civic pride and imperial power. Damasus is remembered for his devotion to the relics and resting-places of the martyrs and for his work in the draining, opening out, and adornment of the catacombs (perhaps his plans were already in hand when the grave-diggers came out in his support). He had the passages widened to make it possible for crowds of pilgrims to visit, opened shafts to admit light and air, constructed flights of stairs leading to the more illustrious shrines, and had the chambers faced with marble. He devised many inscriptions and epigrams for the tombs, some sixty of which are still extant either in originals or copies. They were inscribed in the finest calligraphy by a well-known artist, Furius Dionysius Filocalus. This is now known as "Damasine script."

The glory of Rome was to be based on the blood of the Christian martyrs, not on the old pagan gods; and the rival claims of Jerusalem and Alexandria to be the centre of Christian devotion were to be resisted. Damasus wrote in one epigram that "although the East sent the apostles, yet because of the merit of their martyrdom, Rome has acquired a superior right to claim them as citizens." He was the first pope to speak of Rome as "the apostolic see." Jerome supported this view, advising Damasus that he was "the successor of the Fisherman" and "the rock on which the Church is built."

Damasus instituted a formal system of administration in which papal letters to the bishops took the form of decretals—documents containing rulings designed to secure greater uniformity in the Church—rather than pastoral advice. He built a new library for the papal archives close to his former church of San Lorenzo. The formulation of doctrine, which involved the condemnation of heresies and the development of the institutional framework of the Church, happened in the same period, and the two movements were mutually reinforcing. It was during the pontificate of Damasus that the Western Church finally freed itself from Arianism.

Jerome spent only three years in Rome, but Damasus continued to provide patronage and encouragement for his major task of producing a new translation of the Latin Bible, later to form the main part of the Vulgate. Jerome tells us that Damasus himself was learned in the scriptures, and Damasus wrote him a letter on points of exegesis that supports this claim. Theodoret says that the pope "was illustrious for his holy life, and ready to preach and do all things in defence of apostolic doctrine."

Damasus died on 11 December 384, at the age of about eighty. He wrote a general epitaph for the "papal crypt" of the cemetery of St Callistus, ending, "I, Damasus, wished to be buried here, but I feared to offend the ashes of these holy ones."

He was buried with his mother and sister at a small church which he had built on the via Ardeatina, but his remains were later transferred to the church now known as San Lorenzo in Damaso, where both he and his father had served as priests. The discovery of the epitaphs is due to the work of the archaeologist G. B. de Rossi (1822-94), who toured the catacombs with Fr Marchi, S.J., and wrote the four-volume *La Roma sotteranea cristina*. Among the epitaphs which have been preserved is one that Damasus wrote for himself, an act of faith in Christ's resurrection and his own:

> He who walking on the sea could calm the bitter waves, who gives life to the dying seeds of the earth; he who was able to loose the mortal chains of death, and after three days' darkness could bring again to the upper world the brother for his sister Martha: he, I believe, will make Damasus rise again from the dust.

Jaffé, 1, pp. 37-40; St Jerome, Letters 15, 16, and 35 in N.P.N.F., 6; *Lib.Pont.*, 1, pp. 212-5; *P.L.*, 13, 347-424 contains letters, poems, and epigrams. See also *D.H.G.E.*, 14, 48-53; *N.C.E.*, 4, pp. 624-5. The article in *D.A.C.L.*, 4, 145-97 provides a very full bibliography, and *C.M.H*, pp. 643- 4, has useful references. For background to the pontificate see R. L. Poole, *Lecture on the History of the Papal Chancery* (1915); J. Richards, *The Popes and Papacy in the early Middle Ages* (1979). See also Antony Ferrus, *Epigrammata Damasiana* (1942).

There is a Ghirlandaio fresco showing Damasus wearing his papal tiara in the Sistine Chapel in St Peter's, Rome.

SS Fuscian and Victoricus, *Martyrs* (date unknown)

The account of these martyrs tells us that Fuscian and Victoricus were missionaries from Rome who came into Gaul at the same time as St Quentin (31 Oct.) and set themselves the task of evangelizing the Morini. Victoricus established his headquarters at Boulogne, and Fuscian at the village of Helfaut, near Thérouanne, some distance inland, where he built a small church. Both of them met with opposition from the pagan Gauls and Romans but made a number of converts. After a time they went together to visit St Quentin at the town between Arras and Reims which now bears his name.

On the way they heard that persecution was raging at Amiens, so they passed on to Sains, where they lodged with an old man named Gentian. He was not a Christian but was well disposed toward Christianity. He told them that St Quentin had been martyred six weeks earlier, and they talked with him of the Faith. When the Roman governor arrived with a troop of soldiers to arrest them he was met by the aged Gentian with drawn sword, declaring that he was ready to die for the true God. He was executed immediately, but this story is evidently not accepted by the compilers of the new Roman Martyrology, which omits his name from today's commemoration. Fuscian and Victoricus were taken in chains to Amiens, tortured, and beheaded when they refused to recant.

Though some of the legends surrounding the passion of these martyrs are plainly fabulous, the association with St Quentin and local tradition suggest that a martyrdom did take place, and it was long remembered in Picardy.

C.M.H., pp. 643, 645; *P.B.*, pp. 189-97, from the *Hagiographie du diocèse d'Amiens*. For questions of authenticity, see Duchesne, *Fastes*, 3, pp. 141-52.

St Daniel the Stylite (409-93)

After Simeon Stylites the Elder (1 Sept.), Daniel is the best known of the Syrian stylites, or pillar-hermits, whose strange way of life became a feature of the Eastern Church in the fifth century. They lived a life of extreme asceticism, seeking to share in the sufferings of Christ, while at the same time making the maximum witness. Their mortifications and the holiness of their lives were plain for all to see. They were dependent on disciples or well-wishers for supplies which could be raised on ropes or brought up on ladders; visitors were sometimes allowed to ascend the pillars for advice or healing; and they often attracted crowds of sightseers and pilgrims.

Daniel's biography, written by a younger contemporary who was probably one of his disciples, is confirmed in its general accuracy by other sources for the history of the same period. It begins with a promising child, a native of the town of Maratha, near Samosata, dedicated to God before his birth by devout parents. They would have known the story of the Seven Martyrs of Samosata (9 Dec.), martyred about a century earlier. When Daniel was twelve years old, he went to a nearby monastery and begged the abbot to receive him. The abbot told him that he would be unable to bear the discipline of monastic life, but the boy replied, "I know well that I am young and weak, but I trust in God, and your holy prayers." He was allowed to stay, to the joy of his parents, and in time he became a monk. Some years later he accompanied his abbot on a journey to Antioch, and they lodged on the way in the monastery at Telanissos (Dair Sem'an), where Simeon Stylites had received his training in the monastic life. A discussion developed between the monks of Telanissos and some monks from Mesopotamia on the value of Simeon's witness. The local monks spoke with respect of the hardships he was enduring "for the sake of the Lord," but the Mesopotamian monks contended that it was "but a vainglorious proceeding," saying that ascetic practices pleasing to God might be undertaken quietly in a monastery, without the necessity of living on top of a pillar. They were persuaded to go and visit Simeon and were very impressed with what they found: "When they arrived at that place, and saw the wildness of the spot and the height of the pillar, and the fiery heat of the scorching sun and the Saint's endurance and his welcome to strangers and further, too, the love he shewed towards them, they were amazed."

Simeon asked that the ladder be put in place and invited them to come up, but the monks were ashamed and made excuses. Then Daniel asked if he could ascend. Simeon allowed him to come up, blessed him, and foretold that he would suffer much for his faith. Daniel's abbot died soon after, and the monks would have made him the successor, but Daniel declined and went again to see St Simeon, staying for fourteen days at the monastery near the pillar. He then set out for the Holy Land, but since there was war on the way he went instead to Constantinople, where he built himself a hermitage in an abandoned temple at Philempora. He remained there for nine years under the patronage of the patriarch St Anatolius (3 July).

Simeon died in 459. He left his cloak to the emperor Leo I, but his disciple Sergius was barred from delivering it in person and so gave it to Daniel: the mantle of Elijah fell upon Elisha. Daniel, who must have been over fifty by this time, resolved to follow Simeon's way of life. He chose a spot some distance from Constantinople, where friends provided a pillar "about the height of two men" with a balustrade. (There are no records of pillar-hermits falling off their pillars: many deprived themselves of sleep, and merely dozed, leaning on the balustrade.) There Daniel took up his *stasis*, or station, devoting himself to prayer and meditation. The land on which the pillar had been erected belonged to the emperor Leo's steward. He ordered Daniel to leave, but when he had witnessed the power of his prayers for a sick boy said to be possessed of a demon he was convinced of Daniel's holiness. He had a higher pillar with a broader top constructed, and Daniel consented to be moved to it. Then the steward went to Constantinople and "related everything in detail to the emperor and to all the great folk of the court."

The emperor sent a message, asking Daniel to pray that the empress Verina might bear him a son. Later, when a son was born to them, he went to see Daniel, who allowed the ladder to be set in position. The emperor "went up to the servant of God, and begged to touch his feet." When he saw how mortified and swollen they were, he was amazed at Daniel's endurance. The emperor had two columns built for him, even higher, connected by a bridge of planks held together with iron bars. On one was his "station," and from the other, he could bless the crowds that came for healing. Apparently the design was poor, for when there was a violent thunderstorm, the supports were torn away and the base was shattered. Daniel's disciples "stood trembling and aghast, turning their head from side to side as the column swayed now this way and that . . . but the servant of God answered not a word to anyone, but persevered in prayer and invocations to God for aid." When the emperor heard of this he had the columns made secure and threatened to have the architect executed; but Daniel begged that he should be done no harm, and he was pardoned.

Daniel had no shelter. He was exposed to storms, high winds, burning sun and severe frosts. On one occasion, his leather tunic was ripped from him by the force of the winds, and he was left exposed to the snow all night long. "He came to look like a pillar of salt. . . . His disciples saw the hair of his head and beard glued to the skin by icicles, and his face was hidden by ice as though it were covered by glass . . . and he was quite unable to speak or move." The disciples brought cans of warm water and sponges and gradually thawed him out. When the emperor heard of this he climbed the ladder again and begged Daniel to let him have an iron shelter constructed. Daniel was unwilling, because he knew that Simeon had never had a shelter; but the emperor pointed out that God had given him a task to do, and it was no part of the divine purpose for him to kill himself outright. So the shelter was built and with this addition Daniel remained on his column until he was eighty-four years old. Considering their feats of endurance, the stylites were remarkably long-lived.

Daniel's relations with Gennadius, patriarch of Constantinople, were not easy. At first, Gennadius advised the emperor's steward to drive Daniel off his land, saying that he had no authority to be there. Later, when ordered by the emperor to "go up to the holy man and honour him with the rank of priest," Gennadius temporized until the emperor grew angry. When he finally made the journey with an attendant party of clerics Daniel refused to allow him to climb to the top of the pillar and would not speak to him apart from asking his blessing. It was a very hot day. The crowds pressed round, impatient because of the great heat and the lack of action, and at last the patriarch read the ordination prayers at the bottom of the column. Then Daniel let him climb the ladder, "holding in his hand the chalice of the Holy Body and the Precious Blood of Jesus Christ our God." It must have been a risky journey. Presumably Gennadius laid hands on Daniel, though this is not mentioned in the Life. The two exchanged the kiss of peace, and each received Communion from the hands of the other. The waiting crowds were satisfied, as was the emperor.

Daniel became a wonder of the empire. He was said to have foretold a fire in Constantinople in 465, and the people ran in crowds to the pillar, where the saint, stretching out his hands, prayed for them. The emperor Leo frequently visited and greatly respected him. When the king of the Lazi in Colchis came to renew his alliance with the Romans, Leo took him to see Daniel. The barbarian king prostrated himself before the pillar, and the holy man was witness to the treaty between the two princes. Sick people were often taken to his pillar. Some were brought up to the top of the column and Daniel laid hands on them or anointed them.

The crowds flocked to his pillar. He spoke to them with simplicity of the love of God and the care of the poor, of brotherly love and humility and obedience. He is known to have descended from his pillar once—when, after the death of Leo I, Basiliscus usurped the imperial throne and supported the Eutychian heretics. The patriarch of Constantinople appealed to Daniel for help, and the old hermit came down "with difficulty, because of the pain in his feet." He was received with joy and excitement by the crowds and carried shoulder-high. Basiliscus went to the saint, representing himself as "a simple soldier-man" and promising to annul his orders in favour of heresy. Daniel rebuked him severely and returned to his pillar. A few months later, the emperor Zeno returned with an army, and Basiliscus fled. One of the first things Zeno did after his return was to visit Daniel on his double column.

When he was eighty-four years old, Daniel gave his testament for his friends and disciples: a short document marked by a spirit of charity and affection and setting out clearly the duty owed by created beings to God. After celebrating Mass at midnight on his pillar he knew that he was dying. The patriarch Euphemius was sent for, and there St Daniel died. He was buried in the oratory at the foot of the pillar where he had lived for thirty-three years and three months.

P. G., 116, pp. 969-1038. Delehaye, *Les saints stylites* (1923), includes a critical text of the long Greek Life of St Daniel (pp. 1-94), a critical text of an early compendium (pp. 95-103), and an adaptation of the Metaphrast (pp. 104-47). The preface contains a description of the manuscripts used and a summary of the saint's life. The Life was published for the first time in *Anal.Boll.* 32 (1913); there is a good English version, with introduction and notes, in E. Dawes and N. H. Baynes, *Three Byzantine Saints* (1948).

Bd Franco of Grotti (1211-91)

Franco Lippi was born in Grotti, near Siena, and experienced a remarkable conversion at the age of fifty. As a young man he was violent, insubordinate, and lazy, and his conduct became worse after the death of his father. To avoid a prosecution for murder he joined a group of bandits and led a dangerous and evil life.

When he was fifty Franco lost his eyesight, and the shock of this sudden deprivation brought about a complete change in him. He made a Confession and set out on a long and painful pilgrimage to the shrine of Santiago de Compostela. There his blindness was healed, but his spiritual insight remained. He is said to have made a further pilgrimage, barefoot, from Compostela to Rome—a distance of over a thousand miles.

While praying in a Carmelite church he had a vision of Our Lady in which he was told that he must make public reparation for his past sins. He accordingly went about the streets in sackcloth, beating himself with a whip. Eventually he asked to be admitted to the Carmelite Order, but his age—he was by this time sixty-five—and his appalling reputation made the friars dubious of such a postulant. While they did not deny him absolutely, they told him to try again in five years' time. This he did, and he was allowed to join as a lay brother. He lived for ten years in Carmel, and both his brother Carmelites and the people of the city were amazed at his fervour and the vehemence of his penance. Some of his instruments of penance—a mesh vest, a headband, a collar, a chain, and a small ball he kept in his mouth for recollection, are preserved in Siena. After his death there was a general agreement that he was a very holy penitent. His cult was confirmed in 1670 by Pope Clement X.

In 1590 the Dominican Gregory Lombardelli published *La vita del B Franco Sanese da Grotti*, in which he appears to have confused Franco's life with that of a Servite, Bd Franco of Siena, who died in 1328 and is thought to have been a great preacher and a martyr. Other writers have followed Lombardelli in confusing the two. One is buried at Cremona and the other in Siena, but official exhumations have failed to distinguish the relics.

John Bale's Life in MS. Cotton 73 in the Bodleian Library at Oxford appears to be the most reliable source. For a modern account see Rafael María López-Melús, *Los Santos Carmelitos* (1989), pp. 56-7. L. Saggi, in *Saints of Carmel*, trans. G. N. Pausback (1972), pp. 126-7, deals with the problems raised by Lombardelli's Life.

Bd Hugolino Magalotti (1373)

Little is known about the life of this holy man, whose feast is kept by the Friars Minor. He was born near Camerino in the early part of the fourteenth century and was left an orphan while a young man. He gave his patrimony to the poor, became a Franciscan tertiary, and went to a lonely spot to live as a hermit.

His life was given to manual work, contemplation, and penance, and accounts of his sanctity brought many to his cell, often sick people seeking a cure. He died on 11 December 1373, and a large crowd followed his body to its burial at the parish church of Fiegni. Pope Pius IX confirmed his cult in 1856.

See *Auréole Séraphique*, 4, pp. 177-8, where it is stated that an old manuscript was in existence at the time of Hugolino's beatification. He is also mentioned in Jacobilli's *Santi e beati dell' Umbria*, and by other writers of that district. *F.B.S.*, pp. 923-5; *Bibl.SS.*, 8, 491.

BB Martin Lumberas and Melchior Sánchez, *Martyrs* (1632)

These two Augustinian friars were both Spanish. They were sent to work in the Philippines when the Spanish Empire was at its most extensive. The islands, discovered by the Spanish admiral Gómez de Villalobos in 1543, were named after the crown prince, later Philip II of Spain. Philip was determined to convert the inhabitants to Catholicism and is said to have sent 100,000 missionaries—Augustinians, Franciscans, and Dominicans—to carry out his intention. By 1595 there was a bishop of Manila, and many missions had been set up in the scattered territories of his jurisdiction. The next step was to send missions to Japan, where St Francis Xavier (3 Dec.) had carried out missionary journeys some fifty years earlier. There was no lack of priests eager to follow in his footsteps.

Fr Martin Lumberas was born in Zaragoza and entered the Augustinian Order in 1619 at the age of twenty-three. In July 1622 he sailed from Cadiz for the Philippines with thirteen other missionaries. On arrival he was sent to a monastery in Manila, where he became sacristan and novice-master. Fr Melchior Sánchez came from Granada. He had entered the Order at the age of nineteen and was twenty-two when he was sent to the Philippines with another contingent of friars to work in Mindanao. He seems to have had some skill as a linguist. He studied the languages of the Philippines, including Tagalog, in order to communicate with the people of the islands.

A ministry in the Philippines was relatively safe. Both knew that going to Japan might mean martyrdom. Christianity had been proscribed by a series of edicts from the year 1614. Foreign priests were forbidden to enter the country, and Japanese were forbidden to practise Christianity on pain of death. There had been many martyrs (see the Martyrs of Japan; 6 Feb.) Determined to witness to their faith at all costs, the two sailed for Nagasaki on 4 August 1632 in a Chinese merchant vessel, but they had been in Japan for only a few weeks before they were arrested. The Japanese authorities were not anxious to kill foreign missionaries: their chief concern was to keep their country free from foreign influence. So the governor of Nagasaki begged them in the name of the emperor of Japan to recant so that their faith would be discredited and others would not be drawn to it. This they refused to do, and eventually the death sentence was pronounced.

They suffered a very slow and painful death—less through sadism on the part of their persecutors than through the hope that, even at this stage, they would give way. Both remained resolute. Their witness so impressed observers that twenty-two Portuguese merchants subsequently made a written testimony of their martyrdom.

The two martyrs were beatified together by Pope John Paul II on 23 April 1989.

D.N.H., 3, pp. 107-10.

12

OUR LADY OF GUADALUPE (1531)

This Marian shrine, famous in North and South America, contains an image of the Virgin as a young American Indian woman, painted on the local cactus-cloth. The tradition is that in December 1531, Juan Diego, an American Indian peasant in his fifties, saw visions of the Virgin on Mount Tepeyac, a few miles north-west of Mexico City, and the picture appeared miraculously on his cloak.

The Spanish conquest of Mexico, which must rank as one of the most barbarous of the colonial conquests of the period, had taken place only ten years earlier. The Indians' own cultures had been virtually obliterated and replaced by the alien culture of Spain, but as the country became more settled the religious Orders arrived to learn the languages, set up schools, and instruct the indigenous peoples, trying to understand their traditions.

Juan Diego was a Catholic. Mount Tepeyac was an ancient holy place of his people. There, on 9 December, he heard heavenly singing, and saw a Lady of perfect beauty:

> Her clothing appeared like the sun, and it gave forth rays. And the rock and cliffs where she was standing, upon receiving the rays like arrows of light, appeared like precious emeralds, glowed like jewels, the earth glowed with the splendours of the rainbow. The mesquites, the cactus and the weeds which were all around appeared like feathers of the quetzal and their stems like turquoise, the branches, the foliage and even the thorns sparkled like gold.

The Lady spoke to the "poor little Indian" with respect, calling him "dignified Juan Diego," and told him that she was "the ever-Virgin, Holy Mary, mother of the God of Great Truth, Téotl." She told him to go to the bishop of Mexico and tell him to build a church on the spot, saying:

> In it, I will show and give to all people all my love, my compassion, my help and my defence. Because I am your merciful mother and the mother of all nations that live on this earth. . . . There I will hear their laments and remedy and cure all their miseries, misfortunes and sorrows.

Juan Diego went to the bishop, the Franciscan Fray Juan de Zamórraga, who had a reputation for kindness to the Indians, with his message. The bishop told him to come back on another occasion, so he returned to Mount Tepeyac and had another long and loving conversation with the Virgin, who sent him back to the bishop. On the second occasion the bishop questioned him closely but told him that he must have a sign if he was to believe that this was a true message from the Lady from Heaven. Juan Diego's uncle was very ill and likely to die from smallpox, and Juan made an urgent journey to fetch a priest to hear his uncle's Confession. On his way he passed by the side of Mount Tepeyac, and the Lady came to meet him, asking where he was going. When he told her of his uncle's sickness she assured him that the sick man would recover and sent him to the top of the hill to gather flowers. There, on what was normally scrub-land, he found "all kinds of exquisite flowers from Castille, open and flowering." Then the Queen of Heaven placed the flowers in his rough cloak with her own "precious little hands," and sent him back to the bishop. When he opened his cloak in the bishop's presence, the flowers fell to the ground.

> In that very moment she painted herself, the precious image of the ever-Virgin Holy Mary . . . appeared suddenly, just as she is today, and is kept in her precious home, in her hermitage of Tepeyac, which is called Guadalupe.

On the next day Juan Diego led the bishop to the spot where the Virgin had asked for her chapel to be built and then went to see his uncle, Juan Bernardino. He discovered that his uncle had been cured in the very hour in which he spoke with the Virgin. He and his uncle both went to tell the bishop, who kept them in his home for several days. When the chapel was built the bishop placed the image there "so that all might see and venerate her precious image," and "the entire city was deeply moved."

The documentation for this charming and lyrical story, with its wealth of Catholic devotion, leaves much to be desired. Though the bishop is said to have made special reports of these events, there is no trace of them. Such records of miraculous events were not required by the Church before the Council of Trent. There are translation problems. The bishop did not speak Náhuatl, which was Juan Diego's only language. They had an interpreter named Juan González, eighteen years old at the time, who was training for the priesthood. After his ordination, Fr González joined the Society of Jesus and went off to evangelize the Indians, leaving his papers with a fellow-priest named Juan de Tovar. The original papers apparently disappeared, and the only early record is Juan de Tovar's summary in Náhuatl, which is not detailed. This is in the *Biblioteca Nacional de México*. A fuller account, also in Náhuatl, known as the *Relación*, was written by an Indian theological student named Antonio Valeriano and his fellow-pupils between 1560 and 1570 under the direction of Fray Bernardino de Sahagún, but this was at least thirty years after the events. There are manuscript copies of the *Relación* in several North American libraries, but the original has disappeared.

Since then, strenuous attempts have been made to validate the story of Juan Diego. In 1666 a formal inquiry took evidence from a number of very old Indians, some claiming to be over a hundred years old; but none of them could have been alive in 1531, and what they had to say was vague and unsubstantiated, testifying only to the oral tradition. Inquiries in the eighteenth and nineteenth centuries were similarly inconclusive; but the image on cactus-cloth remains unexplained. It is still the centre of devotion, a picture of a young dark-skinned girl, modest and gentle, known as "the Dark Virgin" (*La Virgen morena*). There are said to be no brush-marks, and there is no explanation of how it came to be formed on a peasant's cloak.

The story of Juan Diego may have its origins in parable rather than in events. The vision is described in sophisticated terms that suggest the concepts and language of a Spanish missionary rather than those of an Amerinidian peasant, and the picture is typical of the Spanish religious art of the period, apart from the dark skin. It bears no resemblance to American Indian art. The first generation of Spanish missionaries in Mexico were very concerned to reach out to the Indians and to find ways of teaching the Faith that would be comprehensible in their culture. The story bears a marked resemblance to that of the story of the Virgin of Guadalupe in Spain; and Guadalupe, in the Spanish province of Extramadura was near the home of Hernán Cortés. Many of his troops came from the same area.

The two young Spanish seminarians, Juan González and Juan de Tovar, may have developed a Mexican version of the Spanish tradition of Our Lady of Guadalupe as an imaginative teaching project, with the picture on cactus cloth as a visual aid. The development of the devotion would be no less miraculous if it were mediated through human agency in this way. It gave the Indians an assurance that Christianity was not merely the faith of their European conquerors but a faith for them also; that the Mother of Christ understood their problems and had compassion for them.

A natural rather than a supernatural origin might explain why the two seminarians left only a summary of the story (later developed by Valeriano) and why there were no episcopal records. Similar teaching methods were often used by Spanish missionaries in California and New Mexico to bridge the gap between cultures. In the same way, Christian art in Africa may portray the Virgin as a young African woman, and in the Far East, her representations frequently have Chinese or Japanese characteristics.

Whatever the origins of the story of Juan Diego, it has become a powerful force in the history of Central and South America. The first chapel at Tepecayo was completed in 1533, and a huge and impressive basilica was dedicated in 1709. There has been re-building since then. In 1737 the Most Holy Mary of Guadalupe was named as the patroness of Mexico City; in 1746 she became the patroness of all New Spain; in 1895 the image was crowned with pontifical approval and celebrated in other parts of the world—California, Spain, the Philippines and elsewhere; and in 1910 Pope Pius X proclaimed her "The Virgin Patroness of Latin America." In 1945, on the fiftieth anniversary of the coronation, Pope Pius XII named the Virgin of Guadalupe as "The Queen of Mexico and Empress of the Americas."

The Virgin of Guadalupe, venerated by the descendants of Spanish and

Indian alike, is of great symbolic importance. More recently, her devotion has provided an inspiration for liberation theologians. She is an advocate for the oppressed, the poor, the marginal populations of the world. The devotion expresses Catholic imagery of a very high order and has become a focus for veneration and social action.

P. F. Velázquez, *La aparición de Sta María de Guadalupe* (1931); D. Demarez and C. Taylor (eds.), *The Dark Virgin: the book of Our Lady of Guadalupe: a documentary anthology* (1958); M. T. Hernández, *Las apariciones de Tepeyac: mita o realidad?* (1974); V. F. Elizondo, *La Morenita: Evangelizer of the Americas* (1980); Jeanette Rodríguez, *Our Lady of Guadalupe: Faith and Empowerment among Mexican American Women* (1994); M. C. Bingemer and I. Gebara, *Mary, Mother of God and Mother of the Poor* (1993); *D.T.C.*, fasc. 127, 475-80; *N.C.E.*, 6, pp. 821-2, includes illustrations of the *Virgen Morena* and the basilica at Tepecayo. Website: http://www.campbellservices.com/johnstown/shrine.html.

ST JANE FRANCES DE CHANTAL, *Foundress* (1572-1641)

Jane (Jeanne) was the daughter of Bénigne Frémyot, president of the *parlement* of Burgundy, and his wife. Mme Frémyot died young while her children were still in their infancy, and M. Frémyot was left to bring them up, which he did with much attention to their religious education. Jeanne took the additional name of Françoise at her Confirmation. When she was about twenty she married Christophe de Rabutin, baron de Chantal, and became the châtelaine of his family seat at Bourbilly. In the next nine years she established good order and management in the house and estate, which had been neglected since the death of her husband's mother.

Her married life was to be marked by tragedy. Her three eldest children died soon after birth; the next three, a boy and two girls, survived, but then her husband died in 1601 as a result of a shooting accident. He survived for nine days, during which he suffered great pain, and he received the Last Sacraments with dignity and resignation. After his death his widow took a vow of chastity and lived with her children either at the home of her own father at Dijon or with her husband's father, the old baron de Chantal, at Monthelon, near Autun. It was while she was staying at Dijon in 1604 that she heard St Francis de Sales (24 Jan.) preach and persuaded him to undertake her spiritual direction. He stressed to her the duties she owed as a daughter, a mother, and a member of society. On his advice she regulated her devotions and followed a strict rule of life, while devoting much time to her children and visiting the poor, sick, and dying of the neighbourhood.

For a time, influenced by her contacts with the Carmelite nuns in Dijon, she thought of entering the cloister; but after much thought and prayer, St Francis proposed a new project, an establishment to be known as the Congregation of the Visitation of the Virgin Mary. It was planned to be a convent for women who, for reasons of delicate health, age, or other considerations were debarred from entering the enclosed Orders. The Sisters would be unenclosed and would work freely in the community.

The convent—the Gallery House, on the edge of the lake at Anneçy, was inaugurated on Trinity Sunday 1610. With Jeanne Françoise de Chantal were clothed two other Sisters, Marie Favre and Charlotte de Bréchard, and a servant, Anne Coste. They were soon joined by ten other women. St Francis wrote his famous treatise *On the Love of God* specifically for this group.

The proposal that the Sisters should live without enclosure roused much ecclesiastical opposition, and eventually St Francis had to agree that the Order of the Visitation would be enclosed, though his drafting of the plan of the Congregation was remarkable in its moderation. Mother de Chantal was certainly free to leave Anneçy in order to attend to the affairs of her children and to found new houses. The year after she took the habit, on the death of her father, she went to Dijon and stayed there for some months to settle his affairs and to place her son in college. She was instrumental in establishing convents in Lyons, Moulins, Grenoble, and Bourges; and in 1619, in spite of much hostility and intrigue, she managed to establish a house in Paris. At the request of St Francis de Sales, St Vincent de Paul (27 Sept.) acted as director, and the abbess of Port-Royal, Angélique Arnaud, was so impressed with the work of the Visitation Order that she tried, unsuccessfully, to resign her office and join it. The attraction seems to have been the teaching of St Francis de Sales— who, unlike many of his contemporaries, placed more importance on the spiritual quality of humility than on corporal austerities—and the good and wise administration of Mother de Chantal. St Vincent de Paul described her as "one of the holiest souls I have ever met."

There was more tragedy to come. The death of St Francis de Sales in 1622 was a great blow to her, and in 1627 her only son was killed fighting against the English and the Huguenots in the Ile de Ré. He left a young wife and a daughter, less than a year old, who was later to become celebrated as Madame de Sévigné. In 1628 a terrible plague raged through France, Savoy, and Piedmont. Mother de Chantal refused to leave, offering the resources of the convent for the needs of the sick and spurring the local authorities to greater efforts. The death of a much-loved son-in-law and of Fr Michel Favre, St Francis' confessor and a close and devoted friend of the Visitandines, added to her trials. Though she remained firm in faith and resignation, she went through periods of great spiritual dryness and interior anguish, expressed in several of her letters.

In spite of setbacks, the convents of the Visitation had continued to multiply. By 1635 there were sixty-five, some of which she had never visited. Mother de Chantal proceeded to visit them all. In 1641, at the age of sixty-nine, she went into France to carry out an errand of charity. The queen, Anne of Austria, invited her to Paris, and—somewhat to her distress, for she preferred to work quietly behind the scenes—she was treated with much distinction and honour. On the way home she fell ill near her convent at Moulins, and there she died on 13 December 1641. Her body was taken to Anneçy and buried near that of St Francis de Sales. She was canonized in 1767.

F. M. de Chaugy, *Mémoires sur la vie et les vertus de sainte Jeanne-Françoise Frémyot de Chantal*, 8 vols. (1874-9): Eng. trans., *The Life of St Jane Frances de Chantal*, intro. R. Boulangé (1852); L. V. E. Bougaud, *Histoire de sainte Chantal et des origines de la Visitation*, 2 vols, (1861, Eng. trans. 1895); A. Gazier, *Jeanne de Chantal et Angélique Arnaud d'après leur correspondance* (1915). Lives by H. Brémond (1912); Ella King Sanders, *Sainte Chantal, 1572-1641* (1918); E. C. V. Stopp, *Madame de Chantal: portrait of a saint* (1962). *Bibl.SS.*, 6, 581-6.

St Spiridion, *Bishop* (Fourth Century)

Spiridion (Spyridon) was a shepherd who became bishop of a small and remote area in the north-east of Cyprus, near Salamis. The historian Socrates says that "so great was his sanctity as a shepherd that he was thought worthy of being made a Pastor of men: and having been assigned the bishopric of one of the cities of Cyprus called Tremithus, on account of his extreme humility, he continued to feed his sheep during his incumbency of the bishopric."

Spiridion was much loved. A story is told of how he caught robbers attempting to steal his sheep. He prayed with them, set them free—and gave them a ram, telling them it was a gift "so that ye may not have watched all night in vain."

He is said to have been present at the Council of Nicaea, though he is not among the signatories. This does not necessarily affect the issue of his presence, as the council transacted a great deal of business and seems to have continued for several months. Athanasius mentions him as among the bishops who maintained the orthodox position against heretical views at the Council of Sardica.

This gentle, humorous bishop suffered in the persecutions of Galerius. According to the Roman Martyrology he lost his right eye, was ham-strung, and was sent to work in the mines. After his death his relics were translated from Cyprus to Constantinople and then to Corfu, where they are still venerated. Spiridion is the principal patron saint of Corfu, Zakythos, and Kephalonia and is widely remembered in his native Cyprus. In Byzantine art he is recognizable by his distinctive shepherd's cap. The Orthodox tradition makes no reference to his sufferings under Galerius.

Early references are made to St Spiridion by historians: Rufinus, *H.E.*, 1, 5; Socrates, *H.E.*, 1, 12; and Sozomen, *H.E.* 1, 11. A Life by Leontius of Neapolis, apparently written at the beginning of the seventh century, is available in the later adaptation of the Metaphrast: *P.G.*, 116, 417-68. An earlier Life of St Spiridion by his pupil Triphyllius of Ledra has not survived. See also P.B., pp. 287-95. For Spiridion's presence at the Council of Nicaea see Hefele-Leclerc, 1, pp. 429, 430. For pictorial representation see, for example, P. Van den Ven, *La légende de S. Spyridon* (1953).

St Corentin, *Bishop* (? 453)

Corentin, or Cury, was a Celtic hermit, the Cornish founder and patron of Cury in the Lizard. An ancient cross stands near his church. In 1890 a fresco was discovered in Breage (the mother church of the Lizard) which depicts him in cope and mitre with a pastoral staff. He is also known in Brittany, where he lived as a hermit, and there are legends about a miraculous fish from which he cut a slice every day for his frugal meal but which was whole again on the following day. He is sometimes shown in art standing next to a spring or a bucket, in which the fish swims.

We do know that he had several disciples and that he was drawn from his hermitage by the people of Cornouaille to be their pastor. From early in the Middle Ages Corentin was venerated as the first bishop of Cornouaille (the see is now at Quimper), and during the seventeenth century his cult became yet more popular as a result of the preaching of the great missioner Bd Julian Maunoir (28 Jan.).

His name occurs in a Winchester missal of the tenth century and a Canterbury litany of the eleventh. An ancient Breton cult in his honour was revived in the seventeenth century, when several old shrines in Brittany were restored.

P.B., from the *Vie des saints de Bretagne*; Duchesne, *Fastes*, 2, pp. 242 and 371-5; G. H. Doble, *St Corentin* (1925); G. H. Doble, *The Saints of Cornwall*, 2 (1962), pp. 45-53; *O.D.S.*, p. 112.

St Finnian of Clonard, *Bishop* (549)

Finnian (Vennianus, Vinnaius, Findén, or Finnio moccu Telduib) was the outstanding figure among the holy men of Ireland in the period following St Patrick (17 Mar.), and many legends have gathered round his name. A tenth-century Life says that he was born and educated in Leinster, probably at Idrone, Co. Carlow, near where he made his first three foundations: Rossacurra, Drumfea, and Kilmaglush. He went to Wales and studied the traditional monasticism of St David (1 Mar.), St Cadoc (23 Sept.), and St Gildas (29 Jan.), which asserted the superiority of the monastic life over the secular life and the importance of learning.

Finnian returned to Ireland and founded churches and monasteries. His great monastery was on the Boyne, at Clonard in Meath, where he was known as the "Teacher of the Saints of Ireland," and some three thousand disciples gathered round him. According to the Book of Lismore, when his monks left Clonard they took with them a Gospel book, a crozier, and a reliquary round which they later built their churches and monasteries. The education of saints who lived long after came to be credited to St Finnian. He was famed for his knowledge of the scriptures, and Clonard for centuries retained a reputation as a centre for biblical studies.

The foundation at Clonard suffered much from the Danes and then from the

Normans. At the beginning of the thirteenth century it ceased to be the religious centre of the diocese of Meath and became a monastery of Augustinian Canons. This continued until the sixteenth century.

St Finnian is said to have died of the plague in December 549. Presumably he was nursing other plague victims, for the writer of an Irish Life says, "As Paul died in Rome for the sake of the Christian people, lest they should all perish in Hell, so Finnian died at Clonard for the sake of the people, that they might not all perish from the yellow pest."

The Penitential of Finnian is probably his; it is based to some extent on Welsh and Irish sources and on St Jerome (30 Sept.) and St John Cassian (23 July), but much of it is original, and it is the oldest surviving example of its kind. It spread the influence of Clonard in penitential discipline and biblical studies. Finnian's relics were enshrined at Clonard until they were destroyed in 887. His feast is testified by a Spanish martyrology of the early ninth century.

Irish Life in W. Stokes, *Lives of Saints from the Book of Lismore* (1890), pp. 75-83 and 222-30; R. Sharpe, *Mediaeval Irish Saints' Lives* (1991), pp. 393-4, has a commentary on the manuscripts: see also notes in Plummer, *V.S.H.*, 2, xv, xvii-xviii, cxv. There is a long entry in *D.H.G.E.* 7, 167-75, under "Findén." There are four major articles by Kathleen Hughes: "The historical value of the Lives of St Finnian of Clonard," *E.H.R.* 69 (1954), pp. 535-72; "The cult of St Finnian of Clonard from the eighth to the eleventh century," *Irish Historical Studies* 9 (1954), pp. 13-27; *Anal.Boll.* 73 (1955), pp. 342-62; and an additional note in *Anal.Boll.* 75 (1957), pp. 337-9. The 1957 paper contains matter translated from the Irish, which the author believed confirmed her hypothesis on the priority of the Irish Life, going back in some respects to the eighth century. See also L. Bieler, *The Irish Penitentials* (1963), pp. 74-95; J. T. Macneill and H. Gamer, *Mediaeval Handbooks of Penance* (1965): the *Poenitentiale Vinniai*, pp. 86-97.

St Vicelin, *Bishop* (c. 1086-1154)

Vicelin, who was to be the apostle of what is now Holstein and district, was born at Hameln (Hamelin) about the year 1086. He studied in the cathedral school at Paderborn and later became the head of the school at Bremen and a canon of Bremen cathedral. He may have studied at Laon in France. He was ordained priest by St Norbert (6 June) at Magdeburg, and in 1126 he began his twenty-year mission among the Slavonic tribes.

His first centre was at Lübeck, where he founded the first church. Later he moved to Wippenthorp, near Bremen. He was a tireless teacher and preacher and a most successful missionary. To provide a more permanent centre Vicelin founded a monastery in Holstein, afterwards called Neumünster, for Augustinian Canons. Later he established another at Högersdorf and started a third at Segeberg.

Like other missionaries he found his work interrupted and even destroyed by war. When pirates descended on the district, devastating the country and burning and sacking the houses, they directed their fury chiefly at the Christians, who were driven out or killed. The priests from Lübeck hid in the marshes with water up to their necks and at last managed to escape, but at Segeberg the monastery was utterly destroyed and at least one Brother killed by the sword.

In spite of opposition from Frederick Barbarossa, Vicelin was in 1149 made bishop of Staargard (now Oldenburg) in Holstein, but there is some doubt as to whether he ever took over his see. Three years later he was struck down by paralysis. He spent the last two years of his life in sickness and suffering at the abbey of Neumünster, where he died. His relics were translated to Bordesholm in 1332.

One of Vicelin's pupils at Neumünster was the chronicler Helmold, who gives an account of his missionary work in his *Chronica Slavorum* (1631 ed.), pp. 44-63; *M.G.H., Scriptores*, 21, pp. 44-50, 52-4, 60-8; *D.Cath.Biog.*, p. 1164; *L.D.H.*, pp. 572-3.

Bd Bartholomew of San Gimignano (1300)

Bartolomeo Buonpedoni, commonly called Bartolo, was born at Mucchio, near San Gimignano, south of Florence. Since he was the only heir of a noble house, his father, the count of Mucchio, wished him to marry and prepare himself for a great position in the world; but Bartolo felt called to the priesthood. After much conflict with his father and some harsh treatment he left home to become a servant in the Benedictine abbey at Pisa. He worked in the infirmary and impressed the monks so much by his gentleness and devotion that he was offered the habit. While Bartholomew was seeking God's will through prayer, he dreamed of the wounded and risen Christ, who told him that he would fulfill his calling through twenty years of suffering rather than through becoming a monk. Accordingly he became a secular priest after some training and was appointed to the parish of Peccioli. There he became a Franciscan Secular of the Third Order and lived and worked in the spirit of St Francis (4 Oct.).

In 1280 Bartholomew contracted leprosy. The disease was progressive, there were no medical cures, and it was regarded—as in biblical times—with such horror that the sufferer was shunned and stigmatized as unclean. Bartholomew remembered the dream about twenty years of suffering. Accompanied by a young man named Vivaldo (Ubald), whom he had taken into his house, he retired to the leper-house of Celloli, about a mile from San Gimignano, where he was made master and chaplain. It is said that the ravages of the disease, painful as they were, never prevented him from celebrating Mass.

He lived at Celloli, ministering to his fellow-sufferers, until his death on 12 December 1200, just twenty years later. He has been called "The Job of Tuscany" on account of his physical and mental suffering, and he is known locally as Santo Bartolo.

A cult was approved by Pope Alexander VI in 1498 and confirmed in 1910.

Bartholomew's tomb lies in the church of St Agostino in San Gimignano, with a shrine above it depicting legends and scenes from his life.

Wadding, 6, pp. 84–7. *Auréole Séraphique*, 4, pp. 165–9, draws on a Life written by one of the Augustinian friars, Fra Giunta, after Bartolo's death. Though Fra Giunta did not know Bartolo personally, he was able to consult many people still living who knew him well. Fr Léon, ex-provincial of the Friars Minor of the Observance, was able to see a manuscript copy of this Life kept at the collegiate chapel of San Gimignano. See also Wadding, 6, pp. 84–7; *F.B.S.*, pp. 940–2; *Bibl.SS.* 2., 845–8. There is a popular Life in Italian, *Santo Bartolo*, by E. Castaldi (1928).

Bd Conrad of Offida (1306)

Conrad became a Friar Minor when he was fourteen years old and was later associated both with the friary founded by St Francis at Forano and with the great convent of Alvernia. Before he was ordained priest and became a preacher he was employed for many years as cook and steward. He lived a very simple life, possessing only one habit and always going barefoot. His love of poverty drew him close to the group known as the Spirituals, or *Zelanti*. He was closely associated with the leaders of the "Celestine" hermits, though his own inclinations were more moderate.

The chief companion of his life was Bd Peter of Treja (17 Feb.), who went with him on his preaching journeys and, according to legend, was with him in the wood at Candlemas when our Lady appeared to Conrad and laid the child Jesus in his arms. The author of the *Fioretti*, who tells this story, adds that Conrad and Peter were "two shining stars in the Marches, like dwellers in Heaven." He calls Conrad "a marvellous zealot of gospel poverty and of the Rule of St Francis." Conrad died at the age of sixty-five, while preaching at Bastia, near Assisi, and was buried there. Some years later his relics were carried off to Perugia, where they now rest in the cathedral. Conrad's cult was confirmed in 1817.

Wadding, 6, pp. 84–7; *Auréole Séraphique*, 4, pp. 174–7; *F.B.S.* pp. 942–4; *Bibl.SS.* 6, 206–7. For Conrad's relations with the *Zelanti*, the main point of interest, see the *Historisches Jahrbuch* for 1882, pp. 648–59, and for 1929, pp. 77–81; also L. Iriarte, O.F.M.Cap., *Franciscan History* (1983), pp. 51–8.

Bd Thomas Holland, *Martyr* (1642)

Thomas Holland's martyrdom came late in the series of religious persecutions in the sixteenth and early seventeeth centuries. He was born in 1600 at Sutton Hall, near Prescot in Lancashire, the son of Richard and Anne Holland, Catholics who had been heavily fined for recusancy. Thomas was educated at the English Colleges at Saint-Omer and Valladolid. For his learning and piety he was dubbed *Bibliotheca pietatis*, "the library of goodness," by his fellow students.

In 1622, having joined the Society of Jesus, he took the missionary oath on the feast of St Thomas of Canterbury (29 Dec.). When in 1623 the Prince of Wales (later Charles I) visited Madrid to negotiate his marriage to the infanta Henrietta Maria, he was chosen to welcome the prince on behalf of the English students. He gave a Latin address said to have given great satisfaction to his Royal Highness and his attendants. There must have been great hopes in Spain at this time that Charles, married to a Catholic princess, would lead England back to Catholicism when he became king.

Thomas was sent on the English mission in 1635. He was fluent in French, Flemish, and Spanish as well as Latin and apparently was an excellent mimic: he could adopt all sorts of accents. He was also a master of disguise, and sometimes his closest friends failed to recognize him. Though his health was poor and he was not easily able to bear the rigours of this secret and dangerous mission, he worked for seven years before he was arrested on suspicion of being a priest from overseas.

He was brought to trial at the Old Bailey. His refusal to swear on oath that he was not a priest was sufficient for the jury to find him guilty. The lord mayor and others on the bench were said to be dissatisfied with this verdict, and the recorder's deputy gave sentence with reluctance. Thomas "calmly said *Deo gratias*" and prepared for his death.

Many people visited him in prison in the two days before his execution, including the duke of Vendôme, who offered to intercede for him. This offer was courteously refused. On the day before his execution, a Sunday, he was able to hear many Confessions and to celebrate Mass. On Monday he celebrated Mass again and then was led off to Tyburn. It was noted that the sheriffs of London and of Middlesex absented themselves from the execution, which may have been a sign of public unease at the sentence. The martyr now declared openly that he was a Catholic, a priest, and a Jesuit and prayed aloud for the king and his people, "for whose prosperity and conversion to the Catholic faith, if I had as many lives as there are hairs on my head, drops of water in the ocean or stars in the firmament, I would most willingly sacrifice them all."

His words were greeted with a shout from the people, and then the execution took place. He was beatified in 1929.

Challoner in *M.M.P.*, pp. 435-9, makes use of a Latin Life published in Antwerp in 1645; Stanton, pp. 597-8; *B.D.E.C.*, 3, pp. 353-4.

St Simon Hoa, *Martyr* (1840)

When the Europeans first came to Indo-China (now Vietnam) in the sixteenth century, there were several warring kingdoms, all subject to greater or lesser degrees of Chinese influence. The Portuguese and Dutch established trading posts, and from the 1770s the French, who had lost India to the British, began to penetrate the country. It was against this background of colonialist expansion and Chinese counter-pressure that the work of the Catholic missions was sporadically attacked. Bishops, priests, and laity, both European and Indo-

Chinese, were martyred. Though the names of many have been lost, 117 are recognized as "the Martyrs of Vietnam" (2 Feb.), and have been beatified, in some cases canonized, in this century.

Those whose feast-days occur in December were martyred in the persecutions of 1838-40, after some twenty years of comparative peace and religious toleration. Gia Long, a successful war-lord, styled himself emperor from 1806. After 1820, when Minh Mang became emperor of China and his suzerain, he shared the Chinese determination to resist social, cultural, and technological change from the West.

Minh was a narrow and rigid Confucian and particuarly opposed to the work of Christian missionaries. Gia Long followed his lead. French influence in Indo-China was relatively weak during this period. In 1832 Gia Long issued an order excluding all foreign missionaries and ordered the churches to be destroyed. The teaching of Christianity was forbidden, and Vietnamese Christians were ordered to renounce their faith by trampling on the crucifix. French Catholics saw Gia Long as a new Nero, but their government took no decisive action to protect the Catholic communities. A warship was sent to Tourane in 1837 and again in 1838, but it failed to make contact with Gia Long's court at Hué. In a sustained outbreak of violence against the foreigners and their beliefs, some seven or eight French missionary priests and an unknown number of Indo-Chinese Catholics were martyred.

Dr Simon Hoa was highly respected in his local community, where he practised as a physician and became mayor. He was a Catholic and attached to the Paris Society of Foreign Missions. He was barbarously tortured and then beheaded. Simon Hoa was beatified in 1900 and canonized in 1988. Six other Indo-Chinese Catholics who were martyred in this period and who have been canonized are noticed in this volume: Peter Duong, Peter Truat, and Paul My (18 Dec.); Dominic Vy and Stephen Vinh (19 Dec.); and Peter Thi (20 Dec).

There was a further outbreak of violence in 1847, when the Catholics were suspected of having supported a rebellion against the Hué government. Napoleon III sent diplomatic protests. When these failed a French naval squadron and a Spanish warship were despatched to the Mekong Delta. The treaty of 1862 ceded three provinces to the French. Between 1833 and 1883, when a French protectorate was set up, between 100,000 and 300,000 Christians died in Indo-China for their faith.

Bibl.SS., 7, 594-5; *N.C.E.*, 14, pp. 198-9, where the names of the martyrs are listed, and pp. 660-2. For background to the persecutions see E. Hammer, *The Struggle for Indo-China* (1954); J. Buttinger, *The Smaller Dragon*, New York (1958), especially ch. 5, "The Flight into Isolation," pp. 270-324. For a general survey in the present work see the Martyrs of Vietnam, 2 February.

13

St Lucy, *Martyr* (*c.* 304)

St Lucy is said to have been a Sicilian, born in the city of Syracuse of noble and wealthy parents and brought up a Christian. She wished to devote her life to God and to give her fortune to the poor, but during the Diocletian persecutions a man, usually represented as a Roman soldier, tried to rape her, and she resisted. He denounced her as a Christian, and she was arrested, tortured, and killed.

Though these traditions have no ascertainable historical basis, her connection with Syracuse and the existence of an early cult connected with her name are well established. A fourth-century inscription mentioning that a girl called Euskia died on Lucy's feast-day survives at Syracuse. Lucy was honoured at Rome in the sixth century as one of the most illustrious virgin martyrs whose lives the Church celebrates. Her name is included in the Canons of the Roman and Ambrosian rites and occurs in the oldest Roman sacramentaries, in Greek liturgical books, and in the marble calendar of Naples. Churches were dedicated to her in Rome, Naples, and eventually Venice. In England two ancient churches were dedicated to her, and she has certainly been known since the end of the seventh century. St Aldhelm, bishop of Sherborne (23 May), celebrated her in both prose and verse, though he unfortunately relied on spurious sources.

Possibly on account of her name, which has connotations of light and purity (Latin *lux*/*Lucia*), legends have long gathered around St Lucy. Some of the legends and many paintings relate to her eyes. One gruesome story is that she tore her eyes out rather than surrender to her attacker, and she is sometimes shown offering them to him. Oddly, she is the patron saint of those with eye trouble, and a gentler interpretation is that this is because the eyes are the source of our awareness of light. Her feast-day has long been the occasion for special ceremonies connected with virginity. It occurs near the shortest day of the year and is especially celebrated in Sweden as a festival of light, with a procession of young girls dressed in white and crowned with lighted candles. The song "Santa Lucia" celebrates her memory.

Hieronymianum, p. 407; *C.M.H.* pp. 646-7. References in Aldhelm's treatise *De Virginitate*, in *M.G.H., Auctores Antiquissimi*, 15 (1919), pp. 293-4; *La Historia di Santa Lucia, Virgine e Martire* (verse, c. 1550); de Villegas, in *E.R.L.* 356 (1977), 2, pp. 533-41; *D.A.C.L.*, 9, 2616-8; A. Beaugrand, *Sainte Lucie* (1882); *Saints in Italy*, pp. 281-3; M. Capdevila, *Iconographia de Santa Lucia* (1949); *Golden Legend*, 1, pp. 27-9.

She is one of the twenty-two virgins in the sixth-century mosaic frieze of the Procession of the Virgins in the basilica of Sant' Apollinare Nuovo in Ravenna, and she appears frequently in *Virgo inter virgines* scenes. The many famous paintings of her include a Titian in the Palazzo Colonna in Rome; a Fra Angelico in the Accademia in Florence, and a Della Robbia relief over the door of the church of St Lucia in Florence. Domenico Veneziano's *St Lucy Altarpiece* (mid-fifteenth century) in the Uffizi Gallery in Florence, shows her carrying her two eyes in a dish. One of Caravaggio's last pictures represents *The Burial of St Lucy*.

St Eustratius of Armenia and Other Martyrs

(? Late Third Century)

According to the Roman Martyrology, Eustratius, Eugenius, Mardarius, Auxenius, and Orestes were all martyred in Armenia during the persecution under Diocletian. Eustratius was an Armenian from a well-known family; Eugenius was his servant; Mardarius and Auxenius were two friends who interceded for him; and Orestes was a soldier who was converted by the sight of his fortitude under torture. All five were tortured and killed. Their bodies were later translated to Rome and buried in the church of Sant' Apollinare, where their relics are still venerated.

The passion of these martyrs is a good example of how such documents were interpolated and even rewritten later for teaching purposes: Eustratius is made to argue with the magistrate, discussing passages from Plato and the classical poets. The story shows some dependence on the story of the Forty Martyrs of Sebastea (10 Mar.). This group of martyrs occupies an important place in the Orthodox calendar.

Fragments of the passion have been found in a ninth-century script, but we have no earlier confirmation of the martyrs' names or their acts.

A late Greek *passio* is printed in *P.G.*, 116, 467-506, and there is a notice in the *Bibliotheca Hagiographica Orientalis* (1910), p. 70. See also Delehaye, *Les passions des martyrs . . .* (1921), pp. 266-8; *Anal.Boll.* 17 (1898), pp. 468-9; 34 (1917-19), p. 35; 46 (1928), p. 159; 57 (1939), pp. 42-3; Quentin, p. 41; *Bibl.SS.*, 5, 313-5.

St Judoc (668)

Judoc (Judicus or Josse) was offered the crown of Brittany about the year 636 when his brother Judicäel (17 Dec.) abdicated and went into a monastery, but after some months he renounced his position and travelled with eleven companions on pilgrimages to Chartres, Paris, and Amiens. He visited Rome, but accounts conflict. It is not clear whether he was ordained in Rome or at the court of Haymon, count of Ponthieu. In either case, he left his fellow-pilgrims and became a hermit in Ponthieu "at Braic on the river Authie," according to Orderic Vitalis, in the place now called Saint-Josse-sur-Mer.

He had one disciple named Wurmar or Wulmar, who had followed him from Brittany, and they spent their lives in celebrating the Holy Mysteries, singing praises to God, meditating on the gospel, and conversing with saints and angels. There Judoc "served God for eight years." He never refused to help the poor as long as he had a scrap of bread left in his hermitage, and he would share whatever he had. There is a story that on one occasion four hungry men came to his door in succession. Three times he halved his piece of bread, until the piece remaining was too small to divide, and that he gave to the fourth. Wulmar, who had grown increasingly agitated as their supply of bread diminished, was greatly relieved to see four ships bearing supplies (probably from Count Haymon, who had remained their friend and supporter) approaching along the river. The legend grew up that the four hungry men had been appearances of Jesus Christ himself, testing the charity of his servant.

Judoc stayed in his hermitage for eight years, at peace with the natural world of woods and water. He "fed birds of every kind, and little fishes from his hand as if they were tame creatures." He built two wooden chapels in the forest, "one for Peter who holds the keys of heaven, and one for Paul the great preacher (*magnilogo*)." Many small miracles were credited to him, including finding the source of a miraculous spring, which healed blindness and other infirmities.

In the eighth or early ninth century Charlemagne gave this hermitage to Alcuin (19 May), the English scholar at his court, as a guesthouse for English travellers. England's connection with the traditions of St Judoc was strengthened in about 902 when some refugees from Saint-Josse came to Winchester, bringing with them relics of their founder. The New Minster at Winchester was then being built, and St Grimbald (8 July), dean of Winchester, enshrined the relics there.

Feasts of St Judoc were given a high rank at Winchester, and we can infer influence from Winchester where they occur in other English calendars. The Wife of Bath in Chaucer's *Canterbury Tales* swears "By God and by Seint Joce." The name Joyce (for both men and women) testifies to his popularity.

When a rival set of relics was discovered at Saint-Josse in 977 the cult of Judoc spread through northern France to Flanders (where he is sometimes called Joost) and then to Germany, Alsace, Switzerland, and Austria; he is represented in the mausoleum of Maximilian at Innsbruck. In art his usual emblem is a pilgrim's staff, with a crown at his feet symbolizing his renunciation of royal power and honour, and sometimes crossed keys, indicating his pilgrimage to Rome.

Propylaeum, p. 581; *Ecclesiastical History of Orderic Vitalis*, trans. and ed. M. Chibnall, 2, (1969), pp. 156-66, 366-7; *D.C.B.*, 3, pp. 467-8; *P.B.*, pp. 242-7. *AA.SS.OSB.*, 2, pp. 542-7.

St Aubert of Arras-Cambrai, *Bishop* (668 or 669)

Aubert was consecrated bishop of Arras and Cambrai in 633 or later. Very little is known about his early years or his family background. He is said to have come from the region of Cambrai and to have been recognized as a man of unusual wisdom and humility.

About the year 650 the hermit Gislenus or Ghislain came to the district to establish a monastery near Mons. Some of Aubert's advisers tried to to prejudice him against the stranger, saying that he might be a false apostle capable of misleading the faithful, but Aubert was open-minded. He refused to condemn Gislenus unseen and sharply rebuked those who were prejudiced against him. He sent for Gislenus and developed a great respect for him. He promised that if Gislenus could build his church he would consecrate it, and this he eventually did. Gislenus became abbot of Mons, and he and Aubert collaborated in encouraging St Vincent Madelgarius (20 Sept.) and his family to enter monastic life. Vincent's wife, Waldetrudis (9 Apr.), and their five children are also venerated locally as saints. Bishop Aubert is associated with other distinguished laypeople who sought the religious life, such as St Amalburga or Amelia (10 July), the mother of St Gudula (8 Jan.). A story is told of his pastoral care for a young man named Landelin who ran away from the seminary at Cambrai: Aubert was very distressed and prayed fervently for his return. When Landelin came back in penitence, Aubert directed him so well that he became a monk and eventually an abbot. He is also named as a saint in the Roman Martyrology (Landelinus, 15 June).

Aubert has sometimes been confused with Audebert, count of Ostrevant, and also with St Aubert of Avranches, the founder of Mont-Saint-Michel, a Benedictine who lived about half a century later.

P.B., pp. 247-51. On the confusion that has arisen between Aubert of Arras-Cambrai and Audebert, count of Ostrevant see *Anal. Boll.* 51 (1933), pp. 99-116; on the confusion with Aubert of Avranches see *D.H.G.E.*, 5, 222-4, and *Bibl.SS.*, 2, 580-2, both of which have separate contributions by different correspondents on the two St Auberts.

St Odilia, *Abbess (c. 720)*

There are many legends concerning Odilia (also known as Ottilia, Othilia, or Odile). She is said to have been born in Alsace near the end of the seventh century, the daughter of a Frankish nobleman named Adalric and his wife, Bereswindis. Adalric, who came of a distinguished line, desperately wanted a son, but the expected child was a daughter, and she was blind. Adalric was appalled and quite unable to accept her handicap. He regarded her at first with irritation and then with unreasoning fury. Though his wife tried to persuade him that Odilia's blindness was the will of God, he regarded it as a personal affront and a reflection on the honour of his family. He was determined to have the child killed and spared her life only in answer to his wife's pleas, on condition that she was sent away and that her origins were kept secret.

Bereswindis gave the child to a peasant woman who had formerly been in her service. She later moved the family to Baume-les-Dames, near Besançon, where her own aunt was abbess of a monastery. Adalric did not know where his daughter had been sent, and nobody dared to mention her in his presence. She was educated by the nuns until she was twelve years old, but at that time she had not yet been baptized.

Bishop Erhard of Regensburg (8 Jan.) had a dream—that he was to go to the monastery near Besançon and baptize a young blind girl, giving her the name of Odilia, and she would receive her sight. He consulted his brother Hidulf (11 July), and together they went to Baume-les-Dames and carried out the Baptism by total immersion. Ehrhard plunged the girl in the holy water; Hidulf lifted her out again; Erhard anointed her head, then touched her eyes with the sacred oil, saying "In the name of Jesus Christ, may the eyes of your body and the eyes of your soul receive light." She became able to see and was baptized Odilia, which means "daughter of light."

Hidulf, who lived not far from Adalric's castle at Hohenburg (a few miles west of Strasburg, and now called Obernai), went to see Odilia's father and told him of the miracle. Adalric made a donation to the monastery at Baume but still refused to see his daughter, saying that she would be a standing reproach to him because he had rejected her. He and Bereswindis had four sons, so his dynastic ambitions were satisfied. The most distinguished of the sons was Hugh, who grew up to be generous and kind. He corresponded with Odilia, and she asked him to help her toward a reconciliation with her father. Hugh asked Adalric to bring her home, but Adalric replied laconically that he had his own reasons for leaving her at Baume, and Hugh did not dare to press him.

Somewhat rashly, Hugh secretly sent a carriage and horses to fetch her. Odilia, believing that her father had relented at last, went willingly; but a violent scene ensued, in which Adalric raised his heavy staff in fury and struck Hugh to the ground. Some accounts say that he killed him. Then, in a complete emotional reversal, he turned to his daughter and was as affectionate as he had formerly been cruel.

Odilia stayed with him for a time, but Adalric was determined that she should marry a German duke, and so she fled from home. She agreed to return only when he promised her his castle of Hohenburg as a monastery and endowed it generously. This castle, which towers over the town of Obernai, stands on a peak which was called the Odilienberg and is now Mont-Sainte-Odile. Odilia became abbess of the new community, where the nuns kept a strict rule of life. She herself lived on bread and vegetables, drank only water, and spent many nights in prayer, sleeping very little. The nuns were devoted to works of mercy, feeding the hungry and caring for the sick and maimed.

Many pilgrims came to Hohenburg, and since the steepness of the mountainside made it difficult for sick and elderly people to reach it, Odilia's mother Bereswindis endowed an auxiliary convent, Neidermünster, on the lower slopes, with a hospice attached.

After her parents died, Odilia cared for patients in the hospice herself, serving them with her own hands. She prayed for her mother and father and is said to have undertaken special penances on her father's behalf. She lived to a great age; when she was dying she told her community that she looked forward to her soul leaving her body, so that she might enjoy the liberty of the children of God.

Though many of the documents concerning St Odilia are historically unreliable, there is a strong local tradition of a devoted and forgiving daughter and a great abbess. Her shrine and her abbey were the objects of great devotion through the Middle Ages. Charlemagne and other emperors made pilgrimages to Hohenburg, as did Pope St Leo IX (19 Apr.) when he was bishop of Toul, and, it is said, King Richard I of England. The pilgrimage was a popular one, and St Odilia was venerated as the patron saint of Alsace before the sixteenth century. The shrine of St Odilia and the remains of her monastery eventually came into the possession of the diocese of Strasbourg, and since the middle of the nineteenth century Mont-Ste-Odile has again become a place of pilgrimage. Odilia's relics are preserved in the chapel of St John the Baptist, a medieval building now usually called by her name.

At the time of the battles of Verdun during World War I, St Odilia became celebrated in France through the attribution to her of a completely apocryphal prophecy. This was again current, though less widely, in 1939-45.

There is a tenth-century Life of St Odilia, edited by W. Levison, in *M.G.H., Scriptores Merov.*, 6, pp. 24-50; cf. *Anal.Boll.* 13 (1894), pp. 5-32 and 196-287. In the judgment of Levison, hardly any of the material can be accepted as reliable history. There is a considerable literature on St Odilia, but the devotional lives are for the most part unreliable. See also P.B., pp. 252-63, from *Les saints de Franche-Comté; D.A.C.L.*, 12, 1921-34; Quentin, pp. 237, 239; *N.C.E.*, 4, pp. 624-5. On St Odilia in art, see C. Champion, *Ste Odile* (1931).

Bd John Marinoni (1562)

Francesco Marinoni was the third and youngest son of a well-to-do family from Bergamo but was born in Venice in 1490. He served as one of the clergy of St Pantaleon's church and, when he was ordained priest, as chaplain and later as superior of a hospital for incurables at Venice. He became a canon of St Mark's church. In 1528 he resigned his benefice in order to join the Theatine Order under St Cajetan (7 Aug.), changing his name to John. The Order was devoted to the restoration of high spiritual and pastoral standards in an age of notorious corruption and to the care of the sick and poor.

When St Cajetan went to Naples he took John Marinoni with him, and John became superior of the Theatine community there. One of their innovations for the poor of Naples and district was the setting up of *montes pietatis*—benevolent pawnshops which would protect them against exploitation.

John refused the office of archbishop of Naples. He died in the city on 13 December 1562, ministered to by St Andrew Avellino (10 Nov.), who wrote an account of his former novice-master. His cult was authorized by Pope Clement XIII in 1762.

There is a biography by J. L. Bianchi, *Ragguaglio della vita del B. Giovanni Marinoni* (1763), and another sketch by J. Silos, re-published in view of the beatification in 1762. See also P.B., pp. 284-5; *D.Cath.Biog.* p. 755.

Bd Antony Grassi (1671)

Vincenzo Grassi, from Fermo in the Italian province of the Marches, joined the Oratorian Fathers at the age of seventeen and took the name of Antony in religion. He was a keen student, said to be "a walking dictionary," and soon acquired a reputation in biblical studies and theology. He had some scruples before his ordination, but these disappeared from the time he said his first Mass, and he was noted for his serenity.

In 1621, when he was twenty-nine, he was kneeling at prayer in the church of the Holy House at Loreto when he was struck by lightning. He left a detailed account of his experience:

> I felt shaken, and as though I were outside myself; and it seemed to me that my soul was separated from my body, and I was in a swoon. . . . Then I was roused with a great crash like thunder, and I opened my eyes and found that I had fallen head-first down the steps.
>
> I saw bits of stone on the floor, and the air was filled with a smoke so thick that it seemed like dust. I thought that plaster must have fallen from the ceiling, but on looking up I saw that it was undamaged. Then I saw that a piece of skin had been ripped off one of my fingers, and I remembered a priest at Camerino who was killed by lightning, on whose body there was no mark except some skin off his hand. So when I saw my finger I thought that I too was going to die. And a sort of heat burning my inside made me feel yet more like it, and when I tried to move my legs there was no feeling in them. I was afraid that scorching heat would reach my heart and kill me.
>
> I was helpless, and lay without moving on the steps thinking that if I could not die in the Oratory, I should at any rate do so in a sanctuary of the Mother of God. Then someone bent over me and I told him I could not move; he called for help and a chair was brought and I was put in it, when I fainted again. But I was conscious that my head and arms and legs were dangling uselessly, and my sight and speech had failed, though my hearing was acute. I knew someone was suggesting the holy names of Jesus and Mary to me.

When he recovered full consciousness, Antony still thought he was going to die and asked for the Last Rites. He was carried to his lodging. "Then I made the discovery that if we believe death to be close at hand we become quite indifferent to this world and know all earthly things to be emptiness."

He recovered in a few days to find that his underclothes had been scorched and that the shock had completely cured him of indigestion. He came to the conclusion that his life belonged to God in a very special manner. He made a daily thank-offering for his preservation, and every year he made a special pilgrimage to Loreto with the same intention. He asked for faculties to hear

Confessions, and this became one of his most notable activities. He brought to it a great simplicity, listening to the penitent, saying a few words of exhortation, imposing a penance, and giving absolution. He preferred not to give direction or suggest rules of life or deal with any matter not directly concerned with the Confession. He used to say that in forming an estimate of a person care should be taken not to judge on the basis of a single act or trait—in most people there was more good than bad.

In 1635 he was elected superior of the Fermo Oratory, and he was re-elected every three years for the rest of his life. He was a gentle superior. When asked why he did not show more severity, he said that he did not know how. In the same way he neither practised nor recommended unusual physical austerities. When an inquisitive person asked him if he wore a hair shirt, he replied that he did not. "Humbling the mind and will," he said, "is more effective than a hair shirt between your skin and your clothes."

This did not mean that he was easygoing: on the contrary, he maintained his community at a very high level of observance and efficiency by personal example. He spoke quietly and would not tolerate loud voices, quietening others by saying, "If you please, Father, only a few inches of voice." His influence extended far beyond his own house: Archbishop Gualtieri of Fermo said that he could not bear to think of losing him, and both Cardinal Facchinetti of Spoleto and Cardinal Emilio Altieri (later Pope Clement X) sought his counsel. When food riots took place in Fermo in 1649 he tried to mediate between the cardinal governor and the people and was nearly shot by the mob for his efforts.

Antony had a great concern for the good of his native town and its people. Nothing would induce him to make social or ceremonial engagements, but he would go out at any time of the day or night to visit sick or dying people or anyone else who needed his help.

As he approached his eightieth year he had the humiliation of losing some of his faculties. He had to give up preaching because he could not make himself understood through lack of teeth; and he had to give up hearing Confessions when he became increasingly deaf. After a fall downstairs he was confined to his room, and at the end of November 1671 he became bed-ridden. Archbishop Gualtieri came every day to give him Communion until his death a fortnight later. One of his last acts was to reconcile two fiercely quarrelling brothers.

Fr Antony's Life was written by his devoted friend and disciple Fr Cristoforo Antici; very shortly after his death an official inquiry into his virtues and reputed miracles was started by the archbishop of Fermo, Mgr Gualtieri, who knew him well and greatly respected him; but owing to civil disturbances and other causes of delay, his beatification was not achieved until 1900. There is a detailed biography in English by Lady Amabel Kerr, *A Saint of the Oratory* (1901). See also E. I. Watkin, *Neglected Saints* (1955), pp. 210-28; *D. Cath. Biog.*, p. 503.

14

ST JOHN OF THE CROSS, *Doctor* (1542-91)

Juan de Yepes y Alvárez was born in Fontiveros, between Avila and Salamanca, in 1542. His father, Gonzalo, came of a family of prosperous silk merchants in Toledo, but Gonzalo was disowned for marrying a poor girl and
became a silk-weaver to support his family. He died when John was about a
year old, leaving his widow, Caterina, in poverty with three small sons. She
and the children went through a period of great hardship, suffering cold and
hunger, and one son, Luis, died. John was sent to an orphanage in Medina del
Campo, where he was fed, clothed, and taught to read and write. At fourteen
he was apprenticed in turn to a carpenter, a wood sculptor, and a printer, but
he had no aptitude for any of these trades. Eventually he found employment as
a nursing assistant in a hospital outside the city. It was popularly known as the
Hospital de las Bubas. Bubo or *buba* in Spanish means a sore or tumour, and it
was a hospital for people with venereal diseases. Here he developed a love for
the sick and the poor and a capacity for undertaking the most menial and
unpleasant tasks. He washed and cleaned and bandaged patients with the most
repulsive conditions. He sang them popular songs and made them laugh. The
directness and honesty of his approach to people, religious and secular, rich
and poor, men and women, is repeatedly stressed in the biographies.

The administrator of the hospital, impressed by his diligence and his intellectual capacity, sent him to the Jesuit College when he was seventeen and
offered him the chaplaincy of the hospital if he became a priest. John studied
Latin and the humanities for four years, but he was developing a vocation for
the monastic life. One night he knocked on the door of the Carmelite priory of
Santa Ana and asked for the habit. He was accepted and professed in the
following year as John of St Matthias. He was sent to the university of Salamanca, then the outstanding centre of theology in Spain, where one of his
tutors was the biblical scholar and poet Fray Luis de León. John worked hard,
learned all he could, and led a frugal and ascetic life. He was not popular with
his fellow-students. They complained that he was always poring over books
and that he reproached them for unsuitable conversation and behaviour.

John was ordained priest in 1567, and he went home to Medina to say his
first Mass in the presence of his mother, as was customary. While he was there
the prior of the Carmelite house, Antonio de Heredia, arranged for him to
meet Teresa of Avila (15 Oct.). At that time Spain was wealthy and had a great
empire. The monastic rule in many houses had grown very lax; Teresa, a

Carmelite nun of outstanding vision and personal qualities, was working with the support of King Philip II to return to the austerities of the original Carmelite Rule of the thirteenth century. Her Discalced (*i.e.*, barefoot) nuns at Avila, dedicated to a strict régime of poverty and a disciplined life, had been approved by the father general of the Carmelite Order in 1567. She was given permission to found other houses for women and two for men, and she was seeking friars. Prior Antonio, who was about sixty years old, was delighted to abandon the dignity of his office for the reform, and John agreed to join him. Teresa said that she had "a friar and a half," which may have been a reference to John's youth in comparison to Antonio's grey hairs, or possibly to his small stature: estimates of his height vary from four feet ten to five feet. John had a final year of theology at Salamanca and then joined Antonio at a small house at Duruelo, about five miles from Avila. There he adopted the Discalced habit and changed his name to Fray Juan de la Cruz, Friar John of the Cross. His mother and his brother, Francisco, who may have been mentally handicapped, came to keep house for the friars. In 1570 John was sent to be rector of a study house at Alcalá, where he suffered acute attacks of spiritual darkness and temptations—experience which was to be used extensively in his pastoral work, his teaching, and his writing. In 1571 Teresa was sent to be prioress of the unreformed Carmelite Convent of the Incarnation at Avila, and she sent for John to be its spiritual director and confessor. The relationship between them was close—it is said that she sewed his first habit with her own hands—but not tender. High-spirited, practical Teresa wanted to get things done. John was pure contemplative and vague about detail; but as her confessor, despite his youth and his lack of inches, he did not scruple to exert his priestly authority over her. She often found him obstinate and narrow, but she appreciated his spirituality and the quality of his direction.

The attitude of the unreformed Carmelites of the Observance toward the Discalced was hardening, and while Teresa was under the protection of Philip II, John was not. The Carmelites appealed to the Carmelite general, who sent Fray Jerónimo Tostado to Spain with full authority to deal with the Discalced movement. John was captured and imprisoned in Medina by the Order in 1575-6 and freed only on the instructions of the papal nuncio; but the nuncio died, and his successor supported Tostado. In 1577, John was captured again and imprisoned in the Carmelite priory in Toledo.

The story of his imprisonment is well attested. After his death a number of depositions about the privations he endured in his prison cell were made by friars and nuns who had known him well. These sometimes differ in minor details, as witness accounts are apt to do, but the general circumstances are clear enough. He spent most of his time in total darkness. There was a tiny slit window high on the wall, two or three inches wide, but this was not on the outside wall of the priory. There was a walkway on the other side, so the light was dim, and he was able to read the divine office only in the short periods when a ray of sunlight penetrated through. He had to stand on a stone (or it may have been a bench) to do so. The cell was freezing in winter and stifling in summer, and he stayed there for eight and a half months. For most of the time he had no communication with anyone except his friar-jailer, who treated him with hatred and calumny. He was half-starved and verminous, and he was regularly flogged in chapter to force him to change his mind and leave the Discalced: he bore the marks for the rest of his life. He was told, though it was not true, that Teresa was also in prison, and that he would die in his cell. He was afraid he was being poisoned. He had no means of reading or writing—it was only in his last few weeks in prison that a more kindly jailer allowed him writing materials and a candle. Worst of all, he had a fear that he might after all be wrong in disobeying the superiors of the Order and thus in danger of losing his immortal soul.

It was in these conditions of stress and privation that John developed great spiritual insight, and it was then that he composed some of his finest poems. In August 1578, at some time in the octave of the feast of the Assumption, he determined to attempt an escape. He had managed to loosen the lock on his door and he tore two small rugs into strips to make a rope. He climbed out of his prison by night and descended the high walls of the priory—only to find that he was in the enclosure of the Franciscan nuns. Confused and calling on the Blessed Virgin for help, he found a way through or over the wall and down to the city walls and the river Tagus below, close to the Alcántara bridge. When he staggered, barefoot and exhausted, through the narrow streets of the city, people thought he was drunk and called after him, but he found his way to the house of the Discalced nuns, who had just come out of chapel.

At the grille he asked to see the mother prioress. The nun who answered his knocking, Isabel de San Jerónimo, said in her deposition that he looked on the point of death. When the mother prioress came, recognizing that he was near collapse and in great danger, she called two more nuns and told them to open the three locks that guarded the door. Though this was in normal circumstances a grave breach of rules, she had the excuse that a sick nun needed to make her Confession. Then the nuns tended him, bound his wounds, and gave him stewed pears with cinnamon, which was all he could eat. When the friars and the constables came searching for him, the mother prioress refused to let them in. They searched the church and the outer part of the house, but did not dare to violate the enclosure. After they had gone John went into the church and began to dictate his poems. Some he had in a small notebook which he had brought from prison, others were in his head. Mother Magdalena of the Holy Spirit, of the convent at Beas, where John acted as confessor for some years after his escape, wrote an account of his life in which she said that she saw the notebook. John left it with her to have a copy made, but someone took it from her cell. She remembered that it contained the first part of his "Romance" based on the Prologue to St John's Gospel, some couplets for another poem

123

with the refrain *Aunque es de noche* ("Though it is night"), and part of *The Spiritual Canticle*, which is loosely based on the Song of Songs. Others said that it included his paraphrase of Psalm 137, "By the streams of Babylon." John knew much of the Bible by heart, and it seems likely that what he managed to complete in prison was largely based on biblical sources.

In the morning Don Pedro González de Mendoza, a canon of the cathedral and member of a famous family who was friendly to the Discalced, took John under his protection. When he was safely away from Toledo and had recovered John was sent as prior of the house of El Calvario, near Beas, as confessor to the Discalced nuns. There he continued to write poetry for some time. When asked how he came to write the poems, he said simply: "Sometimes God gave me the words, and at other times I sought them."

He dreaded administrative responsibility but accepted it as his duty—in 1579 as head of the college at Baeza; in 1581 as prior of Los Mártires, near Granada; and as deputy vicar-general of the Discalced. John would have been happy to pass his days in meditation and prayer close to the mountains and the rivers of the country he loved. "For the love of God, let me be," he said, "for I am not fit to deal with people." He lived very simply and took on the most menial tasks as an example to others, but he carried a heavy burden of duties: his days were spent in setting up new friaries, in teaching and the pastoral care of his friars and nuns, and in his prose writings, *The Ascent of Mount Carmel*, *The Dark Night of the Soul*, *The Spiritual Canticle*, and *The Living Flame of Love*.

After Teresa's death in 1582, John faced mounting opposition not only from the Carmelites of the Ancient Observance but among the Discalced. In 1591 he was stripped of all offices and sent to the remote friary of La Peñuela as a simple friar. He had forecast that he would be "taken and thrown in a corner like an old kitchen cloth." Unsuccessful attempts were made to collect evidence of scandalous conduct against him with the intention of having him expelled from the Order, and when he became ill he went to the friary at Úbeda, where he was badly treated by a hostile and vindictive prior. He suffered great pain but submitted with courage and cheerfulness to the humiliations visited on him. Antonio de Heredia, by this time a very old man, made the journey in wintry conditions from Granada to see him and was shocked to find him neglected and wasted, but John was almost beyond earthly contact, and it was an effort to talk. He died in the first few minutes of 14 December 1591, as the choir began to sing Matins.

The poems and the prose works of John of the Cross have been translated into many languages and run to many editions. In a sense, there is no "definitive edition." John was not careful about documentation, and much of what he had to say was eagerly scribbled down by his friars and nuns and circulated in hand-written copies, with inevitable mistakes and alterations. The nearest we can come to an approved text is that of Sanlúcar de Barrameda (1586 or 1587), which John read through and annotated in his tiny crabbed hand. The poems are full of symbolic imagery—light and darkness, consuming flames, wounding, suffering, pursuing, finding. They are written as love poems, but they are not about earthly love. It was a convention of sixteenth-century Spanish poetry that courtly love between a man and a woman was used as an allegory of the soul seeking the love of God.

Probably his best known poem is the mysterious *Dark Night*, which describes how the soul goes forth under cover of night to meet the Beloved. Many devout Christians have found this poem a source of spiritual enlightenment that touches some very basic chords in human experience. It is important to recognize that it is not about clinical depression. People who suffer from depression, which can be an experience of intense desolation and dereliction, look inward. John looked upward. His spirit did not collapse; it soared. Nor is it an account of a supernatural experience. John wrote later in *The Ascent of Mount Carmel* that "the pure, cautious and humble soul should resist and reject visions and other revelations . . . as it would extremely dangerous temptations." John had nothing in common with the *Alumbrados,* or "Illuminists," of his day, who sought esoteric means of enlightenment and made extravagant claims of ecstatic experiences. *Dark Night* is simply a poetic account of a soul seeking God. At the end, "face to face with Love's own grace," the soul leaves its fears and its cares fading among the lilies—and the lilies are Easter lilies, symbols of the resurrection.

When he was at Beas the nuns asked him to explain the poem further, and he drew for them a diagram of the spiritual path to union with God. On the right lies the path of earthly imperfection, manifested in characteristics such as a love of possessions, pleasure, knowledge for its own sake, and a desire for rest (by which John probably meant spiritual apathy). This path peters out in the mountains. On the left is the path of spiritual imperfection, shown in characteristics such as a desire for glory, joy, and consolation, and this too leads nowhere. In the centre is the path of Mount Carmel, which leads to union with God. Along it is written the word *nada,* repeated: "Nothing, nothing, nothing, nothing, nothing, even on the Mount, nothing." This leads to a high place, where, he writes, "Nothing gives me glory, nothing gives me pain," "Now that I wish for nothing, I have all without wishing," and "Now that I ask for nothing, I have all without asking." The centre path leads upwards to a circle where the Nine Fruits of the Holy Spirit, derived from St Paul's Epistle to the Galatians (Gal. 5:22) are shown. At the centre stands "the honour and glory of God alone."

The repetition of "nothing" is often daunting to modern readers, who are accustomed to think in terms of human rights and self-expression: but John was writing in a society which needed to be told that self-fulfillment was not enough. Spain was at the height of its imperial power, rich with gold from the New World. What John was telling his contemporaries, the *aristócratas* and the *conquistadores*, was that self-aggrandizement was a waste of time. The soul cannot reach God by its own efforts. Without God, the creator of all things, *nada, nada, nada*. Pride and self-interest would only lead them off the path to Mount Carmel and leave them lost in the mountains.

John elaborated his sketch of the road to perfection, and Mother Magdalena wrote that he drew copies in all the nuns' breviaries at Beas; but his "spiritual children" still demanded further explanation, and so he turned to writing his prose works, which describe at length how the mind and body must be cleansed of attachment to earthly things in order to reach out to the divine. These must have been the subject of his lectures, and they are written in the precise and formal language of the lecture room. The theology John had learned at Salamanca was basically Aristotelian, mediated through the close and formal reasoning of Aquinas. This has its own strengths, but it is very different from the lyricism and the visionary reaching out to God that was so marked a feature of the poems. *The Ascent of Mount Carmel* and *The Dark Night of the Soul* are really one work, an exposition of the diagrams in terms of four phases of the path to God. *The Spiritual Canticle* and *The Living Flame of Love* keep more closely to the structure of the poems and explain the meaning of the stanzas in terms of the love between the individual soul and God. All these have become spiritual classics. Yet John was very much aware of the difficulties of trying to "explain" the poems. In the introduction to *The Spiritual Canticle*, he writes to Mother Magdalena:

> Since these Stanzas have been composed under the influence of a love which comes from abounding mystical understanding, they cannot be fully expounded, nor shall I attempt so to expound them, but only to throw upon them some light of a general kind . . . for the sayings of love are best left in their fullness, so that everyone may pluck advantage from them according to his manner and to the measure of his spirit.

John of the Cross was beatified in 1675, canonized in 1726, and declared a Doctor of the Church Universal in 1926. His cult has not been confined to his own Order but has spread through the whole Church and wherever the contemplative life is valued.

Lives by Bruno de Jésus-Marie, *Saint Jean de la Croix* (1929, revised 1961, Eng. trans. 1932); E. Allison Peers, *Handbook to the Life and Times of St Teresa and St John of the Cross* (1954); Crisógono de Jésus (Eng. trans. 1958, Spanish version revised by Matías del Niño Jesús, 1964); Works: *Las Obras de San Juan de la Cruz*, ed. Silverio de Santa Teresa (1929-31), is taken from the version of Sanlúcar de Barrameda; Eng. trans. of the complete works by E. Allison Peers, 3 vols. (1933, revised ed. 1953); K. Kavanaugh and O. Rodríguez (1966). Poems trans. by David Lewis (1912); Roy Campbell (1951); Kathleen Jones (1993). Commentaries: Thomas Merton, *The Ascent to Truth* (1951); A Benedictine of Stanbrook Abbey, *The Mediaeval Mystical Tradition and St John of the Cross* (1954). E. W. T. Dicken, *The Crucible of Love* (1963); L. Saggi, *Saints of Carmel*, trans. G. N. Pausback (1972), pp. 142-69, with a very full bibliography on pp. 169-72; Ross Collings, *John of the Cross*, (1990); John Welch, *When Gods Die*, New York, 1992; *Carmelite Studies VI: John of the Cross*, (1992).

There is a plaque on the wall near the Alcántara Bridge in Toledo to mark where John reached the riverside. There are shrines in Segovia and Úbeda, and a small museum in the priory in Úbeda. A statue in a square there shows him consumed by the "living flame of love," and one in Granada shows him as a cheerful pilgrim, carrying his message across Spain. There are no portraits from life: a "proto-typical" one was painted immediately after his death, a full-length figure the same height as he was. It hangs in the museum in Úbeda, with several derivatives. In the eighteenth century, as his works became more widely known, he was more usually represented writing.

St Nicasius, *Bishop*, and Companions, *Martyrs* (? 451)

An army of barbarians, probably Huns, ravaged part of Gaul and plundered the city of Reims in the mid-fifth century. Nicasius, the bishop, had warned his people of the coming calamity and urged them to prepare by works of penance. When he saw the enemy at the gates and in the streets, forgetting the danger to himself and concerned only for his spiritual children, he went from door to door encouraging them to patience and constancy. When the people asked whether they should yield or fight to the end, he, knowing the city must fall, replied, "Let us abide the mercy of God, and pray for our enemies. I am ready to give myself for my people."

Standing at the door of his church, he tried to save the lives of those nearby, and was himself cut down. His deacon, his lector, and his sister Eutropia were martyred with him.

M.G.H., Scriptores, 13, pp. 417-20; *Anal.Boll.* 1 (1882), pp. 492, 497, 628; Duchesne, *Fastes*, 3, p. 81.

St Venantius Fortunatus, *Bishop* (*c.* 535-*c.* 605)

Venantius Honorius Clementianus Fortunatus, who was born near Treviso, north of Venice, is better known as a poet than as a saint. All that is known of his early years is that he was educated at Ravenna in logic, rhetoric, and law. In his late twenties he was threatened with blindness, which was particularly serious for a scholar. He was cured after rubbing his eyes with oil from a lamp burning before a statue of St Martin of Tours (11 Nov.) in a church in Ravenna. The patron saint of people with eye trouble was St Lucy (13 Dec.), while St Martin was traditionally the patron saint of soldiers, but it is recorded that St Martin was able to cure St Paulinus of Nola (22 June) of an eye complaint, and this may account for Fortunatus' devotion to him. He recovered his sight and resolved to visit St Martin's shrine at Tours to give thanks.

He started on his journey shortly before the Lombard invasion of Italy, which laid waste the northern half of the peninsula. Many other people must have been leaving while they could, but probably few had as pleasing a journey as Fortunatus. His pilgrimage turned into something like a grand tour. He seems to have been a very welcome guest in great houses, staying with bishops and abbots and distinguished noblemen. He enjoyed good living and evidently had the instincts of a courtier, for he repaid hospitality by writing flowery poems extolling the virtues of his hosts. He was at the Frankish court at Metz for the marriage of King Sigebert and his bride, Brunehilda, and he composed an elaborate epithalamium for their wedding. His talents made him very popular with the court and the nobility, who evidently passed him from one noble house to the next.

He completed his pilgrimage to Tours but never returned to Italy, where continual petty wars and Lombard attacks made life hazardous. Yet he could not settle in the uncouth and often brutal society of the Franks. One of the last of the cultured Romans, he was not at home in either setting. He found a haven in Poitiers, where Queen Radegund (13 Aug.) had taken shelter from her brutal and bloodthirsty husband, Clotaire I, after his murder of her brother. At the monastery of the Holy Cross he found a tranquil society of cultured nuns who appreciated his learning and became his friends. Radegund and her adopted daughter, the abbess Agnes, pressed him to be ordained. He became their chaplain, counsellor, man of business, and secretary.

Radegund lived a very austere personal life, but she did not impose this on those around her. Most of the nuns came from the great aristocratic Gallo-Roman families, and the convent life was comparatively luxurious, with Roman baths and gardens and excellent cooking. The nuns kept the Rule of SS Caesarius and Caesaria of Arles (27 Aug. and 2 Jan.), but this was evidently fairly relaxed. It did not prevent them from cosseting their chaplain, sending dishes of meat with rich sauces, butter, fruit, and wine to his lodging. When he visited the monastery there were silver and crystal dishes on the table and bowls of roses. Fortunatus was thus royally entertained and became devoted to Radegund and Agnes. He sent them presents of lilies and wrote charming letters and poems to both, calling them his "mother" and his "sister."

Successive commentators, considering these relationships, have not found them other than innocent. In a society that was often both coarse and cruel the presence of an urbane and cultivated Roman poet who could produce polished verses and who knew how to please must have been a valued addition to the community life. Fortunatus knew all the great churchmen and the high officials and could advise Radegund and the abbess on matters of ecclesiastical politics. There were times when the monastery was in danger, either from warring kings or unsympathetic bishops. He helped them to preserve their way of life. So he continued to enjoy general popularity and to be invited to any public occasion which could suitably be celebrated in a poem.

The relationship between Fortunatus and his bishop Gregory of Tours (17 Nov.) has been the subject of some discussion; for while Fortunatus wrote to Gregory frequently and in very deferential terms, the only extant references to Fortunatus by Gregory are distinctly terse: he describes him as "the priest Fortunatus" or "the Italian priest"; but Fortunatus visited Gregory often, and Gregory urged him to write, suggesting subjects for him, and recommended his writings to other bishops.

When Fortunatus was sixty-nine years old he was elected bishop of Poitiers—a unanimous choice. He applied himself with great zeal and enthusiasm to his episcopal tasks, but they were too much for him, and he died within a year of his consecration.

Fortunatus has been described by some commentators as a flatterer, and by Sir Samuel Dill as a parasite. He could certainly turn a blind eye to the failings of those he praised in such glowing terms: the immorality, the cruelty, and the debased values of the sons of Clovis and their courts were simply ignored; but the panegyric was an established literary form of the time. The idea that assessments of character should be critical, noting faults as well as virtues, is a comparatively modern one—and considerably safer today than it would have been in sixth-century Gaul. The more scathing judgments on Fortunatus do not explain why Gregory of Tours commended his work; why Queen Ragedund, a woman of high standards and great sensitivity, not only tolerated him as her chaplain but trusted him over a period of some twenty years and evidently valued him highly; why he was elected bishop of Poitiers; nor why, after years of very comfortable living and somewhat mechanical tributes to the rich and powerful, he wrote Christian poetry of remarkable quality.

In 569 the Emperor Justinian II sent a relic of the True Cross to the monastery. In medieval Catholic thought the cross was the instrument of salvation: sin came into the world through Adam's tree in the Garden of Eden, and miraculously, Christ's cross, made of that same wood, made redemption possible. Peter Abelard and John of the Cross (14 Dec., above) were later to develop the same theme. Fortunatus made it the subject of the first of his great poems, *Vexilla regis prodeunt* ("The royal banners forward go"), written for the occasion of the relic's reception and deposition. The poem, which Helen Waddell calls "the greatest processional hymn of the Middle Ages," became one of the great hymns of the liturgy, sung through the centuries on Good Friday. The same theme is taken up in his hymn *Pange lingua gloriosi* ("Sing, my tongue, the glorious battle") for Passiontide, and he composed *Salve festa dies* for Easter. If the nuns of the Holy Cross learned about the world from him, he acquired a deep and genuine spirituality from them.

His written works are extensive. He composed other hymns for great ecclesiastical occasions, many of them based on the rhythms of the songs sung by the Roman legionaries on the march. He also wrote Lives of the Saints: in prose, the Lives of St Hilary (13 Jan.), St Radegund (13 Aug.), and St Paternus of Avranches (16 April); in verse, those of St Martin (11 Nov.) and St Médard (8 June). His *In laudem Mariae* depicts the Virgin as Queen of Heaven, receiving homage. Fortunatus was well named. He had found his métier and turned what seemed a rather trivial talent to great themes. Well versed in the classical Latin tradition, he brought to it something new: the devotion and piety that were to mark the best literature of the medieval Christian world. In subsequent generations his reputation as a *bon viveur* may have mitigated against recognition of the excellence of his hymns, which are now rated as among the finest examples of Christian poetry.

Knowledge of Fortunatus is mainly derived from Gregory of Tours and from the poet's own writings and correspondence. The chief references to his relationship with Gregory of Tours are to be found in Gregory's *Historia Francorum*, trans. and ed. O. M. Dalton (1927), especially in the commentary in 1, pp. 20-7, 64 ff., 76-7, and 81-5. The best text of Fortunatus' own work is that edited by Leo Krusch in *M.G.H., Auctores Antiquissimi*, 3, pp. 3-292. See also *D.T.C.*, 6, pt. 1, 611-4; and *D.A.C.L.*, 5, 1982-97. P.B., pp. 296-303 draws on the *Vie des saints de Poitiers*. Text and translation of five lyrics by Fortunatus in Helen Waddell, *Mediaeval Latin Lyrics* (1935 ed.), pp. 58-67, and of *Vexilla regis prodeunt* in *More Latin Lyrics* (1976), pp. 122-3. For a modern assessment of Fortunatus as a poet, see F. J. E. Raby, *History of Christian Latin Poetry* (1953), pp. 86-96; and cf. S. Dill, *Roman Society in Gaul* (1926, rp. 1966), pp. 237, 279 ff., 333 ff. For the cult see Fr B. de Gaiffier in *Anal. Boll.* 70 (1952), pp. 262-84. For comments on the *Vita S Radegundis* see *Anal. Boll.* 111 (1993), pp. 81-91.

Bd Bonaventure Buonaccorsi (1315)

In the year 1276 St Philip Benizi (22 Aug.) came to Pistoia, between Pisa and Florence, to preside at a general chapter of the Servite Order. He took the opportunity to preach to the people of the place, which was torn by factions. Among his audience was Bonaventure, who was about thirty-six years old and a member of the noble Buonaccorsi family. He was a leader of the Ghibellines, the political faction which generally supported the emperor against the pope, and notorious as a desperate character. Bonaventure was so moved by St Philip's exhortations to peace and concord that he went to him and accused himself of creating unrest and causing much misery and injustice. So penitent was he that he asked to be admitted among the Servite friars.

Philip was naturally doubtful at so sudden and complete a change, and he tested the aspirant by imposing a public penance: Bonaventure must openly make reparation for his wrongdoing and personally ask pardon from all whom he had wronged or caused to oppose him. This he did with such thoroughness and goodwill that Philip took him from Pistoia to Monte Senario to make his novitiate at the headquarters of the Order. There he persisted in his good resolutions, and after his profession he was joined to Philip as a *socius* and admitted to the priesthood. For the next few years he was constantly with Philip, who was prior general, and helped him in his efforts, together with the papal legate Cardinal Latino, to bring peace to the troubled cities of Umbria and Tuscany. The spectacle of the reformed Ghibelline going about in the habit of a Mendicant and preaching brotherly love made a deep impression.

In 1228 Bonaventure was made prior at Orvieto, but on the death of St Philip he was called to the aid of his successor and was then made preacher apostolic, with a commission to preach missions throughout Italy. This he did to great effect. In 1303 he was made prior at Montepulciano, and there he assisted St Agnes (20 Apr.) in the foundation of her community of Dominican nuns, whose director he became. Then he was moved to his native Pistoia, where civil war had again broken out and the city was threatened by the Florentines. Bonaventure was tireless in preaching peace and civic unity. He died at Orvieto and was buried in the chapel of our Lady of Sorrows in the Servite Church as a testimony of the respect in which he was held by his brethren. His cult was confirmed in 1822.

A. Giani in *Annalium Sacri Ordinis Servorum* 1 (1719), pp. 118-9; B. M. Sporr, *Lebensbilder aus dem Servitenorden* (1892), p. 621. A.Serra, "Rassegna critica delle fonti riguardante il B. Buonaventura da Pistoia," *Studi Storici dell'Ordine dei Servi di Maria 24* (1974), gives a critical review of sources. There is a brief account in J. M. Chamberlain, *Servants of Mary* (1988), pp. 40-1.

Bd Frances Schervier, *Foundress* (1819-76)

Frances was born in Aachen at a time when the Ruhr was rapidly becoming the industrial centre of west Germany. Her father, Johann Schervier, was a leading businessman. In September 1818 the Austrian emperor attended an industrial congress in the city and, after a visit to the Schervier factory, agreed to become godfather to the child Frau Schervier was expecting. Frances was born in the following January, and the emperor was duly represented at her Baptism.

In 1832, when she was only thirteen, her mother died, and in the following year her two elder sisters also died. Frances found herself responsible for running the household for her father and her younger brothers and sisters. Her father was something of a martinet, and the task must have been a heavy one. Her concern for less fortunate people was already marked: even as a young girl she gave generously to those in need, and one of the servants remarked, "One day, the child will have everything out of the house." Her imperial godfather had sent her expensive gifts. She sold them for the poor.

Industrialization brought poverty and misery, and Catholic organizations began to develop many kinds of welfare work to meet the needs. When she was twenty-one Frances joined the women's organization of her parish, St Paul's. Members were pledged to visit poor and sick people and to care for abandoned children. Frances took this very seriously and was particularly concerned about girls who were being sexually exploited. On one occasion she is said to have dressed as a man and entered a brothel in order to rescue a girl.

In 1844 she became a Franciscan tertiary, and in the following year, after the death of her father, she began to live a community life with four other young women. Their numbers increased to twenty-three; they received the religious habit with the approval of the archbishop of Cologne in 1851 and became the Sisters of the Poor of St Francis. The Congregation had an unusual character, since it consisted of two "families," one dedicated to the contemplative life and one to the active life, each sustaining the other. In 1858 she sent some Sisters to Cincinatti to assist German immigrants, and she visited the United States

131

herself. She was there during the Civil War between North and South and joined her Sisters in ministering to wounded soldiers and the many people who had lost their homes.

In the Franco-Prussian War the Schervier Sisters were behind the front lines helping with the wounded and staffing twenty-eight military ambulances. Mother Frances was with them, coping with shattered bodies and shattered lives. In 1871 the empress of Austria awarded her the Cross of Merit for her work, but she refused it, saying that she did not want any reward: "The care given by the Sisters to sick or wounded soldiers are less personal merits than merits of the society to which they are proud to belong."

Frances Schervier was beatified by Pope Paul VI on 28 April 1974.

Osservatore Romano, 9 May 1974. The report gives Pope Paul's homily, which he delivered in German, and an account of the Life contributed by the under-secretary of the Congregation for the Causes of Saints. See also *F.B.S.*, pp. 935-7; *N.S.B.* 1, pp. 114-5.

15

St Valerian, *Bishop,* and Other Martyrs of North Africa
(457 and 482)

In addition to St Dionysia and other martyrs commemorated on 6 December, some other victims of the Vandal persecutions in North Africa are commemorated today. Under the Arian king Genseric, the aged bishop Valerian, more than eighty years old, was told to give up the sacred vessels of his church. When he steadily refused to do so, he was removed by force: ". . . it was commanded that he be driven out of the city by himself, and that no one be allowed to receive him in his house or on his land; wherefore he remained for a long time in the public street, uncared for, under the open sky, and in this confession and defence of Catholic truth, he ended the course of his blessed life."

On the following day is kept the feast of the many consecrated virgins who suffered under Huneric, being branded, sold into slavery, driven into the desert, and in other ways harried and killed for maintaining the Catholic faith.

As in the case of SS Dionysia, Majoricus, and Companions (6 Dec.), our only knowledge of these martyrs comes from the *Historia persecutionis provinciae Africanae* of Victor, bishop of Vita, who was a contemporary. See *M.G.H., Auctores Antiquissimi*, 3, pt. 1, p. 10. See also *D.C.B.*, 4, p. 1103.

St Paul of Latros (956)

This saint, sometimes referred to as St Paul the Younger, was a solitary who had to work hard for his solitude. His father, an officer in the imperial army, was killed in a battle against the Saracens. His elder brother Basil became a monk in Bithynia, in Asia Minor and after a time retired to Mount Latros (Latmus). When their mother died Paul wanted to live a similar life, but Basil recommended him to the care of the abbot of Kratia, who insisted on keeping him in the monastery. When the abbot died and he was finally free to follow his avocation Paul chose a cave in the most rocky part of the mountain, where for three years he suffered severe temptations. For the most part he lived off the countryside, though peasants sometimes left him a little food. As the reputation of his holiness spread, several men decided to live near him and built up a *laura* of cells. Paul, who had been careless of his own wants, was kept busy in providing for those who lived under his direction; after twelve years, his solitude was so much invaded that he withdrew to another part of the mountain, visiting his brethren from time to time to encourage and cheer them. Sometimes he took them into the forest to sing the divine office in the open air. When he was asked why his moods varied from cheerfulness to sadness, he replied, "When nothing diverts my thoughts from God, my heart overflows with joy, so much that I often forget my food and everything else; and when there are distractions, I am upset."

When Paul wished for even greater solitude he went to the island of Samos and hid in a cave, but he was soon discovered, and so many came to join him that he re-established three *lauras* which had been ruined by the Saracens. The monks at Latros entreated him to return to them, and eventually he agreed. The emperor Constantine Porphyogenitus frequently wrote to him asking his advice. Paul had a great tenderness for the poor and often gave them more of his food and clothes than he could properly spare. On one occasion he would have sold himself into slavery to help some people in distress had he not been stopped.

Paul of Latros died on 15 December 956 after a short illness, instructing his monks and praying until the last. He is not included in the new Roman Martyrology.

The Life of St Paul of Latros, written by an anonymous disciple, is one of the most trustworthy of Byzantine biographies. See *Anal.Boll.* 9 (1892) and the more carefully revised text by Delehaye in the volume *Der Latmos*, issued in 1913 by T. Weigand and other scholars, with abundant illustrations and archeological comments This also contains a previously unprinted commendation from MS. Vatican 704.

Bd Victoria Fornari-Strata, *Foundress* (1562-1617)

Vittoria Fornari was born in Genoa of a wealthy family. As a girl she was attracted to the religious life, but she deferred to the wishes of her father and married Angelo Strata. The marriage was a happy one: Angelo shared in her many charitable works and defended her against criticism that she took little part in the social round of the city. They had six children, four boys and two girls, but Angelo died in 1587, while the children were still young. Victoria, mourning the loss of her husband, doubted her ability to raise her family alone. A nobleman wished to marry her and she thought of accepting for the sake of the children, but she had a vision of Our Lady, who promised her protection if she would live quietly and devote her life to the love of God. She wrote an account of this vision at the direction of her confessor.

Thereafter she took a vow of chastity and lived in retirement, giving her whole time to her devotions, her children, and the poor of Genoa. Her home was austere and simple, and she practised self-denial—for instance, taking only bread and water on fast days.

It was not until her children were grown up and provided for that she reverted to her original intention of entering a religious Order. She went to the archbishop of Genoa with a plan for a new Order of nuns who would have a special devotion to the Blessed Virgin Mary. At first the archbishop withheld his approval because the funds available were not sufficient for such a major undertaking, but when one of Victoria's friends offered to meet the cost of a suitable building he gave his consent. In 1604 Victoria, who was then forty-two years of age, and ten other women were clothed, and they were professed in the following year. Each added Maria Annunziata to her baptismal name. Their special aim was to honour the Virgin in the mystery of her Annunciation and her hidden life in Nazareth. They were an enclosed Order, with a strict Rule.

Mother Victoria administered the new foundation wisely and competently, and eight years later a second house was added. The Order spread to France. Without her knowledge an attempt was made to affiliate the nuns to another Order on the pretext that it was not sufficiently strong to develop on its own, but when she heard of this, she trusted in the continued help of the Virgin Mary, and plans for affiliation were dropped. She continued to govern the Order, setting an example of love and humility, until her death on 15 December 1817 at the age of fifty-five. The Order is known in Italy as the *Turchine*, with reference to the sky-blue colour of their cloaks.

On the occasion of the beatification of Victoria in 1828, an Italian Life was printed with the title *Vita della b Maria Vittoria Fornari-Strata, fondatrice dell' Ordine della Santissima Annunziata detto "Le Turchina."* This Life is anonymous, but official. See also a French Life by Fr F. Dumortier (1902); BS(R), p. 384.

Bd Virginia Centurione-Bracelli (1587-1651)

Though she had a sense of vocation from an early age, Virginia Centurione was unable to convince her parents that she was dedicated to the religious life, and at the age of fifteen she was married to Caspar Bracelli, who came from a family of a similarly distinguished tradition. The marriage was a very unhappy one. Caspar was a young man of vicious habits. He died prematurely, worn out by his excesses, only five years later. Virginia had tried to reconcile him with God, and she nursed him through his final illness. On the day of his death she made a vow of celibacy and determined to spend the rest of her life in bringing up her two small daughters and helping people in distress.

Northern Italy was ravaged by continual wars, and there was misery on all sides. Virginia found a sense of direction when she saw a small girl abandoned and lying in the street. She took the child home, knowing that girls were at particular risk. They were often humiliated and exploited and had little future except as prostitutes. It was not difficult to find others in the same predicament. She gathered them together and started a school for them. When her own daughters married, she devoted all her time and all her financial resources to the school and founded the Order of Our Lady of Mount Calvary to provide teachers for it. She founded a second school in a former monastery, then a third, and a fourth. At least one of these, the Refuge, was well known in Genoa for many years after her death.

Virginia died on 15 December 1651 and was beatified by Pope John Paul II at Genoa on 22 September 1985.

N.S.B. 2, pp. 76-8; *N.D.S.*, p. 320.

St Mary di Rosa, *Foundress* (1813-55)

Paula di Rosa, the daughter of Clemente di Rosa and his wife, Countess Camilla Albani, was born in Brescia, the sixth of nine children. Her mother died young, and she left school at seventeen in order to keep house for her father. She decided not to marry and lived at home, devoting her energies to social work, with her father's approval.

Clemente di Rosa owned a textile mill at Acquafredda, and Paula's first care was to look after the welfare of the factory girls. At Capriano, where the di Rosas had a country house, she established a women's guild, retreats, and special missions with the cooperation of the parish priest. In 1836 there was a cholera epidemic in Brescia, and Paula accompanied a widow, Gabriela Echenos-Bornati, who already had some experience of nursing, in working on the wards.

When the epidemic was over, Paula was asked to run a house for poor and abandoned girls—a difficult task for a well-brought-up young woman of the period. She managed the house successfully for two years, then resigned after a disagreement with the trustees, who did not want the girls to stay in the house overnight. She established a small house of her own for a dozen girls and at the same time, with the help of her brother Philip and the archpriest of Brescia Cathedral, Mgr Faustino Pinzoni, started a school for deaf-mute girls, which she handed over later to the Canossian Sisters.

Paula di Rosa had proved herself an excellent organizer with a quick and lively mind. The Congregation of the Handmaids of Charity, which she and Gabriela Echenos-Bornati founded, took ten years to evolve. The first step was the formation of a religious society devoted to the care of sick and suffering people. Their aim was not simply to nurse the sick but to give all their time unreservedly to their welfare, caring for the whole person. The first four members of the society took up residence in a dilapidated house near Brescia hospital, and the community soon numbered thirty-two.

Before long Clemente di Rosa gave them a better and more spacious house, and their provisional Rule was approved by the bishop in 1843. The death of Gabriela Bornati soon after approval of the Rule, and then in 1848 of their supporter the archpriest Pinzoni, were heavy blows. They came at a time when Italy was suffering from violent political convulsions, and there was armed conflict in the north. Paula di Rosa set up a military hospital—where, like Florence Nightingale some years later, her Handmaids of Charity had to face opposition from doctors who were used to working with military orderlies and thought the women would not be suitable for the work. The Sisters survived the opposition and worked with military and civilian casualties in hospitals and on the battlefields.

In 1849 came the terrible "Ten Days of Brescia." Paula and her Sisters were at the disposal of all the wounded without distinction, but some disorderly soldiers tried to attack the hospital. They were met at the front door by Paula and half a dozen Sisters carrying a great crucifix with a lighted candle on either side, and they went away peacefully.

In the autumn of 1850 Paula set out for Rome, and on 24 October she was received by Pope Pius IX. Two months later, with the most remarkable speed for Rome, the Constitutions of the Congregation of the Handmaids of Charity were finally approved. In the summer of 1852 the first twenty-five Sisters and their foundress were able to take their vows. Paula took the name of Maria Crocifissa, "Mary of the Crucified." There was still work to be done—a renewed threat of cholera at Brescia, convents to be opened in Dalmatia and near Verona. In Mantua she collapsed from physical exhaustion and reached home only to say, "Thank God he has let me get home to Brescia to die." This she did, very peacefully and quietly, three weeks later, at the early age of forty-two. She was canonized in 1954.

There is a full Life in Italian by V. Bartoccetti, *Beata Maria Crocifissa di Rosa* (1940); a good ninety-page summary under the same title by a member of the Congregation; and another Life by Dr L. Fossati. There seems to be no full account of her acts in any language other than Italian, probably because all the houses of the Handmaids of Charity were in or near Italy. See *N.D.S.*, p. 217; BS(R), p. 385.

Bd Charles Steeb, *Founder* (1775-1856)

Charles (Karl) Steeb was the son of wealthy Lutheran parents who lived in Tübingen, near Stuttgart in Germany. The university of Tübingen was a centre of Lutheran influence, and when Charles studied in Verona and became a Catholic this was so unacceptable to his family that he was disinherited. The decision was a very costly one for him, because it left him poor and friendless, with no contact with his homeland. He sought ordination, and with the help of Fr Pietro Leonardi, founder of an evangelical brotherhood in Verona, he turned to working among the poor and dispossessed.

Verona was a centre of philanthropy in the war-torn north of Italy. Charles Steeb became a solitary and austere man but a patient and wise confessor. He worked unsparingly in hospitals, hospices, and *lazarettos* in the city of his adoption, through the period of invasion by the forces of Napoleon, and after, when there were many desperate social problems. He died only five years before Italy was finally united in 1861.

With Sister Luigia Poloni he founded the Institute of the Sisters of Mercy, which now has some two hundred communities in many countries. He was beatified by Pope Paul VI on 6 July 1975.

Lives by G. Cassetta (1964); H. Tüchle (1968); also *Bibl.SS.*, 11, 1374-5; *N.S.B.* 1, pp. 124-6.

16

St Adelaide of Burgundy (931-99)

Adelaide, daughter of Rudolph II of Upper Burgundy, was treated as a political pawn in her early life. She was betrothed at the age of two to Lothair, son of Hugh of Provence, and married to him at the age of sixteen. Lothair was by that time nominally king of Italy, though he was dominated by the forces of Berengarius of Ivrea. A daughter, Emma, was born of the marriage, but three years later Lothair died—it was strongly rumoured that he had been poisoned on the orders of Berengarius. Berengarius tried to force Adelaide to marry his son; when she refused, he treated her with brutality and indignity. She was imprisoned in a castle on the shores of Lake Garda. It is not clear whether she was freed by Otto the Great, the German king who was leading an army to reduce the north of Italy to order, or whether she escaped to his protection.

On Christmas Day 951, Otto married Adelaide—still only twenty—at Pavia. The marriage consolidated his authority in northern Italy, and in 962 he was crowned emperor in Rome. They had five children. Adelaide, a devout and gracious woman, appears to have been a popular empress. Their marriage lasted twenty-two years, until Otto died in 973, but then she faced conflict again. Their eldest son, Otto II, was young, headstrong, and much influenced against his mother by his Byzantine wife, Theophano. Adelaide left the court and went to her brother, Conrad of Burgundy, at Vienne. She appealed to St Majolus (11 May), abbot of Cluny, who brought about a reconciliation. Mother and son met at Pavia, and Otto asked pardon on his knees for his unkindness to his mother. Adelaide sent gifts to the shrine of St Martin of Tours (11 Nov.) in thanksgiving, including Otto's best cloak, and asked the saint's prayers for her son: "You who had the glory of covering with your own cloak Christ the Lord in the person of a beggar."

There was more conflict to come: ten years after his accession Otto II died, leaving as his heir the infant Otto III, for whom Theophano, the child's mother, became regent. The Byzantine princess was still hostile to her mother-in-law, and so Adelaide left the court again for eight years, returning only on Theophano's sudden death, to act herself as regent for Otto III. She found herself in a position of power for the first time at the age of sixty and was advised by the archbishop of Mainz, St Willigis (23 Feb.). She was also assisted and guided at various times in her life by St Adalbert of Magdeburg (20 June), St Majolus (11 May), and St Odilo of Cluny (1 Jan.). She consistently showed a desire for peace and a capacity for being generous and forgiving to her enemies. She founded and restored many monasteries of monks and nuns and looked for the conversion of the Slavs, whose movements at the frontier troubled her closing years before her return to Burgundy.

Adelaide died at a monastery of her own foundation at Seltz, on the Rhine near Strasbourg, on 16 December 999. She was canonized in about 1097.

See the *Epitaphium* of St Odilo of Cluny, *M.G.H., Scriptores*, 4, pp. 635-49; *P.L.*, 142, 967-92; P.B., pp. 210-27; *D.H.G.E.*, 1, 516-7. There is a German Life by F. P. Wimmer, *Kaiserin Adelheid* (1897).

Bd Sebastian Maggi (1496)

During the thirteenth century the family of the Maggi was one of the most powerful in Brescia, but by the time of the birth of Sebastian, early in the fifteenth century, though the name was still honoured it had lost much of its former influence. Sebastian entered the Order of Preachers at the age of fifteen. Through his ministry large numbers were brought to repentance, quarrelling families and communes were reconciled, and the work of his Order was strengthened. He was a powerful preacher and an admirable superior to the many friaries he governed.

Sebastian early recognized the genius of Jerome Savanarola, whose confessor he was for a time. He is said to have heard the Confession of Savanarola more than a hundred times and to have regarded him as a man of pure and blameless life. When Savanarola was only twenty-nine, he appointed him master of novices at Bologna. Sebastian was a strict upholder of monastic observance and worked doggedly for the reform of several houses, especially that of Lodi, where he set an example by begging from door to door for the support of the community.

As superior, he demanded exact obedience from his monks and observed it himself, never missing choir or chapel. He wished to be treated with the openness of a father, and he was then gentle and indulgent; but if his brethren insisted on regarding him as a master, he could be severe. When suffering from sickness, he insisted on carrying out a visitation of his province, but when he reached the priory of Santa Maria di Castello at Genoa he could go no further. This, he told his companions, was to be the place of his rest for ever. He died there on 16 December, and many pilgrims came to his tomb. His cult was confirmed in 1760.

Mortier, 4, pp. 548-50; Procter, pp. 339-45; P.B., pp. 336-7. Bd Sebastian figures in nearly all the Lives of Savanarola.

Bd Mary of the Angels (? 1660-1717)

Marianna Fontanella was the ninth in a family of eleven children born to a count of Santena, near Turin, and his wife. A child of intelligence and promise, she early showed signs of a devout disposition, particularly after a serious illness. She was strongly drawn to the religious life, and in 1676, after some opposition from her family, she was admitted to the Carmel of Santa Cristina at the age of sixteen, taking the name of Sister Mary of the Angels.

After seven years in the convent she experienced a long and severe "dark night," through which she was guided by a very able director, Fr Laurence-Mary, O.C.D. At the end of three years, after some violent struggles and extreme ascetic practices, she came to greater spiritual understanding. At thirty she was appointed novice-mistress and three years later prioress—offices she took up with reluctance but discharged with marked ability. At the suggestion of Bd Sebastian Valfré (30 Jan.), she undertook a new foundation at Moncaglieri in 1702. Though this had only a small house and an inadequate endowment, she was able to establish the nucleus of a community there, and the convent is still in being. She wished to live at Moncaglieri, but she was greatly valued in Turin by the nobility and the people for her advice and prayers and was induced to stay there.

Her writing shows a gentleness and human warmth combined with a strong faith. For instance, she wrote to the prioress of Moncaglieri to console her after the death of the subprioress: "I myself venerated her in a very special manner as my mistress in Jesus Christ. This loss has really pierced my heart. . . . I believe that the Divine Master, finding the fruit perfectly ripe, thought it well to call to himself this precious soul, that she might enter into a happy eternity." The letter, which is undated, is preserved in a kind of reliquary in the Carmelite monastery of SS Joseph and Leopold in Ghent.

Mary of the Angels lived an intense and mystical prayer life. "The love of God" she said, "lightens our darkness," but she was also very practical, keeping accounts, supervising workmen, and carrying out the many tasks that fell to a prioress. When she grew weak the nuns of Santa Cristina wished to elect her prioress again, but she felt unable to sustain the work and prayed that, if it were God's will, she might soon die. Her final illness developed three weeks later.

The cause of Sister Mary of the Angels was introduced at the instigation of King Victor Amadeus II of Savoy, and she was beatified by Pope Pius IX in 1865.

Fr G. O'Neill's *Bd Mary of the Angels* (1909), which is in the Catholic Home Library, includes the letter quoted above (p. 181). It is based on a Life written in Italian by Fr Elias of St Teresa, who had known Mary personally and was able to utilize a partial autobiography she wrote by order of her superiors. A later Italian account is by Fr Benedetto. See also R. M. López-Melús, *Los Santos Carmelitas* (1909), pp. 76-7; and L. Saggi, *Saints of Carmel*, trans. G. N. Pausback (1972), pp. 228-9.

Bd Clement Marchisio, *Founder* (1833-1903)

Clement's father was a cobbler and shoemaker in the town of Racconigi, a few miles south of Turin. There were five sons, of whom Clement was the eldest. The family could not afford to pay for his education, but a priest, Fr Baptist

Sacco, tutored him so that he could enter a seminary. Clement was ordained priest on 20 September 1856 and received instruction under the direction of St Joseph Cafasso (23 June), who trained him to work among the poor and especially with prisoners.

In June 1858 Clement became vicar of Cambiano, where he showed great devotion to the Eucharist. The population was no more than two thousand, but every morning he would give Communion to some four hundred people. In 1860 he was sent to Rivalta, in the suburbs of Turin, where he ministered for forty-three years. He founded the Institute of the Daughters of St Joseph, where the Sisters had a special devotion to the Sacrament and made communion wafers and religious ornaments.

Fr Clement was a quiet and holy man, a good priest and pastor. He did not lack trials and obstacles, but he lived gently and peacefully, spending many hours in prayer. His day was rigorously disciplined, from his rising at five o'clock in the morning until midnight. He continued to celebrate Mass until two days before his death on 16 December 1903.

He was beatified on 30 September 1984 by Pope John Paul II.

N.S.B. 1, pp. 242-3; *N.D.S.*, p. 73.

Bd Honoratus Kozminski (1829-1916)

Wenceslaus Kozminski was born at Biala Podlaska in eastern Poland. His name in religion was Honoratus or Honorius, and he is sometimes called Honorius of Biala. He became a Capuchin Friar Minor and was known for his great spirituality—his constant prayer, his adoration of the Blessed Sacrament, and his devotion to the Virgin Mary. He is spoken of as being "immersed in God." He often said, "Every day I come from Christ, I go to Christ, and I return to Christ."

He grew up in a time when his country was partitioned between occupying powers and eastern Poland was subject to considerable repression by the Russian occupying forces. After the insurrection of November 1830 the Tsar suspended all civil liberties, and the territories were ruled from the palace of the Russian governor in Warsaw. Many Polish patriots—aristocrats and landowners, artists, poets, musicians—left the country, and an émigré community grew up in Paris. In 1861-3 there was a second insurrection, brought about by the Tsar's decree conscripting young Poles into the Russian army. When that failed many more went abroad. Honoratus Kosminski became a leader among those who stayed. When Catholics were persecuted and the religious Orders suppressed he urged his people to return to the spirit of the early Christians, who had similarly suffered for their faith. He wrote in his diary:

> More and more people of various conditions and levels of education who are free come to me and ask me to show them the way. They wish to enter a monastery, and most of all, they ask permission to take vows of chastity. There

are no monasteries. To where and how can I direct these souls? It is not right to send them abroad, because they are a product of this land. They must remain here, because it is not right to deprive this land of its mature and best fruit. What remains here if we remove the holy souls who are specially called? God wills something: he will provide. . . .

He found the answer in organizing groups of lay Catholics to carry on the work of the religious Orders. This led to the disapproval of his superiors, who presumably knew little of conditions in Poland and accused him of changing the character of the Congregations. At one point he was officially deprived of the leadership of the Congregations—a decision he accepted with "deep torment." Today his innovative work, similar to that of the lay Institutes which are now an accepted part of the activities of the Church, has led to the formation of seventeen Congregations, working in four continents.

Honoratus lived well into the twentieth century—but not quite long enough to see his country freed as an independent republic after the First World War or the Church restored to its traditional place in Polish life.

His decree of beatification was promulgated by Pope John Paul II, the first Polish pope, on 22 October 1988.

Osservatore Romano, 7 Nov. 1988; *N.S.B.* 2, p. 194. For background see Roman Dyboski, *Outlines of Polish History* (1985), pp. 201ff.

The Martyrs of Thailand: Bd Philip Siphong and Companions (1940)

Thailand (then Siam) received it first missionaries, Portuguese Dominicans, in 1554. Two of these Dominicans, Jerome of the Cross and Sebastian de Canto, were killed in 1569, Fr Jerome by Muslim traders and Fr Sebastian by a border tribe, although Siam, which then had suzerainty over much of Indo-China and Cambodia, was generally secure and peaceful. Catholics there escaped the persecutions their colleagues faced in Japan (see 6 Feb.), and Indo-China (Vietnam; see 2 Feb.), where martyrdoms were common. Though the king and the court in Bangkok were Buddhist, missionaries were tolerated and even welcomed as bringing Western influence and new knowledge to a nation of peasant farmers. Most of the missionaries were French, and by the nineteenth century the *Missions étrangères de Paris* was particularly active. Christianity was thought not to be incompatible with fairly easygoing Buddhist principles, but there were few conversions: Siam tended to be used as a safe base from which missionary activity could be spread to more dangerous parts of Asia. Catholic communities were regarded as alien enclaves, exempt from national jurisdiction, taxation, and military service.

From the mid-1930s Siam, which had lost much of its influence in the neighbouring areas of South-East Asia, became politically unstable. European influence declined, and there were intense pressures from the growing influence of Japan. The country's name was changed to Thailand in 1939, and there was a strong reaction against the Western powers, which had lost much of their ability to support friendly nations. The threat of invasion by Japan, then in control of much of China and poised for the invasion of South-East Asia, increased the sense of crisis. A strongly nationalistic and military government produced sporadic outbursts of violence against foreigners and against Christianity, the "foreign religion." Some missionaries were interned; churches, colleges, and schools were requisitioned for military purposes; and there was pressure on Thai Christians to recant.

France fell in June 1940. By agreement with the Vichy régime in France, Japan set up military bases in north Vietnam. In November 1940 the Thai army invaded Indo-China, and in December the seven Thai martyrs were killed at Songkhon, a village near the Mekong River, the border with French Indo-China: a catechist, two nuns, three girls, and an elderly woman.

A police patrol had surrounded the village and ordered Christians to recant at gun-point. The mission priest, Fr Paul Fige, was expelled. When the catechist, Fr Philip Siphong Ouphitah, who had been in charge of another mission station near the town of Phaluke, protested at the harassment he was told to report to police headquarters, and he was ambushed on his way there on 16 December. The villagers who later recovered his body found that he had been tortured before being shot. The two Thai nuns, Sister Agnes Phila, aged thirty-one, and Sister Lucia Khambang, aged twenty-three, both of the Order of the Holy Cross, were teachers in the mission school. They continued to run the school, telling the children that Philip was a martyr, while the police shouted insults at them and fired their guns in the air. The most vicious was a constable named Boonlue Muangkote, known as "Luc." The Sisters were ordered to stop teaching Christianity and to dress as Thai women, not as "foreigners."

The Sisters wrote a letter to the police, protesting at this treatment. The signatories were both Sisters, four of the older girls, and a kitchen assistant, Agatha Phutta, who was nearly sixty years old. On 26 December they were marched to the cemetery, where they knelt and prayed. Sister Agnes told the police: "You may kill us, but you cannot kill God. Some day his Church will return to Thailand and be more flourishing than it is now." Then they were shot. Three of the girls, Cecilia Butsi, Bibiana Kampai, and Maria Phong, aged sixteen, fifteen, and fourteen respectively, died with the two nuns and Agatha Phutta. The youngest girl, Soru, escaped the bullets and was taken home by villagers.

This seems to have been an isolated incident: there are no other known martyrdoms in Thailand during this period. "Luc" was not punished by the authorities, though he was transferred to another station. In the following year Japan invaded Thailand to secure air bases and passage for troops for the conquest of Malaya and Singapore, and the Thai government agreed to an alliance with Japan, which lasted until the Japanese surrender in 1945. The six who died on 26 December were buried with Philip Siphong, and in 1986 the remains of all seven were re-interred in the village church of the Holy Redeemer at a service attended by thousands. They were beatified by Pope John Paul II during his world tour, on Mission Sunday, 22 October 1989.

D.N.H., 3, pp. 155-9; *Deux Mille Saints* (Fr. ed. of BS[R], 1991), p. 473. For early missionaries see Mary Jean Dorcy, O.P., *St Dominic's Family* (1983). For background see D. E. Nuechterlein, *The Struggle for South-East Asia* (1965), pp. 45-91; B. Harrison, *South-East Asia: A Short History* (1966), pp. 229-30.

17

St Judicäel (658)

Judicäel was a king of Brittany, elder brother of St Judoc (13 Dec.). He succeeded his father on the throne but had to maintain his position by force of arms. Apparently he was well regarded by the people of Brittany, but he was displaced by another brother, Saloman, and entered the monastery at Gáel, near Vannes. His spiritual director was St Méen (21 June), who tried to dissuade him from extreme mortifications.

One one occasion in winter, he found Judicäel plunged in a frozen stream, with only his head showing through a hole he had made in the ice. He told the former king that, while he respected his fervour, it was necessary to temper fervour with discretion.

When his brother Saloman died in about the year 630, Judicäel's family pleaded with him to return to secular life and become king again. He grew his hair and his beard, abandoned his habit, and married a virtuous wife, with whom he settled down to a life of piety and peace. They cared for the poor and lived with great simplicity, hiding their abstinence from the court. Judicäel is said to have had a special goblet made with a cover, so that the nobles could not see that he was drinking water while they drank wine.

The time he had spent under the direction of St Méen left him with a great regard for the religious life. He had several monasteries and churches built, including the church of Notre-Dame de Paimpont, which was built on a spot where the Druids were said to have practised human sacrifice, in order to purify it. But whatever good works he undertook, Judicäel still felt a secret remorse that he had abandoned monastic life and a growing distaste for the worldly life of the court. At last he abdicated and re-entered the monastery at Gáel. He lived a long time, some say another twenty years, as a monk before he died and was buried next to his master St Méen.

Orderic Vitalis, The Ecclesiastical History, trans. and ed. M. Chibnall, (1969), 2, pp. 156-7; P.B., pp. 319-22, from the *Vie des saints du diocèse de Beauvais*; *Dictionnaire des saints Bretons* (1979), pp. 208-9.

Judicäel is represented in art with a crown at his feet and a broom in his hand: symbols of the luxurious life he renounced at court and the humble offices he performed in the cloister.

St Begga, *Abbess* (693)

Pepin of Landen, mayor to three Frankish kings and himself commonly called Blessed, was married to Bd Itta or Ida. Two of their three children were St Gertrude of Nivelles (17 Mar.) and her elder sister, Begga. Gertrude refused to marry and became abbess of her mother's foundation at Nivelles. Begga married Ansegisulus, son of St Arnulf of Metz (18 July), and spent much of her life as a nobleman's wife. Their son was Pepin of Herstal, the founder of the Carlovingian dynasty in France.

After the death of her husband, Begga in 691 built at Andenne on the Meuse seven chapels, representing the Seven Churches of Rome, around a central church, and a religious house which received nuns from her sister's abbey. This subsequently became a house of canonesses, and the Lateran Canons Regular commemorate St Begga as belonging to their Order.

She is also venerated by the Béguines of Belgium as their patroness, but the common assumption that she founded this Order is a mistake, based on the similarity of the names. The term *beguinae*, first encountered about the year 1200, was originally a term of reproach used of the Albigenses.

St Begga died as abbess of Andenne and was buried there.

Bibl.SS., 2, 1077-8; *D.H.G.E.*, 7, 441-8; *N.C.E.*, 2, p. 224. For the confusion over *beguinae* see *Dict.Sp.*, 1, 1341-2.

St Sturmi, Abbot (779)

Sturm, or Sturmi, the first German known to have become a Benedictine monk, was the son of Christian parents and born in Bavaria. He was entrusted to the care of St Boniface (5 June), who left him to be educated under St Wigbert (13 Aug.) in the abbey at Fritzlar. There he was ordained priest and did mission work in Westphalia for three years, after which he was allowed to go with two companions to lead an eremitical life in the forest at Hersfeld. When they were harassed by marauding Saxons Boniface suggested a district further south where a monastery might be built and the Saxons could be evangelized.

Sturmi rode down into this district on a donkey and selected a site at the junction of two rivers, the Greizbach and the Fulda. Here in 744 the monastery of Fulda was founded. Boniface appointed Sturmi as the first abbot. It was Boniface's favourite foundation. He intended it to be a model monastery and seminary for the whole of Germany. He visited it frequently, and when he died his body was buried in the abbey church.

Soon after its foundation Sturmi went to Italy to study Benedictine observance at Monte Cassino. Pope St Zachary (15 Mar.) gave him a considerable degree of autonomy by withdrawing Fulda from episcopal jurisdiction and allowing it to relate directly to the Holy See.

Boniface was martyred in 754—killed while on a mission to the Frieslanders. Without his support Sturmi faced considerable difficulties, for his successor as bishop of Mainz, St Lull (16 Oct.), demanded that the monastery should be subjected to him. The struggle was protracted and bitter. In 763 an order was obtained from King Pepin for the banishment of Sturmi, and Lull nominated another superior in his place, but the monks refused to accept him and expelled him from the house. They threatened that they would go in a body and appeal to the king. Lull told them to elect a superior of their own, and they elected a lifelong disciple of Sturmi, who took a deputation of monks to court. They were successful in inducing Pepin to recall their beloved Sturmi, who returned to Fulda amid great rejoicing after two years of exile.

The efforts of Sturmi and his monks to convert the Saxons were largely frustrated by the punitive wars of Pepin and Charlemagne, whose actions were not calculated to commend their religion to the heathen. When Charlemagne was called to attack the Moors in Spain the Saxons rose and drove out the monks. Fulda itself was threatened. In 779 Charlemagne returned, and Sturmi accompanied him to the mobilization at Düren, which preceded fresh military success against the Saxons, but he did not live to re-commence his missions. He was taken ill at Fulda and died there. His name was added to the roll of saints in 1139.

Eigil, who was Sturmi's biographer, was related to him and was a monk at Fulda under his direction for some twenty years. He became abbot of Fulda about 817 and died in 822. He is sometimes called "Saint," though his name is not listed in the martyrologies.

Eigil's *Vita S Sturmii* has been many times printed, *e.g.*, in *P.L.*, 105, 423-44, and *M.G.H.*, *Scriptores*, 2, pp. 365-77. There is a translation by C. H. Talbot in *Anglo-Saxon Missionaries in Germany* (1954), pp. 180-202. See also *AA.SS.OSB.*, Saec. 3, part 2, 242-59; *Bibl.SS.*, 12, 43-6; B. Kuhlmann, *Der hl. Sturmi, Grunden Fuldas und Apostel Westfalen* (1890); introduction to M. Tangl, *Leben das hl. Leoba und des Abtes Sturmi* (1920). For Eigil, see *P.L.*, 105, 382-422; C. H. Talbot, *op.cit.*, p. 180; *D.H.G.E.*, 15, 90-1.

St Wivina, *Abbess* (? 1170)

Wivina, a Fleming of noble birth, was determined from an early age to follow the religious life. As a girl she had a number of suitors, including a young man named Richard who had the approval of her parents. When Wivina refused to marry him Richard became very ill, but he was restored to health by her prayers and counsel. She became a hermit for a time, living with one companion in a forest near Brussels. She took her Psalter with her, and this survives at Orbais (Brabant). After a while her solitude was much disturbed by inquisitive visitors, until Count Geoffrey of Brabant offered her land and endowment for a religious house at Bigarden. Wivina became abbess, helped by the abbot of the nearby monastery of Afflighem.

Her abbey prospered in spite of accusations by some of her nuns that her rule was not sufficiently rigorous. She refuted these accusations and died with a high reputation. Her relics were translated to Notre Dame du Sablon, Brussels, in the fourteenth century, and Pope Urban VIII confirmed her cult in 1625.

A Life was written in the thirteenth century by a nun of Bigarden, but it has little historical value: see P.B., pp. 350-6. See also *D.Cath.Biog.*, p. 1210; *O.D.S.*, p. 503: *Bibl.SS.*, 12, 1320-1.

St John of Matha, *Founder* (1213)

John is said to have been born at Faucon, in Provence, and to have been educated at Aix-en-Provence in the accomplishments of a gentleman—grammar, riding, and the use of arms. This way of life was not congenial to him, and when his education was complete he retired to a hermitage to pray and to contemplate. Like many other hermits, he found that the world would not leave him alone, and his privacy was so much invaded that he found it impossible to continue. With his father's approval and assistance he went to study theology in Paris, took his doctorate, and was ordained priest.

While he was celebrating his first Mass he received the inspiration he had been seeking: he felt called to devote his life to ransoming Christian slaves from the Muslims. Though we do not know the date of his birth or of his ordination, it seems likely that the call came during or soon after the Second Crusade (1147-9). At this time the Saracens and the Moors held many thousands of Christians in captivity.

John sought help and direction from Felix of Valois and so inspired Felix that he decided to join in the enterprise. Together they travelled to Rome in the depths of winter (the urgency of their mission may have seemed too great for them to wait for better travelling conditions in the spring). Pope Innocent III was impressed by what they had to say and convinced that they were led by the Holy Spirit. He ordered the bishop of Paris and the abbot of St Victor to draw up a Rule and approved the foundation of the Order of the Most Holy Trinity by a papal Bull in 1198. They were given a white habit with a red and blue cross on the breast. When John returned to France King Philip Augustus approved the establishment of the Order in his kingdom, and a nobleman, the lord of Châtillon, gave them a mansion and an estate for their headquarters. A foundation was made in Paris on the site of a chapel with a dedication to St Mathurin, and the Order became known as "the Mathurins" in France. Felix, who had remained in Italy, developed the work of the Order there.

Evidently the Order grew, and many of the nobility of France and Italy must have provided funds for the difficult and dangerous work of travelling to Muslim held territory and arranging the release of Christians. Members of the Order went to Morocco, to Tunis, and to Spain, and several hundred captives were said to have been set free. John himself encountered hostility: on one occasion the rudder of his ship was damaged and the sails torn by enemies who hoped that the ship would sink on the return journey, but he and his passengers reached their destination in Sicily safely.

John spent his last two years in Rome and died there on 17 December 1213. This is one of the few facts of which we are certain, for much of the story is based on very poor evidence. The official chroniclers of the Trinitarian Order in the fifteenth and sixteenth centuries claimed to base their accounts on documentation, but in fact no records were kept and no archives existed. Two or three hundred years later, when the chroniclers produced the first written records, there were oral traditions within the Order; but these had become so embellished with accounts of supposed miracles and supernatural happenings that they are now regarded as highly unreliable. We can be certain that John of Matha existed, that he came from Provence, obtained a papal Bull from Innocent III, and ransomed captives; but unfortunately the true details of his work, which may well have been interesting and inspiring, have disappeared under the weight of well-intentioned fabrication.

The *Historia documentada del convento de los PP Trinitarios de Avingaña*, which contains the official biographies, was critically examined by Paul Deslandres, who found them to be spurious: see his *L'Ordre Trinitaire pour le rachat des captifs* (1903); also *Anal.Boll.* 46 (1928), pp. 419-20.

Bd Joseph Manyanet y Vivès, *Founder* (1833-1901)

José Manyanet was born at Tremp, in the diocese of Lérida in Catalonia, the eldest of nine children born to Antonio Manyanet, a peasant famer, and his wife, Bonaventura Vivès. At the age of twelve he entered the Piarist college in Barbastro, going on to study at the seminaries of Lérida and Seo de Urgel. He was ordained priest in 1859 and worked for five years in his home town and then in Barcelona, where he became well known as a confessor, spiritual director, and catechist. At the age of thirty-one he established a residential school for boys, the Congregation of the Sons of the Holy Family, and subsequently founded two for girls, the Institute of the Daughters of the Holy Family and the Institute of the Missionary Daughters of the Holy House of Nazareth. He had a great concern for children and for family life. Taking the Holy Family as his inspiration, he published several works of pastoral theology dealing with family virtues and in 1899, two years before his death, started the newspaper *La Sagrada Familia* (The Holy Family). He wrote: "Solidly catholic education and instruction is the most suitable, simple, and practical means of reforming the family and society with it."

In this activity he was representative of a wide movement in Spain in the second half of the nineteenth century. The last quarter of the century in particular saw the foundation of massive numbers of new religious Congregations, primarily of teaching religious, with the Church re-establishing its position as the primary educator of young people, especially of girls. Lay associations, venerating especially the Holy Family and St Joseph, flourished. He described their inspiration: "Our centres are called 'of the Holy Family' because Jesus, Mary, and Joseph are not only the patrons and protectors but also the model that they should imitate in virtue and firm love of work, since this was the principal aim of the hidden life of Jesus in the humble House of Nazareth." Manyanet and his works were influential in inspiring the architect Antonio Gaudí to design his vast church of the *Sagrada Familia*, for which the dedication was selected by the Association of Devotees of St Joseph. Work on this began in 1883, but it remains unfinished. An Association for Gaudí's beatification has been formed in Barcelona.

José Manyanet suffered from chronic ill health but scrupulously observed the rules he had laid down for his Congregation. It is said that he often got up at night to finish the work he had been unable to do during the day. He never refused a child who needed education, whether or not the parents were able to pay for it. He found time to visit poor families and sick people in hospital. Though he faced a good deal of opposition in his work, people who knew him said that he possessed a great sweetness of spirit, even to his opponents, and was much loved.

He died in Barcelona on 17 December 1901 and was beatified by Pope John Paul II on 25 November 1984.

N.S.B. 1, p. 237; *N.D.S.*, p. 176; *D.N.H.*, 2, pp. 35-8. Background works on Catalonia include Victor Alba, *Catalonia: A Profile* (1975); Jan Read, *The Catalans* (1978). See also P. Culshaw, "A Halo for Gaudí," in *The Tablet*, 17 April 1999, p. 521. The quotations above are trans. from the website http://www.manyanet-alcobendas.org/index2.htm, which also has pictures of a statue of him and the beatification ceremony.

18

St Flannan of Killaloe, *Bishop* (Seventh Century)

There are cults of St Flannan in both Ireland and Scotland, and the fact that the feast-day is the same in both cases makes it likely that they refer to the same person. *Flann*, however, means "red," and Flannan was a common name in both countries, so there may have been two red-haired saints whose traditions became fused.

The Irish Flannan is thought to have been the son of a chieftain named Turlough in the Thomond district of the west of Ireland. In youth he is said to have been determined to make a pilgrimage to Rome, and legend tells that he achieved this in the miraculous manner common in Celtic hagiography, by floating on a millstone. It has been suggested that the millstones which accompanied the Celtic saints on their journeys were very small ones, to be used as altars when they celebrated Mass. In Rome he was consecrated bishop by Pope John IV (d. 642), and he returned to his father's district as bishop of Killaloe. When he reached Killaloe all the people assembled to hear the instructions and messages of the Holy Roman See.

Flannan's example caused his father to become a monk in his old age under St Colman at Lismore. This was probably Colman of Kilmacduagh (29 Oct.). Though the name is again a common one, of the four other St Colmans for whom we have reliable records, two lived in the sixth century and the other two were English. According to a Life written after 1162, Turlough asked Colman for a special blessing on his family because three of his sons had been killed. The saint is said to have taken seven strides and prophesied, "From you shall seven kings spring"; and so it was: Turlough's descendents included seven kings, all called Brian.

Though these legends are late and unreliable, it seems that Flannan, like other Irish monks of his period, was an itinerant preacher, and there are traces of his ministry in the west of Ireland and the Hebrides. The cathedral at Killaloe formerly housed Flannan's relics, and churches are attributed to him at Lough Corrib and on the island of Inishbofin. The Flannan Islands, to the west of Lewis and Harris, are named after him, and these islands have long been the centre of prayer and religious customs—perhaps fostered by their remoteness and difficult sailing conditions in the area. On one island, where the lighthouse stands, there are the remains of a tiny drystone chapel called the chapel of Flannan.

Heist, *V.S.H.*, 1, pp. 280-330; *Anal.Boll.* 46 (1928), pp. 124-41; *The Irish Saints*, pp. 177-80; *K.S.S.*, p. 350; S. Malone, *The Life of St Flannan* (1902); R. Sharpe, *Mediaeval Irish Saints' Lives* (1991), pp. 268-70; *D.H.G.E.*, 17, 365 ff.; A. Gwynn and D. F. Gleeson, *A History of the Diocese of Killaloe*, 1, pp. 5-13.

SS Rufus and Zosimus, *Martyrs* (*c.* 107)

When St Ignatius of Antioch (17 Oct.) was at Philippi in Macedonia on his way to martyrdom in Rome, he had with him two laymen, Rufus and Zosimus, citizens of Antioch or of Philippi itself. On the instruction of Ignatius the Philippian Christians wrote a fraternal letter to their fellows at Antioch, and they were answered by St Polycarp, bishop of Smyrna (23 Feb.), to whom St Ignatius had commended the care of his church. In his letter, which during the fourth century was read publicly in the churches of Asia, Polycarp refers to Rufus and Zosimus, who shared in Ignatius' chains and sufferings for Christ. They are thought to have been thrown to the wild beasts in the Coliseum two days before Ignatius was martyred, in the reign of Trajan.

St Polycarp says of them: "They have not run in vain, but in faith and righteousness, and they are gone to the place that was due to them from the Lord, with whom they also suffered. For they loved not the present world, but him who died and was raised again by God for us. . . . Wherefore I exhort all of you that you obey the word of righteousness and exercise all patience, which you have seen set forth before your eyes, not only in the blessed Ignatius and Zosimus and Rufus, but in others that have been among you and in Paul himself and the rest of the apostles."

For St Polycarp's letter see Eusebius, *H.E.*, 3, 36; N.P.N.F., 1, pp. 167-8. The letter is also published in *Early Christian Writing*, trans. and ed. M. Staniforth (1968), p. 147.

Note: Rufus and Zozimus are assigned to 17 October in the new draft Roman Martyrology, and will appear on that date in future editions of this work.

St Gatian, *Bishop* (? 301 or 307)

Gatian is traditionally venerated as the founder of Christian worship in Tours and the first bishop of the Church in that city. All that is firmly established is that St Martin of Tours (11 Nov.) translated his relics to a church built by Gatian's successor, St Lidoric, at the end of the fourth century, which suggests an episcopate earlier in that century.

According to St Gregory of Tours (17 Nov.) Gatian was one of six missionary bishops who came to Gaul from Rome with St Denis of Paris (9 Oct.) about the middle of the third century, but that date now appears to be too early. Another tradition places him even earlier—as one of the disciples of Christ thought to have been sent to Gaul by St Peter himself, but there is no evidence for the first-century colonization of Gaul. As with the legend of St Lazarus (17 Dec.), this early link between Palestine and Gaul seems to owe more to local piety than to history.

Gregory of Tours, *Historia Francorum*, 1, 10; 10, 41; and his *Gloria confessorum*, 4, 39; Duchesne, *Fastes*, 2, pp. 286, 302; P.B., pp. 364-7; *D.H.G.E.*, 20, 2.

St Samthann, *Abbess* (739)

Samthann, whose name is included in both the litany and the Canon of the Stowe Missal, was the founder of Clonbroney Abbey, Co. Longford. She is said to have become a nun at Ernside in Donegal and to have moved from there to Clonbroney. She is remembered for her wise and trenchant sayings: according to her Life, when a monk asked her in what attitude it was appropriate to pray, she replied that it was appropriate to pray in every position, sitting, standing, kneeling, or lying. Another told her that he proposed to give up study in order to pray more, but Samthann told him that he would never be able to fix his mind on prayer if he neglected study. When a third said that he was going on a pilgrimage, she answered that the kingdom of heaven can be reached without crossing the sea and God is near all who call on him.

Samthann would not accept large estates for her abbey, preferring to live very simply, with only six cows to form the community herd. St Virgil (27 Nov.), an Irish monk who became bishop of Salzburg, may have known her: her cult was introduced in southern Germany.

The Irish Saints, pp. 282-4; Plummer, *V.S.H.*, 1, pp. xvi, lxxxvii-lxxxviii; 2, pp. 253-61; *O.D.S.*, p. 427.

St Winnibald, *Abbot* (761)

This saint, whose name is variously rendered Wynnebald, Winebald, or Wynbald, was brother to St Willibald (7 June) and St Walburga (25 Feb.). Their father is thought to have been the West Saxon St Richard (7 Feb.), sometimes called "king of the English." Though there is no certainty even about his name, he is known to have left his native Hampshire with his sons on pilgrimage to the Holy Land and to have died at Lucca. According to the nun Hugebure, who wrote Willibald's Life, the brothers continued their journey "through the vast land of Italy, through the deep valleys, over the craggy mountains, across the level plains," gazing on snowy peaks and passing safely through the ambushes of the "fierce and arrogant soldiery" until they came to Rome. There they gave thanks for their deliverance at the shrine of St Peter, Prince of the Apostles.

In the hot and stifling Roman summer they caught a fever, which Hugebure calls the black plague, but recovered. Willibald went on to the Holy Land, but Winnibald, who had been delicate from his childhood and was not strong enough to complete the pilgrimage, remained at Rome. There he studied for seven years before going back to England, collecting some companions and returning to Rome to dedicate himself to God's service. St Boniface (5 June) came on his third visit to Rome in 739 and enlisted Winnibald to help in the founding of the Church in Germany. Winnibald followed him into Thuringia, where he was ordained priest and given the care of seven churches, based on Sulzenbrücken, near Erfurt. When he was harried by the Saxons he extended his work into Bavaria, and after some years of strenuous missionary work he returned to St Boniface at Mainz. By this time his brother, Willibald, who had also come under the influence of St Boniface, was bishop of Eichstätt. Willibald wanted to found a double monastery on the pattern of Monte Cassino as a model of piety and learning for the Christian communities in Germany, and he asked Winnibald and their sister, Walburga, to undertake this. St Walburga, who had trained at the double monastery of Wimborne (Dorset) and under the English St Lioba, abbess of Bischofsheim (28 Sept.), was said to be skilled in medicine.

Winnibald went to Heidenheim in Würtemberg, where he cleared a wild place of trees and bushes and built little cells for his monks and himself. Later they built a monastery and a separate establishment for St Walburga and her nuns. Winnibald established the Rule of St Benedict in both monasteries. Heidenheim, the first double monastery in Germany, became a centre of evangelism as well as of prayer, work, and study. Winnibald narrowly escaped assassination by hostile pagans.

Winnibald had hoped to end his days at Monte Cassino, but he suffered many years of sickness and was not fit to make the journey. After a gentle exhortation to his monks he died in 761 in the arms of his brother and sister. St Walburga was subsequently entrusted with the rule of both monasteries.

Life by Hugebure, a nun of Heidenheim, ed. O. Holder-Eggar in *M.G.H.*, *Scriptores*, 15, pp. 106-17. Further information is given in the *Hodoeporicon* of St Willibald by the same nun, which is translated in C. H. Talbot, *Anglo-Saxon Missionaries in Germany* (1954), pp. 153-80; scattered references in W. Levison, *England and the Continent in the Eighth Century* (1946); M. Coens, "Légende et Miracles du roi S Richard," *Anal.Boll.* 49 (1931), pp. 353-97; Stanton, p. 600.

SS Peter Duong, Peter Truat, and Paul My, *Martyrs* (1839)

Three Indo-Chinese martyrs who died in the outbreak against foreign missions in Indo-China in 1838-40 are commemorated on this day. Peter Nguyén Dang Dong and Peter Vi Van Truat were both catechists attached to the Society of Foreign Missions of Paris. Paul My also worked with the mission.

The three were canonized by Pope John Paul II in 1988.

N.C.E., 14, pp. 198-9 under "Tonkin" and 661 under "Vietnam." Other sources as for St Simon Hoa (12 Dec.). See also the general entry on the Martyrs of Vietnam, 2 February.

19

St Nemesius and Other Martyrs of Alexandria (250)

During the persecution of Decius, Nemesius, an Egyptian, was arrested in Alexandria on a false charge of being in league with bandits. When cleared of that charge he was immediately re-arrested and accused of being a Christian. He was sent to the prefect of Egypt and, when he witnessed to his faith, treated more harshly than the common criminals, being doubly scourged and then executed with them. Eusebius points out that he was "blest indeed—with a resemblance to Christ" for being executed between two criminals.

With Nemesius are commemorated other Christians who made a similar witness in the face of criminal charges: Arsenius, Heron, and Isodore, with Dioscorus, a boy of fifteen, were charged at Alexandria in the same persecutions. The three adults were tortured and executed. Dioscorus was tortured but finally discharged on account of his youth, being given "time to repent."

St Meuris and St Thea, two women of Gaza in Palestine, suffered a similar fate when persecution raged under the successors of Diocletian. Meuris died at the hands of her persecutors. Thea lived for some time after her ordeal, according to the Life of St Porphyrius of Gaza. She is probably the same person as the Thea commemorated with her sister Valentina on 25 July.

See Eusebius, *H.E.*, 6, 41, for material extracted from St Dionysius of Alexandria.

St Anastasius I, *Pope* (401)

Pope St Anastasius, a Roman, succeeded Pope St Siricius (26 Nov.) on 27 November 399 and died on 19 December 401, so his pontificate lasted only just over two years. Among his friends and admirers were St Jerome (30 Sept.), St Augustine (28 Aug.), and St Paulinus of Nola (22 June). St Jerome called him a man of great holiness, who was rich in his poverty, and commended his blameless life and apostolic solicitude. Anastasius supported the aging Jerome in his controversy with the historian and translator Rufinus of Aquileia. Jerome had been engaged for many years in producing an accurate text of the Bible based on study in the original languages and on previous translations. He was deeply offended by Rufinus of Aquileia's translation of Origen's *First Principles*, a controversial work of the early third century, which proposed an allegorical rather than a literal interpretation of many biblical passages. Jerome, who had once written of Rufinus that "he is inseparably bound to me in brotherly love," was capable of considerable wrath in defence of his scholarship. The conflict

between the two, who were both living ascetic lives near Jerusalem, was protracted and bitter. Jerome referred to those who sought to amend or re-interpret
biblical texts as "presumptuous blockheads" and went to the pope to persuade
him to condemn Rufinus.

Anastasius subsequently wrote to Simplician, bishop of Milan (13 Aug.), to
warn him so that "God's people, in the different churches, may not, by reading
Origen, run into awful blasphemies." He added that "the presbyter Eusebius"
(Jerome) had shown him "some blasphemous chapters which made me shud-
der."

Jerome was grateful for this whole-hearted support and for the pontiff's
encouragement for his own work, and he expressed his gratitude to "the distinguished Anastasius." He wrote that Rome did not deserve to possess such a
pope long: it was not fitting that the world's head should be cut off during the
reign of such a bishop. This was a reference to the threat posed by Alaric the
Goth and his barbarian forces, who finally captured and sacked Rome in 410,
six years after the death of Anastasius.

Anastasius is also remembered for two instructions to bishops: the first required that the clergy should stand for the reading of the Gospel in the Mass as
a mark of reverence; the second stipulated that no cleric from overseas should
be admitted to the Roman jurisdiction without a certificate signed by five
bishops as to his orthodoxy. The aim was to bar priests from the Eastern
Church whose beliefs had been affected by Arianism or dualistic beliefs such
as Manicheism.

Jaffé, 1, pp. 42-3; *Lib.Pont.*, 1, p. 33; St Ambrose: N.P.N.F., 6, *Letters*, 4, 95; references
in papal letters, and in works on SS Jerome, Augustine, and Paulinus; *D.H.G.E.*, 2, 1471-
3; *N.C.E.*, 1, p. 478; C. J. Hefele, *History of the Councils of the Church*, trans. H. N.
Oxenham, (2d ed., 1922), pp. 6, 8, 27, 42, 48, and 446.

Bd Urban V, *Pope* (1310-70)

William (Guillaume) de Grimoard was born in the castle of Grisac in the
Languedoc. His father was a local nobleman and his mother was a sister of St
Elzéar of Sabran (26 Nov.). He was educated at the universities of Toulouse
and Montpellier and became a Benedictine. After his ordination he returned to
his old universities and then went on to Paris and Avignon to study for his
doctorate. He taught canon law and theology at Montpellier and became vicar
general of the diocese of Clermont and Uzès. He was said to be one of the
greatest experts in canon law of his day. In 1352 he was appointed abbot of St
German's at Auxerre.

At this time the popes were in exile at Avignon, and for the next ten years
Abbot William was constantly called upon to undertake diplomatic missions
for Pope Innocent VI. In 1361 the Pope made him abbot of the great abbey of
St Victor's at Marseilles and sent him to Naples as legate to Queen Joanna.
While he was there Pope Innocent died, and there was a difficult problem in

electing his successor. In a rather muddled and hasty election, the cardinals voted without discussion and elected Hughes Roger, brother of Pope Clement V. When he declined (apparently to the general relief) they found themselves so divided that it became impossible for them to elect one of their own members. They chose Abbot William, a Frenchman and a stranger to the Curia, for his scholarship and his skill in diplomacy. He returned at once from Naples to Avignon, where he was enthroned and crowned, and took the name of Urban because "all the popes called Urban had been saints." Austere and unworldly, he continued to live as a Benedictine and to wear the Benedictine habit.

He would no doubt have been happy to continue keeping the papal court in Avignon, but Petrarch, the celebrated Roman poet and scholar, composed a letter urging him to restore the papacy to Rome:

> In your absence . . . peace is exiled: civil and external warfare rages; dwellings are prostrate; walls are toppling; churches are falling; sacred things are perishing; laws are trodden underfoot; justice is abused; the unhappy people mourn and wail, calling with loud cries on your name. Do you not hear them? . . . Must the Queen of Cities be for ever widowed? . . . How can you sleep, under your gilded beams on the banks of the Rhône, while the Lateran, the Mother of all churches, ruined and roofless, is open to the wind and rain, and the most holy shrines of Peter and Paul are quaking, and what was once the Church of the Apostles is but a ruin and a shapeless heap of stones?

Petrarch apparently took much trouble over this letter. He kept it with him for several weeks or months and finally despatched it by personal messenger in the autumn of 1366. We do not know how far it affected the pope's decision, but in the following spring, ignoring the opposition of the French king and the French cardinals, who feared the loss of influence in the Curia, Urban made the difficult decision to return to the papal dominions.

A fragile peace between warring forces had been secured by Cardinal Gil de Albornoz, but there were considerable dangers: the papal territories were in a state of anarchy, harassed by roving bands of mercenaries led by powerful *condottieri*. The great families of Rome were in constant and vicious conflict, and the people of Rome were near starvation. In April 1367 Pope Urban set out with great courage, sailing from Marseilles and taking with him barrels of provisions such as grain, cheese, and salt fish. His journey, escorted by the grand master of the Knights Hospitaller, became a triumphal progress. At Carneto (now Tarquinia) he was met by a host of envoys, ecclesiastical and lay, by a Roman embassy bearing the keys of Sant' Angelo, and by Bd John Colombini (31 July) and his *Gesuati* waving palms and singing hymns.

Four months later Urban entered Rome in state, the first pope it had seen for over half a century. When he saw the state of the city he wept. The great churches, even the Lateran, St Peter's, and St Paul's, were, as Petrarch had said, almost in ruins, and the papal residences were uninhabitable. Immediate steps were taken to start re-building, and food was distributed to the poor. The Pope lived simply, ate frugally, and made anxious inquiries about the help being given to the needy.

In the following year he came to an agreement with the emperor Charles IV, and a new alliance was made between the Church and the Holy Roman Empire. Symbolically, Charles entered Rome leading a mule on which the pope rode, and Urban crowned his queen as empress. Twelve months later the eastern emperor, John V Paleologus, came to Rome, disclaiming schism and seeking Pope Urban's help against the Turks.

But Urban had no help to give, and his own position was far from secure. He was a man of peace: he had failed to curb the activities of the *condottieri*, and his somewhat naïve belief that they could be mobilized to fight against the Turks met with no success. Perugia had revolted, and Rome followed, the mercenaries being led by the Englishman Sir John Hawkwood. When the pope and his court moved to his summer residence at Montefiascone, it was widely rumoured that he was leaving Italy.

His health was failing and he knew that he had not long to live. The Italians were complaining that he surrounded himself with Frenchmen in high office and did not appoint enough Italians. France was at war with England, and the French court pressed him to return to Avignon.

When the Romans realized that he had made up his mind to leave, they implored him to stay. Petrarch wrote to him again, urging him in eloquent prose to remain in the city of St Peter. The letter bitterly criticized the French cardinals and insisted that Rome was the centre of all culture—that the civil and canon law stemmed from Italy, the great Latin orators and poets were all Italian, Latin language and literature were the foundation of the arts. Nothing came from France, said Petrarch. There was no learning in France. He ended by pleading:

> You would be leaving us in dire perils, and peril would beset you even on your journey: in the forests, there are fighting men, in the fields, there are plunderers, in the roads, there are robbers. . . . Stay then, most blessed Father: for if you should not be persuaded by this exhortation, he will meet you on the road who met the retreating Peter, and when Peter said to him, "Where are you going, Lord?" replied, "I am going to Rome to be crucified."

St Bridget of Sweden (23 July), foundress and visionary, who had made her home in Rome, rode out to see the pope on her white mule, prophesying that if he left Italy, his death would swiftly follow.

All this opposition was to no effect. In June 1370 Pope Urban told the Romans that he was leaving them "for the good of the Church, and to help France." In September, "sorrowful, suffering, and deeply moved," he embarked at Carneto; on 19 December he was dead. Petrarch wrote, "Urban would have been reckoned among the most glorious of men if he had caused his dying bed to be laid before the altar of St Peter's, and had there fallen asleep with a good conscience, calling God and the world to witness that if ever the Pope had left this spot, it was not his fault, but that of the originators of so shameful a flight."

The papacy was to be restored to Rome by Urban's successor, Gregory XI, seven years later. Subsequently, Urban was forgiven for what at the time seemed a catastrophic abandonment of his position, and he was praised for the good work he had done: for his attempts to reform the clergy and to check corruption and venality in his own household—though they were not always successful; for his encouragement of learning and his support of the universities, including Oxford; for his influence in the foundation of new universities, such as those of Cracow and Vienna; and his support of many poor students at the new College of Bologna (though his generous bursaries impoverished the papal treasury); for his veneration of the relics of St Thomas Aquinas (28 Jan.), which he entrusted to the Dominicans of Toulouse. He instructed the university of Toulouse: "We will and enjoin on you that you follow the teaching of the blessed Thomas as true and Catholic teaching, and promote it to the utmost of your power."

Pilgrims came to Urban's tomb in the abbey church of St Victor in Marseilles. His canonization was petitioned, and Pope Gregory XI is said to have promised that it would be undertaken, but the times were too troubled. The cult of this learned and conscientious pope continued and was eventually confirmed by Pope Pius IX in 1870.

The best account, with a good bibliography, can be found in G. Mollat, *The Popes at Avignon* (1912, Eng. trans. 1962), pp. 52-8. See also *O.D.P.*, pp. 223-5; Pastor, 1, pp. 95-7; E. Hocedez, *Anal. Boll.* 26 (1907), pp. 305-16; E. H. Wilkins, *Life of Petrarch* (1963), pp. 200-5, 214-5, 220-2, 226-7.

SS Dominic Uy, Stephen Vinh, and Companions, *Martyrs* (1839)

Dominic was a Vietnamese catechist and a Dominican tertiary. He was only twenty-six when he was martyred. He was beatified in 1900 and canonized in 1988.

A small group of Indo-Chinese Catholics, said to have been peasants, were also martyred at the same time. Stephen Vinh, another Dominican tertiary, is the only one of five whose name is known. He too was canonized in 1988.

N.C.E., 14, p. 198-9. Other sources as for St Simon Hoa (12 Dec.). See also the general entry on the Martyrs of Vietnam, 2 February.

20

St Ammon and Companions, *Martyrs* (250)

Like Epimachus (12 Dec.) and Nemesius (19 Dec.) and their companions, Ammon, Zeno, Ptolemy, Ingenes, and Theophilus were martyred at Alexandria during the Decian persecutions in the year 250, and an account of their trials and death reaches us from the letter of St Dionysius of Alexandria (17 Nov.) preserved in the *Ecclesiastical History* of Eusebius.

In the course of this letter, Dionysius describes how a certain Christian, when he was brought to trial, began to fear and to waver. Some of the soldiers on guard duty were also Christians, and they made signs to the prisoner to stand firm. When the magistrate noticed this, he made an inquiry, and in the confusion that followed Ammon and his four companions broke ranks and declared themselves Christians. They were executed with the prisoner.

There have been several other martyrs named Ammon, but this account from Dionysius of Alexandria, the martyrs' contemporary and bishop, is precise and reliable.

Eusebius, *H. E.*, 6, 41: the Latin version is reproduced in Ruinart, p. 174, and there are English versions in N.P.N.F., 1, pp. 283-6, and the Penguin Classics edition (1989), p. 213. See also *D.H.G.E.*, 2, 1308 n. 5.

Note: The new draft Roman Martyrology assigns these martyrs to 6 June, on which date they will appear in future editions of this work.

St Philogonius of Antioch, *Bishop and Martyr* (324)

Philogonius was an advocate who earned a considerable reputation for himself at the bar by his eloquence, integrity, and sense of justice. In 319, while still a layman with a wife and daughter, he was placed in the see of Antioch after the death of Vitalis. St John Chrysostom mentions the flourishing state of that church as proof of his zeal and administrative gifts. In the persecution of the Church by Maximinus and Licinius, Philogonius was imprisoned.

We know no more about his life: all the information available comes from a sermon preached by St John Chrysostom when his feast was celebrated at Antioch in 386, more than sixty years after his death. Chrysostom said little in the sermon about Philogonius' virtues, because the bishop Flavian was to speak on that subject immediately after him: he devoted his own contribution to describing the peace he trusted Philogonius enjoyed in heaven, a society where there are no conflicts, no more of "those icy words 'mine' and 'yours,'" which fill the world with wars, families with quarrels and individuals with disquiet, envy and malice." He said that Philogonius had so renounced the world that he received in this life the spirit of Christ in its fullest degree. A soul must here learn that spirit and state of the blessed and have some acquaintance with the mysteries of grace and the works of love and praise. Those invited to attend an earthly court must learn its manners: similarly, Christians must learn the manners of the court of heaven.

St John Chrysostom's sermon is given in *P.L.*, 48, 747-56. On the degree of credit which may be attached to such panegyrics, see Delehaye, *Les passions des martyrs et les genres littéraires* (1921), 2, pp. 183-235. *D.C.B.*, p. 842; *D.Cath.Biog.*, p. 931.

St Dominic of Silos, *Abbot* (1073)

Dominic was born at the beginning of the eleventh century at Cañas in Navarre, on the Spanish side of the Pyrenees. His people were peasants, and for a time he followed their way of life, looking after his father's flocks among the foothills of the mountains. Here he developed a taste for solitude and quietness, and he decided to become a monk at the monastery of San Millán de la Cogolla. He made great progress in monastic life, was entrusted with works of reform, and became prior of his monastery. In this office he came into conflict with the king, García III of Navarre, who claimed some possessions belonging to the monastery. García eventually drove Dominic and two other monks away, but they were welcomed by Ferdinand I of Old Castile, who sent them to the monastery of St Sebastian at Silos, where Dominic became prior. The monastery was in a remote and infertile part of the diocese of Burgos and was in a state of extreme decay, both materially and spiritually. Under the rule of Dominic, who carried out an extensive ministry of prayer and healing, the decline was arrested, progress was made, and the house became one of the most famous in Spain.

The Roman Martyrology refers to a belief that three hundred Christians, taken captive by the Moors, were liberated when they called upon God in Dominic's name.

Dominic is especially venerated in the Order of Friars Preachers because, nearly a century after his death, Bd Joan of Aza (2 Aug.) made a pilgrimage to his tomb and had a vision in which the saint promised that she should bear another son. The child was named Dominic and became the founder of the Order popularly called Dominicans.

Until the coming of the Republic in 1931 it was the custom for the abbot of Silos to bring the staff of St Dominic to the royal palace whenever a queen of Spain was in labour and to leave it by her bedside until the birth had taken place.

There is a Life by a monk, Grimaldus, thought to have been a contemporary. This has been printed, with a few slight omissions, in *AA.SS.OSB.*, 6, 299-320. A metrical Life by Gonzalo de Berceo, written about 1240, ed. J. D. Fitzgerald (1904), was re-published, ed. A. Andrés, in Madrid (1958). This adds little to our historical knowledge but is perhaps the earliest verse composition in Castilian speech. Much interest has been taken in St Dominic since the treasures of the library of Silos have become known, and a thirteenth-century copy of three early Lives is catalogued as manuscript n. 55 in the archives of Silos: see M. Férotin, *Histoire de l'Abbaye de Silos* (1897), pp. 26-67. See also *España Sagrada*, 27, p. 420; C. Gutiérrez, *Vida y milagros de Santo Domingo de Silos* (1932-51); L. Serrano, *El Real Monasterio de Santo Domingo de Silos* (1934); and a short Life by R. Alcocer (1925). Articles in *D.H.G.E.*, 14, 623-7 and *Diccionario Histórico-eclesiástico de España*, 2, 764. The latter has an extensive bibliography in Spanish.

A painting of Dominic in gold cope and mitre, seated in his episcopal chair, is in the Prado Museum in Madrid.

21

ST PETER CANISIUS, *Doctor* (1521-97)

Peter Canisius has been described as the second apostle of Germany, the first being St Boniface (5 June). He is also honoured as one of the first to use the potential of the printing press for Catholic teaching. Much of the success of the Catholic revival in Germany is considered to be due to his work. He was born in Nijmegen, which was then in the archdiocese of Cologne. His father, Jakob Kanis, was nine times burgomaster of Nijmegen and was ennobled after acting as tutor to the sons of the Duke of Lorraine. Peter's mother died when he was very young, but his father's second wife proved an excellent step-mother. Peter took his Master of Arts degree at Cologne University at the age of nineteen (and later accused himself of wasting his time when he should have been studying). Then he studied canon law at Louvain for a few months to please his father, who wished him to be a lawyer, but he realized that he was not called to this career, refused marriage, took a vow of celibacy, and returned to Cologne to read theology.

Great interest had been aroused in the Rhineland towns by the preaching of Bd Peter Favre (1 Aug.), the senior of the first companions of St Ignatius Loyola (31 July). Canisius attended an Ignatian retreat which Fr Favre gave at Mainz and during the second week made a vow to join the new Order. He lived for some years in the community at Cologne, spending his time in prayer, in study, in teaching, and in visiting the sick. He was already writing: his first publications were editions of the works of St Cyril of Alexandria (27 June) and St Leo the Great (10 Nov.). After his ordination to the priesthood he came into prominence through his preaching. He attended two sessions of the Council of Trent, one at Trent and the other at Bologna, and was then summoned to Rome by St Ignatius, who kept him by his side for five months. He was sent to Messina to teach in the first Jesuit school to be founded, then recalled for his solemn profession and a more important charge.

He was sent back to Germany: he had been selected to go to Ingolstadt with two brother Jesuits to promote Catholic teaching in the university and other teaching centres. The Church, here as in other German cities, was disorganized and demoralized after the attacks of Luther and his followers. Some people became zealous Protestants, but far more, disillusioned by religious controversy, were drifting away from Christian beliefs altogether. Peter found that even among nominal Catholics religious practice was at a very low ebb: fasts were ignored, saints' days went unobserved, and few students came to Mass;

but the Jesuits were popular because they offered free tuition, and with immensely hard work Peter made an impact on the student population and effected a real religious revival by his preaching and teaching. He was so successful in this that the professors unanimously elected him rector—an office that had to be filled every six months. This was a dubious honour which might be declined on payment of a fine of six gold pieces—but he had no gold pieces, so he added the duties to his many other concerns. When his period of office was completed he wrote, "By the grace of God, I am through with this business." He hoped that his time as a university administrator was over, but Duke Albrecht, who much admired his work, insisted that he become vice-chancellor, hoping to keep him in Ingolstadt.

In 1552 he was rescued from this situation by Ignatius, who sent him with a small group of Jesuits to carry out a mission in Vienna. The Austrian Church was in even worse case than the Church in Germany: there were many sects, and Catholic teaching was almost non-existent. Many parish clergy did not have even the most elementary knowledge of theology or doctrine, and parishes were neglected, with the people relapsing into pagan superstitions. The university of Vienna had closed altogether for a time, overwhelmed by a tide of ignorance and indifference. King Ferdinand, brother of the emperor, had requested the mission, and accommodation was found for it in the monastery of St Dominic, by then almost empty of monks.

Peter was the only priest in the team who could speak German—though his Rhineland accent grated on the ears of the Viennese. At first he preached to almost empty churches, but he won acceptance largely through his ministry to the poor of the city and to hospitals and prisons. The Viennese were impressed when they saw him begging for food and clothing for those who needed it and when they heard of his work with condemned men: he would stay with them, walk with them to the place of execution, and comfort them up to the moment of death. In the autumn of 1552 there was an outbreak of plague, and he worked tirelessly bringing food and medicine, hearing Confessions, administering the Last Rites, and comforting relatives.

In that same autumn he inherited the *Compendium*, which was to be a great trial to him but was to lead to his greatest achievement. The idea came from King Ferdinand, who wanted a new manual of Catholic doctrine: "It is to be a methodical work, and to embrace everything a good Christian ought to know. His Majesty wishes it to be composed by his own theologians, printed in Vienna on his commission, and taught, by his express command, in the schools of all his provinces and dominions."

The task was given to Fr Lejay, but on his death it devolved upon Peter Canisius. He found it a burden and wrote to Fr John Polanco, secretary general of the Society of Jesus, to confess that "after so many months, I am stuck fast at the beginning." His best work was done with young people, with the sick and poor, and with prisoners, and he was no great scholar. The problem was that the manual had to be simple enough for the ordinary Catholic to grasp and yet sufficiently learned to satisfy the theologians.

Eventually this difficulty was identified. Another member of the Jesuit mission, Fr Laynez, took over the work of writing a learned treatise, while Peter wrote a primer for students. His famous *Catechism*, or *Summary of Christian Doctrine*, written in Latin, was completed in 1555. It consisted of five chapters, on Faith, Hope, Charity, the Sacraments, and Justice (this last including sin, good works, the cardinal virtues, and the gifts of the Holy Spirit). There were short, pointed questions, and lucid, full answers. King Ferdinand provided a foreword in which he enjoined that "this Catechism and no other is propounded, explained and taught . . . whether publicly or privately."

The *Catechism* was immediately seized upon as a defining document in the battle against Lutheranism. In 1558 Peter produced a *Smaller Catechism*, which was easier for schoolchildren and the general public, and this was translated into German. There was an edition with pictures, woodcuts, and prayers. Later he produced the *Shortest Catechism*, which was easier still but preserved the elements of the Faith. All three ran to many editions and were published in many languages. When he was a very old man Peter edited an edition of the *Shortest Catechism* for those who had only just learned to read, with the words divided into syllables. His aim was not to produce works of scholarship but to reach simple people with his message.

His work brought him unwanted prominence and more administration. King Ferdinand, the nuncio, and even the pope wanted him appointed bishop of Vienna, but Ignatius would allow him to administer the diocese for only a single year, and that without episcopal orders, title, or emoluments. In Prague, where he was sent to found a college, he was dismayed to learn that he was to be provincial of a newly-established province covering southern Germany. During his two years at Prague he established the college on such sound pedagogical lines that Protestants as well as Catholics were happy to send their sons to it. In 1557 he went by special invitation to Würms to take part in a discussion between Catholic and Protestant divines, though he was convinced from past experience that such conferences were useless, since they only hardened the lines of division. Though firm in his own faith, he was always gentle with Lutherans and tried to stress common elements of faith rather than differences.

Apart from the colleges he founded or inaugurated, Peter prepared the way for many others. In 1559 he took up his residence in Augsburg and made his headquarters there for six years. Among the works he produced at this time were a selection of St Jerome's letters, a *Manual for Catholics*, and a revision of the *Augsburg Breviary*. The "General Prayer" he composed is still recited in Germany on Sundays. At the end of his term of office as provincial he settled at Dillingen in Bavaria, where the Jesuits had a college of their own, and directed the university. He occupied himself in teaching, in hearing Confessions, and in the laborious writing of the first of a series of books he had undertaken by order of his superiors.

They were intended as a reply to a strongly anti-Catholic history of Christianity, which was being published by a group of Protestant writers known as the Centuriators of Magdeburg. He continued with this work for some years until 1577, when to his relief he was dispensed from proceeding with it on the grounds of his health. There seems to have been no curtailment of his activities in other directions: he acted as court chaplain at Innsbruck for some years, continued preaching and directing missions, and even filled the post of vice-provincial for a time.

In 1580 Peter was sent to Fribourg in Switzerland, the capital of a Catholic canton wedged between two powerful Protestant neighbours. That city had long desired a Catholic college but had been handicapped by lack of funds and other difficulties. Peter overcame these obstacles in a few years: he raised the money, selected the site, and superintended the erection of the college, which later developed into the university of Fribourg. For over eight years his principal work was preaching: on Sundays and festivals he delivered sermons in the cathedral; on weekdays he visited other parts of the canton. He played a large part in keeping Fribourg Catholic at a critical period of its history.

In 1591 a stroke threatened his life, but he recovered sufficiently to continue writing until shortly before his death. As Fr Brodrick comments, he saw "books as a bulwark of faith." He remained simple, humble, and hard-working as ever, eager to take his part in the daily domestic life of the community. He washed the dishes with trembling hands and swept the dusty corridors, though he could not walk without a stick. St Ignatius preached the right use of illness, and Peter's final long, slow decline was a model of Ignatian teaching, practised with patience and charity. He died very quietly in the presence of his Brothers. He was canonized and declared a Doctor of the Church in 1925 by Pope Pius XI.

Lives by J. H. M. Tesser (1932); J. Brodrick (1935); W. Reany, *A Champion of the Church: Peter Canisius* (1931). Peter Canisius' works are ed. O. Braunsberger, *Beati Petri Canisii societatis Iesu Epistolae et Acta*, 8 vols. (1896-1923); *Meditationes seu Notae in Evangelicas Lectiones*, 3 vols. (1957-63). *Catechisms* in *E. R. L.*, 32 and 382. See also *Anal. Boll.* 16 (1897), pp. 78-82 and 363-4; *N.C.E.*, 1 p. 480; *Bibl. SS.*, 10, 798-814.

St Peter Thi, *Martyr* (1763-1839)

Peter Thi was an Indo-Chinese priest, almost sixty years old when the persecutions developed in the late 1830s. He was beheaded at Hanoi. He was canonized at the same time as other Vietnamese martyrs commemorated in December, in 1988.

N.C.E., 14, pp. 198-9. Other references as for St Simon Hoa (12 Dec.). See also the Martyrs of Vietman, 2 February.

Bd Peter Friedhofen, *Founder* (1819-60)

Peter Friedhofen was a chimney-sweep in the days when this was a dirty and often dangerous job. He was born on 25 February 1819 in Weitersburg bei Vallendar in the Rhine Valley and orphaned young, his father dying in 1820 and his mother in 1828. He had a rough upbringing, being poor and friendless and sickly. The Church was his anchor and, like Adolf Kolping of Cologne (4 Dec.), he determined, whatever the difficulties, to found an organization to help those who led similarly impoverished lives. In 1850 he founded the Congregation of the Brothers of the Charity of Mary, Help of Christians.

Peter faced many trials and difficulties, compounded by chronic ill health, but he showed a remarkable firmness and decisiveness in his plans, and the community was well established when he died at the early age of forty-one.

Peter's faith led to the establishment of an Order that now works in many different parts of Europe, in Brazil, and in Malaysia, running hospitals and old people's homes.

His beatification by Pope John Paul II took place on 23 June 1985.

Osservatore Romano, 22 July 1985; *N.S.B.* 2, pp. 70-72; *D.N.H.*, 2, pp. 62-6.

22

ST FRANCES XAVIER CABRINI, *Foundress* (1850- 1917)

Francesca Cabrini was a small frail woman of indomitable spirit. The tenth child of a fairly prosperous Italian farmer, she was born at Sant' Angelo, Lodigiano, near Pavia, in 1850. Her mother bore eleven children, of whom seven died young and one was brain-damaged, so Francesca grew up knowing about suffering. She studied with the Daughters of the Sacred Heart and passed her examinations as a primary school teacher. At the age of twenty-two she became schoolmistress in Vidardo, near Sant' Angelo, and obtained the permission of the mayor to teach Christian doctrine, which was forbidden by the secular inspector of schools.

Francesca wanted to work more closely with the Church, and she applied to join first the Daughters of the Sacred Heart at Arluno and then the Canossian Sisters at Crema. Neither was prepared to admit her—she was less than five feet tall and in very poor health, but her parish priest, Fr Antonio Serrati, recommended her as the director of an orphanage, the House of Providence in Cadogno. Here she gathered and trained a small group of fellow-workers and ran an orphanage and a workshop for girls, but the scheme was badly organized and ill-funded, and it collapsed for reasons beyond her control.

She sought permission to found a house devoted to foreign missions, perhaps to work in China and other parts of the Far East. There was some resistance to this proposal, because Catholic missionaries had always been men, but eventually she was allowed to found the *Missionarie del Sacro Cuoro* (Missionary Sisters of the Sacred Heart) with seven other Sisters. Her aim was to provide a mixed discipline in which service to people in need would be balanced by regular periods of prayer and meditation and times of silence each day. The keynote was humility and simplicity. There were no special austerities: she thought the work of her Sisters was hard enough if they were really giving all they could to God and the needy. She was always willing to do the most menial tasks herself. In 1880 her Rule of life was approved, and as her reputation for hard work and spirituality grew she was able to set up other houses in Milan and elsewhere in northern Italy.

In the autumn of 1887 she went to Rome to ask for papal recognition of her Institute and a house in Rome and also to explore the possibilities of starting the foreign mission. She was well received: Cardinal Parocchi, the vicar general, after some testing questions, gave permission for the foundation in Rome, and "with five Sisters, in the most dire poverty, but with jubilation in her heart," she set to work. Four months later the Institute received the Decree of Commendation. This was a mark of confidence for a women's Institute working largely for women. The houses in Italy were to form the training base for her missionary work.

But the call did not come from China: it came from the opposite direction. Italy was going through a deep economic depression in the 1870s and 1880s, and desperate families, near starvation and seeking work, emigrated to the United States. Wave after wave of immigration took place, and "Little Italies" developed in American cities, particularly in New York and Boston. Crowded in tenements, exploited by factory owners, the immigrants lived in poverty and squalor, often ignorant of the language or the customs of a strange land. Many of them, particularly from the rural south of Italy, knew little of their faith.

At this time the United States was classified as a mission country. While she was in Rome, Mother Cabrini met the bishop of Piacenza, Giovanni Battista Scalabrini (beatified in 1999: see Supplement at the end of this volume), one of the leaders of the Italian hierarchy. Bishop Scalabrini had been deeply moved by seeing crowds of emigrants waiting to leave from the Milan railway station, sympathizing with their desire for a better life and conscious of the bitter struggle for existence many of them would face. Archbishop Michael Corrigan of New York had asked for "good Italian priests" for New York City. Bishop Scalabrini thought it right that, together with the priests, the Missionary Sisters of the Sacred Heart should go to America.

In November 1887 Mother Cabrini sought an audience with Pope Leo XIII. The Pope had recently received a report from *Propaganda Fide* that gave statistics of the mass exodus to the United States and reported that it had "all the characteristics of a white slave trade." After listening to Mother Cabrini in silence, he gave his decision: her mission was to be "not to the East, but to the West."

Mother Cabrini left Le Havre on 23 March 1889 for New York with six Sisters. It was a stormy and exhausting voyage, and they arrived to find a distinctly unpromising situation: no one met them or expected them, and Archbishop Corrigan was not welcoming. Though he wanted priests, he did not think the work suitable for women. He told Mother Cabrini that the ship which had brought her was still in the harbour and that she should go home, because there was no need for her and her Sisters. She replied, "I have letters from the pope"; and she stayed.

The only accommodation the Sisters could find was filthy, alive with cockroaches and bed-bugs, and they had to beg from door to door for money. Though the diocese and the major religious Orders would not help them, they found friendship and assistance from other women religious, notably the Sisters of Charity and the Bon Secours Sisters, and they began work among the Italian immigrants, teaching the children, visiting the sick, and feeding the hungry. They were soon so well respected that the small shopkeepers in Little

Italy would give them food as they passed by—cabbages, garlic, pumpkin, whatever they had to spare.

There was a good deal of anti-Catholic feeling in New York and prejudice against immigrants from southern Europe in particular, but this small woman with her poor English was convinced that she was obeying the will of God, and she was indomitable. She begged money to found her first orphanage; she convinced Archbishop Corrigan that the work was worthwhile—perhaps helped by a "salty letter" from Bishop Scalabrini.

From the time when she set up the first orphanage, Mother Cabrini's life was one of constant motion in response to demands and offers of help. If the Italian immigrants started their life in the New World in poverty and misery, some of them soon became successful enough to help their own, and they had confidence in her. Her mission was to the Italian community—"our poor Italians, who are abandoned and very much looked down on by the English-speaking public." After a time she was offered a large house in upstate New York. She travelled to Cincinnati, to Pittsburg, to Buffalo, to Saint Louis, to Missouri, to Denver, to San Francisco, setting up schools and orphanages and workshops. In Seattle a site had to be cleared before the builder could start work. Mother Cabrini took up a pick and showed her sisters how to use it, saying, "A missionary must be able to do any kind of work." She went to New Orleans after an ugly incident in which eleven Italians were lynched and founded a house there.

During an epidemic she was asked to start a hospital in New York. At first she refused, saying that she was an educator, not a nurse, but she had a dream in which she saw the Blessed Virgin Mary helping the sick. When she asked Mary why she was doing this, Mary replied that it was because she, Mother Cabrini, had refused to do it. (This episode is commemorated in a large fresco in the chapel of the former St Antony's Orphanage in Carney, New Jersey). She made a heroic start, with a few mattresses and some bottles of medicine. The Sisters had to go begging on the first afternoon, because there was "not a penny in the house," but, as before, what was begun in faith and love brought offers of help. Medical consultants offered their services, and she soon had a well-organized hospital with a medical board. She named it the Columbus Hospital, because it was founded in 1892, four hundred years after the Italian Columbus discovered the New World. Other Italian hospitals, all Columbus Hospitals, developed in Chicago and other great American cities.

She made nine voyages back to Italy—organizing training programmes for her Sisters, who were needed in America in increasingly large numbers, explaining her work to the Catholic hierarchy, and making sure that she had the necessary backing. Above all, she was going back to her spiritual roots, spending time in prayer and meditation, but Pope Leo XIII told her to "hurry all over the earth if possible, in order to take the holy name of Jesus everywhere."

She extended her work to Central America, making an apostolic mission through the jungles of Nicaragua by boat and contracting yellow fever as a result. In 1895, at the age of forty-five, she took a banana boat from New Orleans to Valparaiso, and headed for the Andes. She endured snow, cold, and deprivation before she reached Buenos Aires. She toured Argentina, setting up new schools and orphanages.

Her Rule was finally given definitive approval in 1907, when she was fifty-seven. By that time there were Cabrini foundations in France and Spain as well as Italy, across the United States and in South America, and she set out to visit them all. While she was in Rio de Janeiro there was a smallpox epidemic, and she nursed the sick Sisters herself. Back in the United States, she started a new enterprise in the prisons: Sisters who would work with prisoners, including condemned prisoners on death row, and care for their relatives. When she visited Sing Sing, she addressed the Italian prisoners in their own language as "my good friends." In 1916 she took a six months' spiritual retreat. Her work was nearly done. She was wrapping up presents of sweets for the children in an Italian parochial school in Chicago just before Christmas in 1917 when she collapsed. She died in hospital on the following day.

Mother Cabrini's mission was always to Italian immigrants. Though she became a naturalized American in 1907, this was primarily because it was necessary under corporation law for the many properties of her Institute to be in American hands. She championed the Italian communities and gave them a sense of pride. Her personal warmth, humility, and practicality were outstanding. She combined these qualities with a remarkable organizational competence and an even more remarkable energy—a willingness to work without stint for God's purposes. She was canonized in 1946 by Pope Pius XII and formally proclaimed "the patroness of immigrants." She is known as the "first citizen saint" of the United States.

The Life by Mary Louise Sullivan, M.S.C. (1992), contains much material from the Cabrini archives, an essay on sources, and a full bibliography. Other Lives by C. C. Martindale (1931); E. J. McCarthy (1937); A Benedictine of Stanbrook, (1944); L. Borden (1945); E. Macadam (1946); E. V. Daily (1947); M. A. Farnum (1947); T. Maynard (1948); P. di Donato (1960); S. C. Lorit, trans. Jerry Hearne (1988). Mother Cabrini's writings include *Escortatione della Cabrini* (1954) and *Diario spirituale* (1957); also *Viaggi della Madre Francesca Saverio Cabrini . . . narrati in variae sue lettere* (Milan, 1935). See also *N.C.E.*, 2, p. 1039; *Bibl.SS.*, 5, 1028-45; K. Jones, *Women Saints: Lives of Faith and Courage* (1999), pp. 259-67.

She is represented in the Immigration Museum at the foot of the Statue of Liberty; on the bronze doors of St Patrick's Cathedral, New York; in the National Shrine of the Immaculate Conception in Washington, D.C.; and by a statue in St Peter's Basilica in the Vatican.

SS Chaerymon, *Bishop*, Ischyrion, and Others, *Martyrs* (250)

St Dionysius of Alexandria, in his letter to Fabian of Antioch, speaking of the Egyptian Christians who suffered in the persecution under Decius, refers to the many who were driven or fled into the desert, where they perished from hunger, thirst, and exposure or from the attacks of wild beasts and bandits. Many also were sold into slavery, of whom only some had been ransomed at the time he wrote. He singles out for mention Chaerymon, a very old man and a bishop of Nilopolis, who with his wife had taken refuge in the mountains of Arabia and had never been seen or heard of again. Though searches were made, not even their bodies were found.

St Dionysius also mentions Ischyrion, who was the procurator of a magistrate in some city of Egypt, thought to be Alexandria. His master ordered him to sacrifice to the gods, but he refused, and neither abuse nor threats could move him. The magistrate had him mutilated and impaled.

Both these martyrs are named in the Roman Martyrology.

Eusebius, *H. E.*, 6, 41, in N.P.N.F., 1, pp. 283-6, and the Penguin Classics edition (1989), p. 214. For the Latin version see Ruinart, p. 175.

Bd Jutta of Diessenberg (1136)

Jutta, sister to Count Meginhard of Spanheim, led the life of a recluse in a small house next to the monastery founded by St Disibod (8 July) in the Diessenberg. She was the "noble woman" to whom was confided the care of St Hildegard of Bingen (17 Sept.) when she was a child. It was Jutta who first taught her Latin, taught her to read, and encouraged her love of music. Other disciples came to Jutta and were formed into a community under the Benedictine Rule, over which she presided as prioress for some twenty years.

Hildegard, her successor, said of her, "This woman overflowed with the grace of God like a river fed by many streams. Watching, fasting and other works of penance gave no rest to her body till the day that a happy death freed her from this mortal life." Her relics drew crowds of pilgrims to the Diessenberg, and the prospect of losing them was one of the reasons for the monks' opposition to Hildegard's removal of the community to Bingen.

No Life of Jutta appears to have been printed, but a manuscript account is in existence, copied from the great *Legendarium* of the Augustinian Canons of Bödeken: see *Anal.Boll.* 27 (1908), p. 341; also J. May, *Die hl. Hildegard* (1911); *D.Cath.Biog.*, p. 641; *Bibl.SS.*, 7, 1032-3; *L.D.H.*, p. 298.

Her commemoration has been dropped from the new Roman Martyrology, but she seems worth recording here if only for her influence on Hildegard—whose "canonization" is likewise unconfirmed.

Bd Adam of Loccum (1210)

This monk, with others of the same name, is called Blessed in menologies of the Cistercian Order: the little that is known of him is derived from the *Dialogue of Visions and Miracles* of his fellow-Cistercian, Caesarius of Heisterbach. Adam was priest and sacristan of the abbey of Loccum in Hanover, and he told Caesarius that he had twice been miraculously delivered from sickness. On the first occasion, as a schoolboy, he picked up a piece of stone that was lying among the builders' materials when the monastery at Loccum was being repaired and began to carve it. His schoolmaster saw him and told him sharply to put it down on pain of excommunication. Adam was so frightened that he became ill and thought he was dying, but he had a vision in which two saints told him that he would recover, and he was well within the hour. On the second occasion he was at school at Munster in Westphalia and suffered from eczema. He had a vision of the Blessed Virgin Mary, who cured his condition.

In both cases, the ailments of this devout and nervous boy may have had a psychological rather than a physical origin. What does come through in Caesarius' account is the depth of Adam's devotion to the Blessed Virgin. "It is clear that there is nothing more efficacious and no remedy more sure than the medicine of the Blessed Virgin," observes the novice in Caesarius of Heisterbach's *Dialogue*. To this the monk replies, "And no wonder. For it was she who brought to us the medicine of the whole human race, as it is written, 'Let the earth bring forth the living creature,' that is to say, let Mary bring forth the man Christ."

The monastic buildings at Loccum are now a Lutheran seminary, and the Lutheran land-bishop of Hanover has the official title "Abbot of Loccum."

See Caesarius of Heisterbach's *Dialogue of Visions and Miracles*, 7, 17; 8, 18 and 74: Eng. trans. 2 vols. (1929).

23

ST JOHN OF KANTI (1473)

John Cantius receives his name from his birth-place, Kanti, near Oswiecim in Poland. He came of a fairly affluent family and studied at the university of Cracow. He was ordained priest soon after completing his course and was appointed lecturer. He was known to lead a very strict life, and when he was warned to look after his health, he pointed out that the Desert Fathers were notably long-lived in spite of their ascetic practices.

John's success as a preacher and teacher roused opposition: the circumstances are not altogether clear, but he was removed from his post and sent as parish priest to the parish of Olkusz. Though single-minded and energetic, he was not popular there, and parish life evidently did not suit his talents. After a few years he was recalled to the University of Cracow as professor of Sacred Scripture, and he held this post until the end of his life.

He became famous not only for his academic excellence but for the austerity of his personal life. He was held in such high esteem at the university that for many years after his death his gown was used on degree days to vest each new doctor of the university. He told his students to fight all false opinions, but to do so with moderation and courtesy. His influence stretched far beyond the university. He was a welcome guest at the tables of the nobility, and he was well known to the poor of Cracow. His goods and money were always at their disposition. His own needs were few: he slept on the floor and never ate meat. When he went to Rome he walked all the way, carrying his luggage on his back.

When the news spread round the city that he was dying, there was an outburst of sorrow. "Never mind about this prison which is decaying," he said to those who were looking after him, "but think of the soul that is going to leave it." He died on Christmas Eve 1473 and was canonized in 1767. His feast-day, formerly 20 October, has been moved back one day from the eve of Christmas.

Propylaeum, pp. 464-5; *AA.SS.*, Oct., 8, pp. 1042-73; *Bibl.SS.*, 6, 644-5; A. Arndt, "De loco et anno nativitatis. . . S Johannis Kant," *Anal.Boll.* 8 (1889), pp. 382-8; *O.D.S.*, pp. 263-4.

The Ten Martyrs of Crete (250)

Theodulus, Saturninus, Euporus, Gelasius, Eunician, Zoticus, Cleomenes, Agathopus, Basilides, and Evaristus: these saints, like the Egyptian martyrs noticed earlier in the month (12, 19, 20, and 22 Dec.), suffered in the persecutions consequent on the edict against Christians issued by Decius. There are two kinds of evidence: a Greek Passion of great antiquity and a local tradition in the neighbourhood of Gortyna, the capital of Crete. The village in which they are reputed to have been martyred is still called *Hagioi Deka* (Ten Saints), and a broken slab is shown, with ten hollow depressions, said to mark the places where they received the fatal blows. The slab may be no more than an attraction for pilgrims and tourists, but the ancient name of the village is convincing.

The tradition is that the ten, united in their confession of Christ, were arrested, dragged along the ground to prison, beaten, stoned, and at length brought before the governor at Gortyna. They were ordered to sacrifice to Jupiter, whose festival occurred on that day, but they refused. They were tortured again, and when the mob pressed them to spare themselves by obeying and sacrificing to the gods, they replied, "We are Christians, and would rather die a thousand times." The governor condemned them to die by the sword, and they went to their execution praying that God would have mercy on them and on all mankind and would deliver their countrymen from the blindness of idolatry. Their relics were afterwards taken to Rome.

P.G., 116, 565-73; *Anal. Boll.* 18 (1899), p. 280, has reviews of two complementary papers on the Ten Martyrs in Greek, by A. E. Kopasis and Elias Alexandrides.

St Servulus (590)

Pope St Gregory the Great (3 Sept.) told the story of Servulus in one of his homilies. Servulus was a beggar, paralyzed since childhood and unable to stand upright, lift his hand to his mouth, or turn himself from one side to the other. His mother and his brother carried him to the porch of the church of San Clemente in Rome, where he lived on the alms of passers-by and gave what he could to other people in need. He bought some books of the scriptures, and since he could not read himself, he got others to read to him. He listened with such attention that he learned passages by heart.

He spent much of his time singing hymns of praise and thanksgiving to God, although he was in continual pain. When he was dying he asked the poor who had shared his alms and some pilgrims to sing hymns and psalms by his bed. He sang with them, and then cried, "Do you hear the great and wonderful music in heaven?" and so died. His body was buried in San Clemente.

Pope Gregory gave these details of the life of Servulus to illustrate how his kindness and cheerfulness shamed those who, when blessed with good health and fortune, do no good to others and are impatient with the slightest adversity. He speaks of Servulus with love and respect as one who was well known both to himself and to his hearers, "a pauper in worldly things, rich in merit." The phrase is repeated in another account in his *Dialogues*.

See *P.L.*, 77, 341-2, for the *Dialogues of St Gregory the Great*, 4, 14; and *P.L.*, 76, 1133, for his *Homily 15 in Evangel.*
Servulus is commemorated by a fresco in San Clemente.

St Frithebert, *Bishop* (766)

Frithebert (Frithubeorht or Frithuberht), bishop of Hexham, Northumberland, was the successor of the scholarly Benedictine monk St Acca (20 Oct.). He is mentioned as the administrator of Lindisfarne while its bishop, Cynewulf, was in prison. The Continuator of Bede notes that he was consecrated by Archbishop Egbert in 735, the year Bede died. Frithebert and the archbishop both died in 766.

No other details are known of Frithebert's life. His bones were discovered at Hexham in 1154.

Bede, *H.E.*, Continuator's records for 735 and 766 from the Moore Manuscript; *D.C.B.*, 2 (1880), p. 566; J. Raine, *Memorials of Hexham Abbey*, 1, Surtees Society (1864), pp. 199-200; Stanton, pp. 606-7; *O.D.S.*, pp. 190-1.

Bd Hartmann, *Bishop* (1164)

Hartmann was born at Polling, now in Austria, and educated in the Augustinian monastery of St Nicholas at Passau, where he eventually became a canon. In 1122, when Conrad, archbishop of Salzburg, wished to introduce regular discipline and the communal life among his clergy, he invited Hartmann to become dean of the metropolitan chapter. Subsequently he reformed the monastery of Herrenchiemsee and the House of Canons at Klosterneuberg founded by St Leopold, margrave of Austria (15 Nov.). He became bishop of Brixen in the Tyrol in 1140. Two years later he founded the regular chapter of Neustift in his cathedral city and liberally endowed it. Shortly after, with one of his cathedral canons, he established the hospice of the Holy Cross for poor pilgrims.

Bishop Hartmann was highly respected by the emperors Conrad III and Frederick I. He was involved in the dispute between the latter and Pope Alexander III, but neither threats nor promises could make him serve interests other than those of the Holy See. His cult was confirmed in 1784 by Pope Pius VI.

A medieval Latin Life is printed in Pez, *Scriptores rerum austriacarum*, 1, and also ed. H. Zeibig, *Vita B. Hartmann* (1846). A more modern biography is that of A. Sparber, *Leben und Werken des Seligen Hartmann von Brixen* (1910). See also *D. Cath. Biog.*, p. 532; *N.C.E.*, 6, p. 936; *L.D.H.*, p. 214.

St Thorlac, *Bishop* (1133-93)

Iceland was colonized from Norway and Ireland, and Christianity was introduced by law in the year 1000 as a result of an agreement between pagans and Christians. The faith made such progress that the island was divided into two dioceses, Skalholt in 1056, and Holar in about 1106, which in 1152 were both made suffragans of Nidaros (Trondheim). During the twelfth century two bishops, one from each see, were venerated as saints both locally and in Norway. They were John of Holar and Thorlac of Skalholt. The life of Thorlac is narrated in the Thorlakssaga by a cleric of Skalholt.

Thorlac Thorhallsson was born of poor parents but closely related to influential families. He and his mother moved to Oddi, which was one of the richest church estates in the country and a centre of education, run by his kinsman. He was made deacon at the early age of fifteen and became a priest before he was twenty. After two or three years of parish work he was sent abroad to study, and he is said to have visited England. The fact that there is a Life of St Thomas Becket (29 Dec.) in Icelandic suggests that there were fairly strong contacts between the clergy of Iceland and England during this period. He studied in Lincoln, and it has been speculated that he may have met Bishop Hugh of Lincoln (17 Nov.); but Hugh did not move to Lincoln from Somerset until 1186, and Thorlac returned to Iceland in 1161.

Thorlac was much attached to his mother and sisters, who kept house for him. He kept a strict daily rule of life, which began with the singing of the *Credo, Paternoster*, and a hymn directly he awoke; he is said to have recited a third of the Psalter every day, and he had a special devotion to the titular saints of the churches in which he ministered. He formed an Augustinian community of Canons Regular in Thykkvibaer, of which he was abbot. In 1174 he was elected bishop of Skalholt. Because of political difficulties between Iceland and the crown of Norway, he was not consecrated until July 1178.

Iceland was governed by a general assembly, the Althing, founded in 930. The bishops held an eminent and respected place on this body. There was a church tithe, and the bishops were responsible for using part of this, "Christ's property," for alms to the poor.

Thorlac was a pioneer of church reform. When Christianity was introduced into Iceland, churches had been built in the main centres, often by chieftains and prominent landowners on their own territory and at their own expense. They kept priests for services but regarded the churches as their own property. Thorlac called for financial independence for the Church. The presentation of priests for appointment in these churches by laymen was forbidden, and this led to bitter struggles between Thorlac and some of the most influential men in Iceland, including his own kin, who had traditionally kept the right to present in churches which they or their families had built and furnished. There were angry scenes at the church door. It is said that one wealthy landowner, on being told that his new church must be surrendered to the bishop, declared that he would rather use it as a stable. When Thorlac consistently refused to consecrate it, he was waylaid by the landowner and his supporters on his episcopal travels and forced to carry out the consecration.

Thorlac carried out the principles of Pope Gregory VII on church discipline with great stringency. The abuses of simony were tackled, clerical celibacy was enforced, and the Christian doctrine of marriage was taught. These measures also led to opposition: a particular problem was that his own sister formed a non-Christian union with the chieftain at Oddi. Their son, Pall Jonssen, was to succeed Thorlac as bishop of Skalholt.

Thorlac's episcopate was stormy. Though Iceland was nominally Christian, there was a strong undercurrent of pagan values. His firmness, patience, and care for the poor and needy made him popular with the people, though not always with the chieftains. It is reported that monks from monasteries in other countries came to visit him to learn about the monastic way of life.

In his sixtieth year Thorlac determined to resign his see and retire to the abbey of Thykkvibaer, but he became ill and died before he could carry out this resolution. He was very greatly respected even by the prominent men he had opposed. Five years after his death, the Althing, which included bishops and clergy, formally declared him a saint. It has been argued that the Althing served the double purposes of a parliament and a church synod and was acting in the latter capacity. A popular and liturgical cult of Thorlac developed, extending to Scandinavia, the Norwegian island settlements, and some parts of Britain and Germany. It was known among the Varangians—northerners who served the emperor in Constantinople. Though Thorlac's name was not included by Cardinal Baronius in the Roman Martyrology, Pope John Paul II formally permitted that his name should be added to the proper calendar on 13 January 1984 and named him patron saint of Iceland on the following day. His feast is celebrated in Iceland on 14 January, the date of the translation of his relics, but 23 December is the date of his death.

There are certain fragments of Latin Lives or Breviary lessons relating to St Thorlac, as well as the *Thorlakssage*, printed by Langebek in his *Scriptores rerum Danicarum* 4, pp. 624-30. This material is summarized in S. Baring-Gould, *Lives of the Saints: December* (1877), pp. 262-9. See also a long notice by Gley in the *Biographie Universelle*, 41, 428; *N.C.E.*, 14, p. 140; *Bibl.SS.*, 12, 458-9.

Bd Margaret of Savoy, *Foundress* (1464)

Margaret of Savoy was related to the principal royal houses of Europe: her father was Count Amadeus of Savoy, and her mother was a sister of that Clement VII who claimed to be pope at Avignon during the Great Schism. She married Theodore Paleologus, marquis of Montferrat. On his death in 1418, when she was no more than thirty-six, she resolved not to marry again and went to live on her estate at Alba in Piedmont, where she devoted herself to good works. She became a Dominican tertiary and founded a community at Alba, first of tertiaries and then, by permission of Pope Eugenius IV, of nuns.

Her life was not easy: on one occasion, she had a vision of Christ offering her three arrows, labelled Sickness, Slander, and Persecution, and she suffered from all three. Her health was poor. She was accused of hypocrisy, then of tyrannizing over her Sisters, and a rejected suitor spread the rumour that the convent was a centre of the Waldensian heresy. The friar who was the nuns' confessor and director was imprisoned, and when Margaret went to the castle to demand his release the heavy door was slammed in her face, brutally crushing her hand. Despite these difficulties, her retired life of prayer, study, and charitable works lasted some twenty-five years.

There is in the royal library at Turin a volume of the letters of St Catherine of Siena (29 Apr.) copied and bound "by order of the illustrious lady, Margaret of Savoy, Marchioness of Montferrat." Her cult was confirmed in 1669.

Four or five lives of Margaret of Savoy were apparently published in the seventeenth century: one by G. Baresiano appeared in 1638. There is an Italian biography by F. G. Allaria (1877). See also Procter, pp. 334-7, and *D.Cath.Biog.*, p. 752.

Bd Nicholas Factor (1520-83)

Peter Nicholas Factor was the son of a Sicilian tailor who emigrated to Valencia and his Spanish wife, Ursula. In 1537 he joined the Friars Minor of the Observance in his native town. He made rapid progress in the Order and many times asked to be sent on foreign missions, but he had to content himself with working for the conversion of the Moors—a task involving few hazards in Philip II's Spain.

Nicholas was a vehement person of great zeal: he used to take the discipline before Mass and three times before preaching, once for his own sins, once for those of his neighbour, and once that his preaching might be fruitful. His mortifications were so extreme that he was actually delated to the Inquisition for singularity. He is said twice to have offered to throw himself into a furnace if the Moors he was trying to convert would promise to receive Baptism when he came out unhurt. The offer was refused.

He was known and revered by many of the Spanish nobility, from the king downward, and his personal friends included St Paschal Baylon (17 May), St Louis Bertrand (9 Oct.), and Bd John de Ribera (6 Jan.), all of whom gave evidence at his beatification.

Legends and marvels inevitably became attached to this colourful character. He was said to have known of the victory of the Holy League against the Turks at Lepanto (in the Gulf of Corinth) the day after the battle; to have forecast the election of Pope Sixtus V three years before it took place; to have been so warmed by divine love that when he plunged into cold water it was heated almost to boiling-point; and to have resisted Satan, who appeared to him in the form of a lion, a bear, and a snake. These stories may be more indicative of the culture of his day than of Nicholas Factor's religious experience, but they do indicate the great sanctity attributed to him by his contemporaries.

During the last years of his life he left his house of the Observance of Valencia to join a newly-established community of Capuchin Friars at Barcelona; in doing so, he remained a Franciscan but left his own province. His reasons seem to have been complex. It was said in the process for his beatification that he sought an even more austere way of life, in which more extreme penances would be approved—and also that he deliberately sought a reputation for being fickle and changeable as a means of humiliation. A few months later the province of the Reformed Friars was suppressed, and Nicholas returned to Valencia, saying that he "left those men, who are entirely holy" in order to return to "men who are entirely holy." He told a benefactor of the Order who gave him hospitality on his way back that he was returning most joyfully to Valencia and would end his course there. He died at Valencia soon after his return at the age of sixty-three, having spent forty-six years in the religious life. The decree of his beatification was published by Pope Pius VI in 1786.

The best biography is probably that of G. Alapont, *Compendio della Vita del B Niccolò Fattore*, which claims to be based on the process of beatification and was printed in Rome (1786). A short Life in English was included in the Oratorian Series in the middle of the nineteenth century. See also Wadding, 21, pp. 403, 419-26; *Auréole Séraphique*, 4, pp. 178-91; *F.B.S.*, pp. 933-5; *Bibl.SS.*, 5, 474-5.

St Margaret d'Youville, *Foundress* (1701-71)

Marguérite Dufrost de Lajemmerais was born at Varennes in Canada on 15 October 1701. Her father, an army officer of Breton ancestry, died when she was seven years old, and the family lived in great poverty. Margaret was the eldest child of six. Her great-grandfather Pierre Boucher took her into his house for a time and paid for her education at the Ursuline convent. When she was old enough, she returned to her family and helped to support them by sewing, embroidery, and teaching children, also helping to educate and care for her younger brothers and sisters.

At the age of twenty-one she married François You de la Découverte, or Youville, but the marriage was not a happy one. François and his brothers were fur traders and were involved in the illegal sale of alcohol to the American Indians. Margaret was appalled at his activities, and her compassion for the Indians and their problems may have dated from this time. François had little sense of family responsibilities and was often away from home. Her life must have been a very lonely one, with continued privation and worry about mounting debts. During her eight years of marriage she had five children, of whom only two, François and Charles, survived. When her husband died of his excesses in 1730 she was pregnant again, but the child lived only a few months. She opened a small store to pay off her husband's debts and to support herself and her two sons.

In 1727 Margaret had joined the Confraternity of the Holy Family, and her sense of vocation seems to have dated from this time. She developed a special devotion to the Virgin Mary, spent many hours in prayer, and tried to help other people in need. The story is told in detail by her younger son, Charles, who was to become the Abbé Dufrost and her principal biographer:

> Her piety had grown since she became a widow; bad weather could not prevent her from attending Mass daily, and in the afternoons, going to adore the Blessed Sacrament whenever her occupations allowed her to do so. . . . From the very first years of her widowhood, she was filled with charity for her neighbour, and considered it as an honour to visit the poor, the sick, the prisoners . . . visiting the poor in the city hospital, and mending the ragged clothing of the destitute.

In 1737, when the young François entered a seminary, Margaret and three companions rented a house in the poorer part of Montreal. Charles lived with them until he was old enough to follow his brother to the seminary. It was the custom in French Canadian seminaries for an elder son to take his father's name and a younger son to take his mother's, which is why Charles took the name of Dufrost rather than d'Youville. He recounts vividly how the small group began to accept poor and sick women into their care. Among the first few were an aged blind woman, a woman who was paralyzed and had to be spoon-fed, and one who was mentally disturbed. The project aroused open hostility in the neighbourhood: when the four went to church on All Saints Day, they encountered a violent mob hurling stones and shouting "Down with the *Soeurs Grises*." *Gris* in French means "grey," but it is also slang for "tipsy": the allegation was that the four women were drunk, and that the widow d'Youville was carrying on her husband's liquor trade with the Indians. When they went to Sunday Mass, they were refused the Host by a priest who believed this calumny.

Somehow they survived and won public respect. They made an income by sewing uniforms for the French troops and clothes for the explorers who were opening up western Canada—hard work for women used to embroidery and sewing baby-clothes. They did their washing in the St Lawrence River, and in winter they would come back to their house with their hands red and raw and covered with icicles.

Later that year the four made a private religious profession, and soon after they adopted a simple Rule. In 1745, following a disastrous fire which gutted the house, they demonstrated their faith by signing an act of total renunciation and self-dedication known as the Original Commitment (*engagements primitifs*). This document is still signed by every Grey Nun on the day of her profession.

A wealthy merchant offered them a house rent-free, and the work continued. The General Hospital in Montreal was threatened with closure: the Charon Brothers, who were responsible for it, decided to concentrate their work in the Quebec Hospital, which would have left Montreal without resources for the care of the sick poor. In 1747, following a long battle with the city authorities, Margaret was finally appointed director. The Sisters were officially designated as the Sisters of Charity of the General Hospital, but Margaret preferred the older name. She said, "Keeping the name of the Grey Nuns will remind us of the insults of the beginnings, and keep us humble." The hospital and the hospice wards for old people expanded, meeting the needs created by epidemics and extreme poverty, and won royal approval from Louis XV of France in 1753. In 1755, Bishop de Pontbriand of Quebec formally confirmed the Rule, with Mother Margaret as superior.

It was a desperate time for French Canada. In the Franco-British struggle that culminated in Wolfe's storming of Quebec and the surrender of Montreal in 1759, the Grey Nuns continued their work, nursing military as well as civilian casualties. Mother Margaret insisted on treating French soldiers and English prisoners alike, and on at least two occasions hid Englishmen on the run from the vengeful Indians who were supporting the French. When she heard that the Indians were torturing an English prisoner she paid a ransom for him and had him brought in more dead than alive. When he recovered he stayed on to be her interpreter and to act as an orderly. They were short of beds, short of medicine, short of food. Mother Margaret's prayer was "Give us this day our daily bread—or if not to us, at least to the poor."

Her loyalty was to "our masters, the poor," showing mercy and justice to people of all races, classes, and conditions. When the war was over—and Louis XV had shrugged off his lost Canadian possessions as "a few acres of snow"— the hospital and its associated enterprises continued to grow. There was a saying in Montreal: "Go to the Grey Nuns: they never refuse anybody, or any honest work." On one occasion Mother Margaret found an abandoned baby in the snow, and she took this as a sign that she should open an orphanage. The Grey Nuns developed schools as well as orphanages. They worked with prisoners, with African slaves, with the Indians, with mentally-handicapped and epileptic people, and with prostitutes.

In May 1765, when Mother Margaret was sixty-four years old, disaster struck again: a fire in a nearby house spread rapidly in a high wind, and the General Hospital was engulfed. It seemed that her life's work was in ruins; but other religious Orders offered shelter and hospitality, the governor general sent rations, and offers of help came from all sides—even from two Indian tribes. The spokesman for the Indians said, through an interpreter, "You came to us when sickness entered our tents, when death was claiming our members. You closed the eyes of our old people, and healed our children. Now misfortune has befallen you in turn. Fire has destroyed your house, and you have nothing left … to prove to you that we have not forgotten your kindness, we are bringing you our offering."

They had brought what they had—blankets, moccasins, knives, beads, and a few coins. Eventually the British government paid compensation, and the hospital was rebuilt. A precious possession was a small statue of Our Lady, which had escaped the flames.

Mother Margaret once told her niece: "We need crosses in order to reach heaven," and her life provided many—poverty, insecurity, sickness, and ceaseless toil in a harsh environment—but she was always ready to reach out to those whose lot was worse than her own. When she died in 1771, Sister de Lasource, who had been with her from the beginning, spoke her epitaph: "She loved greatly, Jesus Christ and the poor." At her beatification in 1959, Pope John XXIII called her "the Mother of Universal Charity." She was canonized by Pope John Paul II on 9 December 1990, becoming the first native-born Canadian saint.

The *Vie de Mme d'Youville* by Abbé Charles Dufrost is preserved in the general archives of the Grey Nuns in Montreal, together with his edited version of the *Mémoire pour servir à la vie de Mme d'Youville*, consisting of statements by her Sisters. Lives by A. Sattin (1829); E.-M. Faillon (1852). A. Ferland-Angers (1945) includes extensive correspondence and documentation relating to the foundress. Sister Estelle Mitchell is the author of three modern texts: *Elle a beaucoup aimé* (1959), Eng. trans., *Marguérite d'Youville, Foundress of the Grey Nuns* (1965); *Father Charles Dufrost and his Mother* (1991); and *The Spiritual Portrait of Saint Marguérite d'Youville* (1993). See also *Osservatore Romano*, 10 Dec. 1990, p. 6; *D.Cath.Biog.*, p. 1216; *Catholic Work* 61 (Jan-Feb. 1994), p. 8; K. Jones, *Women Saints:Lives of Faith and Courage* (1999), pp. 208-14.

24

St Delphinus, *Bishop* (403)

The first mention of Delphinus, the second bishop of Bordeaux, occurs in relation to his presence at the Synod of Zaragoza in 380, when the Priscillianists and other groups were condemned for heresy. Delphinus was a valued correspondent of St Ambrose (7 Dec.) and greatly influenced Pontius Meropius Anicius Paulinus, who became St Paulinus of Nola (22 June). Paulinus' conversion was principally due to his wife and St Delphinus, and Delphinus baptized him. Five of the letters of Paulinus to his spiritual benefactor were preserved for many years and give evidence of his great respect for Delphinus.

Sulpicius Severus mentions Delphinus in his *Chronicle*, 2, 48. A *Vie de S Delphin*, published by Fr Moniquet in 1893, has been severely criticized in *Anal.Boll.* 12, pp. 460-2. According to *D.H.G.E.*, 14, 185-7, the correspondence with Paulinus has now disappeared.

St Tharsilla (*c.* 550)

Tharsilla was an aunt of Pope St Gregory the Great (3 Sept.), and what is known about her comes largely from his writings, testifying to the holiness of her life.

Gregory's father, Gordian, had three sisters. When they were young, they lived under strict religious discipline as nuns in their father's house. One of them, Gordiana, who was unsuited to the monastic life, eventually left to marry the steward of her estates, but Tharsilla, the eldest, and a younger sister, Emiliana, continued to maintain their way of life until their eventual death. Tharsilla died on Christmas Eve. Emiliana had a vision or dream in which Tharsilla called to her to celebrate the Epiphany in heaven, and she died a few days after her sister, on 5 January.

The family was aristocratic and wealthy and showed exceptional piety. Gordian was a patrician who held minor orders in the Church (this was possible at the time for married men, particularly wealthy landowners living in Rome), and his wife, Silvia, Gregory's mother, was regarded as a saint. She went into religious seclusion on her husband's death. Gregory the Great was pope from 590 to 604. One of his paternal ancestors, whom he described as *"meus atavus,"* probably his great-grandfather, was Pope Felix III (481-92; 1 Mar.)—more properly Felix II, since the so-called "Felix II," though included in the Roman Martyrology, is now listed in the *Annuario Pontificio* as an antipope. Pope

Felix's father was a priest and his sister a nun. It has been argued that Pope Agapitus I (d. 536) was a member of the same family, the evidence resting on the recurrence of the names Gordian and Emiliana in successive generations and on records of the transfer of property on the Clivum Scauri, where the two sisters lived.

If this is the case, then Tharsilla came of a family that had produced three popes in a little over a century and in which it was a tradition for the women, if they chose to do so, to live an ascetic and sequestered life in their own homes. Pope St Gregory's eulogy of his aunts accorded them an honoured place in a remarkable family history.

See *P.L.*, 77, 348, for the *Dialogues of St Gregory the Great*, 4, 16; and a homily printed in *P.L.*, 76, 1291. Cf. F. H. Dudden, *St Gregory the Great*, 1 (1905), pp. 10-11. For the family background see J. Richards, *The Popes and the Papacy in the Early Middle Ages* (1979), pp. 59-60 and 235-8.

St Mochua, *Abbot* (657)

The tradition is that Mochua's home was in the Achonry district of Connacht and that his father's name was Lonan. His vocation came late, as he was a warrior before he became a monk. His principal foundation was at Timahoe (Co. Laois), on the road from Port Laoise to Castleconer, and the derivation of Timahoe may be from *Tech Mochua*, Mochua's house. He died at another of his monasteries at Derinish, Co. Cavan. One story is that he was killed by a band of marauders and that their leader, the O'More, was subsequently killed in revenge.

Some monasteries in Scotland also claimed Mochua as their founder. There are said to be more than fifty Celtic saints named Mochua, and a number of them seem to have preached and founded monasteries in both countries.

Irish Saints, pp. 248-9; *O.D.S.*, pp. 341-2; Plummer, *V.S.H.*, 2, pp. 184-9; but see the editor's comments on the reliability of the *vita* in 1, pp. lxxix-lxxxi.

SS Dagobert II (679), Irmina (*c.* 710), and Adela, *Abbess* (*c.* 724)

Dagobert succeeded to the throne of Austrasia, in northern Gaul, in 656, when still a minor, but he was exiled by his guardian Grimoald, who gave the throne to his own son, Childebert. Dido, bishop of Poitiers, took Dagobert to Ireland and placed him under the care of St Wilfrid, archbishop of York (12 Oct.). Grimoald spread the rumour that Dagobert was dead and actually held a magnificent funeral for him.

Dagobert lived *incognito* during his exile. He was well educated, and Wilfrid arranged his marriage to a Saxon princess, by whom he had a son, Sigebert, and four daughters. In 675 or 676 he was restored to his kingdom with Wilfrid's help. Wilfrid provided him with arms and sent him back in considerable state with a suitable escort.

According to Eddi's Life of Wilfrid, St Theodore of Canterbury (19 Sept.) divided Wilfrid's diocese without his consent. Wilfrid journeyed to Rome to appeal to the pope and was "most graciously received" by Dagobert when he visited his court. Dagobert wanted Wilfrid to stay and to become bishop of Strasbourg. When Wilfrid refused, Dagobert "sent him on his way with lavish presents."

His reign was not to last long. He had been exiled because of the intrigues of one mayor of the royal palace, Grimoald. Another, Ebroïn, fostered a revolt against him within four years of his return to the kingdom. Dagobert was preparing to lead his troops into battle on the borders of Lorraine and Champagne when he was killed in the forest of Woëuvre. It was said that he met with a hunting accident, but the local tradition is that he was ambushed. St Audoenus, archbishop of Rouen (24 Aug.), had his body conveyed to the nearby monastery of Stenay, of which Dagobert was patron, and the monks of Stenay arranged his burial and venerated his relics.

A cult grew up in consequence, and Dagobert was mentioned as king and martyr in the martyrology of the cathedral of Verdun. In 872 Archbishop Hincmar of Rheims had the remains encased in a silver reliquary ornamented with gold fleurs de lis, but this disappeared during the Huguenot riots of 1591.

Dagobert II has sometimes been confused by hagiographers with his grandfather Dagobert I. The latter made magnificent endowments to the abbey of Saint Denis in Paris, but his life was in some respects less edifying than that of his grandson.

According to tradition, Dagobert's daughter, Princess Irmina, was to have been married to a Count Herman, but a rival suitor killed Herman and then committed suicide. After these tragic events Irmina became a nun. Dagobert founded or restored a convent for her near Trier. Irmina was a strong supporter of the missionary work of St Willibrord (7 Nov.) and in 698 gave him the manor on which he founded his monastery of Echternach.

Adela, another daughter, became a nun after the death of her husband, Alberic. She is probably the widow Adula who about 691-2 was living at Nivelles with her young son, who was later to become the father of St Gregory of Utrecht (25 Aug.). She founded a monastery near Palatiolum, now Pfalzel, near Trier, became its first abbess, and governed it for many years. Adela seems to have been among the disciples of St. Boniface (5 June): a letter in his correspondence from Abbess Aelfled of Whitby to an Abbess Adola is addressed to her.

The tenth-century Life of Dagobert, best edited by B. Krusch in *M.G.H., Scriptores Merov.*, 2, pp. 511-24, is of little value, but see Krusch's supplement in vol. 7, pp. 474 and 494. See also *Eddi's Life of St Wilfrid of York*, trans. J. F. Webb (1965, rp. 1981), ch 28; Bede, *H.E.*, 2, 20; P.B., pp. 424-9, based on the *Histoire des saints d'Alsace* and the *Histoire de Verdun et du pays Verdunois*; *D.H.G.E.*, 14, 14-15; *N.C.E.*, 4, p. 611.

The Latin Life of St Irmina, ed. Weiland in *M.G.H., Scriptores*, 23, pp. 48-50, comes from the monk Thiofrid. It was written nearly four hundred years after her death and is of dubious provenance: see *Anal.Boll.* 8 (1889), pp. 285-6. See also P.B., pp. 439-42 and 444, from the *Histoire des saints d'Alsace*; Quentin, p. 237. On Adela see *D.H.G.E.*, 1, 525-6.

Bd Bartholomew dal Monte, *Founder* (1726-78)

Bartholomew (Bartolomeo) was born in Bologna on 3 November 1726. His father, Orazio, had been left a business as a reward for his virtuous way of life and quickly built this up into one of the wealthiest banks in Bologna. His mother, Anna Maria Basseni, had lost three children in infancy before giving birth to Bartholomew at the age of forty-three. He was confirmed at the age of seven by Cardinal Prosper Lambertini, the future Pope Benedict XIV (1740-58), and in his adolescence he was educated by the Jesuits.

His father tried to settle him gently into the banking world by giving him routine tasks, but a friend introduced him to a devout parish priest, Alessandro Zani, who had founded a Congregation to care for the young poor and sick, and he became a major spiritual influence on Bartholomew. Early writings setting out an agenda for daily life show a young man somewhat obssessed with self-control, devoting long hours to prayer, with a spirituality focussed on the Eucharist and the Blessed Virgin—more like a religious already than a wealthy young layman. In 1743 he went to hear a mission preached by the "reformed" Franciscan Leonard of Port Maurice (26 Nov.), from which he came away convinced that he should be a priest and missioner himself. He was ordained on 20 December 1749, at the age of twenty-three and went on to study for a doctorate in theology, which he achieved in one year. He was to remain an assiduous student for the rest of his life, leaving a library of over two thousand volumes ranging from the Fathers through the medieval Schoolmen to modern preachers such as Bossuet.

His father died in 1752. He inherited a considerable sum of money, but he freed himself from any involvement in the affairs of the bank. He bought a house, which was to become the headquarters of his Institute, the *Pia Opera delle Missioni*. He started preaching missions in parishes in Bologna, at the same time travelling to Milan, Rome, and elsewhere to hear the finest preachers of the time, making assiduous notes to help himself with both style and subject-matter. Over the next decade his activity spread beyond the diocese of Bologna, and his reputation grew. He preached in the great cities, including Rome in 1758, and in rural areas, where, as in other European countries, a nominally Christian population in fact had very little idea of the meaning of the faith it outwardly practised. In 1763 he made his profession as a Franciscan in Assisi, confirming the inspiration provided by Leonard of Port Maurice.

In 1768 he went to Vienna to preach to the large Italian community settled in the capital of the Hapsburg Empire, at the invitation of Cardinal Migazzi, who had heard of his reputation in Rome. It was not to be a happy or succesful experience, as after a horrendous journey across the Alps in winter he slipped in an icy street and broke several bones in his left foot. He was unable to preach the Lent course, and it was three months before he was able to return to Bologna. From Pentecost onward he was again active preaching missions and giving courses of spiritual exercises to the clergy in several dioceses.

The years 1769 to 1774 saw his activities extend still further. Besides his preaching he was invited by bishops, cardinals, and the pope, Clement XIV (1769-74), to resolve cases of clerical abuse as well as ecclesiastical and even civil disputes. His mission extended into Lombardy in 1771, and in 1774 he was called to Rome to preach in preparation for the Jubilee Year of 1775. There he preached sermons lasting over an hour several times a day, often having to draw to a premature close because of the clamour from his audience to make general Confessions. In Rome he applied to join the overseas missions and go to the Indies, but he was politely told by *Propaganda Fide* that at nearing fifty he was too old and that his activities in Italy made him too valuable to be spared. These were to last for a further four years.

He was an outstanding exponent of the technique of popular missionizing developed by the Jesuits and other newer Orders, designed to implement the evangelizing decrees of the Council of Trent and thereby rouse the mainly rural population from religious apathy and ignorance. The *Novissimi*, the Four Last Things—death, judgment, hell, and heaven—featured prominently, followed by catechesis for children and adults and leading up to a general Confession and Communion. Missions were prepared well in advance; their days were divided into preaching, catechesis for children and adults, and processions. They used theatrical aids to various degrees, largely to terrify audiences with images of the death of sinners and its consequences, and had the threefold objective of convincing minds, stimulating wills, and moving hearts to conversion. They enjoyed mass support and achieved considerable long-term success.

Bartholomew was greatly affected by the suppression of the Jesuits in various countries in 1769: he had been educated by them; he used the Spiritual Exercises in his courses for clergy; and he had many close Jesuit friends. Bologna offered hospitality to many ex-Jesuits, notably from Spain and Mexico. The latter brought the cult of the Virgin of Guadalupe (12 Dec.) with them, and Bartholomew, already gravely ill, agreed to preach to them on her feast-day in 1778. Twelve days later he was dead. He was buried in the church of San Michele in Bologna, behind closed doors, as crowds would have torn his body to pieces in quest of relics, on 28 December. During Napoleon's occupation of Italy many churches, including San Michele, were de-consecrated, and his relics were secretly translated to the basilica of San Petronio on 23 August 1808. He was beatified by Pope John Paul II in Bologna on 27 September 1997. His activities and achievements offer an Italian parallel to those of his near-contemporary St John-Francis Régis (31 Dec.) in France.

Bartholomew left a number of writings setting out his principles for missions and practical guidelines for their proper conduct, his main message being "Jesus as the heart of the priest." He also made a practical contribution to the mission movement in the shape of his foundation: the *Pia Opera delle Missioni*. Membership of this Institute was limited to the diocesan clergy of Bologna, and it was headed by an elected director, whose main task was to plan missions throughout the diocese of Bologna so that each parish received one every five years. The members were then to take the formation they received to other dioceses and States, "above all the most needy."

The above entry is based on the biography produced on the occasion of his beatification: Giandomenico Gordini, *Il Beato Bartolomeo dal Monte: Un predicatore di missioni popolari nel Settecento* (1997).

Bd Paula Cerioli, *Foundress* (1816-65)

Costanza Cerioli was born at Soncino, near Bergamo, the last of the sixteen children of Don Francis Cerioli and his wife, Countess Frances Corniani. She was educated by the Visitation nuns. At the age of nineteen she passively agreed to a marriage arranged for her by her parents to a wealthy widower of sixty, Gaetano Buzecchi-Tassis. This was in accordance with custom at the time, but her biographer, Fr Federici, describes how difficult the match was for her. The marriage lasted for nineteen years but it was not a happy one. Costanza endured a painful situation with resignation. Though she had three children by her elderly husband, two died in infancy. The third, Charles, died at the age of sixteen. His memory was to become an important influence in her life.

When her husband died she was still in her thirties, and she was left with a considerable fortune. Since she no longer had a family of her own, she determined, with the advice of her parish priest, to devote herself and her resources to the welfare of orphans, the children of peasants from the surrounding countryside, where there was acute poverty. Her advisers and faithful friends were Canon Valsecchi and the bishop of Bergamo, Mgr Speranza. The bishop told her that some people thought she was "cracked," "So I am," she replied, "by the lunacy of the Cross." Other helpers soon joined her, including Louisa Corti, who was later to write of the project at length in her memoirs.

In 1857 Costanza made her religious vows, taking the names Paula Elisabeth. Her foundation was shortly officially recognized as the Institute of the Holy Family at Bergamo. The work increased and developed, and five years later a Brothers' branch of the Congregation was formed for boys at Villa Campagna, near Soncino. This was entrusted to John Capponi, a hospital official from Leffe. Sister Paula saw her task as preparing children and young people specifically for rural life, and the agricultural training given to the boys was copied in other parts of Italy.

Paula had always been delicate, with a slight spinal deformity, and she suffered increasingly from heart trouble. Three years after the foundation at Villa Campagna she died in her sleep on Christmas Eve. She was beatified by Pope Pius XII in 1950.

189

In addition to the documents of the beatification process there are the memoirs of Mother Corti and Paula Cerioli's own writings. A biography by Mgr. P. Merati was published in 1899. These were all fully used by E. Federici in his official Life, *Suor Paola Elisabetta Cerioli* (1948). See also *N.C.E.*, 3, p. 407.

St Sharbel Makhlouf (1828-98)

Joseph Makhlouf was born in the remote village of Beqaa-Kafra, in the highest part of the Lebanon, near the great cedars. His family was poor, and his father died in his early childhood, so he and his younger brothers and sisters were brought up by his mother and an uncle. It was a devout, almost monastic atmosphere. Joseph became a shepherd but was taught to read and write, served Mass, and sang in the choir of the village church. As a boy, while tending his sheep, he found a cave where he could spend hours in prayer and meditation. He often visited the hermitage of Kozhaya, where two of his other uncles were monks, and learned about their way of life. In 1851, when he was twenty-three, he made a long and difficult journey over the mountains to the monastery of Our Lady of Maifouk and entered the novitiate there, taking the name Sharbel from a Syrian martyr of the second century. He was sent to the great monastery of St Maro at Annaya, where he took solemn vows in 1853, then to the neighbouring monastery of St Cyprian of Kñfan, where he studied theology and philosophy. He was ordained priest in 1859 and returned to Annaya, where he lived for fifteen years in all. The régime was a very austere one, combining long hours of prayer, silence, fasting, and mortification with hard physical work, but Sharbel was content, delighting in singing the office, working in the fields, and meditating on the mystery of the Mass.

While many Maronite monks engaged in pastoral and parochial work, the Order also made provision for those called to solitude; and in 1866 Sharbel, who had been drawn to what he had read of the lives of the early Desert Fathers, resolved to follow their way of life. He moved to a small hermitage called St Peter and St Paul's, which was owned by the monastery and consisted of four tiny stone cells and a chapel. Food was brought to him once a day from the monastery. Here he lived for over twenty-three years, devoting himself entirely to preparing for, celebrating, and giving thanks for his daily Mass. He would rise while it was still dark and spend hours in preparation, praying in Aramaic, the language Jesus spoke. He would celebrate the Mass at about eleven o'clock in the morning with great reverence and recollection, and then spend most of the afternoon and evening kneeling before the holy tabernacle in adoration and contemplation.

He slept on a mattress stuffed with leaves on the floor, with a block of wood wrapped in an old habit for a pillow. He had no means of heating, even in the bitter winter. In this life of prayer and penance he experienced the temptations of the hermits of the early Christian period, and many people came to him for spiritual advice and healing.

In 1898 he suffered a stroke while celebrating Mass in the Maronite rite, just before the prayer of consecration. Fr Makarios, who was serving for him, took the chalice from his hand and set it down, then led him back to his cell. The prayer Sharbel was unable to finish runs: "Father of truth, behold your son who makes atoning sacrifice to you. Accept the offering: he died for me that I might have life. Behold the offering! Accept it. . . ." He repeated this prayer before he died eight days later, on the night of Christmas Eve.

He was buried in the nearby cemetery, and many pilgrims have visited his shrine: in 1950, they were said to average fifteen thousand a day. There have been many reports of miracles and conversions. He was beatified at the Second Vatican Council on 5 December 1965, and was canonized by Pope Paul VI in 1977.

P. Daher, *Vie, survie et prodiges de l'ermite Charbel Maklouf* (1953); other Lives by J. Eid (1955), M. Hayek (1962), and S. Garafolo (1965). See also D. Attwater, *Saints of the East* (1963), pp. 184-6; *Bibl.SS.*, 8, 568-9; Catholic Truth Society Pamphlet, no date. Website of St Jovite Monastery, Quebec: http://magnificat.qc.ca/english/index.html.

ST PETER NOLASCO (p. 197, below)
The bell refers to his call to those in need, i.e., Christian captives.
Gold bell with silver rays on black field

25

St Anastasia, *Martyr* (? 304)

The legend of Anastasia is that she was the daughter of a noble Roman named Praetextatus and had St Chrysogonus (24 Nov.) for her spiritual adviser. She married a pagan, Publius, and cared for the Christians in prison during the persecution of Diocletian. Her husband forbade her to leave the house, but when he died on a mission to Persia she went to Aquileia to help the Christians there. After the martyrdom of SS Agape, Chionia, and Irene (1 Apr.) she was arrested and eventually executed.

These and other stories about Anastasia are almost certainly apocryphal. Anastasia's name was included in the Canon of the Mass in the fifth century but, so far as is known, she was not born in Rome and did not live there. Her cult originated at Sirmium in Pannonia, where she was perhaps martyred under Diocletian, but no reliable details of her life and passion have come down to us. When St Gennadius was patriarch of Constantinople, the relics of St Anastasia were transferred from Sirmium to that city, and a considerable cult followed.

The explanation of how her commemoration became associated with Christmas is of liturgical interest. The commemoration of the birth of Christ as a separate feast began at Rome and eventually spread from Rome to the East; but when the pilgrim lady Etheria visited Jerusalem near the end of the fourth century the Nativity was still observed there as part of the Epiphany on 6 January, though the birth of Christ took precedence over his "shewing forth" and the homage of the Magi. Etheria describes how on the vigil the bishop, clergy, monks, and people of Jerusalem went to Bethlehem and made a solemn station at the cave of the Nativity. At midnight a procession was formed, and they returned to Jerusalem and sang the morning office just before dawn. The dawn Mass was originally in honour of St Anastasia of Sirmium. Later in the morning of the Epiphany there was a solemn celebration of the Holy Eucharist, which was begun in the great basilica of Constantine (the *Martyrion*) and consummated in the chapel of the Resurrection (the *Anastasis*).

Fr Delehaye, in his commentary on the *Hieronymianum*, lays stress on the reluctance of the Church of Jerusalem to adopt a separate feast of the birth of our Lord, though a sermon of St John Chrysostom makes it clear that it had been adopted in the Syrian city of Antioch as early as 376. It is plain from one of the sermons of the patriarch Sophronius (11 Mar.) that Jerusalem had conformed to the usage of the rest of Christendom before his death in 638.

In the sixth century the "poliliturgy" of the Jerusalem observances was duplicated or imitated in Rome on Christmas Day. At cockcrow the pope celebrated Mass in the basilica of Santa Maria Maggiore, to which the reputed relics of the wooden crib were brought in the seventh century; then, later in the day, a procession was made to St Peter's, where he sang Mass again. In between these two celebrations came another, which took place in the church of St Anastasia, below the Palatine. This practice, which continued through the medieval period, is specified in the Roman Missal. Duchesne points out that in the late fifth century, about the time when the cult of Anastasia of Sirmium reached Rome, the church was the chapel royal of the Byzantine court officials and the central place of worship for the Greek quarter. It was originally called the *Anastasis* basilica, being, like the one in Constantinople, a copy of the *Anastasis* basilica in Jerusalem. It acquired a dedication to St Anastasia, whose feast occurs on 25 December.

The American archaeologist P. B. Whitehead notes a further possibility: he points out that the church of St Anastasia is one of the twenty-five original *tituli*, or parish churches, of Rome and the only one that is actually in the centre of the city. All these churches had their origins in the chapels of private houses, but St Anastasia is sited in the part of Rome where the imperial palace stood, not in the residential district. The nineteenth-century Italian archeologist G. B. de Rossi discovered an inscription in the church, which recorded that it had been decorated with wall-paintings by Pope Damasus (11 Dec.). Damasus died in 384, which means that the church must have been founded well before his time. The architecture of the church supports this finding: a small part of the building can be dated back to the time of Constantine, who was emperor in Rome from 312 to 324, when he moved the capital to Byzantium. Constantine had a sister named Anastasia, of whom very little is known apart from her name and the fact that she married Bassianus Caesar, to whom Constantine entrusted the rule of Italy.

The church of St Anastasia clearly had a great significance for Christian Rome. The adoption of St Anastasia as titular saint may be purely fortuitous, based only on the similarity of "Anastasia" and *Anastasis*. The dedication may be a Greek import, an older church acquiring a dedication to Anastasia of Sirmium as her cult spread and Byzantine influence in Rome increased. The church may have been within the part of the imperial palace occupied by Constantine's sister and may later have acquired her name; or it may have had another Roman foundress named Anastasia. The possibilities are not necessarily exclusive: more than one of them may apply; but though the church is now relatively obscure and the linguistic and historical traditions are tangled, its history gave Anastasia of Sirmium for centuries the distinction of being commemorated at the second pontifical Mass of Christmas. In the Byzantine rite her feast is kept on 22 December.

H. Delehaye, *Étude sur le legendier romain*, pp. 151-71, deals with some very suspect sources, probably compiled to substantiate the claim to Anastasia as a Roman saint. See also

L. Duchesne, *Christian Worship* (1919), pp. 265, 265a, 421, 490-1, 497-8; and *Mélanges d'archéologie et d'histoire*, 7 (1887), pp. 387-413; J. P. Kirsch, *Die romischen Titelkirchen* (1918), pp. 18-23; P. B. Whitehead, "The Church of St Anastasia in Rome," *Am. J. Arch.*, 2nd series 31 (1927), pp. 405-20.

St Eugenia, *Martyr* (date unknown)

Eugenia, a Roman virgin martyr, was buried in the cemetery of Apronian on the via Latina. A basilica was later built in her honour and restored during the eighth century.

The legend of Eugenia, like that of St Marina or St Reparata, is a popular folk-myth about a woman who disguised herself as a monk and lived undetected in a monastery. This may have happened on a number of occasions in the early days of the monastic system, for there were as yet no separate monastic establishments for women, and monks were careful about personal privacy; but the situation was likely to give rise to local gossip, of which this is a comparatively mild example.

According to the legend, Eugenia was accepted in the monastery as "Eugenius." A woman named Melanthia, believing her to be a man, made advances to her and was "energetically repulsed." In revenge she laid charges of sexual misconduct with the governor of Alexandria, and all the monks in the monastery were condemned to death. When Eugenia revealed that she was a woman, the monastery was spared, and Melanthia was struck by a thunderbolt.

The story seems to have an Oriental origin and is attributed to Eugenia in several different accounts. Delehaye has commented exhaustively on the manuscripts. He shows that the legend is baseless but that there are sufficient grounds for honouring Eugenia as an authentic Roman martyr. An account which may have more substance is that she founded one of the early monasteries for women and led an exemplary religious life until she was martyred in a persecution of Christians in the time of the emperors Valerian and Gallinus (253-60).

H. Delehaye, *Étude sur le légendier romain* (1936), pp. 171-86; *C.M.H.*, p. 501. For the legends see the *Sanctuarius* of Mombritius, printed in Rosweyde, *Vitae Patrum*, and in *P.L.*, 21, 1107-22. Two or three different Greek adaptations are known in manuscript, and that of the Metaphrast is printed in *P.G.*, 116, 609-52. There are also Syriac and Armenian versions: the former translated into English by A. Smith-Lewis in *Studia Sinaitica* 9 and 10, the latter by F. C. Conybeare in *The Armenian Apology of Appolonius* (1912).

Bd Peter the Venerable, *Abbot* (1092-1156)

Pierre de Montboissier was born in the Auvergne. His date of birth is variously given as 1092 or 1102. The earlier date seems more likely, as he had already served as prior of Domène when he was elected abbot of the great monastic house of Cluny in 1122. Cluny was the motherhouse for many other monasteries. His predecessor, Pontius, had managed the affairs of the abbey incompetently, but during the thirty-four years that Peter governed Cluny it rose to a level of prosperity and influence that it was never to reach again.

The early days were not auspicious. Pontius literally made war on Peter, driving out the monks who were loyal to him and conducting the affairs of the monastery in an unseemly way. Eventually he was summoned to appear before the pope and removed from office. Peter still faced controversy from the rigorist St Bernard of Clairvaux (20 Aug.), who repeatedly alleged that the rule at Cluny was lax. Eventually Peter, like abbot Suger of Paris, had to tighten the rule to meet Cistercian criticisms.

Peter was a scholar with wide academic sympathies and interests. He encouraged his monks to study, secured manuscripts for them, and built up at Cluny a theological library remarkable for the time, consisting of some five hundred volumes of the works of the early Fathers and about a hundred other great works. Since he had been brought up in the south of France he was very conscious of the threat posed to Christianity by the Moors, and he made several long visits to Spain for discussion with abbots and bishops. One of his major projects was the translation of the Koran into Latin in the school of interpreters in Toledo. He set up a team under Peter of Toledo consisting of two scholars, of whom one was an Englishman named Robert Kennet, his own secretary, and the other an Arab named Mahomet. The work was finished in 1143, and despite some errors it formed the basis for translations of the Koran into European languages until the middle of the seventeenth century.

When the translation was completed, Peter wrote his own treatise *Adversus nefandem sectam Sarracenorum*, in which he described Islam as a Christian heresy denying the divinity of Christ and the uniqueness of his earthly mission. The two great founders of religion, he argued, were Moses and Jesus, and Mohammed's personal failings and his career of bloodshed made him unworthy to be called a prophet. When we remember that he was writing in the aftermath of the First Crusade (1096-9) it is remarkable that he wished to have an intellectual understanding of the people who were then seen as the greatest enemies of Christendom.

He made two visits to England, and an attempt was made to bring the abbey of Peterborough under Cluniac rule, but this did not succeed. During King Stephen's disputed reign (1135-54) Peter was in touch with Henry of Blois, Stephen's brother and bishop of Winchester, who was a monk of Cluny. When Stephen died and his rival, Matilda's son, became king of England as Henry II, Bishop Henry went back to Cluny. He gave his great wealth to the abbey and after a lifetime of political scheming and warfare, earned something of a reputation for piety under Peter's direction.

Abbot Peter is probably best known for his championship of Peter Abelard. When Abelard's theological writings were doubly condemned, at Sens and in Rome, he obtained a mitigation of the sentence from Pope Innocent II, offered Abelard shelter at Cluny, and helped to bring about a meeting of reconciliation with Bernard of Clairvaux. After Abelard's death two years later he sent his body to the nuns of the Paraclete, where Héloïse was then abbess, with his assurances that Abelard had lived a holy life at Cluny. He had died absolved from his sins and in communion with the Church. This was a generous and risky gesture in view of the earlier scandal and the theological controversy that had surrounded Abelard's teaching. He subsequently wrote to Héloïse expressing his respect for her learning, offering spiritual counsel, and promising to help the career of her son Peter Astrolabe. He also wrote an epitaph comparing Abelard's philosophy with that of Socrates, Plato, and Aristotle.

His outstanding intellectual generosity extended to many unorthodox groups. At times Peter defended Jews and heretics against persecution, though his own theology was always orthodox. He was constantly involved in theological controversy and made six visits to Rome in all, despite frequent ill health and the difficulty of crossing the Alps. He had a great reputation among his contemporaries as a scholar and theologian. He wrote treatises, sermons, and hymns and kept up a large correspondence with those who consulted him—though he was apt to let letters from Bernard of Clairvaux pile up at Cluny while he wrote quietly in some remote hermitage. The hymn *Caelum gaude, terra plaude* is his.

The emperor Frederick Barbarossa named him "the Venerable." Peter was revered as a saint by the faithful at large as well as by his own Congregation. His cult has never been formally approved by the Holy See, but his name occurs in French martyrologies.

P.L., 189, 15-42, contains a medieval Life written by the monk Rodulf, Abbot Peter's constant companion, a collection of extracts from the chronicle of Cluny, and some other materials, including Peter's own writings: songs, poems, and letters. See also P. Séjourné in *D.T.C.,* 2 (1935), 2065-82; J. Leclercq, *Pierre le Vénérable* (1946); David Knowles, *The Controversy between St Bernard and Peter the Venerable* (1935); *The Letters of Abelard and Héloïse,* trans. and intro. B. Radice (1974), with an appendix containing letters from Abbot Peter, pp. 275-88; *The Letters of St Bernard of Clairvaux,* trans. and intro. Bruno Scott James (1953, rp. 1998), especially 305-9, 398, and 400; J. Kritzeck, *Peter the Venerable and Islam* (1964).

Bd Bentivoglio de Bonis (1232)

Bentivoglio, or Bentivoglia, a native of San Severino (now San Severino Marche, north-east of Assisi), joined the Franciscan Order during the life of St Francis, and a number of his near relatives followed his example. We are told of his great charity, his zeal, and the inspiring nature of his sermons. The parish priest of San Severino is said in the *Fioretti* to have been brought to order by witnessing Bentivoglio in ecstasy while praying in a wood. The same source describes how he was ordered by his superior to move to a place some fifteen miles distant but was unwilling to abandon a leper for whom he was caring: he carried the leper on his back all the way with great fervour and charity. According to legend, "if he had been an eagle, he could not have flown in so short a time, and this divine miracle put the whole country round in amazement and admiration."

He died where he was born, at San Severino, on Christmas Day 1232.

Mazzara, 2, pp. 276-7; Wadding, 2, pp. 326-8; *Auréole Séraphique*, 2, pp. 31-3; *F.B.S.*, pp. 906-8; *Bibl.SS.*, 2, 1250.

St Peter Nolasco, *Founder* (1256 or 1258)

Little is known for certain about Peter Nolasco's life. Though there is considerable documentation, much of it consists of seventeenth-century documents written to promote the cause of his canonization. These represent Peter as having been born in the Languedoc, possibly at Saint-Papoul or Masdes-des-Saints-Puelles, of a noble family. His father died when he was fifteen, and he was guided up by a pious mother who encouraged him in his determination to devote his life to God's service. According to some authors, he was present during Simon de Montfort's campaign against the Albigensians. When the king of Aragon was killed in battle his son James was taken prisoner, and Simon de Montfort appointed Peter Nolasco to be his tutor, sending them both into Spain.

At that time the Moors ruled most of Spain, and many Christians were held prisoner both there and in North Africa. Peter is said to have spent most of his estate in redeeming prisoners and then to have developed the idea of a religious Order to undertake this work. There were many difficulties, and there is a story of a miraculous vision of Our Lady who appeared to Peter, to the king of Aragon, and to Raymund of Peñafort (7 Jan.) telling them to undertake the project under her special patronage and protection. Raymund was the spiritual director of both the king and of Peter Nolasco. At that time he was archdeacon of Barcelona with a special mission to the poor. The king declared himself the protector of the new Order, and on 10 August 1223 the king and Raymund conducted Peter to the church and presented him to Berengarius, bishop of Barcelona, who received his three religious vows, and a fourth: to devote his whole substance and his personal liberty if necessary to the work of ransoming slaves. Peter received his new habit from Raymund, who drew up the Rule and Constitution for the new Order. It was to be a military Order. The friars carried swords, and the Mercedarian habit, unchanged since the early days, still has provision for arms. The superior of the Order has the military title of *comendador*. They were popularly called Mercedarians, *merced* being the Spanish for ransom or reward.

Two other friars were professed at the same time. When Raymund went to Rome in 1235 he obtained from Pope Gregory IX the confirmation of the foundation and its Rule. Peter Nolasco founded other Mercedarian houses in Valencia and Granada. He sent his friars out in pairs to bargain with the Muslim authorities and is said to have ransomed a great number of captives himself, both in the southern coastal regions of Spain and in Algeria, where he was imprisoned for a time. He resigned the offices of ransomer and master general of the Order some years before his death. In his last moments he exhorted his Brothers to perseverance and concluded with the words of the psalmist: "The Lord hath sent redemption to his people; He hath commanded His covenant for ever." Many miracles were attributed to his relics.

These are the outlines of the documentation that was presented in Peter Nolasco's cause before his canonization in 1628 and which formed the basis of an assessment of his life for nearly three centuries. An iron casket full of previously unknown documents had, it seemed, been discovered behind a wall in the Mercedarian house in Barcelona while the cause was actually being pressed in Rome. The chief of these documents, known as the *documento de los sellos* (the deed with the seals) was apparently drafted by a notary named Pedro Bages in 1260 with the express object of being submitted to the Holy See in support of Peter Nolasco's claims to sanctity. Ironically it fell to to a Mercedarian, F. D. Gazulla Galve, the principal champion of the Order's cause, to establish conclusively that Bages died before 4 February 1259, and therefore could not have drafted a document in 1260. When Fray Gazulla read a paper before the Literary Academy of Barcelona, *Al Margen de una Refutación*, in 1921, the whole evidence of the documents in the iron casket was widely dismissed as spurious. It is now accepted by the Order that Peter was born in or near Barcelona, not in the Languedoc. Naming the Languedoc as his birthplace provided an ingenious rationale for his involvement in the campaign against the Albigensians and the relationship with the young king of Aragon. His family was of the merchant class rather than the nobility; and the date of his ceremonial presentation to bishop Berengarius may have been 1218, 1228, or even 1234 rather than 1223. There has been a heated controversy between the Dominicans and the Mercedarians concerning the rival claims of Peter Nolasco and Raymund of Peñafort to be the main founder of the Order— though Raymund was a secular archdeacon at the earliest date suggested for the foundation of the Order: he did not become a Dominican until 1222.

The story of Peter Nolasco is an object lesson in hagiographical assessment. In the first edition of the present work Alban Butler accepted the evidence of the documents without question. In the 1956 edition, the editors were inclined to reject it all out of hand. They write, "When this primary instrument is thus proved to be spurious, what possible value can attach to the rest of the contents of the iron casket? It would serve no good purpose to pursue the matter further." Yet the second reaction is as sweeping as the first. Sixteenth-century evidence on a thirteenth-century saint is not good evidence, and it is clear that the story has suffered from pious accretions—the noble birth, the royal connection, and some of the less probable miracles; but there must have been oral traditions relating to the founder in the Mercedarian house at Barcelona, and these cannot be entirely dismissed, though they require careful assessment.

We do know that Peter Nolasco lived and worked in Barcelona; that a ceremony took place there (in whatever year) in which he was presented to Bishop Berengarius to take his religious vows and commence work on the new Order; that Raymund of Peñafort was there (he preached the sermon); that Peter undertook the difficult and dangerous work of ransoming captives from the Moors and built up the Mercedarian Order, which still exists in Spain and has extended its work in central Africa and Latin America. The basic elements in the story are not disproved by the overenthusiasm of some seventeenth-century friars who wanted to honour their founder, and Fray Gazulla's integrity in presenting the evidence on Pedro Bages, even though it destroyed some elements in his own case, commands respect.

P. N. Peres, O.Merc., *San Pedro Nolasco, fundador de la Orden de la Merced* (1915); F. D. Gazulla Galve, O.Merc., *La Orden de Nuestra Señora de la Merced: Estudios histórico-criticos 1218-1317* (1934); *Anal.Boll.* 39 (1921), pp. 209 ff.; 40 (1922), pp. 442 ff.; 55 (1937), pp. 412-15; *N.C.E.*, 11, p. 225. For the Dominican claims see V. Galindo, O.P., *San Raimondo de Peñafort* (1919).

Bd Jacopone of Todi (*c.* 1230-*c.* 1306)

Jacopone, baptized Jacopo or Jacomo, was born into the Benedetti family at Todi in Umbria. He had a very harsh upbringing: his father beat him savagely and frequently for real or imagined misbehaviour, and the boy often wished that his father would die. He was to carry a load of guilt into his adult life on that account. There are no details of his student life, but he is thought to have read law at the university of Bologna, then the most famous university in Europe after Paris. He gives no details in his writings of his studies. Later he was to dismiss all learning as a waste of time but to lament his wildness as a student: released from parental control, he says, he gambled, indulged in drunken revelling, and became involved in violent brawls and street fights. He seems to have stayed on at university and taken his doctorate, because he was spoken of afterwards as "a very learned man."

When he finally left university, he became very wealthy and lived a life of ostentatious display and selfish gratification. He was quite indifferent to religion until, when he was thirty-seven or thirty-eight, he married Vanna di Guidone, who was young, noble, reputedly beautiful, and very devout. Jacopo wanted to parade his bride in local society: she obeyed his wishes but continued with her devotions in private. About a year after they were married she was tragically killed at a wedding, when a balcony on which she and other guests were standing collapsed. Vanna was the only fatal casualty. When her body was prepared for burial she was found to be wearing a hair shirt under her rich wedding garments as a form of mortification.

Jacopo's life was shattered, and he seemed to lose his reason. He gave up his profession, put on the habit of a Franciscan tertiary and began to practise extreme penances. On one occasion he crawled on his hands and knees across the town's main square wearing a donkey's harness. On another he arrived at a wedding party at his brother's house tarred and feathered all over. A friend told the story of how he asked Jacopo to carry two chickens home from the market. Jacopo took them to the parish church and placed them on the family sepulchre, saying that the grave was the only true home of mankind. For ten years this formerly wealthy and respected citizen was a familiar sight in the streets of Todi. He became a local joke, the crazy man. The children jeered at him and called him familiarly "Jacopone," and the name stuck.

After this long period of intense guilt and wild regret he sought the calm and structure of religious life. St Francis of Assisi (4 Oct.) had founded a house of Minorites in Todi. In 1278 Jacopone applied for admission. At first the Franciscans hesitated, but at length he was admitted and became a Friar Minor. He allied himself with the stricter party in the house, the *Spirituali*, or *Zelanti*, who were drawn not to the gentle tradition of the *Fioretti* but to the more harsh and violent forms of mortification.

Jacopone was one of the friars who in 1294 petitioned the pope (Celestine V; 19 May) for permission to live apart from the Order, but Celestine died in the same year, and Cardinal Gaetani, the opponent of the Spirituals, became pope as Boniface VIII. Jacopone was one of the three Franciscans who drew up a manifesto claiming that Boniface had been invalidly elected. He was said to have written material for the Colonna party, which opposed Boniface, including the savage satire "*O papa Bonifacio molt ay jocato al mondo*," though some modern commentators have argued that "*O papa Bonifacio*" is an interpolation, others that the most bitter passages were added subsequently to Jacopone's work by another hand. Whatever the truth of the matter, Jacopone's opposition to Boniface was sufficiently serious for him to be arrested and thrown into prison for five years. For a time he was even denied the sacraments. Loaded with chains in his evil-smelling dungeon, perhaps he satisfied his instinct for self-mutilation, for he seems to have reached a new maturity, no longer obsessed with guilt and self-accusation but stretching out to the love of God. In some of these later poems he reaches the heights of contemplation. In one he writes of what it means to be "based secure in nothingness":

Made one with Truth in singleness
Now is the heart to kingship brought,
And stilled is every restless thought,
By love in transmutation wrought.

Both at the Franciscan house in Todi, San Fortunato, and in his prison, Jacopone wrote a stream of lyrical poems in the Umbrian dialect. In Umbria, as in other parts of Italy, lay brotherhoods, or *Laudesi*, sang and acted religious songs in the vernacular in the streets and the marketplace, so his work was in a recognized tradition. The poems were very popular, particularly among the *Spirituali*. They were deeply religious and mystical verses, written with fervour and powerful in cadence. Bernardino of Siena (20 May) made long extracts from Jacopone's writings, and some are still preserved in Bernardino's own handwriting with the heading: "Here begin certain canticles or laude of our holy modern David, Fra Jacopone da Todi."

Jacopone is best known as the putative author of the hymn *Stabat Mater dolorosa*. He is also credited with the companion hymn, or as some critics say, the parody, the less well known *Stabat Mater speciosa*, written for Christmas. The *Dolorosa* is said to have been ascribed to him in a fourteenth-century manuscript, and both hymns appear in an edition of his *Laude* printed at Brescia in 1495. However, there are other candidates for the authorship of the *Dolorosa*, notably Pope Innocent III, who wrote the *Veni creator spiritus*. The *Speciosa*, described by one critic as "tame and servile," is not in keeping with either his character or his other writings. There is no proof that Jacopone wrote any Latin poems at all.

On the death of Boniface VIII at the end of 1303 Jacopone was set at liberty, and he went to live first in a hermitage near Orvieto and then at a Poor Clare convent at Collazzone between Todi and Perugia. Here he died on Christmas Day, probably in 1306. He received the Last Rites from his friend John of Alvernia. In 1433 his relics were translated to the church of San Fortunato at Todi, and how he was regarded there can be read on his tomb: "The bones of Blessed Jacopone dei Benedetti of Todi, by Order of the Friars Minor. He became a fool for Christ's sake and, having deceived the whole world by a new artifice, took Heaven by storm."

In 1906, on the 600th anniversary of Jacopone's death, a monument was erected in his memory at Todi.

Wadding, 6, pp. 87-93; *Bibl.SS.*, 7, 618-28. Much has been written about Fra Jacopone. In the *Bollettino Francescano storico-bibliografico*, 2 (1931), pp. 81-118 and 201-23, no less than 994 books and articles in some way concerned with him are enumerated. There is a more recent bibliographical note in George T. Peck, *The Fool of God: a Life of Jacopone da Todi* (1980), pp. 225-33. Apart from what can be gathered from his poems, we learn little of his life except for the sketch in the *Franceschina* of Jacopo Oddi (fifteenth century). A Life by Evelyn Underhill (1919) contains the poems in the original dialect, with translations by Mrs Theodore Beck. George T. Peck finds these translations "prettied-up," and those in F. Ozanam's *The Franciscan Poets*, trans. and intro. A. E. Nellen and N. C. Craig (1914), pp. 186-328, may be closer to the originals. There is a good critical edition of the *Laude, Jacopone da Tod—Laude* (1974), ed. and intro. M. Mancini: Eng. trans., *Jacopone da Todi: The Lauds*, trans. Serge and Elisabeth Hughes (1982). In a review of the centenary literature in *Anal. Boll.* 28 (1909), pp. 231-4, Fr Van Ortroy states that Jacopone's cult was confirmed by the Holy See in 1868 and points out that further evidence has been found that *O Papa Bonifacio* is not his work. Commentaries: N. Sapegno, *Frate Jacopone* (1923); F. Maccarini, *Jacopone da Todi e suori critici* (1952); P. Barbet, *B Jacopone de Todi, l'auteur du Stabat* (1943); G. T. Peck (see above) (1990); Alvaro Cacciotti, "Jacopone da Todi: the Cross," *Studies in Spirituality* 2 (1992), pp. 59-98.

Bd Michael Nakaxima, *Martyr* (1628)

Michael Nakaxima was born at Maciai in Japan. During a period of persecution, when the European missionary priests were in danger of their lives, he sheltered some of them in his own house, and he became a member of the Society of Jesus. After he was arrested he was held a prisoner for nearly a year, tortured at Ximabara, and executed at Mount Ungen. He was beatified in 1867.

BS(R), p. 401. See also references for Simon Yempo (4 Dec.), and the general entry on the Martyrs of Japan, 6 February.

Bd Mary of the Apostles, *Foundress* (1833-1907)

Marie Thérèse, eldest daughter of Baron Joseph von Wullenweber, was born in the castle of Mullendoch at Gladbach in Germany. From an early age she had a strong vocation to the religious life and a desire to renounce the advantages of her aristocratic background.

She took the name Mary of the Apostles to indicate her devotion to the spreading of the gospel, and she became the foundress and superior of the Congregation of Sisters of the Divine Saviour. She wrote: "My principal aim has always been to devote my life to mission, and to give of my best in this service."

She died in Rome on Christmas Day 1907 and was beatified by Pope Paul VI on 13 October 1968.

N.S.B., 1, pp. 105-6.

St Albert Chmielkowski, *Founder* (1845-1916)

Adam Chmielkowski was born on 20 August 1845 at Iglomia, near Cracow. He spent a year in the Russian cadet school at St Petersburg but evidently had no sympathy with the Russian military forces that were occupying his homeland. He returned to Poland to study in Warsaw, and like many patriotic young Poles of his day he took part in the uprising against Tsarist oppression in 1863 (see Bd Honorius Koszminski; 16 Dec.). Adam was wounded, and his left leg was amputated. His parents sent him to safety in Paris, where he studied art and engineering. He became a painter, and he did not return to Poland until after the amnesty of 1874. His experiences as an émigré had given him a great sympathy with the dispossessed, and his studio became a refuge for homeless and poor people. He became a Jesuit in 1880 but had to leave the Order because of bad health. When he recovered he took up painting again, and he became a member of the Third Order Secular of St Francis in 1888. Following the example of St Francis he renounced all his possessions and went to live and work among the homeless, taking the name Albert in religion.

Other men, moved by the misery of tramps and social outcasts, joined him, and he founded the Brothers of the Third Order of St Francis, Servants of the Poor. Under his guidance a group of women, led by Bernardyna Jablonska, began work for homeless women, and they became the Albertine Sisters.

In all, Brother Albert set up twenty-one refuges in different parts of Poland, helping anyone in need regardless of nationality, age, or religion. He lived as the poor lived, and he died on Christmas Day 1916 in a pauper institution in Cracow. The Albertine communities have continued his work in Poland and also in Italy, the United States, and Latin America. He was beatified by Pope John Paul II during a visit to Cracow on 22 June 1983 and canonized in Rome in the context of a Papal Mass attended by many pilgrims from eastern Europe, on 12 November 1989.

Lives in Polish by Cz. Lewandowski (1926); A. Florczak (1935); K. Michalski (1946); and in French, M. Winowska, *Frère Albert, ou la face aux outrages* (1953); also *Bibl.SS.*, 3, 1244-5; *Osservatore Romano*, 13 Nov. 1989; *D.N.H.*, 2, 145-9; 3, 325-6.

ST STEPHEN (over page)
Silver stones, for the manner of his death;
gold palm, for his spiritual victory, on red field

26

ST STEPHEN, *Martyr* (*c.* 34)

All that is known of Stephen, the first deacon and the first martyr, comes from the New Testament. He was a Jew and probably one of the Hellenists of the Dispersion. His name, Stephanos, is Greek, meaning a crown or a king. The Hellenists were Jews from outside Palestine. They had their own synagogues in Jerusalem, where the scriptures were read in Greek. The Hebrews, including the twelve apostles, were Palestinian Jews, and in their synagogues the scriptures were read in Hebrew. Stephen appears first in the sixth chapter of the Acts of the Apostles. There were many converts, and difficulties arose between the Hebrews and the incomers: the Hellenists complained that their widows (which probably means the poor and needy in general) were being neglected in the daily distribution of food. The apostles called a full meeting of the disciples and said that it was not right for them to neglect the word of God in order to give out food, so they proposed to appoint deacons for this purpose, "seven men of good reputation, filled with the Spirit and with wisdom." Stephen is mentioned first among the seven and described as "a man full of faith and the Holy Spirit." The apostles prayed and laid hands on them.

According to the record in the Acts of the Apostles the seven seem to have carried out duties similar to those of the apostles, preaching and baptizing, and it is unlikely that the task of distributing food was left wholly to the Hellenists. After the difficulties that had arisen, this task would probably have been best served by a group in which both Greeks and Hebrews were represented. The seven seem to have fulfilled a different purpose: to have been, or to have developed into, a hierarchy for the Hellenist community, parallel to the twelve apostles for the Hebrews.

Stephen "was filled with grace and power, and began to work miracles and great signs among the people," but he spoke with such force that he roused the opposition of the elders of certain synagogues. When they could not get the better of him by argument they accused him of blasphemy. Stephen was indicted before the Sanhedrin and summarily arrested. The main charges against him were that he had said that the Temple would be destroyed and that the Mosaic Law had been set aside by Jesus of Nazareth. Stephen was given leave to speak, and he made an eloquent and learned defence, set out in Acts 7:2-53. He showed that Abraham, the father and founder of their nation, had been guided to settle in a strange land; that Moses was commanded to set up a tabernacle but foretold that there would be a new law and that the Messiah would come to Israel; that Solomon built the Temple, but God was not to be confined in houses made by human hands.

His speech expresses the polemic against the Temple that was to become a feature of some early Christian groups. The Temple, a huge complex of buildings, was the commercial and religious centre of the whole of Judaism. He ended by calling the people "murderers" for what they had done to the Messiah when he came:

> You stubborn people, with your pagan hearts and pagan ears. You are always resisting the Holy Spirit, just as your ancestors used to do. Can you name a single prophet your ancestors never persecuted? In the past they killed those who foretold the coming of the Just One, and now you have become his betrayers, his murderers. You who had the Law brought to you by angels are the very ones who have not kept it.

His hearers were infuriated when they heard him, and we are told that they ground their teeth at him. Stephen, being filled with the Holy Spirit, gazed into heaven and said: "Behold, I see heaven thrown open, and the Son of Man standing at the right hand of God." The members of the council shouted out and stopped their ears with their hands. He was dragged outside the city walls and stoned. Stephen called on the name of the Lord Jesus and fell to his knees, asking God to forgive his attackers. "And when he had said this, he fell asleep in the Lord."

It seems that this was a judicial execution, not an act of mob violence, because there were witnesses: we are told that they took off their outer garments and left a young man named Saul to look after them. Normally the Jews had no right to execute prisoners without the approval of the Roman authorities, but the events may have occurred during the interregnum between governors after the end of Pontius Pilate's tour of duty in the year 36 (see the Conversion of St Paul; 25 Jan.). Afterwards, devout people buried Stephen and mourned his death.

There was a great persecution of the Christians, and many fled from Jerusalem. Probably most of them were Hellenists: the apostles certainly stayed in Jerusalem and were unharmed. The young man Saul, who had "entirely approved of the killing," worked for the total destruction of the Church until the day when his intellect and emotions revolted and he met Christ on the road to Damascus. The work of the first martyr was fulfilled in the work of St Paul, the great apostle to the Gentiles.

According to Duchesne, St Stephen's festival goes back "considerably earlier than that of the discovery of his tomb, which took place in 415." St Stephen is the patron of many churches, including several French cathedrals, such as Bourges, Sens, and Toulouse. In England, forty-six ancient churches are dedicated to him, most of them built after the Norman Conquest.

C.M.H., pp. 10-1; L. Duchesne, *Christian Worship*, pp. 265-8; M. Simon, *St Stephen and the Hellenes in the Primitive Church* (1958); M. H. Scharleman, *Stephen: a Singular Saint*

(1968); F. M. Abel, "Étienne (saint)," *Dictionnaire biblique*, suppl. 2 (1934), 1132-46; *Bibl.SS.*, 11, 1376-92.

In art his usual attributes are a book of the Gospels with a stone and perhaps a palm, and he is usually shown wearing a dalmatic to show that he was a deacon. Among many other representations there is a fine cycle of paintings by Fra Angelico in the chapel of Nicholas V in the Vatican (1447), a painting by Fra Filippino Lippi in the Duomo at Prato (1460-4), and a splendid mosaic at Monreale in Sicily. His stoning is shown in a painting by Giulio Romano in the church of S. Stefano in Genoa (1523) and in one of the tapestries designed by the school of Raphael for the Sistine Chapel (*c.* 1515).

St Dionysius, *Pope* (268 or 269)

Because of persecution, the Roman See was vacant for nearly a year after the martyrdom of St Sixtus II (7 Aug.) in 258. Dionysius (Denys) was a Roman priest, probably of Greek descent, described by his namesake of Alexandria as an admirable and learned man. Some months after the beginning of his pontificate the emperor Gallienus promulgated an edict ensuring toleration for Christians. This brought persecution to an end for the time being and gave the Church a legal existence, freeing churches, property, and cemeteries for ecclesiastical administration. Dionysius became responsible for re-establishing and consolidating the work of the Church after a period of great hardship and suffering.

He also had to deal with a pre-Arian controversy in Libya and Egypt, where several bishops denied the distinction between the three Persons of the Trinity. Dionysius of Alexandria (17 Nov. in this edition; 8 Apr. in future), attempting to correct them, was accused of ignoring the unity of substance of the three Persons and was denounced to Rome. Pope Dionysius summoned a council in Rome and issued an encyclical to the Egyptian Churches stating that the Word (the Son) was not a created being but co-existent with the Father. Dionysius of Alexandria replied in a letter, backed up by a lengthy treatise, that he accepted the decisions of the council, and the affair seems to have ended there.

The same sort of trouble broke out when Paul of Samosata, bishop of Antioch, instructing the Jewish queen of Palmira, Zenobia, in the mystery of the Incarnation, proposed two persons in Christ—one pre-existent as Son of God, the other born in time as son of David. The Eastern bishops held a total of three synods at Antioch condemning Paul, who refused to submit, and Pope Dionysius supported them in several letters. Paul died unrepentant in 258.

A century later, St Basil the Great (2 Jan.) wrote of Dionysius' generosity in supporting the Church in Cappadocia, where persecution still raged after an invasion by the Goths. Dionysius had sent a large sum of money for ransoming Christians in captivity.

The *Liber Pontificalis* describes Dionysius as a martyr, but he is thought to have died peacefully. Though not the first pope to die naturally, he is the first to whom the title of martyr is not accorded liturgically.

Jaffé, 1, p. 22; *Lib.Pont.*, 1, p. 157; scattered references in Eusebius, *H.E.* 7, 7 and 7, 30; and in St Athanasius and St Basil the Great, etc. E. Caspar, *Geschichte des Papsttums*, 1 (1930), pp. 92 ff.; Leclercq in *D.A.C.L.*, 13, 1186-8; *O.D.P.*, pp. 22-3.

St Zosimus, *Pope* (418)

Zosimus is said by the *Liber Pontificalis* to have been a Greek by birth. He was possibly of Jewish descent, since he was the son of a presbyter named Abram. He succeeded Pope Innocent I in 417, and nothing is known of his previous life or career. During the brief two years of his pontificate he made two major decisions that have led to criticism from commentators.

The first concerned the problems of Pelagianism. Innocent I had condemned the Pelagians, who denied the doctrine of original sin, as heretical, on the representation of the North African bishops. Pelagius and his supporter Caelestius appealed to Zosimus. Pelagius wrote a skillful letter defending his own new treatise on free will, and Caelestius had a personal audience with the pope. Zosimus, impressed by their earnest entreaties, and perhaps by their appeal to his own authority, reversed his predecessor's judgment, informing the African bishops that they had been too hasty and had listened to prejudiced accounts. Much alarmed, they told him bluntly that Innocent's condemnation must stand. Zosimus hesitated for six months. The bishops met in November 417 and approached the emperor Honorius, who agreed to banish Pelagius and Caelestius. Zosimus bowed to the emperor's decision, and Pelagianism was again pronounced a heresy.

Zosimus had further difficult relations with the North African bishops arising out of an irregular appeal made to Rome by a priest, Apiarius of Sica. Apiarius had been condemned by the bishops of his own jurisdiction for leading an immoral life. North African canon law forbade appeals to Rome, but the pope heard the appeal and acquitted Apiarius. Again the African bishops protested and insisted that their own decision must stand, but the matter dragged on and was not settled by the time Zosimus died.

Zosimus has been criticized for heavy-handed and tactless handling of the Church in North Africa and for following divisive policies; but these were the decisions of a pope new in office and with not long to live. In his last few months he is known to have had several cataleptic seizures of such severity that he was repeatedly assumed to be dead.

The *Liber Pontificalis* does suggest a more positive side to his pontificate. He promulgated several decrees on matters of liturgy and clerical discipline, including the wearing of the maniple by deacons and the dedication of Easter candles in country parishes.

Jaffé, 1, pp. 49-51; *Lib.Pont.*, 1, p. 157; *P.L.*, 20, 659-85; *O.D.P.*, pp. 38-9; *D.Cath.Biog.*, p. 1222; *D.A.C.L.*, 13, 1263.

St Tathai (Fifth-Sixth Century)

Tathai (Tathan, Tathar, Tatheus) was said to be "sprung from a royal line" of the kings of Ireland. According to the twelfth-century Life he "crossed over to Britannia," that is, to Wales, with eight disciples and went to Caerwent (Gwent), where he taught and set up a monastery "by angelic exhortation and by donation of the most noble King Caradoc, son of Yrnyr."

There he raised a church and appointed twelve canons with the advice and consent of the bishop of Llandaff. Later he is thought to have founded the monastery of Llandathan (St Athan). He became famous in the neighbourhood as a holy man and was called "the Father of all Gwent":

> He was the defender of the woodland country . . . whatever was given to him, he gave to others. . . . The hungry, beset with famine, and the thirsty with parching thirst, this man satisfied from his abundance. Expelling cold from the sides of the naked, he brought consolation to those punished in prison. To the sick and to widows, he gave succour, seeking eternal things, not transitory.

The Life says that he died at Caerwent and was buried in the floor of his church, though Llandath also claimed to be the site of his burial.

Stanton, p. 608; *N.L.A.*, 2, pp. 361-3; *S.B.I.*, p. 153; A. W. Wade-Evans, *Vitae Sanctorum Britanniae et Genealogiae* (1944), pp. 270-87; J. Daryll-Evans, *Patron Saints of Gwent Churches* (1991), pp. 15, 21.

Bd Vincentia López y Vicuña, *Foundress* (1847-90)

Vincentia López was born in Navarre. The decisive point of her early life was when she was sent to school in Madrid and came under the influence of her aunt, Doña Eulalia, who had founded a home for orphans and domestic servants. Vincentia made a vow of celibacy at the age of nineteen and was drawn to the religious life, though not to living in an enclosed Congregation. Her parents were at first unwilling to accept her wishes, advising her either to marry or to enter an enclosed Order, but eventually they allowed her to return to Madrid to work with Doña Eulalia. She was concerned about what would happen to the orphanage when her aunt died. With the help of the Jesuit Fr Hidalgo, Vincentia drew up plans to form the home into a religious community, and Doña Eulalia devoted herself and her whole fortune to it. In 1876 Vincentia and two others were given the habit by Bishop Sancha of Madrid. Fr Hidalgo afterwards asked her what her feelings were during the ceremony:

"Father, to tell what I suffered during the ceremony, and the joy our Lord gave me at the same time, is impossible . . ." and she stopped.

The Father asked her why she had suffered so much, and with great difficulty she answered, "I saw all the sufferings at once."

"Your own, or those of others?" he asked.

"All," she replied, as though lost in the thought of them.

Mother Vincentia's intense spiritual life was combined with a very practical and far-seeing charity: she did not make the mistake of expecting too much of people worn down by the difficulty of keeping body and soul together. She refused to finance the work by conducting schools, as many other Orders did: instead she chose the harder way of begging and insisted to her nuns that those who helped the poor must be prepared to be poor themselves. Many came to join her Order, six similar establishments were opened in other cities, and in 1888 the Holy See issued a decree of praise of the Institute of Daughters of Mary Immaculate for the Protection of Working Girls.

Just before the Feast of the Assumption in 1877, she wrote to her novices:

Love one another in God and for God, and see God himself in your Sisters, as the Rule tells us; fix your eyes on their qualities, and not on their faults, unless it be for the sake of compassion and of mutual help on counselling them. . . . As for love of the girls in our own houses, it is not necessary to say anything. I know that you love them. . . . It is the work to which God has called us.

She said, "I count myself happier in the service of these my Sisters than the great ones of this world in the service of their lords and kings. May our Lord give me grace to fulfil my undertaking." She was not yet forty-four when she died. After her death her Congregation spread to South Africa and other countries, including England.

Among Vincentia's works was the formation of a "triple alliance" between the houses of her Congregation and the convents of Carmel and the Visitation in Spain, for special devotion to the Sacred Heart.

She was beatified by Pope Pius XII in 1950.

E. Federici, *La Beata Vincentia María López y Vicuña* (1950); W. Lawson, *All You Need is Love* (1969); Catholic Truth Society pamphlet, trans. and adapted from the French by an English nun of the Handmaids of the Sacred Heart (1941); *N.C.E.*, 8, p. 987.

Note: BB Agnes Phila and Lucia Khambang, Sisters of the Order of the Holy Cross and teachers in a mission school in Thailand; Agatha Phutta, a kitchen assistant, nearly sixty years of age; Cecilia Butsi, Bibiana Kampai, and Maria Phong, schoolgirls aged sixteen, fifteen, and fourteen respectively, are commemorated separately today. See the general entry on The Martyrs of Thailand, 16 December, above.

27

ST JOHN, *Apostle and Evangelist* (*c.* 100)

St John the Evangelist is traditionally held to be "the disciple whom Jesus loved," the author of the Fourth Gospel, three Epistles, and the Revelation of John. He is often called in England, as by the Greeks, "the Divine" (*i.e.*, the Theologian). He is identified with the Galilean John, son of Zebedee and brother of St James the Greater (25 July). James and John were fishermen, called by Jesus as they were mending their nets in their boat (Matt. 5:21-2) soon after the call to Peter (29 June) and Andrew (30 Nov.). Jesus gave the brothers the nickname of *Boanerges*, "Sons of Thunder." When a Samaritan village refused Jesus hospitality because he was making for Jerusalem, their immediate response was, "Lord, do you want us to call down fire from heaven to burn them up?" (Luke 9:54)—suggesting ardent faith but impulsive and vehement reactions.

The Fourth Gospel portrays "the disciple whom Jesus loved" as having a privileged position but never gives his name. The usual interpretation is that St John is writing of himself. This disciple leans against Jesus at the Last Supper and asks who will betray him (13:23-6). He is present in Gethsemane and is probably the "other disciple" who followed Jesus after his arrest with Peter and heard Peter's double denial before the cock crew (18:15-16). Alone among the apostles, he stands at the foot of the cross, and Christ's grief-stricken mother is commended to his care: "Woman, behold thy son"; "Behold thy mother" (19:26-7). He is the first of the men to reach the empty tomb—running in response to the call from Mary Magdalene (22 July) and outstripping Peter, who was older and slower, but waiting to let Peter enter first (20:2-6). He is with the resurrected Jesus in the upper room (20:19-22) and on the shores of the Sea of Tiberias (21:7), and the rumour goes out among the disciples that he will not die but will live until Christ comes again in glory (21:23).

We know that John was prominent in the life of the early Church and that he had a very long life. His brother James died in Herod's persecution of the Christians. John worked with Peter and then later settled in Ephesus. St Irenaeus (24 Mar.) received a tradition from St Polycarp of Smyrna (26 Jan.), who died in 155 or 166, that John lived at Ephesus until the time of Trajan (emperor 98-117). He is thought to have died peacefully in about the third year of Trajan, that is, the hundredth of the Christian era, being then about ninety-four years old. He seems to have outlived all the other apostles, and he is the only one of whom it is certain that he did not die a martyr.

St Jerome (30 Sept.) recounts a tradition that, when age and weakness made it impossible for him to preach to the people, John would have himself carried down to the assembly of the faithful and would say only "My little children, love one another." When they asked why he always used the same words, he said, "Because it is the word of the Lord, and if you keep it, you do enough."

The tradition that John son of Zebedee was the author of the Fourth Gospel goes back to the second century. Thanks to the discovery of the Chester-Beatty fragment, we now know that this Gospel was in writing in the early second century or even earlier. One view is that John writes as an eyewitness, with a detailed knowledge of events. He writes in maturity, perhaps as an old man, about events that occurred when he was young. He writes after much meditation, emphasizing the theological import of his story and presupposing in his readers a knowledge of the events of Christ's life as portrayed by the Synoptic Gospels, written earlier. And he ends with a note that suggests something of his early vehemence:

> This disciple is the one who vouches for these things and has written them down, and we know that his testimony is true.
>
> There were many other things that Jesus did: if all were written down, the world itself, I suppose, would not hold all the books that would have to be written.

However, this subscript suggests that more than one person was involved in the version of the Gospel we have in the Bible, and most modern scholars hold that it went through a number of phases, reaching completion only at the end of the first century. Though John son of Zebedee may stand at the root of the traditions that form the basis of the Gospel, the "redaction theory" is that he must at least have had a number of scribes or collaborators or editors, who developed what he had to say into a coherent narrative.

Some scholars now hold that the unnamed "disciple whom Jesus loved" may have become a symbolic figure, representing all those whom Christ loves, that is, his followers. This disciple is shown as being present at all the key events in Christ's passion, and he is the repository of the gospel tradition. It is argued that too much is attributed to this one disciple for the narrative to be a literal account of what occurred. If this is the case, then the omission of his name could have been deliberate.

The Revelation, or Apocalypse, though also ascribed to John, is very different in style and content from the Gospel. Translation tends to obscure the stylistic differences; but while the Fourth Gospel is written in correct Greek with a fairly limited vocabulary, the Apocalypse gives evidence of a more sophisticated vocabulary. Some scholars think that the inattention to style and syntax in the Apocalypse could be accounted for by the urgency of conveying an intense spiritual experience; others that the differences in style result from the evangelist dictating his vision to a younger man with a wider command of

Greek—possibly another John. Some have concluded that the Apocalypse shows evidence of a completely different authorship.

John's symbol is the eagle—representing the fourth of the living creatures about the throne of God (Rev. 4:6-8) which have become the emblems of the writers of the four Gospels, or, it has been suggested, representing the soaring thought of the Prologue to the Gospel that bears his name. Many churches are dedicated to him, including the Lateran Basilica in Rome (with St John the Baptist; 24 June and 29 Aug.), and he is a familiar figure in medieval iconography. In paintings of the Italian Renaissance he is often depicted as a young man with red hair—perhaps an allusion to his quick temper. John is the patron saint of theologians, writers, and all who work at the production of books.

F. L. Cross (ed.) "St John on Patmos," *New Testament Studies* 4, (1963), pp. 75-85; *Bibl.SS.*, 6, 757-97; *N.C.E.*, 7, pp. 9, 1005-6 and 1080-8. On the liturgical aspects see L. Duchesne, *Christian Worship*, pp. 265-8. Modern studies of the Fourth Gospel include F. L. Cross (ed. 1957); C. H. Dodd (1953 and 1963); C. K. Barrett (1955); R. H. Lightfoot (ed. C. F. Evans, 1956); E. Malatesta, *St John's Gospel, 1920-65: a cumulative and classified bibliography* (1967); R. Schnackenberg, 3 vols. (Eng. trans. 1968-82), and on the Epistles, *The Johannine Epistles* (Eng. trans. 1992).

In art he appears either as a young, beardless man, in scenes from the Gospels, or as an old man, often meditating on the island of Patmos. In Leonardo da Vinci's *Last Supper* (begun before 1497) in Santa Maria delle Grazie, Milan, he is not reclining on Jesus' bosom or "next to Jesus" (*NRSV*) but in a group of three with Peter and Judas, in an attitude of trusting, grieving acceptance of Judas' betrayal. The Giotto frescoes in Santa Croce, Florence (early fourteenth century), follow the apocryphal Acts of John (used in *The Golden Legend*) in showing him being raised from his grave by Christ himself. He is shown young and beardless on Patmos in a painting by Hieronymus Bosch (*c.* 1500) in Berlin, absorbed in a vision of the Virgin and Child with an angel; and, also in Berlin, seated in a magnificent landscape, by Geertgen. The legend of his raising from the dead is the subject of a fresco by Correggio in the dome of San Giovanni Evangelista in Parma (1520-3). See P. and L. Murray, *The Oxford Companion to Christian Art and Literature* (1996), p. 253.

St Fabiola (399)

Fabiola was one of the patrician Roman ladies who were much influenced by St Jerome (30 Sept.), but she was not a member of the circle that gathered round him while he was living in Rome. She was a determined and independent woman of considerable wealth; and when her husband's dissolute life made married life impossible, she obtained a civil divorce, which was not difficult under Roman law. She then married another man, but after the death of her second husband she submitted to the canons of the Church, presenting herself for penance at the Lateran Basilica, and was readmitted to the communion of the faithful by Pope St Siricius (26 Nov.).

Thereafter Fabiola devoted her great wealth to works of charity. She gave large sums to churches and communities in Italy and the adjoining islands and founded a hospital for the sick, whom she gathered from the streets and alleys of Rome, waiting on them in person. This was the first recorded Christian hospital in the West, though there were similar developments in Egypt and Asia Minor, where St Pachomius (9 May) and St Basil of Caesarea (2 Jan.) are generally regarded as the pioneers.

In the year 395 Fabiola went to visit St Jerome at Bethlehem in company with a relative named Oceanus, and stayed there with St Paula (26 Jan.) and her daughter St Eustochium (28 Sept.). Jerome was in conflict with the bishop of Jerusalem because of his controversy with Rufinus about the teaching of Origen. Attempts were made to enlist Fabiola's sympathies on the side of the bishop, but she remained loyal to Jerome. She wanted to spend the rest of her days at Bethlehem, but the life of a consecrated woman was not suited to her temperament: she needed company and activity. Jerome commented that her view of the stable at Bethlehem was that it ought to be in constant touch with the inn. However, he praised her as "a chaste matron and a Christian woman."

When the Huns threatened to overrun Jerusalem, Jerome and his followers moved to the coast, and Fabiola eventually went back to Rome. It seems that she was thinking of marrying for the third time, since a priest named Amandus put a complex question relating to the status of a divorced woman to Jerome, and this was generally thought to be a "feeler" put on behalf of Fabiola. In the event Jerome was cautious, and she did not marry again but spent the last three years of her life in works of public and private charity, notably being associated with St Pammachius (30 Aug.) in the foundation at Porto of a large hospital for poor and sick pilgrims. She was still restless and was about to sail for Jaffa when she died. It was said that all Rome attended her funeral.

St Jerome was in touch with Fabiola to the end and wrote two treatises for her: one, on the priesthood of Aaron and the mystical significance of the sacerdotal vestments, he completed while her ship was being got ready to sail; the other, the "Forty-two Mansions or Healing Places of the Israelites" in the wilderness, was not completed until after she died. It was eventually sent to Oceanus together with an account of Fabiola's life and death, the wanderings of the Israelites being compared to her own restless wanderings.

St Jerome, Letter 77, N.P.N.F., 6, pp. 157-62; *P.L.*, 22, 690-8; Leclercq in *D.A.C.L.*, 7, 2274-5; *D.C.B.* (1911), pp. 361-2; *N.C.E.*, 5, p. 783.

St Nicarete (c. 410)

Nicarete was an elderly woman of wealth who, according to the Roman Martyrology, "flourished in holiness during the reign of the Emperor Arcadius." She left her family, who lived in Nicomedia, and devoted herself to good works in Constantinople, where she is thought to be the lady skillful in the healing arts mentioned by St John Chrysostom (13 Sept.). She is said to have treated Chrysostom, archbishop of Constantinople, when he was ill and to have supported him staunchly. She refused his suggestion that she might become a deaconess and supervise the unattached consecrated virgins of the city: that was evidently not her calling, and she preferred to work quietly behind the scenes.

According to the historian Sozomen, "by modesty of character and philosophy, she was always studious of concealment." She suffered persecution for her support of Chrysostom, like St Olympias (17 Dec.), but when she was unjustly deprived of most of her goods and property she managed the remainder so well that she supplied all the wants of her household and was still able "to contribute largely to others." Eventually she is thought to have been driven into exile.

Sozomen, *H.E.*, 8, 3, in N.P.N.F., 2, p. 414. The reference by Chrysostom is in his fourth letter to Olympias.

SS Theodore and Theophanes (841 and 845)

These brothers were born in Kerak, across the Dead Sea from Jerusalem in what was formerly the land of the Moabites. They grew up in Jerusalem, where their parents settled. In their youth they both became monks in the monastery of St Sabas (5 Dec.) and by their progress in learning and virtue acquired a high reputation. The patriarch of Jerusalem insisted that Theodore should be ordained priest and, when the emperor Leo the Isaurian supported the Iconoclasts, sent Theodore to exhort the emperor not to disturb the peace of the Church. Leo had Theodore scourged, and sent the two brothers to an island at the mouth of the Black Sea, where they suffered much from hunger and cold. When Leo died, they returned to their monastery at Constantinople, but the new emperor, Theophilus, a violent Iconoclast, who ascended the throne in 829, had them scourged and banished again.

Two years later they were brought back to Constantinople, and when they still persisted in their opposition to Iconoclasm Theophilus commanded that twelve lines of iambic verse, composed for that purpose by a courtier, should be cut into the flesh of their faces. The sense of the verses was as follows: "These men have appeared at Jerusalem as vessels full of the iniquity of superstitious error, and were driven thence for their crimes. Having fled to Constantinople, they forsook not their iniquity. Wherefore they have been banished from thence, and thus stigmatized on their faces."

They were laid upon benches, and the letters were allegedly cut into their skin. Since the message was a long one, it seems possible that it may actually have been pricked or tattooed; but whatever the process was, it was painful and disfiguring, and it took two days to complete. Then they were again banished, this time to Apamea in Bithynia, where Theodore died. The emperor Theophilus died about the same time. St Methodius (14 June) became patriarch, and the images were restored. St Theophanes was then honoured for his confession of the Faith and made bishop of Nicaea. He wrote a number of hymns, including one on his brother. Theodore is distinguished by the Greeks as "the Poet," but both brothers are more commonly called "*Graptoi*," that is, the Written-on.

A Greek Life of Theodore, attributed to the Metaphrast, is printed in *P.L.*, 116, 653-84. The brothers are also spoken of by such later historians as Cedrenus and Zonaras in their accounts of the reign of the emperor Theophilus. There is a notice in *Synax. Const.*, pp. 130-1.

ST JOHN (p. 210, above)
The Eagle of St John. Wood engraving by Eric Gill
from The Four Gospels *(1931)*

28

THE HOLY INNOCENTS (The Year of the Birth of Jesus Christ)

King Herod, who governed Jewry under the Romans at the time of the birth of Jesus, was an Idumaean—not a Jew of the house of David or of Aaron but the descendant of people forcibly Judaized and the vassal of imperial Rome. When he heard that there was one "born king of the Jews" and that wise men were coming from the East to worship him, he feared for his throne. He called together the chief priests and scribes and asked them where the prophet had foretold that the Messiah would be born. They told him, "At Bethlehem in Judaea" (Mic. 5:1). Then he sent for the Magi secretly, cross-examined them about their movements and intentions, and finally sent them on their way with orders to return and tell him where the child was, making the excuse that he too would go and worship the child; but the Magi were warned in their sleep not to return to Herod and went back to their own country by another route. Then Joseph, fearing for the child, took Mary and the infant Jesus into Egypt, where they stayed until Herod was dead (Matt. 2:12-5).

Herod, realizing that the wise men would not identify the child for him, ordered all the male children under the age of two in the Bethlehem district to be killed. This fulfilled the prophecy of Jeremiah: "A voice is heard in Ramah, lamenting and weeping bitterly: it is Rachel weeping for her children, refusing to be comforted for her children, because they are no more" (Jer. 31:15).

This was probably not a large-scale massacre. It is unlikely that there would have been more than a few male children of that age in a small village like Bethlehem. Such a deed would not be out of character for Herod the Great: toward the end of his life he became highly suspicious about claimants to his throne, and he was certainly ready to eliminate them. Josephus says of Herod that "he was a man of great barbarity toward everybody." The number of Herod's victims is said to have been great: the Byzantine liturgy speaks of fourteen thousand, the Syrian menologies of sixty-four thousand, though these must be exaggerations.

Matthew's message is not purely a record of events. He is concerned to show a parallel between the infancy of Jesus and the infancy of Moses, the fate of the Innocents resembling that of the Hebrew children killed on Pharaoh's orders when Moses was born (Exod. 1:13-22).

The feast of these Holy Innocents, who in the East are called simply the Holy Children, has been kept in the Church since the fifth century. Through-

216

out the Western Church they have been commemorated on 28 December since the sixth century. They are venerated as martyrs who died not only for Christ but actually instead of Christ. In the *Hieronymianum* they are called "the holy babes and sucklings," and in the calendar of Carthage simply "the infants." The Spanish poet Prudentius wrote to honour them in his *Hymn for Epiphany*, in a passage beginning "*Salvete, flores martyrum*":

> All hail, sweet flowers of martyrdom,
> Cut down in life's bright dawning hour,
> And shattered by the foe of Christ,
> As rosebuds in a whirling storm . . .
>
> Amidst the streams of blood that flowed
> From tender babes of equal age,
> Alone, the Virgin's Son escaped
> The sword that pierced the mothers' hearts.

These first martyrs of Christ are pictured, in their simplicity, playing by God's altar with the crowns and palms that are their reward.

Bede wrote a long hymn about them. In England their feast was formerly called Childermas. They are specially venerated in Bethlehem, where the Franciscan friars and children of the choir visit their altar under the Church of the Nativity and sing Prudentius' hymn from Lauds of the Feast. Some tiny stone sarcophagi reputed to be those of the Innocents are preserved in the same cave as the altar.

The Innocents are mentioned by a number of the early Fathers, including St Irenaeus, *Adv. Haeres.*, 50; St Cyprian, Epistle 56, 3, ch. 58; St Gregory Nazianzen, Sermon 38 on the Nativity; St John Chrystosom, Homily 9 on Matthew. See also *C.M.H.*, p. 13; *Propylaeum*, p. 605; Duchesne, *Christian Worship*, p. 268; *The Poems of Prudentius*, trans. M. C. Eagan (1962), pp. 89-90; J. E. Raby, *A History of Christian-Latin Poetry* (1927, rp. 1953), p. 48, for a hymn by Rabanus Maurus; *D.A.C.L.*, 7 part 1 pp. 608-16.

St Theodore the Sanctified, *Abbot* (? 314-68)

Theodore was a disciple of St Pachomius (9 May), the founder of community (cenobitic) monasticism in the Egyptian desert. He was born in the Upper Thebaid and entered Pachomius' community at Tabennesi. There are conflicting manuscript accounts of his entry: those who wished to join the community had to wait at the gate for some days, to learn the Lord's Prayer and some psalms, and to receive instruction. Theodore may still have been at the gate when his wealthy mother and brother arrived, bearing "letters from bishops" (or it may be only one letter from one bishop) and demanding that the boy be given back to his family. There was evidently an angry scene. Theodore was determined to enter the community and refused to speak to his mother. Pachomius personally mediated and finally accepted Theodore; but thereafter he ensured that families had been consulted and property matters settled before a new monk joined the community. Though the monks lived out of the world, he did not wish them to live in opposition to their relatives.

Pachomius made Theodore his companion when he visited his other monasteries in what became a large federation, and after Theodore's ordination to the priesthood committed the rule of Tabennesi to him, himself retiring to the small monastery of Pabau. Theodore was very close to him and was virtually trained as his successor, but when Pachomius became ill and the heads of the monasteries asked that Theodore be named as the next abbot, Pachomius taxed him with lack of humility. Theodore replied honestly enough, "For seven years now I have been sent by you to visit the monasteries, and to settle everything as you do. And never did it enter my heart that 'after him, I will be in charge'; but now I am plagued by the thought, and I have not yet been able to conquer it."

Pachomius had him stripped of all authority and left him in disgrace for two years, though many monks assured Theodore that "what had occurred was not a sin." There must have been many earnest discussions as to whether Pachomius resented Theodore's abilities or whether Theodore had failed in deference to the older man. In these circumstances the development of factions in the communities was almost inevitable.

At the end of Theodore's two years of disgrace, in 346, there was an outbreak of plague, in which three of the superiors of the monasteries died. When Pachomius also became a victim, there was a real crisis of leadership. Though Theodore was with him when he was dying, Pachomius still refused to name him as the next abbot. At the last he summoned "all the great ones among the brothers" and told them to choose a successor for themselves; but they could not agree, and eventually he named Petronios, who was already ill, and who died only thirteen days after him. Petronios, pressed by the anxious elders in his final hours to name his own successor, named St Orsiesius (15 June), but Orsiesius knew that the task of reconciling the factions and carrying the administrative responsibility was too much for him and placed Theodore in charge. Theodore accepted the responsibility but constantly deferred to Orsiesius asking his advice and telling the monks that particular decisions were taken with his approval: he did not wish to fail in humility again.

Theodore had the ability to pull the federation together. He was well known in the monasteries, and he visited each in turn, assembling the monks, investigating their complaints, and exhorting them to unity. He instructed, comforted, and encouraged individual monks and won their confidence by his prayers and his tireless efforts on their behalf. So mutual charity was restored.

Theodore ruled the communities for twenty-two years. At the celebration of Easter 368, when all his monks were gathered together, he was taken ill and died shortly afterwards. His body was carried to the top of the mountain and interred in the monks' cemetery, but it was removed soon after and buried with that of St Pachomius. St Athanasius (2 May) wrote to the monks to comfort them for the loss of their abbot, bidding them to keep before their eyes the glory into which he had entered. His commemoration has been dropped from the new Roman Martyrology.

Anal.Boll. 87 (1979), pp. 5-55, 241-79; sources on the life of Pachomius, particularly A. Boon, *Pachomiana Latina* (1932); T. H. Lefort, *Oeuvres de S Pachôme et ses disciples*: Coptic texts with French translation (1965); the Rule and letters of Pachomius, translated in *P.L.*, 23, 61-106; H. G. Evelyn White, *The Monasteries of the Wadi n'Natrun*, 2 (1932): but see criticisms by P. Peeters in *Anal.Boll.* 51 (1933), pp. 152-7; P. Rousseau, *Pachomius: the making of a community in fourth century Egypt* (1985).

SS Rumilus and Conindrius (*c.* 450)

Though St Patrick (17 Mar.) is venerated as the patron of the Isle of Man and sent a mission there from Ireland, it is not known whether he visited the island in person. Rumilus and Conindrius are reputed to have been the first bishops of Man. The *Tripartite Life of St Patrick* tells how the saint converted an Irish robber chief named Maccaldus and sent him out in a boat, without rudder or oars, to be prepared to serve God wherever it might take him:

> And a north wind arose, and bore him to the south, and cast him on the island called Evonia; and he found there two wonderful men, glowing in faith and doctrine, who first taught the word of God and baptism in Evonia. And the men of the island were converted to the Catholic Faith by their teaching, whose names are Conindrius and Rumilus . . . and he spent the remainder of his life with these holy bishops till he was appointed their successor in the bishopric.

Little more is known of St Maccaldus (Maughold or Marghold), also commemorated locally on 28 December.

Another tradition in Manx folklore names St Germanus or Coemanus as the first bishop of Man. Coemanus may have been the son of a Welsh prince named Brecan. This prince and his family were disciples of St Patrick; they were connected by birth to some of the Ulster chieftains, and their territory lay on the coast opposite the Isle of Man. An Irish Catholic Truth Society pamphlet reconciles the two traditions with the ingenious suggestion that Rumilus may have been Coemanus, and Conindrius his brother Canoc: Irish or Welsh names often became confused in the translation to medieval Latin records, and the sons of Brecan would have been a likely choice as missionary bishops. Both have been dropped from the new Roman Martyrology but are retained here for their local interest.

W. S. Dempsey, *The Story of the Catholic Church in the Isle of Man* (1958); Dean Walsh, *Ireland and the Isle of Man* (Irish C.T.S., n.d.); Stanton, p. 609.

St Antony of Lérins (*c.* 520)

Antony was born in Valeria, in Lower Pannonia, during the time of the barbarian invasions. His father died when he was eight years old, and he was entrusted to the care of St Severinus Boethius (23 Oct.). When this great scholar and philosopher died the boy was cared for by his uncle Constantius, bishop of Lorch in Bavaria. He became a monk and for a time attached himself to a monk named Marius, who had a group of disciples near Lake Como, but Antony's vocation was for the solitary life, and he joined two hermits at the other end of the lake. Here he lived in a cave, spending his time in prayer and study and cultivating his garden. A murderer, hiding from justice, is said to have simulated devotion and attached himself to Antony as a disciple, but Antony "read his soul," and the man fled.

Antony also had to leave, for the news of this incident brought him many visitors, whom he found distracting. At last, despairing of finding complete solitude and fearing that the attention he had received would make him vain, he went over the Alps into southern Gaul and became a monk at Lérins. His Life was written by St Ennodius, bishop of Pavia (17 July).

For Ennodius of Pavia's Life see *M.G.H., Auctores Antiquissimi*, 7, pp. 185-90; also *P.L.*, 63, 239-46; *D.H.G.E.*, 3, 739.

Bd Matthia of Matelica, Abbess (*c.* 1300)

The convent of Poor Clares at Matelica, in the March of Ancona, is said to date back to about 1233, when St Clare (11 Aug.) herself was still alive. Originally it was dedicated to St Mary Magdalene (22 July), but since 1758 it has been known as the convent of Bd Matthia. A late Life seems to be the sole source of information about her, though nearly all the Franciscan chroniclers give an account of her. According to the *vita*, she was born about the same time as the convent was founded, the only child of Count Guarniero Nazzarei. His ambition for her was that she should marry and have children, but she had other ideas and sought admission to the local community of Poor Clares.

When the abbess, who happened to be related to Guarniero, refused to accept her without her father's permission, Matthia went to the convent chapel, put on a habit, and cut her own hair. At this point Guarniero, finding her so determined, reluctantly gave his consent. All that is known for certain after this is that she held the office of abbess for some forty years and died on 28 December, perhaps in 1300.

Miracles were reported so frequently at her grave that her remains were soon moved to a tomb next to the high altar in the convent chapel. In 1756, when the tomb had to be moved to allow for repairs, the bishop of Camerino took the opportunity to examine the relics. They were enshrined under the altar of St Cecilia (22 Nov.). Some believe that the convent in Matelica was originally founded for some Benedictine nuns and that it became Franciscan during

Matthia's lifetime—which they would put at an earlier date of 1171 to about 1213.

B. Mazzara, *Leggendario Francescano*, 1 (1676), pp. 875-6; G. Baldassini, *Italian Lives* (1852); V. da Porto San Giorgio (1877); *Auréole Séraphique*, 1, pp. 332-8; A. M. Zimmermann, *Kalendarium Benedictinum* 3 (1937).

St Gaspar del Bufalo, Founder (1786-1837)

Gaspar (Gaspare) was born in Rome on 6 January 1786 to Antonio and Annunziata Quarterione. As he was born on the feast of the Epiphany, he was given the names of all three Magi at his baptism the following day. His family circumstances were modest. He showed early signs of a devout nature, occasionally taken to excess, as when he ran away from school at the age of seven to convert the heathen and earn martyrdom. He studied at the Collegio Romano, at the time run by secular clergy following the suppression of the Jesuits. At the age of twelve he donned the minor seminarian's cassock and soon began organizing local works of spiritual and material relief for the poor, including the rebirth of the *Opera di S. Galla*, of which he was elected director in 1806. He was ordained priest on 30 July 1808 and intensified his relief work among the poor, specializing in evangelizing the carters and peasants of the Campagna Romana, known as *barozzari*.

The church of S. Nicola in Carcere in Rome contained a little-known relic, a presumed piece of the centurion Longinus' cloak, stained with the blood of Jesus. In 1808 Gaspar's friend Francesco Albertini instituted a confraternity dedicated to the Precious Blood, either to honour this relic or to draw people's attention to the redemptive power of Christ's blood. Gaspar was one of his staunchest collaborators in this venture, and devotion to the Precious Blood was to provide the driving force of his spirituality for the rest of his life.

In 1809 Napoleon took Rome and began to introduce harsh measures against the Church in Italy. Pope Pius VII (1800-23) was arrested and deported in the night of 5-6 July. All Roman clergy were required to sign an oath of allegiance to Napoleon, which involved abjuring allegiance to the Holy See. Most, including Gaspar, refused and were exiled from Rome. Gaspar was first exiled to Piacenza, on 13 July 1810, and then imprisoned successively in Bologna, Imola, and Lugo. He endured four years of prison serenely, planning with Albertini what they would do to help put the Church back on its feet after their release. When Napoleon fell in 1814 Gaspar was on his way to further imprisonment in Corsica; he was returned to Italy and set free in Florence. He made his way back to Rome and placed himself at the service of the pope. Pius VII ordered him to devote himself to preaching missions aimed at restoring religion and morality in Italy, which for five years had been effectively deprived of priests and sacraments. He left Rome and his family to dedicate the rest of his life single-mindedly to this one great purpose.

Taking devotion to the Precious Blood as his major theme, he launched into a programme of preaching missions to combat the widespread irreligion and bring people back to the Faith. In this he appeared to be fulfilling the words of Sr Agnes of the Incarnate Word, who in 1810 had told Gaspar's spiritual director that a zealous priest would appear to shake people out of their indifference through devotion to the Precious Blood. Whatever weight can be attached to this, he decided on the foundation of a Congregation of missionaries dedicated to the Precious Blood after preaching a mission at Giano, in the diocese of Spoleto, in 1814. He was actively supported in this both by his friend Cardinal Cristaldi and by Pope Pius VII, who gave him a house and the adjoining church of S. Felice. The Congregation was established there and formally approved by the pope on 15 August 1815, the feast of the Assumption. Gaspar had a great devotion to Mary and always took an image of her, vererated as the "Madonna of the Chalice," on his missions. The future Pope Pius IX (1846-78) was an early member of the Congregation, and it was to be his encyclical *Redempti sumus*, issued in 1849, that gave worldwide impetus to devotion to the Precious Blood.

A second foundation was made in 1819 and a third shortly afterwards, at Albano, near Rome. His ambition was to found a house in each diocese of Italy, choosing the most abandoned or wicked city as its location. In 1821 the pope wrote personally to him asking him to found six in the kingdom of Naples. Gaspar responded energetically to the pope's request but again and again met resistance and difficulties in raising funds. Naples, the Papal States, and most of the rest of Italy were prey at the time to brigands. Originally partisans fighting against the French occupation, they had developed into lawless bands living in safe hideouts in the mountains, from where they plundered the towns, carried out vendettas, and organized crime and violence of every kind. Successive popes—Puis VII, Leo XII (1823-9), and Pius VIII (1829-30)—had tried to curb the scourge, but without success. Leo XII, who had originally been far less supportive than his predecessor, eventually entrusted Gaspar with a particular mission to the brigands: armed only with the gospel, he had some success in reducing their activities in the area around Rome.

His missions made an enormous impression all over Italy. His dramatic methods, similar to those employed earlier by Bd Bartholomew dal Monte (24 Dec.), were physically and emotionally draining for him. The Passionist St Vincent Strambi (25 Sept.), who was his companion on several missions, described him as a "spiritual earthquake," while the people acclaimed him as "an angel of peace." He brought about large-scale and often explosively emotional conversions, but he also made many enemies, particularly among the Freemasons, who even made attempts on his life. He attacked them head-on in his mission sermons as anticlercials and atheists, and he even managed to convert some whole lodges, earning himself the title "Hammer of the Sectarians."

In 1834, with the collaboration of Bd Mary de Mattias (20 Aug.), whom he personally had chosen for this work, he made a parallel foundation for women, the Institute of Sisters Adorers of the Precious Blood. He preached his last mission at the Chiesa Nuova in Rome in 1836 during an outbreak of cholera. His health, never robust, was now failing and the following year he retired to Albano for several months, returning to Rome after the feast of St Francis Xavier (3 Dec.) knowing that he was dying. He died on 28 December 1837 in a room in the Orsini Palace. St Vincent Palotti (22 Jan.), the Roman founder of the Pallottine Fathers, reported seeing his soul ascending to heaven in the form of a bright star and being received by Jesus.

His fame soon spread beyond Italy, especially in France. There, Françoise de Maistre, daughter of the governor of Nice and niece of the Ultramontanist writer Joseph de Maistre, was apparently healed through his intercession; Gaston de Séjur wrote and lectured extensively about him; Peter Julian Eymard, founder of the Blessed Sacrament Fathers (1 Aug.), spread his influence by constantly appealing to his inspiration.

Gaspar del Bufalo was beatified by Pope St Pius X (1903-14; 21 Aug.) on 18 December 1904 and canonized by Pope Pius XII (1939-58) on 12 June 1954 in the piazza in front of St Peter's. His remains are enshrined in the church of S. Maria *in Trivio* in Rome. In his closing speech to the Roman synod of January 1960 Pope John XXIII (1958-63) called him the "wholly splendid glory of the Roman clergy, who was the true and greatest apostle of devotion to the Most Precious Blood of Christ in the world." He was originally commemorated liturgically on 29 December; this was moved to 21 October in 1962, but he is here noticed on the actual date of his death.

Bibl.SS., 6, 40-3; *D.I.P.*, 4, 1038-42, with fuller bibliog. Biographies include M. Armellini, *Il venerabile Gaspare del Bufalo* (1901); V. Sardi, *Vita del Beato Gaspare del Bufalo, romano* (1904); G. del Libero, *San Gaspare del Bufalo romano* (1954). In English: E. Kaiser, C.PP.S., *St Gaspar del Bufalo, Herald of the Precious Blood* (1957); R. Bernardo, C.PP.S., *Saint Gaspar del Bufalo, Saint of the People* (n.d.); L. Contegiacomo, C.PP.S., *St Gaspar's Prison Experiences* (1988); J. Klopke, C.PP.S. (ed.), *Essays in Honor of St Gaspar del Bufalo*, 2 vols. (1992 and 1993)—all publisher by the Congregation's Messenger Press in Carthagena, Ohio. On the Congregations see J. M. Behem, *Religious of the Precious Blood* (1957); *D.I.P.*, 5, 1458-60 (men's); 1, 115-8 (women's). On devotion to the Precious Blood see *D.I.P.*, 7, 812-5. His over three thousand letters are in the course of publication in Italian (1968-), and an English edition is in preparation (n.d.).

He is usually represented in devotional art in the act of preaching, holding up a crucifix or an overflowing chalice. There is an anonymous portrait from life dating from 1836 in the museum devoted to him in Rome, reproduced in *D.I.P.*, 4, facing 1032. A twentieth-century effigy of *Gaspar Dying*, by Aurelio Mistruzzi, adorns his tomb.

Houses closely linked with the Sisters Adorers were founded in 1834 in Dayton, Ohio, and Löwenberg, Switzerland, with a later foundation at O'Fallon, Missouri, in 1878. In the late 1970s there were over seven hundred members of the Missionaries (men), in 116 houses spread over fourteen countries; the Sisters Adorers had 398 communities with over 2,500 members, one thousand of them in the U.S.A.

29

ST THOMAS BECKET, *Bishop and Martyr* (1118-70)

He said that only his enemies called him "Becket" and styled himself "Thomas of London" until he went to Canterbury. Thomas was of Norman stock, the son of a burgess and sometime sheriff of London named Gilbert. He studied with the Canons Regular at Merton Abbey in Surrey. When his parents died he was left ill provided for and for some years had to work as a clerk. At the age of twenty-four he obtained a post in the household of Theobald, archbishop of Canterbury. He received minor orders and was greatly favoured by Theobald, who provided him with a number of benefices. In 1154 he was made deacon, and the archbishop nominated him archdeacon of Canterbury, which was then the first ecclesiastical dignity in England after the bishoprics and abbacies. Theobald sent him to Rome on several occasions on important missions. He was involved in gaining the approval of the pope, Eugenius III, for the succession of Henry of Anjou as king of England after the usurpation of Stephen.

Henry II was crowned at Westminster on 19 December 1154, and in the following year he appointed Thomas as his chancellor. His energies and abilities had full scope in this post, and the legal and political reforms that Henry II carried out after the years of civil war which had left England exhausted must have owed much to the advice and influence of his chancellor. King and chancellor were on terms of close personal friendship. Thomas enjoyed his new status and the magnificence that went with it. When he was sent to France to negotiate a royal marriage for the infant prince Henry his personal retinue numbered two hundred men. There were several hundred more—knights and esquires, clerics and servants, in the column, with eight wagon-loads of presents, music and singers, hawks and hounds. His entertainments were on a correspondingly generous scale and his liberality to the poor proportionate. In 1159 he fought for the king in France with seven hundred of his own knights and showed himself to be an excellent tactician. Cleric as he was, he wore armour and engaged in hand-to-hand fighting.

The prior of Leicester, meeting him at Rouen, exclaimed, "What do you mean by dressing like that? You look more like a falconer than a cleric. Yet you are a cleric in person, and many times over in office: archdeacon of Canterbury, dean of Hastings, provost of Beverley, canon of this church and that, procurator of the archbishopric—and likely to be archbishop too, the rumour goes!" Thomas took the reproach in good part and said that he knew three poor priests in England, any one of whom he would rather see archbishop than himself, for he would inevitably have to choose between the king's favour and God's.

Thomas was proud, irascible, violent, and impetuous and remained so all his life; but despite his love of secular grandeur, he made retreats at Merton, followed penitential practices, and prayed long and earnestly. His confessor during the first part of his career testified to the blamelessness of his private life under conditions of extreme danger and temptation.

Theobald, archbishop of Canterbury, died in 1161. King Henry resolved to make his chancellor archbishop to end the resistance of the Church to royal encroachment on its rights and privileges. Thomas told him flatly:

> Should God permit me to be archbishop of Canterbury, I should lose your Majesty's favour, and the affection with which you honour me would be changed into hatred. For several things you do in prejudice to the rights of the Church make me fear that you would require of me what I could not agree to; and envious persons would not fail to make this the occasion of endless strife between us.

The king paid no attention to this warning, and Thomas refused to accept the king's wishes until Cardinal Henry of Pisa, the papal legate, pressed him to agree. The election was made in May 1162. Thomas set out immediately from London to Canterbury. On the road he gave private charge to several of the clergy travelling with him to warn him of his faults, "for four eyes see more clearly than two." On Saturday in Whit-week he was ordained priest, and on the octave of Pentecost he was consecrated.

Soon after that he received the *pallium* from Pope Alexander III, and by the end of the year there was a notable change in his way of life. He wore sober clerical dress and a hair shirt next to his skin. He rose early to read the scriptures, keeping his secretary Herbert of Bosham by him so that they might discuss the meaning of passages together. At nine o'clock he sang Mass or was present when he did not celebrate himself. At ten daily alms were distributed, and he doubled all the ordinary alms of his predecessor. He dined at three o'clock among his guests and household in the great hall. He kept a notably good table for the sake of others, but was himself very temperate and moderate. He visited the infirmary and the monks working in the cloister nearly every day and sought to establish a certain monastic regularity in his own household. He took an especial care for the selection of candidates for Holy Orders, examining them personally. He exerted a rigorously even-handed justice: "The letters and requests of the king himself were of no use to a man who had not right on his side."

Conflicts with the king became increasingly serious. At Woodstock, Thomas refused to pay a levy on ecclesiastical lands to the crown. When a canon named Philip de Brois was accused of murder he refused to have him handed over to the king's courts and had him tried by his own court. In October 1163 Henry called the bishops to a council at Westminster and demanded the ending of benefit of clergy and the separate jurisdiction of the ecclesiastical courts. Thomas stiffened the resistance of the bishops. Then the king demanded an observance of all royal customs, many of which he did not even specify. The bishops temporized, and the king, in anger, demanded the return of castles and honours that Thomas had held since he was chancellor. For a time Thomas, who was getting very little support from the pope, was conciliatory; but when he saw the details of the new royal customs set out in the sixteen Constitutions of Clarendon, he exploded: "By the Lord Almighty, no seal of mine shall be put to them!" They included provisions that no prelate should leave the kingdom or appeal to Rome without the king's consent; that no tenant-in-chief should be excommunicated against the royal will; that the custody of vacant benefices and their revenue should be held by the king; and that clergy sentenced and convicted by ecclesiastical courts should be subject to the royal officers. Many of these were matters that had been in dispute between kings and archbishops since the early days of Norman rule.

Thomas was bitterly remorseful for having weakened in his opposition to the king, thus setting an example the other bishops were only too ready to follow. "I am a proud, vain man, a feeder of birds and a follower of hounds," he said, "and I have been made a shepherd of sheep. I am fit only to be cast out of the see which I fill." For forty days or more, while awaiting absolution from the pope, he would not celebrate Mass. He tried to heal the breach with the king, but Henry was vengeful. He refused Thomas an audience, twice stopped him from crossing the Channel to put his case before the pope, and demanded money alleged to be owing from the time when he was chancellor (though Thomas had received a clear discharge from all debts on becoming archbishop). After a stormy council at Northampton, in which he was attacked by barons and prelates supporting the king, Thomas secretly embarked for France and had an audience of the pope at Sens. Pope Alexander III pronounced some of the provisions of the Council of Clarendon to be intolerable. Thomas resigned his archbishopric into the hands of the pope and withdrew; but the pope called him back, reinstated him, and ordered him not to abandon his calling, for that would be to abandon the cause of God.

Negotiations between the pope, the archbishop, and the king dragged on, while Thomas stayed first in the Cistercian abbey at Pontigny and then, as the guest of the French king, Louis VII, at the abbey of Sainte-Colombe, near Sens. He remained abroad for six years.

His return to England was brought about by a crisis in the long-standing and bitter dispute between the archbishops of Canterbury and York concerning the primacy of the archbishop of Canterbury. In his absence Archbishop Roger of York had defied his orders by crowning the heir to the throne, Prince Henry. It was a common practice on the Continent for the heir to be crowned during his father's lifetime to ensure continuity of rule, though the practice had not previously been followed in England. Pope Alexander, perhaps not fully understanding the issues, granted a licence authorizing the archbishop of York to carry out the coronation ceremony. The date of the licence is not known, but it is established that (possibly on representations from Thomas) the pope subsequently cancelled it, in a letter dated 26 February 1170. The prince was actually crowned on 14 June 1170, and there is some doubt whether the letter of cancellation was actually delivered before the coronation took place. It was a long, slow journey from Rome to London, and some leading churchmen had an obvious motive for suppressing news unwelcome to the king.

Thomas had a brief and unsatisfactory meeting with Henry II at La Ferté Bernard, north of Vendôme, as a result of which he agreed to return to England. His farewell words to the bishop of Paris were, "I am going home to England to die."

He procured letters from the pope supporting his authority and served sentences of suspension on Archbishop Roger and the six bishops who had assisted at the young prince's coronation. He landed at Sandwich on 1 December 1170 to a very mixed reception. The sheriff of Kent attempted to prevent him from coming ashore. He was welcomed at Canterbury, but he faced hostility from the court, and young Henry, formerly his friend and his pupil, refused to receive him. Thomas retaliated by publicly denouncing and excommunicating the archbishop of York and the assisting bishops from the pulpit of Canterbury Cathedral on Christmas Day. He gave an address to his monks in the chapter house on the text "Here we have no abiding home, but look for one from above."

The archbishop of York and the bishops of London and Salisbury were already in Normandy, laying their complaints before the king at Bur, near Bayeux. In one of his fits of ungovernable rage, Henry II asked who would rid him of Thomas, though his actual words are not established. Four knights took them as permission to kill and at once set out for England. Their names were Reginald FitzUrse, William de Tracy, Hugh de Morville, and Richard le Breton.

On the afternoon of 29 December the four reached Canterbury. They demanded to see Thomas, and found him sitting in his bedroom. He knew why they had come. He did not rise to greet them and acknowledged only one of them, Hugh de Morville. Though the interview began quietly, it ended with oaths and threats from the knights. Thomas, urged and hustled by his attendants, moved slowly toward the church, the traditional place of sanctuary, his cross carried before him. The monks were singing Vespers. As he entered the church he was met by a crowd of terrified monks who tried to close the door behind him. He turned round saying, "A church is not a castle," and opened the door himself. The knights rushed in shouting: "Where is Thomas the traitor? Where is the archbishop?" "Here I am," he replied, "no traitor, but archbishop and priest of God." And there, between the altars of Our Lady and St Benedict, he was brutally hacked to death. Of the four knights, only Hugh de Morville struck no blow. The murderers dashed away, shouting, "The king's men! The king's men!"

The incident was over in ten minutes. The great church filled with people, and a thunderstorm broke overhead. The archbishop's body lay alone, stretched in the middle of the transept, and for a long time no one dared to touch it or even to go near it. Thomas had not lived like a saint, but he died like one. A man of many parts, he sought glory; in the end, by courage and self-denial, he found it.

The assassination of a metropolitan in his own cathedral while acting with the authority of the pope was a deed of sacrilege that produced universal horror both in England and on the Continent. It is doubtful whether Henry II can be held directly and deliberately responsible for the murder. Certainly he showed every sign of extreme grief when the news was brought to him. He shut himself away, lamenting and fasting for forty days. The public revulsion demanded a public penance of the most severe kind, and this he performed— first at Avranches in May 1172 when he received absolution from the papal legates, and then at Canterbury in July 1174, eighteen months after the solemn canonization of Thomas as a martyr by Pope Alexander at Segni.

On 7 July 1220 the body of St Thomas was translated from its tomb in the crypt to a shrine behind the high altar by the archbishop, Cardinal Stephen Langton, in the presence of King Henry III, the papal legate, and the archbishop of Reims. The shrine became a major place of pilgrimage until it was destroyed by Henry VIII's men in 1538. The Pilgrims' Way, from London to Canterbury, can still be traced. Chaucer immortalized it in *The Canterbury Tales*, and the stained-glass windows in Canterbury Cathedral commemorate it. Some eighty English churches were dedicated to Thomas before the Reformation, but dedications, statues, and pictures of his martyrdom were removed in Henry VIII's reign. There is a stone carving of his murder by the knights in the cathedral at Chartres.

C. Robertson and J. B. Sheppard, *Materials for the History of Thomas Becket*, 7 vols. (R.S., 67, 1875-85); Lives by A. Duggan (1952); Dom David Knowles (1970); and F. Barlow (1986). For the iconography see Tancred Borenius, *St Thomas Becket in Art* (1932) and "Some further aspects of the Iconography of St Thomas," *Archaeologia* 87 (1934). For the conflict with Henry II, see D. Whitelock *et al.*, *Councils and Synods*, 1, pt. 2 (1981), pp. 914-50; C. Duggan, *Canon Law in Mediaeval England* (1982); B. Smalley, *The Becket Conflict and the Schools* (1973); M. Brett *et al.* (eds.), "The Primacy Dispute," in intro. to *Hugh the Chanter, The History of the Church of York* (1990).

In July 1995, a twelfth-century Limoges casket which is believed to have held a relic of St Thomas until the dissolution of the monasteries in the sixteenth century, and to have been kept at Peterborough Abbey, was put up for auction in London. The casket is of copper. The cloisonné and enamel decoration depicts the murder of Thomas by the four knights on the front, and his lying in state, attended by angels, on the lid. It was described in the press as " an irreplaceable national treasure," and a fund was raised to save it for the nation. Among the major contributors was the widow of T. S. Eliot, whose play *Murder in the Cathedral* is based on these events. The reliquary was purchased for £4 million by a private collector from abroad, but the National Heritage Secretary issued an order forbidding its export, and it was eventually sold for a lesser sum to the British Museum. A smaller example of the reliquary, also from Limoges, and showing Thomas with only two of his assassins, is in the Cluny Museum in Paris.

St Trophimus, *Bishop* (? Third Century)

When Pope St Zosimus (27 Dec.) wrote to the bishops in Gaul in 417 he referred to Trophimus, saying that he had been sent as a missionary into Gaul and that his preaching at Arles was the source of the spreading of the Faith in the province. A century and a half years later St Gregory of Tours (17 Nov.) says that St Trophimus of Arles, its first bishop, was one of the six bishops who came from Rome with St Dionysius (St Denys of Paris; 9 Oct.) in the third century. Nothing is known of Trophimus of Arles apart from these references and the dedication of Arles Cathedral.

He was presumably named for Trophimus of Ephesus, a Gentile who accompanied St Paul on his third missionary journey (2 Tim. 4:20). Later, when the bishops of Arles asserted a claim to primacy in Gaul, some attempt was made to identify the two as the same person in order to give the claim additional weight, but neither the attempt nor the claim met with any success.

Albánez and Chevalier, *Gallia Christiana Novissima* (1901), 3, 11, lists Trophimus as the first archbishop of Arles. See also Quentin, pp. 303 and 603; Duchesne, *Fastes*, 1, pp. 246-7; *D.C.B.*, 4, p. 1055; *D.Cath.Biog.*, p. 1018.

St Marcellus Akimetes, *Abbot* (*c.* 485)

The *Akoimetoi* differed from other Eastern monks by a rule that the divine office was sung continuously day and night by successive choirs without interruption. From this practice came their name of the "not-resters."

Marcellus, the third abbot of a house sited on the Bosphorus opposite Constantinople, was the most distinguished of the *Akoimetoi* monks. He was born at Apamea in Sicily. Having a distaste for secular pursuits, he employed his time in sacred studies at Antioch and Ephesus and was drawn to the *Akoimetoi* by their reputation for austerity and solitude. He became assistant to the abbot and on his death was elected in his place.

As abbot he was insistent on the rule of poverty and would allow no hoarding or investment. He thought a ten-days' supply of food in hand too much. The *Akoimetoi* had always been rather contemptuous of manual work, but he insisted that all the monks should undertake some physical labour. The community numbered three hundred monks, and from all parts of the East applications were made to Abbot Marcellus for individual monks to be made abbots or for groups to form the nuclei of new establishments.

Marcellus was an outstanding figure in contemporary movements against heresy in Constantinople. He was one of the archimandrites who signed the condemnation of Eutyches in 448, and he assisted at the Council of Chalcedon. He governed his monastery for some forty-five years.

Synax. Const., p. 353. There is a detailed Greek biography attributed to the Metaphrast in *P.G.*, 116, 705-45. See also *D.A.C.L.*, 1, 315-8; *N.C.E.*, 9, p. 191; *Echos d'Orient*, 2, pp. 305-8 and 365-72.

St Ebrulf, *Abbot* (596)

St Ebrulf (Evroul or Evroult) was born in Normandy, probably at either Bayeux or Beauvais, and brought up at the court of King Childebert I. He became cup-bearer to the king and was eventually given charge of the administration of the royal palace. He married, but after a time he and his wife agreed to separate in order to enter the religious life. She took the veil, and he distributed his goods among the poor. It was some time before he was given leave to go from court, but at length he was able to enter a monastery in the diocese of Bayeux. He was much respected by the other monks, but this respect became a temptation to him, and he withdrew with three others to avoid it.

They settled at first in a quiet spot near Exmes, but crowds came out to see them and disturbed their solitude, so they moved to a remote part of the densely-wooded forest of Ouche in Normandy. They settled near a spring of water, made an enclosure with a hedge, and built themselves wattle huts. A robber came across the little settlement and tried to warn Ebrulf that there were brigands and wild beasts in the forest, saying, "Poor solitary creatures, what terrible fate has forced you to live in this deserted spot? Don't you know that this place is a refuge for brigands, not for hermits?" Ebrulf said, "We have come here to weep for our sins. We put our confidence in the mercy of God, who feeds the birds of the air. We fear no one." The robber went away impressed by the faith of the monks and the weight of his own sins, and the next day he returned with three loaves baked in the ashes and a honeycomb, offering his small presents and asking to be admitted to the company.

Ebrulf wanted to live as an anchorite without being burdened by the care of others; but he could not be indifferent to the salvation of those around him. He therefore received those who wished to live under his direction and was obliged to build a monastery for them. His community increased in numbers. Members of the nobility came to him, offering him their treasures, their land, and their houses, and he asked them to build other monasteries for both men and women. In all there were some fifteen monasteries, and he appointed superiors whom he could trust to institute his own Rule. He used to exhort his religious to manual labour, telling that they would gain their bread by work and heaven by serving God through work.

Ebrulf continued to guide his communities for many years. There was a time when pestilence broke out and many of the monks died. He comforted them in their last hours and prayed for their souls. Eventually the pain and the terror subsided, and the communities returned to tranquillity. The fame of his work spread. King Childebert III and his queen made a State visit, accompanied by a retinue of the nobility and the clergy. Pope John VII sent relics from Rome, including a relic of St Peter. Ebrulf died in peace and humility in his eightieth year.

The forest is now known as the forest of Saint-Evroult, and the village as Notre-Dame-de-Saint-Evroult. The abbey of Ouche was eventually abandoned but re-founded in the eleventh century. The chronicler Orderic Vitalis (1075-1142) was one of its monks in its period of greatest intellectual and spiritual influence.

A full life compiled by an anonymous ninth-century writer is printed by Surius. An abridged version is available in *The Ecclesiastical History of Orderic Vitalis*, trans. and ed. M. Chibnall, 1 (1969), app. 2, pp 204-11, where it is described as "a late and unreliable *vita*." See also the preface to Le Prévost and Delisle's edition of Orderic's *Historia Ecclesiastica* (vol. 1, 1840), pp. 79-84; P.B., pp. 576-91, from the *Vie des saints du diocèse de Séez;* Quentin, p. 33; *D.H.G.E.*, 16, 220-1.

Bd William Howard, *Martyr* (1680)

William Howard was a grandson of St Philip Howard, earl of Arundel and Surrey (19 Oct.). He was arrested and imprisoned in the Tower of London in 1675 for shielding Catholics and died there under sentence of death five years later.

William became Viscount Stafford in 1637 as a result of his marriage to the sister of the last holder of the title. Charles I created him and his wife baron and baroness respectively. He supported the Royalist side in the ensuing Civil War and lost his lands, which were restored after the accession of Charles II in 1660, but he felt that his loyalty to the Crown had not been sufficiently rewarded and seems to have borne a grudge against Charles II. In 1678 he had a very public "altercation" with the earl of Peterborough in a debate in the House of Lords, which made him enemies. In the same year he was denounced for complicity in the so-called "Popish Plot" invented by Titus Oates, which was alleged to aim at the assassination of Charles II in order to secure the succession of his Catholic brother, later James II. The plot was entirely fictitious and the elderly William Howard, then over sixty years of age, an unlikely participant, but in an atmosphere of public suspicion and apprehension the fact that he was a Catholic and something of a malcontent was enough. He was imprisoned in the Tower and tried by his peers in Westminster Hall in an atmosphere of great pomp and solemnity.

The diarist John Evelyn records that even some of William's own kinsmen voted against him. Evelyn, who knew him personally, could not believe that a man of William's maturity and experience would enter into such a plot and engage total strangers to murder the king. He found William's composure impressive. He "spake but little . . . and indeed behaved himself modestly, and as became him," but he was found guilty. He said, "God forgive those who have falsely sworn against me" before he was beheaded on Tower Hill in 1680. His death was shortly followed by the execution of St Oliver Plunket, archbishop of Armagh and primate of Ireland (11 July), at Tyburn on related charges.

D.N.B., 10, pp. 81-3; Stanton, pp. 610-13; *John Evelyn's Diary and Correspondence*, 2 (1857), pp. 127-9 and 154-5; George Clark, *Oxford History of England: The Later Stuarts*, pp. 92-5.

ST THOMAS BECKET (p. 224, above)
The Cornish choughs were known in the Middle Ages as St Thomas' birds
(and form the Burns & Oates colophon). Black choughs with
red legs and beaks, on silver field

30

St Anysius, *Bishop* (*c.* 410)

Anysius lived in Thessalonica about a century after St Anysia, who is commemorated today in the Orthodox calendar, and he may have been named in
her memory. He became bishop in 383, when St Ambrose (7 Dec.) wrote
commending his zeal and expressing great hopes for his episcopate.

He is known in church history on account of the action of Pope St Damasus
(11 Dec.) in making him patriarchal vicar in Illyricum, which was later to
become debated ground between Rome and Constantinople. His powers were
renewed by the two following popes.

Bishop Anysius was a strong supporter of St John Chrysostom (13 Sept.) and
went to Constantinople to uphold his cause. In 404, together with fifteen other
Macedonian bishops, he appealed to Pope Innocent on Chrysostom's behalf
after he had been exiled from his see. Chrysostom wrote Anysius a letter
thanking him for his efforts. It was during the episcopate of Anysius that the
shocking massacre took place in Thessalonica for which Emperor Theodosius
subsequently did penance (see St Ambrose; 7 Dec.). The virtues of Bishop
Anysius were highly praised by both Pope St Innocent I (28 July) and Pope St
Leo the Great (10 Nov.).

Anysius is named in the Roman Martyrology but is now thought not to have
been martyred himself, though many of his flock suffered martyrdom.

There is no Life of St Anysius, and we are dependent on scattered references in general
church history. These are discussed in, for example, Tillemont, *Mémoires*, 10, pp. 156-8.
See also L. Duchesne, "L'Illyricum ecclésiastique," in the *Byzantinische Zeitschrift*, 1
(1892), pp. 531-50; J. Zeiller, *Les origines chrétiennes dans les provinces danubiennes*, 1 (1918),
pp. 310-25; L. Petit, "Les Evêques de Thessalonique," in *Echos d'Orient* 4 (1901), pp. 141
ff.

St Egwin, *Bishop* (717)

Egwin (Ecgwine) was of royal blood, related to Ethelred, king of Mercia. He
became bishop of Worcester about 692 or 693. His zeal in reproving vice and
remedying abuses incurred the enmity of a faction in his see, who denounced
him to the king and the archbishop of Canterbury and forced him to withdraw.
He performed a penitential pilgrimage to Rome to answer to the pope, and he
was vindicated. On his return, with King Ethelred's help, he founded Evesham
Abbey.

Later, probably about 709, he undertook a second journey to Rome in the company of two kings, Cenred of Mercia and Offa of the East Saxons, and received considerable privileges for his foundation from Pope Constantine. Evesham became one of the great Benedictine houses of medieval England. According to Florence of Worcester, Egwin died at Evesham and was buried in the monastery.

After the Norman Conquest the cults of Saxon saints were investigated in the time of Archbishop Lanfranc, and in many churches Norman dedications were substituted for Saxon ones, but Egwin's cult was accepted, and the monks of Evesham carried out an extensive fund-raising tour, carrying his relics, in order to buy wood and stone for a church for their flourishing community. Two ancient churches were dedicated to Egwin.

An eleventh-century Life of Egwin, claiming to incorporate older elements, is printed in W. D. Macray, *Chronicon Abbatiae de Evesham*, R. S. (1863), pp. 1-26. J. C. Jennings, "The Writings of Prior Dominic of Evesham," in *E.H.R.* 77 (1962), pp. 298-304, establishes Dominic's authorship of this Life. See also Florence of Worcester, *Chronicon*, trans. and ed. T. Forester, 1, pp. 33 and 37-9; William of Malmesbury, *Gesta Pontificum*, R.S., 52, pp. 296-7, 383-6; Stanton, p. 615; A Benedictine of Stanbrook, *St Egwin and his Abbey of Evesham* (1904).

Bd Sebastian of Esztergom, *Bishop* (1036)

On New Year's Day in the year 1001, King Stephen of Hungary was crowned at Esztergom. The day was the first of the new millennium. The occasion signified the foundation of the Christian Hungarian State. King Stephen, now St Stephen of Hungary (16 Aug.) and the country's patron saint, had asked for and received a crown from Rome—probably from Pope Silvester II, after consultation with the Holy Roman Emperor Otto III. Stephen's queen, Bd Gisela (7 May), was Otto's sister. The sending of the crown changed the status of Hungary and the Magyars: from being regarded as a barbarian horde against whom Christian princes had a duty to take up arms, they became accepted as part of Christendom.

Sebastian (Sebestyén) became the second archbishop of Esztergom in 1002 and was consecrated in the presence of the royal couple. He became King Stephen's chief ecclesiastical adviser. Together they set about the task of converting the Magyars, organizing dioceses, founding abbeys, and bringing Hungary into the Christian tradition. At first this was not popular with the Magyars, who enjoyed fighting and looting and were not initially attracted by the prospect of self-denial and suffering, but a great cultural change was made, and Catholic Christianity has survived through many foreign occupations. The memory of Archbishop Sebastian, together with that of St Stephen and his queen, has long been reverenced as symbolizing Hungary's golden age.

Archiepiscopi Strigonensis (1758), 1, 14-21; E. Szentpétery, *Scriptores rerum Hungaricarum*; E. Kovács and Z. Lovac, trans. P. Balabán, *The Hungarian Crown*, (1980); BS(R), p. 501.

Bd Margaret Colonna (1280)

The earliest information about Margaret (Margherita) Colonna, daughter of Prince Odo Colonna, who died in about 1256, comes from two Lives, one written by Giovanni, the eldest of her four brothers, and the other by a Poor Clare of San Silvestro. Both appeared within about twelve years of her death. Margaret lost both her parents while she was still a child and grew up in the care of her brothers. When the time came for them to arrange a marriage for her, she refused to cooperate and retired with two attendants to a villa in Palestrina, twenty-four miles east of Rome. There she put all her energy and everything she possessed into serving the sick and the poor.

Prevented by ill health from joining the Poor Clares at their house in Assisi as she so longed to do, she decided to establish a convent of that Order in Palestrina. She was helped in this by her brother Giacomo, who had by then been made a cardinal. (He is described on this account as her *dignior frater*, while Giovanni is referred to as her *senior frater*.) Giacomo obtained the necessary permission from the pope, and the new community was given the Rule of the Poor Clares as modified by Pope Urban IV (1261-4), but Margaret's continued ill health prevented her from either joining the community or taking an active part in its government. For the last seven years of her life, during which she acquired a reputation for working miracles, she suffered from a painful cancer, which she faced with great courage and patience. She died while she was still young and was buried at Palestrina. Later, when the nuns moved from there to San Silvestro in Capite, they took her relics with them. Some seven hundred years later, when the house at San Silvestro was turned into a general post office, the relics were moved again, this time to the community's new home at Santa Cecilia in Trastevere. The cult of Bd Margaret Colonna was confirmed by Pope Pius IX in 1847.

B. Mazzara, *Leggendario Francescano* (1680), 2, pt. 2, pp. 775-80; also other Franciscan chroniclers. See also L. Oliger, *B. Margherita Colonna* (1935); *Auréole Séraphique*, 4, pp. 170-3.

31

ST SILVESTER I, *Pope* (335)

Silvester was the son of a Roman named Rufinus. He succeeded Miltiades in 314, less than a year after the Edict of Milan had granted some degree of toleration to Christians, and his pontificate lasted twenty-two years, through the reign of the Emperor Constantine. Since this was the period in which the Church, which had been subject to periods of persecution, became a powerful and accepted institution in the Roman Empire, it has often been assumed that Pope Silvester had a major influence in bringing this change about.

The most significant legends about him are those relating to the "Donation of Constantine." The tradition is that Constantine suffered from leprosy, that he was converted to Christianity, and that his leprosy was cured when he received Baptism from Silvester. In gratitude, the emperor granted numerous rights to the pope and his successors and endowed the Church with the provinces of Italy. A twelfth-century mosaic in the chapel of St Silvester in the church of the Santi Quattro Coronati in Rome shows Constantine on foot, leading the pope, mounted on horseback, into the city in triumph.

This and similar stories were embroidered and used for political and ecclesiastical ends during the Middle Ages. The *Acts of St Silvester*, a romanticized fifth-century version of his pontificate, enjoyed great popularity but has long been recognized as largely fabrication. The relationship between emperor and pope was less straightforward. Constantine certainly adopted the *Chi Rho* monogram as a battle emblem before his battle against Maxentius in 312, but after the battle he gave thanks for his victory to the Unconquered Sun, and appears to have seen no conflict between Christianity and popular solar monotheism. He issued a number of edicts granting toleration to religious groups, including Christians, but he did not make Christianity the official religion of the empire. He was generous to the Church in Rome, giving the pope the palace of the Lateran, where Silvester set up his *cathedra*, and established the Latin basilica as the cathedral church of Rome, enriched with gold and silver images. He built the first churches of St Peter on the Vatican, Holy Cross in the Sessorian Palace, and St Laurence outside the Walls. The *Liber Pontificalis* contains a long list of magnificent gifts to the Church from the emperor, including heavy silver chalices and patens, candlesticks, chandeliers, "basins for baptism," and revenue-producing farms and properties. There is no doubt of his generosity to the Church. This is the period when the Christian community began to develop as a corporate body in Rome, holding property and exercising temporal power, but Constantine did not regard Rome as the institutional centre of the empire. In 330 he moved his imperial capital from Rome to Byzantium.

Silvester does not appear to have been one of Constantine's confidants, and he did not baptize him. Constantine remained a catechumen until he was baptized on his death-bed by an Arian bishop in Nicomedia, eighteen months after Silvester's death. The timing of his Baptism may not be of great significance, since death-bed Baptisms were common at the time, particularly among those who had to wage war or were responsible for executions and who anticipated having much to repent of. It is perhaps more significant that Pope Silvester did not preside at the two great doctrinal councils of his pontificate, the Council of Arles in 314 and the Council of Nicaea in 325, and was not present at either. He was new in office at the time of the Council of Arles and may have thought it unwise to leave Rome. He sent representatives to the council, where the bishops dealt with the Donatist dispute, and the bishops actually commended him for not coming in person and for remaining in Rome "where the Apostles sit in judgement."

The Council of Nicaea, eleven years later, was called together by Constantine. The letters of invitation went out in his name; he placed imperial transport at the disposal of the bishops; he was personally present at some of the sessions; and the conference ended with a magnificent banquet at his imperial palace. It was the first ecumenical or general council of the Church, of major doctrinal importance, since it drafted the Nicene Creed, condemned the Arian heresy, and promulgated a number of important canons. Though some 220 bishops attended, they were nearly all from the Eastern Church, and they met in what is now Izmir in north-west Turkey. Silvester of Rome sent only two priests and two deacons as legates. The presiding bishop was Hosius (Ossius) of Córdoba, the emperor's own ecclesiastical adviser. There is no record that Pope Silvester formally confirmed the signature of his legates to the acts of the council, though Pope Damasus (11 Dec.) was later to claim that he did so.

Pope Silvester's name, joined to that of Pope Martin I (13 Apr.), is now given to the cardinal-titular church founded near the Baths of Diocletian by a priest named Equitius. Pope Silvester also built a church at the cemetery of Priscilla on the Salarian way, and there he was himself buried in 335. In 761 his relics were translated by Pope Paul I to St Silvester *in capite*, now the national church of English Catholics in Rome, where his stone papal chair still stands in the cloisters.

For Constantine's edicts see J. Stevenson (ed.), *The New Eusebius* (1960), pp. 297-304. Jaffé, 1, pp. 28-30; *Lib.Pont.*, 1, p. 157; *O.D.P.*, pp. 27-8. Cf. N. H. Baynes, *Constantine the Great and the Christian Church* (1929). For discussion on the Council of Nicaea and the question of the primacy of Rome see C. J. Hefele , *History of the Councils of the Church*, trans. H. N. Oxenham (2d. ed., 1922), pp. 394-401.

There is a fourteenth-century painting of the story of St Silvester in the church of Santa Croce, Florence.

St Zoticus (*c.* 350)

The story of Zoticus, a priest in Rome, provides an interesting addendum to that of Pope Silvester (see above). When Constantine decided to transfer his imperial capital from Rome to Byzantium in 330 and to rename the ancient eastern city, Zoticus followed him.

The acceptance of Christianity as the religion of the imperial power meant that Christian works of mercy, which had previously been carried out on a small scale, had to be adapted to the needs of the wider community. In Constantinople Zoticus built a hospital for the poor and a shelter for orphans. This work probably anticipated the *ptochotropheion*, or institute for the needy, set up in Caesarea by St Basil the Great (*c.* 329-79; 2 Jan.), which became a model for similar centres in other parts of the empire.

Zoticus remained loyal to the Faith as defined at the Council of Nicaea under Constantine's successor Constantius, who was an Arian.

Bibl.SS., 12, 1505-6; *D.Cath.Biog.*, pp. 122-3.

SS Melania the Younger (? 383-439) and Pinian (? 379-440)

Melania the Younger was the daughter of a Roman senator, Publicola, and his wife, Albina. She is designated "the Younger" to distinguish her from her father's mother, Melania the Elder, who, widowed at the age of twenty-two, went to Jerusalem, built a monastery, and devoted herself to charitable causes.

The younger Melania's father, Publicola, though a Christian, was ambitious for his family, and he seems to have been in conflict with his mother, who was profoundly influenced by the ascetic movement, which had reached Rome from North Africa and the Middle East. The elder Melania had given away most of her own possessions and was vowed to celibacy. There is some evidence that the younger Melania may have had a brother, who was "led away" by his grandmother into the ascetic life, so that young Melania was Publicola's only hope of having a male heir. In 397, in order to further this hope, he arranged an ambitious marriage with her kinsman Valerius Pinianus, son of the prefect Valerius Severus. Melania was only fourteen and Pinian seventeen.

Melania, also influenced by her grandmother, wished to remain a virgin; but Publicola insisted that the marriage should be consummated. According to her biographer Gerontius, she pleaded with Pinian "with much piteous wailing" to live with her "according to the law of continence," but Pinian refused. The young husband and wife must have been subject to intense and contradictory pressures from their relatives. Young Melania became pregnant, and her first child, on whom so much depended, was a girl. Publicola, still determined to have a male heir, stopped Melania from associating with Christians (presumably including his own mother), who might encourage her in celibacy. Melania became pregnant again and on the feast of St Laurence (10 Aug.) 399, she went into premature labour. After a difficult and dangerous confinement she gave birth to a boy, who died on the following day. If the date of her birth is given correctly, she was still only sixteen years old.

Shortly afterwards the infant daughter also died. Melania was desperately ill, and Pinian, who was sincerely attached to her despite all the family pressures, swore that if she lived they would both be celibate. Her father bitterly disapproved. It was only when he was dying five years later that he willed all his estates to Melania and begged her forgiveness for opposing her "heavenly vocation."

When Publicola died Melania became extremely wealthy. She owned property in Rome and great estates in other parts of Italy, in Sicily, in Spain, in North Africa, in Britain, and probably in Gaul and Aquitania. In modern terms she must have been a millionairess many times over, and Pinian was also wealthy in his own right. Melania's biographer makes it plain that they were determined "to make themselves enemies to the confusions of secular life" in spite of their wealth. Pinian was now Melania's "brother in the Lord" rather than her husband. Together with her mother, Albina, they left their palace in Rome, never to return. They went to an estate they owned in the country, where they devoted themselves to "training in the practice of the virtues."

They assisted the poor and needy, visited prisoners and redeemed them if they were imprisoned for debt, sheltered strangers, and visited the sick—living out quite literally the corporal works of mercy listed in Matthew 25:42-5. They wore cheap clothes—though Pinian seems to have found this more difficult than Melania did and was slow to abandon his fine linen. They were joined by young girls, widows, and over thirty families; the estate became a centre of hospitality, of charity, and of religious life.

Melania and Pinian decided to sell all their Italian properties. Their relatives, particularly Pinian's brother Severus, were appalled at this break-up of the family fortunes, and they may have had some legal grounds for preventing it. Severus seems to have provoked a slave revolt, persuading some thousands of Melania's slaves that they would be better off sold to him than placed on the open market. An unknown city prefect attempted to confiscate the properties for the city treasury, but he was killed before he could take action. So many obstacles were placed in their way that Melania and Pinian went to Serena, mother-in-law of the emperor Honorius, and secured her support in asking the emperor to protect the equitable sale of the properties. The sales went through: the proceeds were enormous and were applied to needy causes in many parts of the empire. Poor and sick people, captives, bankrupts, pilgrims, churches, and monasteries were relieved and endowed in large numbers. Palladius in his contemporary *Lausiac History* says that the monasteries of Egypt, Syria, and Palestine received very large benefactions. In two years Melania gave their freedom to eight thousand slaves and sold many more to Severus, probably at their own request.

These events become more explicable if it is recalled that they took place in 405-7, when the barbarians were devastating Gaul and had crossed into Italy. Melania's recent biographer, Dr Elizabeth Clark, takes the view that these sales of property were so extensive that they may have been sufficient to destabilize the Roman economy—at a time when huge amounts of gold were required to fend off Alaric the Goth and other barbarian chiefs. This may explain why the city prefect obtained the support of the Senate for his plan to take over the estates, and perhaps why many of the slaves sought the protection of Severus. It may also explain why Melania and Pinian left their palace in Rome so precipitately and divested themselves of all their Italian possessions. Their haste suggests that they anticipated the end of the civilized world as they knew it.

The end was to come very quickly. In 408 or early in 409 Serena was executed by order of the Senate, possibly for her part in helping to liquidate the estates. She was regarded as a traitor to Rome; and by that time Alaric was blockading the Tiber to prevent supplies getting through. The imperial city was starving and plague-ridden, and corpses rotted in the streets.

Melania and Pinian had fled to their estates in Sicily; but when the Goths reached Calabria and burned Reggio, just across the Straits of Messina, they determined to go to North Africa. They were evidently still very wealthy refugees. When their ship was driven to seek harbour from a storm, probably in Lipari, they found that the island was being held to ransom by pirates, and to save the people from catastrophe Melania bought the freebooters off with a huge sum in gold.

They had North African estates to go to, and they eventually settled at Tagaste in Numidia. St Augustine (28 Aug.) called them "real lights of the Church," and Pinian made as profound an impression as his wife. When he went to Hippo to visit Augustine the people wanted him to be ordained priest so that he could minister to them, and there was a riot because they thought he was being prevented from doing this by the bishop of Tagaste. Pinian evidently had no intention of being ordained, but order was restored only when he promised that, should he ever become a priest, he would exercise his ministry at Hippo. While they were in North Africa Melania established and endowed two new monasteries, one for men and one for women, for people who had been slaves on her lands there. She herself lived with the women but would not let them live as austerely as she did. She took food only every other day and sometimes fasted for long periods. She usually slept for only two hours a night, prayed constantly, and wore sackcloth. She also worked hard: her biographer Gerontius says that she "wrote without mistakes in notebooks." The skills of a really conscientious and accurate transcriber were much valued, and five hundred years later manuscripts were still in circulation that were attributed to Melania's hand.

In the year 417 Melania, Pinian, and Albina left Africa for Jerusalem and lodged in the pilgrims' hospice near the Holy Sepulchre. By this time they had given away all their possessions except those in territory occupied by the barbarians, and they were poor enough to think of adding their names to the city's register of those needing alms. A friend was able to sell part of their estates in Spain and brought them the money. Melania "seized it as from the lion's mouth," and proposed to Pinian that they should make an expedition to visit the monks of the Egyptian deserts. They did so and continued to distribute money freely. Their habits were still the habits of the rich. They tried to give some gold to one monk, but he said he had no use for it and threw the pieces in the river. They were so impressed by the ascetic example of the Desert Fathers that they returned to settle at Jerusalem to a life of solitude and contemplation. Here Melania's cousin Paula introduced her to St Jerome (30 Sept.). She became one of his closest friends and colleagues. He called her "the devout Lady Melanium," and wrote that she was "eminent among Christians for her true nobility."

After fourteen years in Palestine, Albina died, and Pinian died in the following year. He is named with Melania in the Roman Martyrology. She buried her mother and her "spiritual brother" side by side on the Mount of Olives, and herself lived in a small cell close by. This became the nucleus of a large community of consecrated virgins, but she refused to act as superior. Her own contribution to the community life was remarkable for its mildness and care for individuals. She also built a monastery for men on the Mount of Olives— Gerontius was a monk from this monastery and her disciple. It is possible that in his desire to praise the holy acts of "the blessed woman" he does not do full justice to Pinian and Albina.

On Christmas Eve 439 Melania went to Bethlehem, and after the Mass at dawn she told her cousin Paula that she was dying. On St Stephen's Day she attended Mass in his basilica and then read the account of his martyrdom to her companions. She wished them well and told them that they would never again hear her read the lesson. She made a farewell visit to the monks, then summoned the sisters again, asking for their prayers, "for I am going to the Lord." She told them that if she had ever spoken to them severely, it was for love of them, reminding them of her words: "The Lord knows I am unworthy, and I would not dare compare myself with any good woman, even of those living in the world. Yet I think the Enemy himself will not at the Last Judgment accuse me of ever having gone to sleep with bitterness in my heart." In the evening, repeating the words of Job, "As the Lord willed, so it is done," she died. She was fifty-six years old.

Melania the Younger has been venerated liturgically from early times in the Byzantine Church, but there was no cult in the West until 1905, when Cardinal Rampolla published a monumental work on her life.

Considerable fragments of a Latin Life of St Melania had long been known to exist in various libraries, and these are available in *Anal. Boll.* 8 (1889), pp. 16-63. The Metaphrast produced his own sophisticated version of the biography: see *P. G.*, 116, 753-94. The Greek text was edited from a manuscript in the Barberini Library by Delehaye in *Anal. Boll.* 22 (1903), pp. 5-50. In 1905 Cardinal Rampolla discovered a complete copy of the Latin in the Escorial and printed both Latin and Greek in a sumptuous folio volume, *Santa Melania Giuniore Senatrice Romana*, with a long introduction, dissertations, and notes. In a long contribution to *Anal. Boll.* 25 (1906), pp. 401-50, Fr Adhémar d'Alès examines the variations between the two texts. His conclusion is that the Life was compiled by Melania's disciple Gerontius about nine years after her death in a first draft written in Greek, but that the texts in Greek and Latin which we now possess were elaborated a few years later from this original. See also St Jerome, Letters 4 and 39, in N.P.N.F., 6, pp. 6-7 and 53; Palladius, *Historia Lausiaca*, ed. Cuthbert Butler, 2 (1904), p. 156. For a modern critical text, Eng. trans., and discussion of the textual problems see Elizabeth A. Clark, *The Life of Melania the Younger* (1984).

St Columba of Sens, *Martyr* (date unknown)

The tradition is that Columba was a Spanish girl who, when she was sixteen, came into Gaul with other Spaniards and settled at Sens, posibly in the third century. She is said to have been the child of noble but pagan parents and to have left them to avoid the worship of false gods. She was baptized at Vienne. When the Emperor Aurelian came to Sens he ordered Columba and her companions to be put to death. She was beheaded at the fountain of Azon on the road to Meaux.

The cult of St Columba spread over France and Spain and to Italy. The abbey of Sainte-Colombe, which sheltered her relics, was the chief religious house of Sens. Its third church was consecrated by Pope Alexander III in 1164. In the next year Archbishop Thomas Becket (29 Dec.), then an exile from England, arrived at the monastery after he was forced to leave Pontigny. He stayed at Sainte-Colombe until he returned to England and to martyrdom.

G. Chastel, *Ste Colombe de Sens* (1939), contains a new text of the passion and an account of the cult; Tillemont, *Mémoires*, 4, 347; P.B., pp. 629-38.

St John-Francis Régis (1597-1640)

Born in the Languedoc at Font-Couverte, in the diocese of Narbonne, John-Francis Régis was educated at the Jesuit college of Béziers and in 1615 entered the Society of Jesus at Béziers at the age of eighteen. It was said that he was so grounded in humility that he vilified himself but canonized everyone else. When he had completed the first year of his novitiate he followed courses in rhetoric and logic at Cahors and Tournon. While he was at Tournon he accompanied the priest who served the little town of Andance every Sunday and holiday, and he gave catechetical instructions while the priest was hearing Confessions. These were so helpful that he was said to have influenced the older members of the congregation as well as the children He was then only twenty-two years old.

In 1628 he was sent to Toulouse to begin his theology course. A companion who shared his room told the superior that John spent much of the night in prayer in the chapel. "Take care not to disturb his devotions," said the superior, Fr Francis Tarbes, "nor to hinder his communion with God. He is a saint; and if I am not greatly mistaken, the Society will some day celebrate a feast in his honour."

In 1631 John was ordained, and he spent the rest of his life ministering to the peasant communities of the Languedoc and the Auvergne. The summers were spent in the towns, but in the winter months he visited the villages and the more remote farms. He preached, he taught the illiterate, and he had a special concern for people in trouble. His discourses were plain and even homely, unlike the formal Jesuit discourses of his day, but they were so expressive of the fervour that burned within him that they attracted large congregations drawn from all social classes. He addressed himself particularly to the poor. The rich, he said, never lacked confessors. When warned that this view was unpopular in aristocratic circles, he retorted: "So much the better: we are doubly blest if we relieve a poor brother at the expense of our dignity."

His mornings were spent in the confessional, at the altar, and in the pulpit. The afternoons he devoted to prisons and hospitals. Very often he was so busy that he forgot to take his meals. Before he left Montpellier he had formed a committee of women to carry out prison visiting and had rescued many other women from prostitution. To the critics who contended that such rescue efforts seldom last long, he replied: "If my efforts do no more than hinder one sin, I shall consider them well expended."

After Montpellier he made his temporary headquarters at Sommières, and from this base he visited the most out-of-the-way places, winning the confidence of the people by talking to them in their own patois. His success at Montpellier and Sommières prompted Mgr de la Baume, bishop of Viviers, to ask for his services and those of another Jesuit in his diocese. No part of France had suffered more from prolonged civil and religious strife than the wild, mountainous regions of the Vivarais and the Velay. Law and order seemed to have disappeared, the nobles were often no more than brigands, and the peasantry were lapsing into savagery. Absentee bishops and negligent priests had allowed the churches to fall into ruin, and whole parishes had been deprived of the sacraments for twenty years or more. Traditionally, many of the inhabitants were Calvinist, but they had fallen so far away from religion that there was little to choose between them and those who were nominally Catholic.

With the help of his Jesuit assistants, Bishop de la Baume undertook a thorough visitation of his diocese. Fr Régis went everywhere a day or two in advance of him, conducting a mission. This was the beginning of a three-year ministry, during which he had a considerable effect in bringing back religious observance to this neglected area.

Such a vigorous campaign was hardly likely to go unopposed. At one point in his ministry baseless charges were made against him by those who resented his activities. Fr Régis never said a word in his own defence, but the bishop recognized the falsity of the charges and continued to give him his support.

About this time Fr Régis made the first of several unsuccessful applications to be sent on the Canadian mission to the North American Indians. His superiors were no doubt satisfied with the work he was doing in France, but he regarded it as a punishment for his sins that he was not allowed to go into this dangerous territory and to risk martyrdom for the Faith. Instead, he redoubled his efforts to reach the most desolate parts of the mountainous region of the Velay, where no man went unarmed and the winters were bitterly cold. On one occasion he was held up by a snowdrift for three weeks, with only a little bread to eat and sleeping on the bare ground.

Graphic and touching descriptions of these expeditions are to be found in the depositions for his canonization. The curé of Marlhes stated:

No cold, no snow-blocked path, no rain-swollen torrent could stop him. . . . I have seen him stop in the middle of a forest to satisfy a crowd who wished to hear him. I have seen him stand all day on a heap of snow at the top of a mountain, instructing and preaching, and then spend the whole night hearing confessions.

Another witness had been passing through the district when he saw a procession winding its way in the distance. "It is the saint," he was told, "and the people are following."

The last four years of his life were spent at Velay. All through the summer he worked in Le Puy, where the Jesuit church proved too small for congregations numbering four or five thousand. His influence reached all classes and brought about a real and lasting spiritual revival. He established and organized a complete social service with prison visitors, sick-nurses, and guardians of the poor, most of them women. The well-to-do gave him money freely: he established a granary for the poor and a refuge for women and girls.

This last enterprise got him into trouble again: some of the men of the area objected to the women's refuge and blackened his character, while even his own Order questioned his prudence. For some time his work was stopped by a timorous superior, and Fr Régis, as when he was wrongfully accused at Viviers, made no attempt to justify himself. He was much loved by the people of the area, and stories began to circulate about the cures he had performed and the way in which, however great the demands on the granary, there always seemed to be enough corn for the hungry. His work went on.

In the autumn of 1640 he seems to have realized that his life was coming to an end. He was due to give a mission at La Louvesc toward the end of Advent, and before he did so he made a three days' retreat at the college of Le Puy and settled a few small debts. On the eve of his departure he was invited to stay for the semi-annual renewal of vows. He said that he was unable to stay and that he would not be returning, though his companion would. They set out in bad weather, lost their way, and had to spend the night in a ruined house in the woods, open to the piercing wind. Fr Régis, completely exhausted, contracted pleurisy; but he insisted on continuing painfully to La Louvesc, where he preached three times on Christmas Day and three times on St Stephen's Day, spending the rest of those two days in the confessional. At the close of the last address he attempted again to hear Confessions but fainted twice. He was carried to the curé's house, and there he died on the last day of the old year at the age of forty-three.

Fr Régis was canonized in 1737 by Pope Clement XII. His body remains at Louvesc, where he died, and is visited annually by thousands of pilgrims. It was on a pilgrimage to his resting-place that St Jean-Marie Vianney, the Curé d'Ars (4 Aug.), came to a realization of his own vocation, and he subsequently wrote a Life of Fr Régis.

Lives by C. La Broüe (1654); G. Dauberton (1717); F. Curley (1893); J.-M. Vianney, in the series Les Saints (1914); G. Guiton, *Après les guerres de religion . . .* (1937). See also *C.E.*, 8, pp. 464-5; *D. Cath. Biog.*, p. 980; Sandra Miesel, *National Catholic Register* (U.S.A.) 68, 14 June 1992, p. 4.

St Catherine Labouré (1806-76)

Zoë Labouré was born on 2 May 1806. She was the eighth of the ten children of a French yeoman farmer, Pierre Labouré, and his wife, Madeleine Goutard, who lived at Fain-les-Moutiers in the Côte d'Or. She was the only member of her large family who did not go to school, and she never learned properly to read and write. When she was only eight her mother died, and not long after this she inherited from her sister Louise, who left home to become a Sister of Charity, the combined role of housekeeper and helper to her father. From the age of fourteen she felt called to the religious life herself, but her father was opposed to the idea and, in order to distract her, sent her to Paris to be a waitress in a café belonging to one of her brothers. This had no effect on her, so in 1830 M. Labouré gave in and allowed her to join the Sisters of Charity of St Vincent de Paul at Châtillon-sur-Seine. She took the name Catherine, and once her postulancy was over she was sent to the convent in the rue du Bac in Paris.

She arrived four days before the relics of St Vincent de Paul (27 Sept.) were transferred from the cathedral of Notre-Dame to the Lazarist church on the rue de Sèvres, and on the evening of the opening day of the festivities she had the first of the visions for which she was to become famous. Three more visions took place in mid-July, and then, on 27 November, Our Lady appeared to her standing on a globe, with shafts of light streaming from her hands and the words "O Mary, conceived free from sin, pray for us who have recourse to thee" surrounding the image. When Our Lady turned round, Catherine saw a capital M with a cross above it and below it two hearts (one thorn-crowned, one pierced with a sword). Catherine seemed to hear a voice telling her to have what she saw struck as a medal and promising that those who wore the medal with devotion would receive great graces at the intercession of Mary. The visions continued until September 1831.

Catherine confided in her confessor, M. Aladel, who after thorough investigations, obtained permission from the archbishop of Paris to have the medal struck. The first fifteen hundred of what came to be known as the "Miraculous Medal" (because of its origin rather than its properties) were issued in June 1832. In 1834 M. Aladel published a *Notice historique sur l'origine et les effets de la Médaille Miraculeuse*, 130,000 copies of which were sold in six years, with translations into seven languages, including Chinese. When in 1836 the archbishop of Paris ordered an inquiry into the alleged visions, Catherine could not be persuaded to appear—she had taken such precautions to keep herself unknown and did not want to lose that anonymity now. So the tribunal went on without her, coming down, in the end, in favour of the authenticity of the visions.

The popularity of the medal increased daily, particularly after the conversion in 1842 of an Alsatian Jew, Alphonse Ratisbonne. Having reluctantly agreed to wear it, he had a vision of Our Lady in the same form, became a Christian, and went on to become a priest and to found the Congregation of Notre-Dame de Sion and the Fathers of Zion.

Alphonse Ratisbonne's vision was subjected to canonical inquiry, and the reports of this, as well as of the archbishop of Paris' inquiry into Catherine's visions, were used in Catherine's beatification process. Almost nothing is recorded about her personal life. From 1831 until her death on 31 December 1876 she lived unobtrusively in the convent at Enghien-Reuilly—as portress, or minding the poultry, or looking after the old people in the hospice. Her superiors spoke of her as "rather insignificant," "matter-of-fact and unexcitable," "cold, almost apathetic." Not until eight months before her death would she speak to anyone other than her confessor about the graces she had received, and then only to her superior, Sister Dufès. But there was an outburst of popular veneration at her funeral, and a twelve-year-old child crippled from birth was reported to have been cured at her grave soon afterwards. Catherine Labouré was canonized in 1947. Her relics remain in the chapel of the convent in the rue du Bac, where she had her visions.

See J. I. Dirvin, *St Catherine Labouré of the Miraculous Medal* (1984); C. Yves, *La vie secrète de Catherine Labouré* (1948); G. Fullerton, *Life and Visions of a Sister of Charity* (1880); other biographies in Eng. trans.: E. Crapez (1920), E. Cassinari (1934). See also *O.D.S.*, p. 286; *N.C.E.*, 8, pp. 301-2; *Bibl.SS.* 3, 1045-7.

Alphabetical List of Entries

(Names are listed for those saints and blessed who have entries in the main body of the text.)

Supplement

This Supplement includes major beatifications since the relevant volumes were written, some that were overlooked, and one unfortunate omission through the loss of a computer file. Like the monthly volumes, it does not claim to be comprehensive: beatifications proceed at an unprecendented pace, and it has not been considered appropriate to include all those about whom little more is known than appears in, for instance, the weekly English edition of the *Osservatore Romano*. Early volumes have been reprinted in the United States, and the reprints have been updated with the inclusion of the relevant entries below. These are repeated here so that subscribers to the original printing have the same information. Entries were "closed" at 30 September 1999.

Several people have contributed to the compilation of this supplement, and I should like to thank Fr Andrew Brizzolara, C.S., for the entry on John Baptist Scalabrini; Br Frederick McMahon, F.M.S., for the entry on St Marcellin Champagnat; Christa Pongratz-Lippitt for checking and contributing to the entry on Aloysius Stepinac; Jean Olwen Maynard for alerting me to many beatifications, particularly of Blessed from the Third World, for the entry on Bd Vincent Lewoniuk and Companions, and for providing a mass of information.

Paul Burns
30 September 1999

---

7 January

Bd Mary-Theresa of the Sacred Heart, *Foundress* (1782-1876)

She was born Johanna Haze in Liège in Belgium. There seems to be some doubt as to the actual year of her birth: the *Dizionario degli Instituti di perfezione* gives it as 1782, but the *Bibliotheca Sanctorum* puts it forward by five years to 1777, making her ninety-nine at the time of her death. Her father worked in the secretariat of the archbishop of Liège; the family had to flee from the French Revolution in 1794, and her father died the following year.

She had several sisters who married, but she and one other, Ferdinanda, vowed to devote their lives to the service of God as religious. Conditions during the Revolution and the period following, however, prevented them from finding an Order in which they could be professed. They lived with their family, devoted themselves to good works among the poor and sick of the

251

parish, and worked in a school started by another sister in 1824. With renewed freedom for religious Orders promulgated in Belgium in 1830, Johanna returned to her project and in 1832 was given approval for a new Congregation, the Daughters of the Holy Cross of Liège, taking the name Mary-Theresa of the Sacred Heart of Jesus in religion. As superior, she oversaw the establishment and then considerable growth of the Congregation for over forty years.

The Congregation, dedicated to education, care of the sick, and evangelization spread during her lifetime to Germany in 1851, India in 1862, and England in 1863; after her death it expanded to the then Belgian Congo, Ireland, Brazil, and to the U.S.A. in 1958. It currently numbers some 1,500 Sisters in 113 houses. Mother Mary-Theresa died rich in years and achievements in Liège on 7 January 1876 and was beatified by Pope John Paul II on 21 April 1991.

Bibl.SS., 8, 1144; *D.N.H.*, 3, pp. 248-50, with portraits.

14 January

St Nino of Georgia (early Fourth Century)

Little is known about the beginnings of Christianity in the former kingdom of Georgia, but the story of the beginnings of its evangelization told by Rufinus is accepted (and elaborated) by the Georgians themselves and by other Byzantine sources. The story was told to Rufinus by a Georgian prince named Bakur, who was recounting events that took place in the lifetime of his parents or grandparents.

Rufinus tells us that early in the fourth century an unnamed young woman—whom the Georgians called Nino and the Roman Martyrology, not knowing her name, Christiana—was taken to Georgia as a captive. She made a great impression on the people by the sobriety and chastity of her life and her devotion to prayer. When questioned, she simply told them that she worshipped Christ as God. It was the custom for the mother of an ailing child to take it round to the other women to ask about possible remedies. One such child was brought to Nino; when she laid it on her hair cloak and prayed over it, the child got better.

After that many people went to her for healing, and the queen, who had an ailment, went to see her. Nino laid the queen on her hair cloak and prayed, and the queen was cured. When the queen wished to thank her, she is reputed to have said, "It is not my work but Christ's; and he is the Son of God who made the world." The king sent her presents, but Nino refused them. At last the queen went to her husband and said, "O King, the captive woman prizes none of these things. She rejects gold, despises silver, and nourishes herself by fasting as if by food. The only way in which we can reward her is by worshipping that God Christ, who cured me, according to her prayers." Shortly afterwards, the story goes, the king was lost while hunting: he swore that if Christ would show him the way home he would believe. The mist cleared, and the king kept his word. He and his wife were instructed by Nino. He announced his change of religion to the people, gave Nino licence to preach and teach, and had a church built. He then sent an embassy to the emperor Constantine, telling him what had happened and asking that bishops and priests might be sent.

Rufinus' narrative, which dates from the late fourth century, has been translated into Greek, Syriac, Armenian, Coptic, Arabic, and Ethiopic and considerably amplified. In Georgian literature, there is a whole cycle of Nino legends. Rufinus gives no localities for his events. He does not give the name of the king and queen or even the name of the saint, her nationality, or place of origin. Later versions have attempted to supply these omissions: Nino is said to have come from Cappadocia, from Rome, from Jerusalem, from the kingdom of the Franks; the pseudo-Moses of Khorene, an Armenian writer, credits her with the conversion of Armenia, associating her with their St Hripsime. In some accounts she is said to be a niece of Patriarch Juvenal of Jerusalem or a fugitive from the persecutions of Diocletian; in others, to have been miraculously preserved from martyrdom. In Egypt she is sometimes known as *Theognosta*.

After seeing Christianity firmly established in Georgia, Nino is said to have retired to a cell on a mountain at Bodbe in Kakheti. Here she died and was buried. It may be the case that the conversion of Georgia was begun in the reign of Constantine and that a woman had a prominent part in it. The kingdom was certainly Christian at the time Rufinus wrote; but it is now impossible to say what is the truth behind the story he heard form the Georgian prince.

Rufinus, *H.E.*, 1, 10; *P.L.*, 21, 480-2. The story of Nino has been greatly elucidated by Fr Paul Peeters' article "Les Débuts du Christianisme en Géorgie," *Anal.Boll.* 50 (1932), pp. 5-58. The legend does not appear in its best-known form before 973, and the texts written in Georgian are of still later date. A Life of St Nino has been translated into English from the Georgian by M. and J. Wardrop: see the Oxford *Studia Biblica et Ecclesiastica*, 5, pt. 1 (1900). A somewhat cognate Armenian text is made accessible in the version of F. C. Conybeare, but the early dates there assigned to these documents are unwarranted. See also D. M. Lang, *Lives and Legends of the Georgian Saints* (1956, rp. 1976), pp. 13-39. For background, see Nicholas Zernov, *Eastern Christendom* (1961), p. 73.

16 January

Bd Joseph Vaz (1651-1711)

According to a legal agreement with the papacy known as the *Padroado*, the Portuguese crown—in return for resourcing the promotion of Christianity in its huge maritime empire—enjoyed extensive jurisdiction over the local churches thereby established. The sixteenth century saw the formation of enduring Catholic communities in many parts of Asia, though the close alliance between Christian mission and colonial aggression also provoked a heavy backlash of local resentment. In the seventeenth century, when most of Portugal's Asian possessions were seized by the Dutch, the missionaries fled or were expelled. Only a few small enclaves remained Portuguese, including Goa, on the west coast of India, the administrative and ecclesiastical headquarters of the former empire. Since Portugal could no longer fulfill its responsibilities in the rest of Asia, the Holy See began appointing vicars apostolic through *Propaganda Fide*—an intervention jealously opposed by Portugal. Goa was producing a healthy surplus of Indian priests who would have been ideal to serve under *Propaganda* had not its Portuguese archbishops been so extremely unwilling to relinquish control over them, resenting with particular ferocity their advancement by Rome to the episcopate. Within Portuguese territory these priests, however dedicated and competent, were barred on racist grounds from all positions of responsibility.

Joseph Vaz was born in 1651 in Sancoale, Goa, to a Catholic family of the Brahmin caste and ordained in 1676. Some years later he chanced to hear of the plight of Catholics in Ceylon (now Sri Lanka), where the practice of their faith had been totally proscribed since the Dutch takeover in 1658. The Dutch East India Company, which controlled the coastal strips where most of them lived and virtually all the seaports, permitted no priests to disembark on the island. He sought permission to go and help them, pointing out that a dark-skinned Indian like himself should be able to enter unnoticed. Instead he was appointed as *vicar forane* to Kanara, just south of Goa, in the hope that he could be used as a catspaw to re-establish *Padroado* rights there. He was under orders to treat the *Propaganda* vicar apostolic—another Goan Brahmin named Thomas de Castro, based in Mangalore—as an interloper and to forbid the faithful to have anything to do with him or his priests. Instead he treated de Castro with humble respect and gave him full co-operation. As a consequence he narrowly escaped suspension and was also made to bear the brunt of de Castro's recriminations against the *Padroado* authorities. During the three years he spent in Kanara he came to be revered by people of all religions as a true *sanyasi*, a holy ascetic. But on his return to Goa he found himself in disgrace as a disloyal priest.

Shortly afterwards he joined a group of Goan clergy seeking to form their own religious community, existing congregations being open only to those with European blood. Elected superior, he worked for six months to form the community after the Oratorian model. Then he resigned his office and set off for Sri Lanka, accompanied by a young man named John Vaz, a servant from his family home. Dressed as coolies wearing only a coarse ankle-length cloth round the waist, the pair reached Jaffna exhausted after a dreadful ferry passage in bad weather, had to beg for scraps and sleep rough, and quickly contracted dysentery. Carried into the forest to die, they were saved by a woman who brought them a little rice gruel each day.

Wandering the streets of Jaffna as a beggar, with a rosary round his neck, Fr Vaz made contact with Catholic families who established a safe base for him in an outlying village, from where he was able to exercise his ministry throughout the region for just over two years. Shortly before Christmas 1689, however, the Dutch authorities strengthened their anti-Catholic measures. Eight men, the richest and most influential of the Tamil Catholics, were flogged, imprisoned, and so badly treated that they all died soon after.

Fr Vaz sought refuge in Kandy, a Sinhalese Buddhist kingdom which still maintained independent sovereignty over the undeveloped, jungle-covered interior. He was at first thrown into a dungeon on suspicion of being a Portuguese agent, but King Vimaladharma Surya II, convinced of his sincerity, had him released from prison. He was not, however, allowed to leave the capital. Finally, in 1692 when the coming of the monsoon after a time of severe drought was attributed to his prayers, he was given complete liberty. He sent John home with a letter, in response to which volunteers began arriving from the Goan Oratory to join him.

While working to revitalize Sri Lankan Buddhism, Vimaladharma Surya II and his successor Narendrasimha never ceased to honour Fr Vaz. Under royal protection the Oratorians travelled freely throughout Kandy, tramping barefoot through the jungle, living on two meals a day of plain rice, and sleeping on the ground like the poorest of their flock. They could enter the Dutch-controlled coastal areas only disguised as labourers or fishermen, and they had to carry out their ministry at night in private houses. But since they easily blended in with the general population they were never caught.

Fr Vaz expected them to master both Sinhalese and Tamil thoroughly. The Sinhalese writings of the gifted Fr James Gonsalvez, who studied under Buddhist monks, are considered literary classics: a selection was republished in 1993 by the Sri Lankan government. Fr Vaz also composed prayers, hymns, and para-liturgical material in the two vernaculars. Church buildings and music used simple, local forms.

Whereas European priests customarily charged a fixed fee for their services, Fr Vaz forbade his missionaries to accept fees or stipends: only almsgiving of a purely voluntary nature, as practised by Buddhists toward their own monks, was permitted. The faithful responded so generously that not only was the mission essentially self-supporting but there was plenty left over for the poor. Donations in rice were kept in a sack at the church door so those in need could help themselves. On Fr Vaz' insistence, humanitarian assistance was always offered freely to all, with no discrimination between Catholics and non-Catholics. When an epidemic of smallpox broke out in Kandy, Fr Vaz wore himself out caring for the sick. His heroism was recorded in the Buddhist chronicle *Vijitavalle Rajavaliya*, which is now in the British Museum.

Pope Clement XI took a keen interest in Fr Vaz's work. He was given the offer of being made a bishop, which he refused. If he had accepted, the outraged archdiocese of Goa would probably have retaliated by refusing to allow any more priests from the Oratory to depart for Sri Lanka. He died in Kandy on 16 January 1711, leaving in Sri Lanka a vibrant Catholic community numbering around seventy thousand, of whom forty thousand were from traditionally Catholic families restored to the practice of their faith, while thirty thousand were fresh converts. The Goan Oratory, of which he was effectively the founder, continued to provide the island with clergy until it was suppressed by an anticlerical Portuguese government in 1834.

The missiological approach exemplified by Joseph Vaz—eschewing political or economic manipulation, untainted by cultural imperialism, respectful toward non-Christians, and commending itself solely by the sincerity and humble charity of the evangelist—was centuries ahead of its time and is seen today as having foreshadowed the insights of Vatican II. The story of his pioneer intra-Asian mission inspired Jeanne Bigard to found of the Society of St Peter the Apostle to raise funds for the training of indigenous priests in the Third World. His beatification, the cause for which was introduced in 1713 but delayed by a succession of procedural obstacles, was proclaimed during a special papal visit by Pope John Paul II to Colombo in 1995, and the further process for his canonization was set in motion.

There are several studies published in India and Sri Lanka, including C. Gasbarri, *A Saint for the New India* (1961); R. H. Lesser, *Joseph Vaz—India's First and Greatest Missionary* (1992); W. L. A. Don Peter, *Star in the East* (1995); C. J. Costa, *Life and Achievements of Blessed Joseph Vaz* (1996). The only biography published in England is A. Cator (trans.), *The Apostle of Ceylon* (1913). On the background see C. R. Boxer, *The Dutch Seaborne Empire 1600-1800* (1965), pp. 156-66; V. Perniola, S.J., *The Catholic Church in Sri Lanka— The Dutch Period, Vol. 1, 1658-1711* (1983); W. L. A. Don Peter, *Historical Gleanings* (1992), pp. 71-107; A. Soares, *The Catholic Church in India* (1964); M. Quéré, O.M.I., *Christianity in Sri Lanka under the Portuguese Padroado 1597-1658* (1995).

Signature of Bd Joseph Vaz

20 January

Bd Cyprian Michael Iwene Tansi (1903-64)

The first Nigerian, or indeed West African, to be beatified was born in the village of Igboezunu, near Aguleri in south-east Nigeria in September 1903. His parents, who practised the traditional religion of the Ibo people, named him Iwene, short for Iwegbuna, meaning "Sorrow will not kill you." His father had been imprisoned by the colonial rulers, so the name indicated considerable magnanimity. His father died when he was young, and his mother sent him to be educated by the Irish Holy Ghost missionaries at St Joseph's, the local Catholic school. She was to die tragically in 1922 when a medicine man accused her of being responsible for the deaths of several young people and forced her to swallow poison. Iwene was baptized in 1912 with the name Michael and grew up to become a teacher, being appointed headmaster of St Joseph's at the age of twenty-one. The time of his baptism was the pivotal time in a mass conversion to Christianity in Igboland, in which schools were a key factor. The direct impact of white missionaries was minimal: "The Igbos converted themselves" (Hastings, p. 449). Drawn to the priesthood, he entered the newly-opened seminary near Aguleri and was ordained in Onitsha Cathedral on 19 December 1937. He was one of the first ten Nigerians to be ordained priests.

He worked tirelessly in the rapidly-spreading archdiocese of Onitsha from his ordination to 1950, starting a new parish in 1939. There one of his catechumens was a boy who was to become Cardinal Arinze. Fr Michael baptized him, heard his first Confession, gave him his first Communion, and later prepared him for Confirmation. Arinze has said that Fr Michael, the first priest he ever knew, was "under God" the inspiration for his own vocation and that he "wanted to be like him." Fr Michael was ascetic in his personal life and an inspiring preacher. He built a weekly boarding school to which pupils would arrive on Mondays with enough provisions to last them till the following Friday. He trod the mud bricks himself, acting as a catalyst for the whole community. Aided by Sisters, he paid great attention to the preparation of girls for marriage, encouraging domestic skills and refusing to countenance the traditional cohabitation before marriage. In common with most of Christianity at the time, he was fiercely opposed to certain elements of traditional religion. He chased secret-society members wearing masks and supposedly spirit-possessed out of his church with a stick, declaring that "the spirit has been confronted by a more powerful spirit" (Hastings, p. 335). He was also unusually willing to denounce scandalous behaviour by the rich and socially prominent.

Fr Michael had long wanted to be a contemplative monk, but there were no contemplative monasteries in Nigeria. In 1950 he was accepted at Mount St Bernard Abbey near Leicester in England, where he took the name Cyprian in religion. The original intention was that he and other Nigerians should eventually return to Nigeria to make a monastic foundation there, looking to Mount St Bernard as its motherhouse, but the plans were frustrated, largely through lack of finance. In 1951 another Nigerian priest, Fr Clement, also came to Mount St Bernard, and at the end of 1953 both made the decision to stay on there. Though ordained priests, they went through the same formation process as any other newcomer. As novices they would take part in farm work in the fields (often in intense cold, to which they were completely unused), and in the ordinary cleaning and domestic work within the monastery.

The fame of Fr Cyprian's holiness in Nigeria followed him, and he received frequent visitors from his home country, to whom he would eloquently explain the purpose and universal value of the contemplative life. His replies to correspondents show his continuing love and concern for his people and the Church in Africa. In the community the impression he made "was one of quiet, conscientious regularity, self-effacing and thinking of others" (Wareing). In 1959 he was seriously ill with what proved to be the recurrence of an old stomach ulcer. For two years he was an invalid and was put on a special diet, taking his meals in the monastery infirmary, though he still worked in the refectory and the bookbindery as well as taking a full part in the offices in choir. In 1962 a tubercular gland was removed from his neck; his régime was changed to one of fresh air, and he was put to work in the garden. In 1963 arrangements were finally made for an African foundation, but the location was to be Bamenda in Cameroon. Cyprian (who was furious at the decision to make the foundation outside Nigeria) was due to go as novice-master, but he was never to leave. The then Fr Arinze saw him late in 1963 but found him in failing health, though he was able to celebrate the Silver Jubilee of his ordination to the priesthood on 19 December, with cards and letters pouring in from all over the world. Arinze's next visit was to attend his funeral; Fr Cyprian had developed a thrombosis in his leg and was being prepared for an operation on his stomach when a sudden aortic aneurism brought about his death in Leicester Royal Infirmary on 20 January 1964. Arinze was determined that his memory should be perpetuated, and he organized a group of older priests to start collecting documentation on his life and hold a symposium in 1974.

As Fr Cyprian had died in the diocese of Nottingham, it would normally have been the province of the bishop of Nottingham to begin the diocesan process, but he waived this right in favour of the archdiocese of Onitsha, and the promotion became an African process, aided by the promoter general of the Trappist Order, who suggested that Fr Tansi's remains should be brought back to Nigeria to aid the people's devotion. The diocesan process was formally opened in 1984, and the cause was given great impetus when a remarkable cure was attributed to Tansi's intercession. A young Nigerian woman named Philomena had, after an operation, been diagnosed as terminally ill; her parents told the mission Sisters that they would be to blame for her death as they had prevented them from consulting fortune-tellers and using charm-medicines. Sr Mary de Sales of the local congregation of the Immaculate Heart of Mary took Philomena, by then unable to stand, to touch the coffin when it was brought back to Onitsha. She immediately stood up and suggested that Sr Mary and she should go to Mass, which she did unaided. By the next day she was eating normally and by the time of Fr Tansi's beatification was healthy and married with three children. A thousand pages of documentation were presented to the Congregation for the Causes of Saints, who concluded unanimously that he had practised heroic virtue. He was declared Venerable in 1995, the decree of beatification was issued the following year, and the ceremony took place at Onitsha in Nigeria on 22 March 1998. The "young African Church" had learned the ways of Rome and achieved a relatively speedy successful outcome. Cardinal Arinze declared that the beatification of Fr Tansi sends a clear message to African Christians that "saints are ordinary men and women who come from your own villages."

The above is indebted to Gerard O'Connell, "An African Miracle," in *The Tablet*, 28 Feb. 1998, pp. 276-7, and to Gregory Wareing, O.C.S.O., *A New Life of Father Cyprian Michael Iwene Tansi* (1994). The text of this is available, with some further information, on the Internet at http://members.aoi.com/wacdevlin/nunraw/cyprian.htm and http://geocities.com/Athens/Academy/7644/tansi/. See also E. Isichei, *Entirely for God: The Life of Michael Iwene Tansi* (1980); Mgr P. M. Idigo (comp.), *Our Memories of the Reverend Father Michael Cyprian Tansi* (two eds., n.d.). For the background see Adrian Hastings, *The Church in Africa* (1994). There is a play based on his life by Veronica Umegakwe, *The Footprints of Father Tansi*, subtitled "The Tomb is not his Goal" (1984), and a regular bulletin listing favours in answer to prayers is published by Veritas Press in Onitsha. A wall sculpture of Bd Cyprian by Leicester Thomas has been erected in the public part of the Mount St Bernard Abbey church.

24 January

Bd Vincent Lewoniuk and Companions,
Martyrs of Podlasie (1874)

Ever since the 1595 negotiations leading up to the Union of Brest, which brought Orthodox Ukrainians living under Polish rule into communion with Rome while retaining their Eastern liturgy and customs, dissension had coloured the relations between Orthodox and Catholic Ukrainians (cf. St Josaphat; 12 Nov.). Over time both communities developed their own separate identities. Contrary to what had been promised by the Polish government, Eastern-Rite Catholics were not granted full civil rights, and Polonization of the Ukrainian élite continued: the nobility and educated classes adopted Latin-Rite Catholicism together with the Polish language and ethnic identity. Paradoxically, because only the peasantry continued to identify themselves as Ukrainians and as Eastern-Rite Catholics, they came to love their Church more deeply than ever: despised and powerless it might be, but it was *theirs*.

Meanwhile the Ukrainian Orthodox had been drawn into the orbit of the Russian Church, which itself underwent drastic and traumatic change as the czars subjected it to rigid State control. Following the partition of Poland in the late eighteenth century, Catherine the Great and her successors forcibly suppressed Eastern-Rite Catholicism in the areas taken under Russian rule. This was a key element in the policy of "Russification": the imposition of a Russian identity on subject peoples and denial of their right to self-determination. In successive operations culminating in 1839 troops were used to effect mass conversions of Ukrainians to Orthodoxy. While many submitted quietly, many others resisted and were punished with imprisonment, torture and killing, abduction of children, and swingeing financial exactions. But always the pretence was maintained that they were pathetically grateful at being restored to their "true" ethnic, linguistic, and religious allegiance. Czar Nicholas I issued a celebratory medal with the inscription: "Separated by hate 1595, reunited by love 1839."

The eparchy of Chelm had escaped suppression because it lay within the "Congress Kingdom" of Poland, belonging to the Russian crown but granted a degree of autonomy by international agreement at the Congress of Vienna. This autonomy was revoked in 1863 following a Polish nationalist uprising. In 1873 Czar Alexander II decided the time had come to suppress the eparchy of Chelm. As a preliminary move Fr Markel Poppel, a Russophile Ukrainian Catholic priest who had voluntarily transferred to Orthodoxy, co-ordinated a drive to bring the liturgical life of the parishes into outward conformity with current Orthodox practice. Meanwhile he was readying a large team of Ukrainian priests, likewise recent converts to Orthodoxy, for the forthcoming takeover.

The Eastern Catholic parishioners of Pratulin were deeply upset when the government stripped their church of its accumulated "Latinizations": the organ was thrown out, and devotional equipment such as rosaries and monstrances were confiscated. Maksym Hawryluk, thirty-four-year-old father of three and one of the better-informed villagers, warned them that this was probably the thin edge of the wedge.

The parish priest, Josef Kurmanowicz, conducted his last service at Christmas before fleeing to Galicia, the Austrian-ruled part of Ukraine. The church was closed, and the women took away the key and hid it. When the new government-appointed priest arrived, the parishioners refused to let him into the church, knowing he had gone over to Orthodoxy. The district governor, Kutanin, was called in to deal with their recalcitrance. He gave them a few days to think about it.

Kutanin returned to Pratulin on 24 January 1874, accompanied by the new priest and a Cossack unit commanded by Colonel Stein. Lukasz Bojko, a twenty-two-year-old farmer not yet married, raised the alarm throughout the villages served by the parish, and hundreds of peasants gathered around the Eastern Catholic church. The men in their long frock coats stood massed in front of the main doors, barring access. Kutanin demanded the church key. The parishioners refused to hand it over.

Daniel Karmasz, a respected farmer aged forty-eight, was among the group defending the doors. Holding in his hand a large crucifix, he explained to Kutanin that after their organ was taken away they had resolved not to permit any further interference with their religion. Katunin argued with the peasants, but neither promises of reward nor threats of punishment would induce them to move away from the church.

Onufry Wasyluk, though only twenty-one, was a natural leader and had been elected chair of the village council. He was confident that a determined peaceful demonstration by the entire population would get their message across to the authorities. Others had come to Pratulin in a very different frame of mind. Ignacy Franczuk, aged fifty, had said goodbye to his wife, Helena, and seven children as if he would never see them again. Before leaving home he changed into clean clothes: he had an intuition he would not be coming back. Jan Andrzejuk, aged twenty-six, had also said a special goodbye to his wife and two sons. Being among the few village leaders who could read and write, he had some intimation of what was likely to happen. During the morning several people remarked, "How sweet it is to die for the Faith!"

Colonel Stein ordered his soldiers to fix the bayonets to their rifles. He expected the peasants to break and run. Instead they stood their ground. The Cossacks advanced into the church grounds and began using the butts of their rifles to clear a path. The Catholics resisted the pushing. Some threw stones. Colonel Stein ordered his men to withdraw and regroup, unfurl the regimental standard, beat the drums, and sound the attack. Karmasz called to the Catholics to throw down any sticks and stones they were holding: "This is not a fight. This is a struggle for the Faith and for Christ." The peasants knelt down in the snow. Someone began singing a hymn and everyone joined in. The colonel ordered the Cossacks to open fire.

Wincenty Lewoniuk, aged twenty-six, was the first to be hit, followed by Daniel Karmasz. As Karmasz fell, the cross was grabbed from his hand by Franczuk, who in his turn a moment later slumped to the ground. Lukasz Bojko died at his post in front of the main door. A bullet hit Anicet Hyciuk, a nineteen-year-old who had come to bring food to the men defending the church. His neighbour Filip Geryluk, aged forty-four, cradling the boy's dead body in his arms, tried to remonstrate with the Cossacks. They shot him too. Wasyluk's wife, who saw him killed instantly by a bullet in the head, bravely consoled his weeping mother: Onufry had done nothing wrong, and they must be glad that he had given his life for his faith. Konstanty Bojko, a poor labourer of forty-nine, and Michal Wawryszuk, aged twenty-one, were also killed by the volleys. Konstanty Lukaszuk, aged forty-five, lay dead in the graveyard, run through by a bayonet.

The Cossacks were running amok, and the massacre might have gone on longer had not one of them accidentally wounded another. They ceased firing, broke down the church door with an axe, and led the government-appointed priest inside. Meanwhile the villagers picked up the wounded and took them to safety. About 180 people had been injured. Andrzejuk died soon after reaching home. Hawryluk, wounded in the stomach and dying in agony, was carried home under cover of night. Bartlomiej Osypiuk, a thirty-year-old farmer, also died of his injuries in the presence of his wife and two children. He told them he was happy to lay down his life for God, and prayed for the persecutors.

Many of the survivors, still defiant, were rounded up, loaded with chains, and marched off to prison. The bodies of those killed outright were left lying all day in the graveyard, then thrown unceremoniously into a common grave. The ground was carefully levelled to leave no trace of the burial, but the local people took note of the spot.

The Pratulin massacre is among the better recorded of many violent incidents during the suppression of the eparchy of Chelm. Pratulin today is in the diocese of Siedlce in the region of Podlasie, eastern Poland. Wincenty Lewoniuk and his twelve companions were beatified by Pope John Paul II in a ceremony in Rome on 6 October 1996. In June 1999, concelebrating Mass in Siedlce with both Latin and Eastern Catholic bishops from Podlasie, Ukraine, and Russia, the pope preached a long homily in honour of the Pratulin martyrs, saying, "Today we venerate the relics of the martyrs of Podlasie and we adore the Cross of Pratulin, which was the silent witness of their heroic fidelity. They held this Cross in their hands and they bore it in the depth of their hearts, as a sign of love of the Father and of the unity of the Church of Christ."

Osservatore Romano (English weekly edition), 9 Oct. 1996; 23 June 1999. For the background see N. Davies *God's Playground—A History of Poland* (1981), especially vol. 2, pp. 210-1; D. Pospielovsky *The Orthodox Church in the History of Russia* (1998), pp. 102-

3. Websites: http://www.sim.pl/~KLObp/unia.html; http://free.polbox.pl/u/unici/
pratulin.html.

29 January

Bd Boleslawa Lament, *Foundress* (1862-1946)

She was born into a large family in Lowicz, some forty miles west of Warsaw,
on 3 July 1862. At the age of twenty-two she joined the Congregation of the
Family of Mary, one of several religious bodies founded by Bd Honoratus
Kozminski (16 Dec.), who became her mentor and inspiration. He asked her to
leave Poland and move into White Russia, to Mogilev on the river Dneiper on
a mission to schismatic Orthodox groups. Her efforts to bring these into communion with the Catholic Church led her to found the Congregation of Missionary Sisters of the Holy Family in 1905. Two years later she moved the
administration of the new Congregation to St Petersburg, where her Sisters
engaged in an intensive apostolate. In 1913 their mission was extended to
Finland, where she opened a school for girls.

The October Revolution of 1917 put an end to their activities, and Sr
Boleslawa and her Sisters were forced to flee back to Poland, abandoning their
expansive missionary plans and the considerable material foundations she had
laid. She could only accept this reversal as the will of God. In 1922 she established a new house in Chelmno in northern Poland, re-defining the objective of
her Congregation as a mission to the Orthodox living in the eastern parts of
Poland, where they generally formed the poorest sections of the population.
This mission was to be carried out in a spirit of ecumenism, aimed at the relief
of the people's condition rather than their conversion. The Congregation grew,
and she was able to open houses in the dioceses of Vilna (then in Poland, now
Vilnius, capital of Lithuania) and Pinsk, followed by foundations in Warsaw
and Rome. In 1935 she moved the motherhouse to Bialystok in north-eastern
Poland, where she opened children's homes and a school.

On the outbreak of the Second World War several provinces of eastern
Poland were overrun by the Soviet army and annexed into the Soviet Union.
Once again she saw her achievements destroyed and once again accepted this
as the will of God. By this time she was suffering from a progressive paralysis.
She inspired her Sisters to carry on their mission as best they could in a
situation she defined as *passio catholica*, universal suffering affecting her Congregation, the Catholic Church, and the culture of Christendom. Her health
deteriorated further, and she died in Bialystok on 29 January 1946. She was
beatified there on 5 June 1991 by her countryman Pope John Paul II, who
spoke of her resignation in suffering and courage and perseverance in the face
of the two great upheavals she and her Congregation had undergone.

D.N.H., 3, pp. 251-4, with the text of the pope's address at the beatification ceremony.

10 February

Bd Aloysius Stepinac, *Bishop and Martyr* (1898–1960)

Aloysius (Alojzije) Stepinac was born on 8 May 1898 in the village of Brezaric, in the parish of Krasic, twenty-five miles from Zagreb in what is now Croatia and was then part of the Austro-Hungarian empire. He was the fifth of eight children, and his devout mother prayed constantly that he might become a priest. He attended secondary school in Zagreb, staying as a boarder at the archdiocesan orphanage. He sent in his application forms for the seminary at the age of sixteen, but on leaving school he was drafted into the imperial army in the First World War and sent as an officer to the Italian front in 1917. In July 1918 he was captured by the Italians and held as a prisoner of war until a month after the end of the war, in November, when he was released. After serving in Greece as a "Salonika volunteer" for a short time, he was demobilized in the spring of 1919. For the next five years he studied agronomy in Zagreb, during which time he was active in church affairs, joining the Catholic Youth Movement, and in the social life of the town. His father wanted him to marry, and he became engaged, but all the time he was debating within himself whether he had a vocation to the priesthood: deciding that he did, he broke off the engagement.

At the end of 1924 he enrolled as a philosophy and theology student at the Gregorian University in Rome and from that time never doubted his vocation to the priesthood. He received his doctorate in philosphy in 1927, was ordained in 1930, and returned to Croatia the following year. He served for a while as a parish priest and was placed in charge of liturgical ceremonies in the diocese of Zagreb, where he also started a branch of Caritas. In 1934 he was appointed coadjutor bishop of Zagreb, which made him, at thirty-six, the world's youngest bishop and successor designate to the incumbent archbishop, Anton Bauer.

There were pressing reasons for not leaving sees empty. The union of the southern Slavic territories with Serbia and Montenegro as part of the Treaty of Versailles after the First World War had brought into being the country known from 1929 as Yugoslavia. It contained a mix of (Serbian) Orthodox, (Croatian) Catholics, and Muslims, with the Orthodox the dominant religious group. An agreement between the government and the Holy See provided that large tracts of church lands would be managed by the kingdom if a see became vacant. A concordat guaranteeing religious freedom for Catholics was accepted by the (lower) House of Delegates in July 1937 but not by the Orthodox Holy Synod of Yugoslavia, which effectively vetoed its approval by the Senate. In practice, however, the spirit of the concordat was observed, and Catholic life was flourishing when Aloysius Stepinac was appointed archbishop of Zagreb on the death of Archbishop Bauer in 1937. He was relatively unknown but was quickly accepted by his flock. Two weeks after his consecration he led a pilgrimage to the Croatian national shrine at Marija Bistrica, leading fifteen thousand pilgrims along the twenty-mile route. Within three years he had made an episcopal visitation to all the 208 parishes in the diocese, receiving an enthusiastic welcome wherever he went. By 1939 he had founded new parishes, started a Catholic newspaper, initiated a new translation of the Bible into Croat, headed the preparations to celebrate thirteen hundred years of Christianity in Croatia, participated in numerous congresses, and made a pilgrimage to the Holy Land.

In 1935 he spoke out against Serbian acts of terror against Croatians but also against "exaggerated nationalism, wherever in the world it rules." He asked that the next council of the Church should condemn such nationalism as the "first among the contemporary heresies, as the biggest plague of the human race." In 1936 he agreed to sponsor a committee set up to help Jewish refugees from Hitler's Nazi régime. In 1938 he asked the parish priests of Zagreb to help Jews as their "Christian duty" and spoke against the evils of racism to university students.

When the Axis forces of Germany and Italy invaded Yugoslavia in March 1941, Croatia became a nominally independent State governed by the pro-Nazi Ustasha régime led by Ante Pavelic, which lasted from 1941 to 1945. It was in effect a satellite of the Axis powers. The régime was very accommodating to the Catholic Church but at the price of forcing it to collaborate in actions directed against the Serbian partisans. It was responsible for the murder of an estimated 200,000 Croatian Orthodox, Serbs, and Jews, and large numbers of the Catholic clergy are said to have taken part in pogroms and forced conversions. Stepinac opposed these but gave his clergy permission to receive people into the Church when their lives were threatened, remarking philosophically that those who were convinced would remain in the Church while those who were not would return to their own religion once "this time of insanity and barbarity passes."

Like most Croatians, Stepinac had initially welcomed the Ustasha, writing a letter to Pope Pius XII (1937-58) defending what he saw as positive measures taken by the régime (though this is claimed by some commentators to be a forgery), but as news of their crimes reached him his criticisms became more public, and by 1942 he was their most outspoken critic. When new racial laws were enacted in April he sent a note of protest to the authorities, and he declared in a sermon in Zagreb Cathedral on 25 October 1942: "Each member of every nation and race on earth has the right to a life worthy of a person and to treatment worthy of a person. Everyone, without differentiation, whether they are members of the Gypsy race or any other race, whether they are black, or Jewish or Aryan, they all have the right to say 'Our Father, who art in heaven!' And if God has given this right to everyone, what human authority can violate it?" In 1943 he was even more explicit: "We always preach the holy principles of God's law, no matter whether Croats, Serbs, Jews, Gypsies, Catholics, Orthodox, or others are involved." He supported this by condemning Allied bombing of civilians in Zagreb and by taking to Rome evidence of atrocities committed alike by German Nazis, Italian Fascists, Serbian Chetniks, Croatian members of the Ustasha, and Communists.

Stepinac and other Catholic leaders were nevertheless later reviled for complicity in the crimes of the Ustasha, and when the war ended in 1945 partisan forces destroyed many churches and monasteries and killed over two hundred priests. After the end of the war, when Croatia came under Communist control as part of the federated People's Republic of Yugoslavia, Archbishop Stepinac was arrested but released after a few weeks. A meeting with President Tito left him with with the impression that Tito wanted a nationalist Church in Croatia, separate from Rome, though Tito may have been asking him simply to dissociate the Croat bishops from certain aspects of Vatican policy. Whether or not there was a misunderstanding, Stepinac flatly refused any accommodation and issued a pastoral letter detailing the persecution of the Church in Yugoslavia. Both he and Cardinal Mindszenty of Hungary based their views of Communism on Pius XI's pre-war encyclical *Divini Redemptoris*, which condemned it as "intrinsically evil." There could therefore be no recognition that the post-war Communist or socialist régimes of Eastern Europe might be attempting to build a more equal society. Pius XII's view was that the Church in these regions had no alternative but to "cling together behind its martyrs" (Luxmore)—a view that received its most extreme expression in his later decree excommunicating all Communists and denying the sacraments to any Catholics who helped them in any way. Stepinac and Mindszenty followed this line, whether out of conviction or obedience, whereas in Poland Cardinal Wyszynsky managed to steer a more understanding course.

In November 1945 Stepinac was attacked near Zagreb and stoned, after which he did not leave the archbishop's palace. In January 1946 the authorities asked the papal envoy to have him removed from Zagreb. In September he was arrested again and put on trial, accused of complicity in the crimes of the wartime government. Condemned after a show trail, he was sentenced to sixteen years hard labour plus a further five years of deprivation of his rights as a citizen. He had expected a death sentence. He was imprisoned in Lepoglava, where his jailers did not dare force him to work but instead tried to poison him slowly. Seriously ill, he was then moved in 1951 from there to his home village of Krasic, where he remained under house arrest in an old rectory until he died on 10 February 1960. The announcement in 1952 that he was to be elevated to the rank of cardinal early in 1953 caused a worsening of relations between President Tito of Yugoslavia and the Vatican, leading to the expulsion of the papal nuncio. He did not go to the consistory following Pope Pius XII's death in 1958, for fear that he would not be allowed back into Yugoslavia, where he was determined to remain at all costs. After his death the situation gradually eased, and an agreement with the Holy See in 1966 guaranteed the liberty of the Church but also affirmed the Church's loyalty to Yugoslavia. His internal organs had been removed and burned after his death, but when his remains were exhumed and tested in 1996 his bones were found to contain traces of poison, which cleared the way for him to be declared a martyr.

Aloysius Stepinac was beatified, after what was recognized as a difficult process, by Pope John Paul II at Marija Bistrica on 3 October 1998. The pope expressed the hope that the legacy of both Fascism and Communism could be overcome, and that "this part of Europe will never again see a repeat of the inhuman situations which we have repeatedly witnessed in this century, and that the tragic experience of the last war will be a lesson that will enlighten minds and increase the will for dialogue and co-operation." Stepinac's record was defended by the Co-ordination of Jewish Municipalities in Croatia, which issued a statement saying that "The Jews in Croatia are grateful to Cardinal Stepinac for advocating the salvation of many Jews during the Ustasha Independent State of Croatia" and that they would not object to the beatification. Cardinal König, the retired archbishop of Vienna (who was nearly killed in a car crash on his way to the beatification ceremony), described Stepinac as a patriot but not a nationalist and as someone who made "a deep impression" on him by his behaviour during his trial and during his period of house arrest. König described his last will and testament as "a text without any bitterness, [written] in the full awareness that as a Christian and a bishop this was the path he had to take for his faith and the Church." The thousands of letters he wrote to bishops, priests, and laypeople during his confinement, some seven hundred of which have survived, show his unshakeable faith and are full of forgiveness of his persecutors. But, as in the case of Cardinal Schuster of Milan (30 Aug.), there are many who take a different view of his political actions, and his beatification is bound to remain controversial.

The Tablet, 10 Oct. 1998, for reports on the beatification; Jonathan Luxmore, "Pius XII and the Reds," in *ibid.*, 12 June 1999, pp. 802-4; Josip Stilinovic, "A Patriot, Not a Nationalist" in *The Catholic World Report*, Aug./Sept. 1998. Biographical studies (not in Croat) include R. Pattee, *The Case of Cardinal Aloysius Stepinac* (1953); T. Dragouin, *Le Dossier du Cardinal Stepinac* (1958); F. Eterovic, *Aloysius Cardinal Stepinac: A Spiritual Leader* (1970); M. Raymond, *The Man for This Moment: The Life and Death of Aloysius Cardinal Stepinac* (1971); M. Landercy, *Le Cardinal Stepinac* (1981); S. Alexander, *The Triple Myth: A Life of Cardinal Alojzije Stepinac* (1987). For the background see S. Alexander, *Church and State in Yugoslavia since 1945* (1979); M. Tanner, *Croatia—A Nation Forged in War* (1997). A fuller list, as well as polemic about his dealings with Jews, can be found on the Internet at croatians@dalmatia.net.

22 February

Bd Vincent Vilar David, *Martyr* (1889–1937)

This lay martyr of the Spanish civil war was born in Manises, a small town near Valencia famous for its ceramics, on 28 July 1889. His parents were Justo Vilar Arenes, who owned a ceramics works, and Carmen David Gimeno; Vincent (Vicente) was the youngest of eight children. He was sent as a boarder to the Piarist College in Valencia and then studied for six years in Barcelona, gaining a degree in industrial engineering with a view to joining the family business. He took a lively interest in Catholic social teaching, especially the forms of "lay apostolate" encouraged by Pope Pius X, a very live issue at the time in industrial Barcelona, as well as practising regular religious observances and exercising a social apostolate under the aegis of the St Vincent de Paul Society.

The four sons of the family took over the ceramics works after their father's death in 1911, and Vincent was appointed technical director when he had finished his studies. He set about applying progressive social policies to the factory, introducing sickness benefit and an old-age pension scheme for the workers. He also opened a technical school to train workers in the ceramics industry, seeing that only specialized skills could improve both their personal prospects and those of the backward Spanish industry. This started with teachers giving their services free but then received State support and was officially inaugurated in 1925. Its fame grew, and it attracted students from all over Spain and some from Latin America. His brothers, however, found his policies too much to bear and persuaded him to leave the family firm in 1924. He applied the same principles in another ceramics works and was again forced to leave, this time after only two years. Together with a wealthy widow and others he then started a plant making chemical products, where, as joint owner, he was able to put his advanced social principles into practice. He had been offered a post in the civil administration of Valencia under the dictatorship of General Primo de Rivera in 1923 but refused it, saying that his work in Manises was too valuable.

In 1917 he had been struck by a young visitor to the ceramics works. She was not quite seventeen: after three years of considering and consulting, followed by two of formal engagement, he married Isabel Rodes Reig in November 1922. The marriage, based on deep Christian commitment, was extremely happy from the start. Vincent, who was a prominent member of several pious confraternities, donated all his share of the profits from the chemical works to the seminary of Valencia, despite the protests of the rector, who was also his uncle, that this was far too much. He visited Rome on business and had private audiences with Pope Pius XI; in 1933 he and his wife also visited Assisi, which delighted him as he had a particular devotion to St Francis (4 Oct.).

With the proclamation of the Republic in April 1931 the climate changed: education and social action were to belong to the State, not the Church. Some Catholics decided that they had to take matters into their own hands, and Vincent Vilar was the leading spirit in establishing a centre in Manises for the religious instruction of the local population. He provided a house and even persuaded the local authorities to support the project in July 1931. It started evening classes in 1932, with 170 pupils. At the outbreak of civil war in July 1936 Valencia remained staunchly Republican. It was subject to outbreaks of violence from anticlerical units of the Popular Front (see the general entry, Martys of the Spanish Civil War; 22 July). Mass was celebrated openly for the last time on 19 July. Vincent Vilar opened his house as a refuge for Carmelite nuns; it was officially searched in November, and he was told that if he ceased his militant Catholic actions he would be left in peace. He categorically refused.

By this time he was working in the ceramics industry once more. The factory was taken over by the Communist C.N.T. union, and he stayed on as an ordinary worker. In February 1937 he gave most of the clothes and blankets from his house to freezing Republican militiamen. He and his wife went to Valencia to buy more and visited a priest, who heard their Confessions and gave them consecrated hosts to take home. The following day they gave most of the food they had in their house to refugees from Málaga. That same night Vincent was arrested and taken before the local revolutionary committee, accused of helping priests, supporting the Church, and teaching young people to pray. Two union representatives spoke in his favour, knowing how he had always sought to benefit his workers. Asked to deny the value of all he had done, he replied, "My greatest mark of honour is to be what I am and to have acted as I have done. I do not deny the truth." The committee, seeking to save him from execution, ordered his transfer to the Model Prison in Valencia, but some Communists objected in the street outside. There was an altercation between them and the militiamen, during which Vincent was shot in the legs and fell to the ground, where he was despatched by a shot to the head.

His death caused widespread consternation in the locality. He had not been involved in party politics and was immediately regarded by Catholics as a martyr, killed purely out of hatred for the Catholic Church. The factory was closed for a week as a mark of respect. The diocesan process for his beatification was opened in 1963 and completed in 1990. His body was translated to the parish church of St John the Baptist in Manises on 20 November 1967, and he was beatified in St Peter's by Pope John Paul II on 6 July 1993.

The above is based on A. Llin Cháfer, *Vicente Vilar David: un santo seglar de nuestro tiempo* (1994).

2 April

Bd Mary of St Joseph, *Foundress* (1875–1967)

Laura Evangelista Alvarado Cardozo was born in Choroní in Venezuela on 25 April 1875. Her parents ran a small store in the town, but around 1880 they moved to the larger town of Maracay in search of better prospects. Laura worked in her teenage years in order to be able to instruct poor children at home, and during a smallpox epidemic in 1892 she cared for the sick in a small hospital opened by the parish priest, Fr Vicente López Aveledo, which provided the only medical facilities in the town. He was also her spiritual director, and under his guidance she made a vow of perpetual virginity. In 1896 he appointed Laura director of the hospital. She lived there, forming a community around her known as "the Samaritans."

She grew up in a time when the number of priests and religious was diminishing, bishops were being expelled, and President Antonio Guzmán Blanco (1870–88) was passing a series of anticlerical laws and closing seminaries. By the end of the nineteenth century Church-State relations had improved somewhat, with governments re-admitting religious Orders so that they could run schools and hospitals, and in 1901 Laura and Fr López founded a Congregation of Sisters to care for the sick, the elderly, and orphans, named first the Sisters Hospitalers of Saint Augustine, later changed to Augustinian Recollects of the Heart of Jesus. A special dispensation of the Holy See in 1903 recognized her work as foundress of the Congregation and allowed her to take perpetual vows of chastity, poverty, and obedience. She took the name Mary (María) of St Joseph in religion.

In 1905 she founded the first home for orphans in Maracay, and she went on to found thirty-seven homes for orphans and the elderly in towns all over Venezuela. Her ministry was defined as being to all the needy whom no one else would care for: "The most downtrodden of all are ours, the ones nobody wants to receive," she told her nuns. She combined this activity with a deep prayer life, showing especial devotion to the Eucharist and to Our Lady. She made hosts with her own hands and encouraged her nuns to do the same. She had a great veneration for the priesthood and encouraged native Venezuelans to become priests so that the country would not depend so heavily on missionaries from overseas.

She tried to resign her position as superior general as her age advanced, but her Congregation would not accept this until 1960, when she was already eighty-five. She died at the age of ninety-two on 2 April 1967 and was buried in the chapel of the Immaculate Conception Home in Maracay, where her tomb has become a shrine visited by thousands of pilgrims every year. She was beatified by Pope John Paul II in the piazza in front of St Peter's on 7 May 1995, becoming the first Venezuelan Blessed.

Pastoral letter of the bishops of Venezuela, in *Vida religiosa* 79, no. 10, 15 Sept. 1995; Eng. trans in *Catholic International* 7, no. 1, Jan. 1996. For the background see R. de Roux, "The Church in Colombia and Venezuela," in E. Dussel (ed.), *The Church in Latin America: 1492–1992* (1992), pp. 271–84.

13 April
Bd Scubillion Rousseau (1797–1867)

Jean-Baptiste Rousseau was born on 22 March 1797 at Annay-la-Côte, near Dijon in Burgundy, western France. His father, Bernarde, was a stonemason, married to Regina Peletier. He joined the De La Salle Brothers in Paris, became Brother Scubillion in religion, and worked for a time in France, serving at Alençon, Poitiers, and Chinon before being sent in 1833, at his own request, to the remote French colony of Réunion, in the Indian Ocean to the east of Madagascar.

He was to serve there for thirty-four years as a teacher and catechist. At St-Leu he gave up his evenings, after completing his normal duties, to teaching catechism to the slaves who worked on the coffee and vanilla plantations. He took great care in adapting his catechesis to the understanding of illiterate adults and became their friend. His representations on their behalf to their owners and the civil authorities led many of the slaves to regard him as a saint and contributed to their eventual emancipation in 1848. He had a gift for fostering vocations to the priesthood and the religious life and inspired many to join the De La Salle community.

Brother Scubillion is remembered as a pioneer of human rights in a society where oppression and extremes of inequality were only too common. He was beatified by Pope John Paul II at Saint-Denis, the capital of Réunion, on 2 May 1989.

Osservatore Romano, 3 May 1989; *D.N.H.*, 3, pp. 128-32.

25 May

Bd Christopher Magallanes and Companions,
Martyrs (from 1915 to 1937)

The twenty-two priests and three laymen commemorated here were all killed in Mexico, the first in 1915, the last in 1937, and the remainder in the period of intense persecution of the Church associated with the *Cristero* uprising between 1926 and 1929. The triumph of the Mexican revolution in 1920 brought in anti-ecclesiastical feeling and legislation. The hierarchy had used the dictatorship of Porfirio Diaz (1876–1910) to consolidate its position after decades of at least intermittent suffering at the hands of liberal governments. A new Constitution, approved in 1917, severely curtailed the civil and political rights of clergy and the Church's right to hold property. Its relevant articles finally became law under President Plutarco Elías Calles in 1926, provoking a strong reaction from the hierarchy, which declared the suspension of all public worship. This hardly affected the wealthy élite, who treated the clergy as domestic chaplains and could still get the sacraments virtually on demand. The rural clergy were ordered into hiding in the cities by the bishops, and in the countryside peasants took up arms with the slogan "Long live Christ the King and the Virgin of Guadalupe." The official Church did not support this armed rebellion, but a wider movement, the League for the Defence of Religious Freedom, formed around it, involving the Church at most levels. A partial end to the *Cristero* revolt was arranged in 1929 on the basis that the "Calles law," though remaining in force, would not be applied rigorously, but the conflict smouldered on in seven States of the Republic for a further decade.

The few priests who decided to remain in rural areas to adminster the sacraments varied in their degree of involvement with the *Cristeros*. They were all liable to be shot if found, and some ninety were, but all those recognized as martyrs were personally dedicated to non-violent means.

The one who died in 1915 was David Galván Bermúdez, born in 1881. After some years studying in the seminary of Guadalajara he left to pursue a life of dissipation, but after a time he changed his ways, returned to the seminary after a year of probation, and was ordained in 1909. He taught at the diocesan seminary, and during Carranza's uprising he was arrested as a priest and then released. On 30 January 1915, during an exchange of fire between Carranza's supporters and those of Pancho Villa, he went to help the wounded lying in the street, was arrested by a group of soldiers, taken away, and shot.

The first of those to die during the *Cristero* uprising were Fr Luis Batiz Sainz and the three laymen, David Roldán Lara, Salvador Lara Puente, and Manuel Morales. They were arrested and accused of fomenting rebellion through the National League for the Defence of Religious Freedom.

Luis Batiz, born in 1870 and ordained in 1894, was the spiritual director of the seminary of Durango and parish priest of Chachihuites, where he built a workshop and a school and catechized both adults and children. After telling a meeting of the League that the closure of public worship was a church and not a government decree and so should be respected, he left the presbytery and took refuge in a private house. He was found there by a platoon of soldiers on 14 August 1926. The authorities decided that he should be taken to Zacatecas, but on the way there the soldiers who were escorting him stopped the car he was in, took him out, and shot him.

The three laymen were members of ACJM (Catholic Action of Mexican Youth), a militant movement forming part of the League, of which Fr Luis was chaplain. Manuel Morales was born in 1898 and had entered the seminary at Durango but had been forced to leave to work to support his family. He later married, had three children, and became president of the National League. He tried to remonstrate at Fr Luis' arrest, but he was himself imprisoned with him and shared his fate, even though the priest has begged the soldiers to spare him so that he could take care of his family.

David Roldán, born in 1907, had also been a seminarian and had to leave to support his family, his father having died before he was one year old. A committed Christian, he was elected president of ACJM in 1925 and vice-president of the League shortly after. He and Salvador Lara were in the second car on the way to Zacatecas and were shot in the same place as the first two.

Salvador was born in 1905 and, like the other two laymen, had had to leave the seminary of account of his family's poverty. He was secretary of the League and local president of Catholic Action. He tried to organize Fr Luis' release but instead shared his fate. Though both he and David had explicitly denied their movement's involvement in violence, they both died with the *Cristero* slogan, "Long live Christ the King and the Virgin of Guadalupe," on their lips.

A further eight martyrs were killed between January and May 1927. Jenaro Sánchez was born in 1886 and ordained in 1911. He served in several parishes and was known as a devoted parish priest with a gift for preaching. He was arrested by a group of soldiers when walking in the countryside with some of his parishioners. He was hanged from a tree on 18 January at Tecolotlán in the State of Jalisco after being so savagely beaten and bayonetted that it was some time before the body was recognized and taken down.

Mateo Correa, born in 1866, had been parish priest in several parishes,

271

including Concepción del Oro, where he became a close friend of the family of Bd Miguel Pro (23 Nov.), to whom he gave his First Communion. In 1926 he was parish priest of Valparaíso and was arrested on the orders of General Ortiz, together with several members of the ACJM, but released, to the general's fury. He was re-arrested early in 1927 and taken to the barracks in Durango, where Ortiz ordered him to hear the Confessions of several prisoners and then tell him what they had said. Fr Mateo was shot on 6 February for refusing to break the seal of the confessional.

Julio Alvarez Mendoza, also born in 1866, had been ordained in 1894. He refused to go into hiding and was on his way to celebrate Mass on a ranch when he was arrested. He was tied to the saddle of a horse and taken through several cities to León, where he was sentenced to be shot. This took place early in the morning of 30 March, and his body was thrown on to a rubbish dump, on the site of which there now stands a memorial to him.

David Uribe Velasco was born in 1888 and ordained in 1913, after which he worked with the bishop of Tabasco. Forced into hiding several times, he had returned to his people when he was arrested. He was shot in the back of the head in Cuernavaca on 12 April.

Sabás Reyes Salazar was born in 1879, studied at the seminary of Guadalajara, was ordained in 1911, and was parish priest of Totolán in Jalisco at the time of the persecution. He was returning from performing a Baptism when troops attacked the village. He hid in a house for several days, but his hiding-place was revealed to soldiers, who tortured and then shot him on 13 April.

Román Adame Rosales was born in 1859 and also studied at Guadalajara, where he was ordained in 1890. A parish priest with a deep devotion to the Virgin Mary, he founded the Association of Daughters of Mary. Forced into hiding, he carried on his ministry in private houses and ranches, and it was at one of the latter that he was denounced. He was taken to the local barracks and shot on 12 April. One of the members of the firing squad refused to fire and was himself shot after Fr Román.

Christopher (Cristóbal) Magallanes, who gives his name to this group of martyrs, was a pastor of considerable stature who from 1914 to his death in 1927 pioneered the re-evangelization of the Huichole Indians, who had virtually lost touch with the Church since the expulsion of the Jesuits in the eighteenth century. He was born in 1869, growing up in a poor family and working on the land till the age of nineteen, when he entered the seminary in Guadalajara. He was ordained in 1899 and in 1910 was appointed parish priest of Totalice. He established catechetical centres and schools in the villages in his parish, built a dam to provide a water supply, and enabled peasants to buy small plots of land. He was totally dedicated to non-violence but was caught up in a battle between *Cristeros* and government troops on 21 May 1927. He was arrested and accused of supporting the uprising and was shot four days later. Before he died he declared his innocence and expressed the hope that "my blood may serve to bring peace to divided Mexicans."

His curate at Totalice was Fr Agustín Caloca, born in 1898 and ordained in 1923. He was also prefect of the local auxiliary seminary and responsible for ministering to the ranches. He was arrested while arranging for the seminary students to disperse and was shot with Fr Magallanes.

Between June 1927 and the end of the year a further six of this group of martyrs met their deaths.

José Isabel Flores was born in 1866, was a distinguished student at the seminary of Guadalajara, and was ordained in 1896. He was parish priest in a number of places, was known for his dedication, and founded several Associations, such as the Daughters of Mary. Arrested, he was offered his freedom if he subscribed to the "Calles law," but he refused to do so and was shot on 21 June in Zapotlanejo.

José María Robles was another of Guadalajara's brightest students, born in 1888 and ordained in 1913. He had a deep devotion to the Sacred Heart and in 1918 founded the Congregation of "Victims of the Eucharistic Heart of Jesus." Forced into hiding under the persecution, he was arrested while preparing to say Mass in a private house and taken to the local barracks, then on horseback into open country, where he was hanged from an oak tree on 26 June.

Miguel de la Mora was born into a peasant family in 1874 and helped to work the land until he decided he had a vocation to the priesthood. He was ordained in 1906 and worked as parish priest in the diocese of Colima, of which he became the first martyr. He was arrested when the persecution began but released, only to be re-arrested on a ranch after a woman had asked him if he was a priest and, if so, to perform a marriage ceremony for her daughter. He was taken to Cardona and shot in a stable on 27 August.

Rodrigo Aguilar Alemán, born in 1875, studied at the auxiliary seminary of Guzmán, where he showed great literary talent. He was ordained in 1905 and worked in various parishes. In 1927 he was acting parish priest in Unión de Tula when he was denounced and forced to hide on a ranch. Discovered there, he was taken to the main square of Ejutla, where he was hanged from a mango tree on 28 October.

Margarito Flores was born in 1899 and worked on the land with his peasant family until he entered the seminary of Chilapa, where he was ordained in 1924 and shortly afterwards was appointed professor. During the persecution he took refuge in Mexico City and taught in a school. He was captured and then released, returned to Chilapa, and offered his services to the bishop, volunteering to go to a parish where the municipal governor had threatened to shoot any priest found there. He was arrested on his way there and shot in Tuliman on 12 November.

Pedro Esqueda Ramírez was born in 1887 and studied at Guadalajara until the seminary was closed in 1914, when he went back to his native town of San Juan de los Lagos, working there as deacon until he was ordained in 1916 and served as assistant priest. When persecution intensified in 1926 he worked underground in the parish, but he was eventually found in a private house, where he had hidden the sacred vessels in a hole in the floor. He was dragged out, tortured for several days, taken to Teocaltitlán, and shot on 22 November 1927.

A further four of this group were martyred in 1928, while the last died in a renewed outbreak of persecution in 1937.

Jesús Méndez Montoya was born in 1880, studied at the seminary of Michoacán, and was ordained in 1906. He was parish priest of Valtierilla when the persecution broke out, a dedicated priest noted for his devotion to the Eucharist, long hours in the confessional, and concern for parish Associations. When federal troops entered the village, he attempted to escape with the ciborium full of consecrated hosts hidden under his cloak. He managed to consume the hosts before the soldiers sat him on the trunk of a tree and fired at him. They missed, perhaps on purpose, and their commanding officer made him stand, when he was killed. His body was placed on a railway line so that it would be cut to pieces, but the officers' wives took it away for a proper wake and burial. The date was 28 February 1928.

Toribio Romo González, born in 1900, was prominent in the social ministry in Catholic Action during his time at the seminary of Guadalajara, where he was ordained in 1922. As assistant priest in various parishes, he was noted for his powerful preaching. He lived a nomadic life during the persecution, hiding and setting up an oratory in a disused factory and ministering in the city of Tequila by night. Early in the morning of 25 February soldiers broke in, shot him, stripped his body, and dragged it to the city hall, in front of which they left it.

Justino Orona Madrigal was born into an extremely poor but religious family in 1877. The need to work to help support his family interrupted his studies at Guadalajara, but he worked hard and was ordained in 1904. He was parish priest in four different urban parishes, where anticleralism and indifference were the rule. When persecution broke out he preferred to stay with his people and family in Cuquío, but he was seized on a ranch belonging to friends and shot on 1 July, together with his brother and his assistant priest, Atilano Cruz Alvarado.

Atilano was born in 1901 and was of indigenous descent, though his parents were practising Catholics. He spent his childhood working the land until his parents took him to Teocaltiche so that he could learn to read and write. He entered the local auxiliary seminary in 1918 and moved on to Guadalajara two years later. He was ordained in 1927 and had been sent to the ranch only the day before the soldiers arrived and shot him in his room. His body and that of Fr Orona were dumped in the town square, but parishioners took them away and buried them the same day.

Tranquilino Ubiarco, also of Indian descent, was born in 1899 and spent his childhood in extreme poverty. His studies for the priesthood were continually interrupted during the Carranza revolution, but he persevered and was ordained in 1923. He started catechetical study centres and a journal of Christian doctrine. He had been assistant priest of Tepatitlán, working out of private houses, for fifteen months when he was seized on 5 October. He was allowed to hear the Confessions of those arrested with him and was then shot together with them.

Pedro de Jesús Maldonado was born in Sacramento in 1892. His studies for the priesthood at Chihuahua were also interrupted by the revolution, and he spent a time learning music; he was eventually ordained in El Paso in Texas in 1918 and returned to Santa Isabel in Chihuahua. His ministry concentrated on catechism for the children, night adoration, and the formation of Marian Associations. He survived the years of intense persecution, but this broke out again in 1931, when the churches were closed once more. He was arrested, maltreated, and released in 1932 and again in 1934, when he was exiled to El Paso. He returned, and in 1937 a fire broke out in the public school, which the authorities blamed on him. He was seized by a group of armed and drunken men, who made him walk barefoot from the village where he was to Santa Isabel, where he was beaten unconscious. He was taken to the hospital in Chihuahua but died there on 11 February 1937.

These twenty-five martyrs were beatified by Pope John Paul II on 22 November 1992, and miracles attributed to their intercession have (1999) been accepted, so the cause for their canonization is being promoted.

Information from website (in Spanish): www.aciprensa.com/santmexi.htm; fuller details of their deaths in particular, with photographs, in Ann Ball, *Faces of Holiness* (1998). For the background see Jean Meyer, *The Cristero Rebellion* (1976); also summary in M. A. Puente, "The Church in Mexico," in E. Dussel (ed.), *The Church in Latin America: 1492–1992* (1992), pp. 217-29.

1 June

Bd John Baptist Scalabrini, *Founder* (1839–1905)

John (Giovanni) Scalabrini was born at Fino Mornasco near Como in northern Italy on 8 July 1839, the third of eight children born to Luigi Scalabrini and his wife, Columba Trombetta. His father, Luigi, was a wine merchant, and the couple were held in high esteem in the locality. Luigi actively provided for the Catholic education of his children, and John was remembered by his classmates for spending many hours in study and prayer. After completing his elementary schooling in his home town he was sent to high school in Como. There he developed a love for the Eucharist and a devotion to the passion of Christ and his sorrowful Mother.

His parents were delighted when he expressed a desire to study for the priesthood. He entered the junior seminary of Sant'Abbondio and progressed from there to the theological seminary, where he served as prefect of discipline with his friend Luigi Guanella (24 Oct.). He continued on to the major seminary, coming first in his class in both "academics" and "disposition." He was ordained by the bishop of Bergamo on 30 May 1863. In the early years of his ministry he was a professor at, and then rector of, Sant'Abbondio. He then became pastor of San Bartolomeo in Como, where he involved himself in ministering to young people and textile and other factory workers. He founded a kindergarten, for which he wrote his first catechism, which he dedicated to the memory of his mother, who had died in 1865.

In 1875, at the age of thirty-six, he was consecrated bishop of Piacenza. He proved to be a tireless and dedicated pastoral bishop, making five visitations of the 365 parishes under his care, half of which could be reached only on foot or on mule-back, during his twenty-nine years as bishop. He organized and personally supervised three diocesan synods and worked to bring the Eucharist back to a central position in the often superstitious piety of the time, dedicating two hunded churches in the process. He reorganized the diocesan seminaries and used his theological expertise to reform their curriculum. Wherever he went he administered the sacraments, taught the Faith, and devised educational programmes. He encouraged devotion to the person of the pope at a time when anticlericalism was rife in newly-unified Italy. At the same time he advised Pope Pius IX (1839-78) to work for reconciliation between Church and State so that Catholics could play a part in the volatile politics of the time without being forced into moral dilemmas. His charity was both abundant and discreet: he ministered to victims of cholera; visited the sick and prisoners; aided both the poor and noble families who had lost their wealth; sold his own belongings; and opened the bishop's residence as a dispensary, serving sick farmers and workers. He founded an institute for those with hearing and speaking difficulties; organized protection for the young women employed in the rice fields, who were often subject to sexual as well as economic exploitation; and established mutual aid societies, worker's associations, rural banks, co-operatives, and Catholic Action centres.

His pastoral visitations showed him that emigration, particularly from the rural parishes, was turning into an exodus. The young men were deserting the region in great numbers, leaving behind them villages populated only by the elderly and young women. He became a passionate champion of the welfare of emigrants. Inspired by the sight of them cramming the Milan railway station, he gave an address in Piacenza in 1887 in which he spoke of "the vast waiting room filled with three or four hundred individuals, poorly dressed . . . marked by premature wrinkles drawn by privation. They were emigrants. They were leaving. They belonged to the various provinces of northern Italy and they were waiting . . . for the train to the Mediterranean . . . from where they would embark for the Americas . . . to find less hostile fortune." From 1887 to 1892 he researched into, lectured on, and wrote pamphlets on the phenomenon of emigration, forcing it into the arena of national debate. He worked and corresponded with many other great figures deeply concerned with this and other social issues, including Don Bosco (31 Jan.), Louis Orione (12 Mar.), Cardinal Andrew Ferrari of Milan (2 Feb.), the future Pope Pius X (1903-14; 21 Aug.), and Frances-Xavier Cabrini (22 Dec.), whom he persuaded to work in the United States rather than go to the Far East.

Bishop Scalabrini saw the need for an organized body to care for the pastoral needs of the migrants and founded the Missionaries of St Charles, who were to be migrants with the migrants. The community was formally recognized by Pope Leo XIII (1878-1903), who actively supported its aims, in November 1887. Eight years later Scalabrini, together with Fr Giuseppe Marchetti, founded a parallel Society for women, the Missionary Sisters of St Charles.

In the last ten years of his life he made two pastoral visits to his missionaries. His first was to the eastern United States from 3 August to 12 November 1901. His three-month itinerary was covered by both the Italian and the American press, and his visits to Italian immigrant ghettos brought reporters into neighbourhoods that previously had received publicity only for crimes.

By his own account, given during an interview in New York City, Scalabrini's travels took him to New Haven, Boston, Utica, Syracuse, Buffalo, Cleveland, Detroit, Canada, Chicago, St Paul, Kansas City, St Louis, Cincinnati, Columbus, and Washington, D.C., where he was received by President Theodore Roosevelt. The tour was arranged through Archbishop John Ireland of St Paul, and it afforded Scalabrini the opportunity to speak out against injustice toward Italian immigrants and to defend them to the president of the Republic.

His second international visit was to his missions in Brazil, starting on 13 June 1904. Here too he was received as the personal envoy of Pope Leo, and in later years he would reflect on these visits to Cardinal Merry del Val, the secretary of state of Pope Pius X, asking him to encourage the pope to establish a commission or a pontifical congregation for the pastoral care of immigrants.

All his activity was nourished by a deep devotion to Christ in the Eucharist and to the Blessed Virgin, as his homilies and pilgrimages testify. He died in the early hours of 1 June 1905, which that year was the feast of the Ascension. His last words were indicative of a life lived for others and in the service of God: "My priests, where are my priests? Let them come in; do not make them wait too long. . . . God's will be done." He was beatified by Pope John Paul II on 9 November 1997.

M. Caliaro and M. Francesconi, *John Baptist Scalabrini: Apostle to the Emigrants* (1977); A. Brizzolara, *The Visit of Bishop Scalabrini to the United States and Its Effects on the Image of Italian Immigrants as Reflected in the American Press of 1901* (1996); Archivio Generale, Pia Società dei Misionari de S. Carlo-Scalabriniani, *Visita all Missione degli Stati Uniti D'America* (B-IV 1091, nn. 169-72).

6 June

St Marcellin Champagnat, *Founder* (1789–1840)

Marcellin Champagnat, founder of the Marist Brothers of the Schools, was born into a sound Christian family on 20 May 1789, barely two months before the French Revolution; he was, nevertheless, affected in some ways by that great movement of history. His father, Jean-Baptiste Champagnat, became a senior official in the small town of Marlhes on the high plateau of the Mont-Pilat district, not far from the city of Saint-Etienne. Jean-Baptiste's official duties under the Revolution included acting as town clerk of Marlhes and colonel of the National Guard. His son Marcellin eschewed politics throughout his life of fifty-one years, but the principles of the Revolution may be seen in the egalitarianism of his approach to people and the classless structure of the Institute of Marist Brothers.

National education was quite chaotic during this period of French history, and Marcellin received practically no schooling until the age of fourteen, when a diocesan recruiter found that the boy had an interest in becoming a priest. Some education under his teacher brother-in-law led the latter to declare to Marcellin's family that the boy did not have the capacity to pursue studies for the priesthood. Despite this uncompromising verdict, at the age of sixteen a determined Marcellin entered the minor seminary of Verrières. After one year the seminary authorities recommended that he should not return after the holiday break. This did not deter Marcellin's mother, who, having ascertained that he still wanted to become a priest, employed means both spiritual (a pilgrimage) and human (influential friends) to have him readmitted.

After eight years at the minor seminary, where his conduct and his application to study improved steadily (a fact attested to by the resolutions recorded in his notebooks), Marcellin entered the major seminary of St Irenaeus at Lyons toward the end of the reign of Emperor Napoleon I. Here he encountered professors steeped in the principles of Sulpician formation, but he also came in contact with a charismatic character among the students, Jean-Claude Courveille, whose eloquence, drive, and enthusiasm concerning the foundation of a Society of Mary led to the formation of a group imbued with the idea of becoming members of a Society bearing the name of Mary. At meetings of this group the shape of the new Society was hammered out. There were three branches contemplated—a Society of priests, an Institute of religious Sisters, and a Third Order for lay members. One persistent voice held out for a fourth branch, an Institute of Teaching Brothers. The voice was that of Champagnat, whose own lack of early education and awareness of the country's dire need for Christian educators drove him to worry his starry-eyed companions with his reiterated request. In exasperation, they finally gave way and appointed Champagnat to found the teaching Brothers' branch. Champagnat took this charge as a special commission from his peers.

On 23 July 1816, immediately after their ordination ceremonies, twelve of the companions climbed the hill of Fourvière and, at the shrine of the Black Virgin, placed their written and signed pledge on the altar (under the corporal) while their then leader, Courveille, celebrated Mass. Then the new priests went to their respective placements as clergy of the archdiocese of Lyons. It would be a long twenty years before they came together as priests of the Society of Mary.

Champagnat was allocated to La Valla, on the side of the steep hill leading to the plateau of the Mont-Pilat range. Here, as curate, he carried out his parish duties with zest but was ever conscious of his task for the unborn Society of

Mary. He soon came in contact with a prospective candidate in the person of Jean-Marie Granjon, a former Grenadier of Napoleon's Imperial Guard, to whom Champagnat started to give the first elements of formal education. It was a sick call, however, that stirred him to action in regard to the founding of the teaching Brothers. After attending to the spiritual needs of a dying youth whose knowledge of religion was abysmally poor, Champagnat determined to act, a determination that was strengthened when a second recruit came his way, as if prompted by Providence.

On 2 January 1817 Champagnat brought his two followers to a house he had acquired and personally cleaned and provisioned. It was the first breath of the infant Society of Mary. Universal approval was not, however, forthcoming. The parish priest, Fr Rebod, worried about financial commitments that could possibly become his responsibility, opposed the project, and influenced other priests against his curate. Later, the authorities of the local College, worried about the effect on their enrollments of Champagnat's growing cluster of primary schools, stirred up more opposition, but the greatest early trial in this sphere was provided by the vicar general, Mgr Bochard, who wanted Champagnat's group of Brothers to be absorbed into his own Congregation, the Society of the Cross of Jesus. Pressure on Champagnat mounted, but a sudden influx of vocations (the answer to prayer and pilgrimage to the La Valla shrine of Our Lady of Pity) and a semi-miraculous deliverance from certain death when he and a Brother were caught in a snowstorm early in 1823 convinced Champagnat that he had to "stiffen the sinews, summon up the blood," and resist the threat to his Institute. By happy chance a specific church event rescued Champagnat.

A new pope, Leo X, removed Cardinal Fesch, Napoleon's uncle, from his control of the archdiocese of Lyons. When Archbishop de Pins was appointed apostolic administrator of Lyons, Bochard, in high dudgeon, resisted the appointment and soon left the archdiocese. The harassed Champagnat breathed a sigh of relief, for not only was the danger of Bochard removed, but Champagnat also gained the approval and support of the new archbishop for the work he had undertaken in founding schools staffed by his Marist Brothers.

As Shakespeare wrote, "When troubles come, they come not single spies but in battalions." Internal problems now challenged Champagnat. Courveille, the charismatic inspirer of the would-be Marists, had not proved to be a stable leader. He came to join Champagnat in the house Champagnat built, the five-storey motherhouse, Notre Dame de L'Hermitage. In his frustration with his diminishing influence among the priests of the group, he sought to have himself elected as superior of the Brothers. Despite Champagnat's sympathetic support for his candidacy, Courveille could not convince the Brothers to accept him as leader. Their vote was heavily in favour of the man they knew and admired, Champagnat.

Champagnat was seriously ill at the beginning of 1826, which brought creditors clamouring for their money. At this time the disappointed Courveille fell into a grave moral lapse and, through the energetic action of another Marist priest aspirant, Terraillon, was not successful in his effort to return to the motherhouse. It is of interest to note that Champagnat, through his recruiting of young chaplains who came to help him with the formation of the Brothers at the motherhouse, was able to imbue young priests with a longing to join the priests' branch of the Marists. Indeed, when the clerical Marists were approved in 1836 (mainly because of their acceptance to be the Church's missionaries in the south-west Pacific), no fewer than ten of the twenty-one who arrived for the vow ceremony at the town of Belley had been influenced by Champagnat in the archdiocese of Lyons. The others came from the diocese of Belley, where Jean-Claude Colin, the new leader of the general Marist movement, gathered a following. Champagnat was also instrumental in sending a good number of young women to the incipient Congregation of Marist Sisters.

Courveille's fall was not Champagnat's only problem at this time. After ten years of apostolate some among the Brothers had lost their initial fervour. There were those who were disaffected, particularly in regard to educational method and the matter of dress. The founder's illness and period of convalescence also had some influence on exacerbating the problems, particularly when, perforce, they had been put under the authority of the unstable Courveille. With the latter removed from the scene, Champagnat's immediate problems were twofold: he had to induce some of the Brothers to change to a modern, more effective method of teaching reading (no easy task, for some of the older Brothers were fixed in their ways), and he had difficulties concerning the Brothers' attire, which, for some, was becoming too showy. Both could have become major crises, but Champagnat's skillful handling of affairs soon settled the situation. After a trial year or so the new technique for teaching reading was accepted by the Brothers, and those who resisted the dress reform—two notable rebels—left the Institute.

Champagnat was a thoughtful, progressive educationalist, thoroughly concerned for the welfare of the students. This was why he insisted that his Brothers employ the "simultaneous method" of education used by the De La Salle Brothers. His insistence on this method led to the loss of the school at Feurs, where the anticlerical local council tried to force him to adopt the newly-devised "mutual method." The reason for Champagnat's insistence on the simultaneous method was that, through this system, the teacher could have more direct contact with, and thus more good influence on, the children. In brief, Champagnat's educational concept was that in their teaching the Brothers should integrate faith with education and should create a family spirit in the school environment. He believed that the Brothers should be with the young, should love them, should lead them to Jesus, and form them to be good Christians and good citizens. In a circular letter to the Brothers (19 January 1839) he said: "I desire and wish that, following the example of Jesus, you have a tender love for the children. With holy zeal break for them the spiritual bread of religion."

A major difficulty for Champagnat was that of obtaining official government recognition of the Institute. There was early promise for this, but as French governments became increasingly anticlerical, Champagnat's quest, although it waxed and waned during his many attempts, was finally not crowned with success. Indeed, the progress of the Institute was often affected by the political climate of the country. Champagnat had trouble with some local government officials, with the threat of compulsory military service for his Brothers, and even with a special government-authorized visitation of the motherhouse in a fruitless quest for a "marquis" who was supposed to be giving military training to anti-government rebels! Government recognition finally came to the Institute only after the founder's death, when Louis Napoleon's government, more favourably disposed toward the Church, granted the long-sought authorization.

Champagnat's cause was hardly furthered by some clerical friends who tried to solve his lack of government recognition by amalgamating his Institute with other groups who possessed the vital authorization. Several such attempts were made, the most serious being that of a projected joining of the Marist Brothers to Fr Querbes' Clerks of St Viateur, an attempt carried out by Fr Pompallier (later a bishop leading the first Marist party to the missions of Oceania) and the vicar general, Cholleton (later a Marist priest and novice-master). Neither Querbes nor Champagnat was enthusiastic about this proposal because they knew that the distinctive spirits of their respective Institutes were not compatible. Nevertheless, the two "plotters" came close to effecting the union. Fortunately the archbishop, although at first favourable to the union, changed his mind. A presumably tear-stained draft of a letter concerning this matter shows how deeply Champagnat was moved by this affair.

By the time of his death in 1840, Marcellin's Institute of Marist Brothers numbered forty-eight establishments and 280 Brothers. Champagnat himself had become a priest of the Society of Mary in 1836, a consecration that placed him under religious obedience to Fr Colin, who was elected leader of the clerical branch. To the end of his life Marcellin believed in an integrated Society, all four branches under the leadership of one man. Later in the century Rome decreed otherwise, separating the branches under their respective superiors general.

During the time Champagnat was subject in obedience to Colin as his religious superior, the two leaders, by and large, worked well together, although it was clear that they did not share the same concept of the role of the Brothers. Colin thought the Brothers could be used as auxiliaries to the priests in their apostolates anywhere, whereas, essentially, Champagnat wanted the Brothers for the school apostolate and for life in community with their own Brothers. In spite of this difference of opinion, Champagnat, who was enthusiastic about the apostolate of the missions, sent his Brothers to Oceania under the superiorship of Marist priests, a procedure that continued for some time after the founder's death. Unfortunately the identity of these generous volunteers became blurred with that of the Joseph Brothers, a group of religious Brothers whom Colin recruited as a lay-brother section of the Marist Fathers. Eventually these Marist Brothers in the missions were advised by the Brother superior general to remain with the priests' branch, the Society of Mary.

Exhausted by his apostolic exertions, Champagnat perceptibly declined in health in 1839, dying at the comparatively early age of fifty-one on 6 June 1840. During the twenty-year generalate of his successor, Br François Rivat, the Institute expanded vastly, at a rate of one new opening every three weeks over the twenty years.

In 1856 the Marist Brothers entered the field of secondary education when the Marist Fathers asked them to take over the school at Valbenoîte, near Saint-Etienne. At the beginning of the third millennium, in different parts of the world, the Marist Brothers are working not only in primary, secondary, and tertiary education, but also in many mission situations and in other apostolates associated with young people. Numbers peaked at above nine thousand in the late 1960s, and the Marist Brothers enter the new millennium with scarcely five thousand. Vocations in First-World countries have dropped considerably, but a good response continues in other parts. Marcellin Champagnat was named Venerable in 1920 and beatified in 1955. His canonization on 18 April 1999 was an occasion to fan the flame of the characteristic virtues of humility, simplicity, and modesty already very much alight in Marist hearts.

J. Coste, S.M., and G. Lessard, S.M., *Origines Maristes (1786-1836)*, vols. 1-4 (1961); Stephen Farrell, F.M., *Achievement from the Depths* (1984); Pierre Zind, F.M.S., *Les Nouvelles Congrégations de Frères Enseignants 1800-1830* (1969); *Life of Joseph Benedict Marcellin Champagnat* (1947). Frederick McMahon, F.M.S., *Strong Mind, Gentle Heart"* (1988); *ibid.*, *Travellers in Hope* (1994).

6 June

Bd Raphael Guízar y Valencia, *Bishop* (1878–1938)

Raphael (Rafael) was born in Cotija in the State of Michoacán in Mexico on 26 April 1878. Ordained priest, he worked tirelessly in various States of the Republic of Mexico and also in Cuba, Guatemala, Colombia, and the southern States of the U.S.A., dedicating himself above all to children and the poor. He was consecrated bishop of Veracruz in 1919 and as bishop was noted for his concern for the spiritual and academic formation of his priests and seminarians, for his devotion to the Eucharist and Our Lady, and for his close adhesion to the Holy See.

He died with a great reputation for holiness in Mexico City on 6 June 1938. His remains were taken to the city of Xalapa in Veracruz and interred in the cathedral amid scenes of wide popular enthusiasm. He was beatified by Pope John Paul II on 29 January 1995.

www.aciprensa.com/santmexi.htm (in Spanish).

14 August

St Meinhard, *Bishop* (1196)

Venerated as the apostle of the Church in Latvia (Livonia in the Middle Ages), Meinhard was an Augustinian Canon of Segeberg Abbey in Holstein. Merchants from Lübeck, probably trading for the costly furs that fetched a high price in western Europe, brought him to the mouth of the Dvina (or Daugava) River in the 1170s or early 1180s to begin a mission to the pagan Livs, Latgali, and Zemgali there. He established himself at Ikskile, some twenty miles east of Riga, where he built a stone church dedicated to Our Lady and also a stone fort in which the local people would be safe from raiders from Lithuania seeking to carry off slaves. The community grew, and when Meinhard made a return visit to Germany in 1186, Archbishop Hartwig of Bremen consecrated him first bishop of Ikskile, which was later confirmed by Pope Clement III, who gave him papal approval for his mission in 1193.

He was venerated as a man of outstanding virtue, and a cult began soon after his death, which occurred probably on 14 August in 1196. There was, though, a pagan reaction in the area, and Christian fortunes had to be restored through a campaign undertaken by Albert of Buxhövden, consecrated bishop of the Livs in 1199, who declared Livonia to be "the property of the Mother of God." The master of the chronicler Henry of Livonia, who compiled the chronicle of the mission, Albert founded Riga in 1201, and this became his episcopal city. Meinhard's body was translated there in 1226, where it remains in what is now the Lutheran cathedral.

The eighth centenary of the Christianization of Latvia was celebrated in 1986, the event being dated to Meinhard's consecration. In September 1993 Pope John Paul II visited the Baltic States, by then independent of the former Soviet Union, and on 8 September solemnly proclaimed and formally restored veneration of St Meinhard in these words: "Therefore, fulfilling the desire of my brothers in the episcopate and of many Christian faithful, by my apostolic authority I duly re-establish the veneration of St Meinhard, bishop of Ikskile, especially in this particular Church whose apostle and founder he was. Moreover, I grant permission for his feast to be celebrated each year on 14 August in the places and manner determined by law."

An account of Meinhard's evangelizing activity is in *Henrici Chronicon Livorniae*, 1, 2, written between 1225 and 1229. See R. Fletcher, *The Conversion of Europe* (1997), pp. 492-3. For a summary history see Jedin-Dolan, 4, p. 219. For the papal visit see *Osservatore Romano*, weekly edition, 15 Sept. 1993, pp. 8, 9.

Some remains of Meinhard's original church can still be seen.

24 August

Bd Mary Incarnation of the Sacred Heart (1820–86)

María Vicenta Rosal Vásquez, the first Guatemalan to be beatified, was born in Quetzaltenango, the capital of Guatemala, on 26 October 1820. Determined from the age of fifteen to follow a religious vocation, on 1 January 1837 she joined the Sisters of Bethelehem, founded by Bd Peter de Betancur (25 Apr.), taking the name Mary Incarnation of the Sacred Heart. She found them falling away from the standards of their calling and moved to the convent of the Catalinas, but she found this no more to her liking and returned to her original "Bethlehem." She was appointed prioress in 155 and revised the Constitutions to bring them back into line with the original ideal. This angered some of the older Sisters, leading Mary to found a new *beaterio*, as the convents were called, in Quetzaltenango in 1861. Here she was able to lead a community reformed according to her ideals, deeply dedicated to prayer, especially of reparation to the Sacred Heart, to which the 25th of each month was dedicated.

She started two schools in the capital, but her work was interrupted when President Justo Rufino Barrios (1873–85) began expelling religious Orders. She went to Costa Rica, where she started the first school for women in the country, and then to Colombia, where she started an orphanage and refuge for women in the city of Pasto. Moving on to Ecuador, she established the Bethlemite Sisters in Tulcán and Otavalo.

This indefatigable champion of women's education and protection died on 24 August 1886 after falling off her horse on her way from one of her foundations in Ecuador to the other. It was the eve of the feast of the Sorrows of the Sacred Heart, which she had been inspired to institute. Her body was later transferred to Pasto in Colombia, where it remains. She was beatified by Pope John Paul II on 4 May 1997 with four others, including the first Gypsy to be beatified, Ceferino Giménez Malla (8 Aug.). The Bethlemite Sisters now work in Italy, Spain, Africa, India, U.S.A., four countries of Central America, Venezuela, Ecuador, and Colombia, with the motherhouse in Bogotá.

Osservatore Romano, weekly English edition, 7 May 1997; www.aciprensa.com/santos.htm (in Spanish).

31 August

St Aidan, *Bishop* (651)

Aidan (or Aedan) was a Scot (of Irish origin if not born in Ireland) and a monk of Iona noted for his asceticism and gentleness. He was an obvious choice to help in the task of christianizing the English, "an uncivilized people of an obstinate and barbarous temperament." Bede's account, on which we rely for details, is especially adulatory: "He never looked or cared for any worldly possessions, and loved to give away to the poor whatever he received from the king or rich people. Whether in town or country, he always travelled on foot unless he was forced to ride, and whenever he met anyone, whether high or low, he stopped to speak to them. . . . His life was very different to the apathy of our own times, for everyone who was with him, monk or lay person, had to meditate: that is, either to read the Bible or to learn the Psalms. . . . If wealthy people did wrong he always spoke out."

St Oswald, king of Northumbria (d. 642; 9 Aug.), who became Aidan's friend, had been converted to Christianity when in exile on Iona, and he asked Aidan to leave Iona to revive and extend St Paulinus' (10 Oct.) missionary work among non-Christian Saxons in Deira, the southern part of his kingdom. A very austere monk had already been sent to help Oswald, but he had returned complaining of the uncouthness of his prospective converts. In 635 Aidan was consecrated bishop of Lindisfarne (Holy Isle), the island off the coast of Northumbria between Berwick and Bamburgh, which he made his centre of operations. He established a monastery under the Rule of St Columba (or Colmcille; 9 June) and became the first abbot. He went on long trips to mainland England to encourage Christian communities and to establish new missionary centres, mainly in the northern kingdom of Bernicia. Until Aidan learned English properly, Oswald, who had fluent Gaelic from his years of exile, acted as his interpreter.

Aidan was a Celtic ecclesiastic and taught by the standards of his Church (Bede stresses his keeping of Easter in the Irish and Pictish fashion). His lifestyle was austere, and he tried to make ordinary people follow monastic practices. He built churches and established monasteries. He ransomed, trained, and ordained suitable slaves. He planned the education of twelve English boys, including St Chad (2 Mar.), who were former slaves, in order to make them ecclesiastical leaders of their nation. St Oswin (d. 651; 20 Aug.), who succeeded Oswald, also treated Aidan as a close friend and presented him with a splendid horse, which Aidan, to the king's initial chagrin, promptly gave away.

In 651 Aidan, who had retired to Inner Farne Island for his Lenten penance, watched the castle at Bamburgh, which he had used as a mission centre, burn after an attack by King Penda of Mercia. He died at Bamburgh the same year and was buried on Lindisfarne. His bones were eventually translated to St Peter's church there, and some of them were later taken to Ireland by Bishop St Colman of Lindisfarne (18 Feb.) when he left England after refusing to give up Celtic usages after the Synod of Whitby. The island was abandoned during the Viking invasions. In the tenth century the monks of Glastonbury enhanced their holding of relics with some reputed fragments from Aidan's body, and his feast-day entered the Wessex calendars. Bamburgh church was named after him.

Bede, *H.E.*, trans. L. Shirley Price (1955), bk. 3, ch. 3, 5ff., pp. 141-2, 145-8; A. C. Fryer, *Aidan, the Apostle of the North* (1884); J. B. Lightfoot, *Leaders in the Northern Church: Sermons* (1890); E. W. Grierson, *The Story of the Northumbrian Saints* (1913), pp. 45-69; H. Mayr-Harting, *The Coming of Christianity to Anglo-Saxon England* (1972), pp. 94-9.

1 October (previously 5 December)

St Nicetius of Trier, Bishop (*c.* 566)

Several distinguished men, including St Gregory of Tours (17 Nov.) and St Venantius Fortunatus (14 Dec.), bear witness to the acts of Nicetius of Trier, who was the last Gallo-Roman bishop of Trier in the early days of Frankish domination in Gaul. Gregory called him "a man of eminent holiness who enjoyed great fame among his people alike for the admirable eloquence of his preaching and for his good works and miracles."

Nicetius was born in the Auvergne and became a monk. When he was abbot of his monastery, which was probably at Limoges, he attracted the attention of King Theoderic I, who nominated him bishop of Trier. When the royal officers were escorting him to Trier he showed what sort of prelate he was going to be: they halted for the night, and the officers turned their horses out into the fields of the local peasants, careless of what damage they did. When Nicetius ordered the horses to be removed, the officers laughed at him. He drove the horses out himself, threatening excommunication to those who oppressed the poor.

Nicetius often preached to his monks from the text that "a man may fall out in three ways—by thought, word, and deed," and he was not afraid to rebuke the irregularities of Theoderic and his son Theodebert. Clotaire I was less tractable, and when Nicetius excommunicated him for his crimes, he retaliated by banishing Nicetius. The exile was a short one. Clotaire died soon after, and his son Sigebert saw that the bishop was restored to his see.

Nicetius assisted at several important synods at Clermont and elsewhere and was indefatigable in restoring discipline to a diocese that had suffered much from civil disorders. He called in Italian workmen to rebuild his cathedral and founded a clergy school, but his own actions provided the best lesson for both clergy and laity. Though he enjoyed the favour and protection of King Sigebert his zeal brought him enemies: for instance, he attacked incestuous marriages and excommunicated offenders, some of whom opposed him bitterly.

Several of Nicetius' letters have been preserved. One, written about the year 561, was to Clodesindis, daughter of Clotaire I and wife of Alboin, the Arian king of the Lombards. He tells her to endeavour to convert her husband to the Faith and writes trenchantly about the fruits of Catholic belief: "Let the king send messengers to the church of St Martin. If they dare enter it, they will see the blind enlightened, the deaf recover their hearing, and the dumb their speech: the lepers and sick are cured and return home sound, as we see." He wrote of the blessings brought through the relics of three holy bishops: "The very demoniacs are forced to confess their virtue. Do they do so in the churches of the Arians? They do not. One devil never exorcizes another."

Another letter is addressed to the emperor Justinian, who had been influenced by his wife toward Monophysitism, the belief that the human nature in Christ was totally subordinate to the divine. In it Nicetius, who was quite fearless on matters of theology and church discipline, tells the emperor that his lapse is bewailed through Italy, Africa, Spain, and Gaul, and that he will be lost if he does not repudiate his errors.

See the *Historia Francorum* of St Gregory of Tours, trans. and intro. O. M. Dalton (1927), 2, p. 465; Duchesne, *Fastes*, 3, pp. 37-8; *D.C.B.* (1911), pp. 758-9; *D.Cath.Biog.*, p. 849; *L.D.H.*, p. 411. For Nicetius' letters see *M.G.H.*, *Epistolae*, 3, pp. 116-22.

11 November

Bd Eugene Bossilkov, *Bishop and Martyr* (1900–52)

Eugene Bossilkov was born into a family of Latin-Rite Catholics in Belene, a village in the Danube Valley in northern Bulgaria, on 16 November 1900 and was given the name Vincent at his baptism. At this time the mission to northern Bulgaria was entrusted to the Passionist Fathers, who had originally established it in 1781. He received his secondary education first at the Passionist minor seminary in Oresc and then at the diocesan seminary in Nikopol. In 1914 he was sent to the Order's seminary in Ele in Belgium, where he received the Passionist habit in 1919, taking the name Eugene of the Sacred Heart in religion, and completed his philosophy course. He began his theology in Holland, but when the Belgian/Dutch Passionist province divided in 1924 the mission seminary was transferred to Ruse in Bulgaria, and he completed his theology there. He was ordained on 25 July 1926, at a time when Catholics in Bulgaria numbered less than 1 per cent of a total population of some 3.5 million, of whom the great majority were Eastern Orthodox, with a sizeable Muslim minority.

In 1927 he was sent to Rome to study for a degree at the Pontifical Oriental Institute, and in 1932 he gained a doctorate with a thesis on the union of Bulgaria with the Roman Catholic Church in the early thirteenth century (1204). On his return home in 1933 he served first as personal secretary to the Passionist Bishop Damian Theelen and then, having expressed a preference for more pastoral work, as pastor in Bardaski-Gheran, where he concentrated on improving the level of religious education among his flock with particular emphasis on young people.

The government of Bulgaria agreed to cooperate with Hitler's forces in March 1941, thereby avoiding actual occupation by Germany. This put a stop to all missionary endeavours, though it also prevented the Nazi excesses that took place in other eastern European counries. In summer 1944 the government tried to change sides, but it did so just too late, three days after Stalin had declared war on Bulgaria on 5 September. A "Fatherland Front" government was installed with partisan participation and Soviet military support, and moves were begun to control religious activity. All religious feasts were suppressed, any religious manifestation had to be within church buildings, church schools were confiscated, and all Catholic charities were suppressed. A special law passed in 1949 forbade any religious activity not under state control and all contacts with ecclesiastical bodies outside the country.

Bishop Theelen died in August 1946, and Fr Eugene was chosen as apostolic administrator in anticipation of the nomination of a successor. Despite the prohibitions in force he ordered a mission to be conducted in each parish and personally took part in these. He was named bishop of Nikopol by Pope Pius XII on 26 July 1947, the first Bulgarian Passionist to hold the office. The authorities seem to have softened their stance somewhat, as the civic authorities played a part in the ceremonies attending his consecration in October. He was also permitted to make his *ad limina* visit to Rome, where he arrived on 3 July 1948, having visited his Passionist brethren in Holland on the way, and where he was received in audience by the pope on 17 September. He left to go back to Bulgaria on 1 October despite being advised against returning because of danger of imprisonment or even death, telling a friend, "I am the shepherd of my flock. I cannot abandon the flock."

After his return the political situation deteriorated, and he advised the Passionist provincial in Holland to recall the missionaries; most left in early 1949. He stayed behind, writing to his provincial, "If it comes to the worst, so be it. I have the courage to go on living. I hope I also have the courage to suffer the worst, always remaining faithful to Christ, the Pope, and the Church." Arrests of priests began the following year, when two Capuchins were accused of being anti-Communist, harbouring anti-Soviet sentiments, and spying for the Vatican and imperialist powers. Bishop Bossilkov was under constant surveillance and unable to move around freely: "I can't take a step without my 'guardian angel' always at my heels. What a feeling!" he wrote to his provincial. He resorted to writing in a simple code, with the government his "dentist" and his troubles his "toothache": "My health is fine, but the dentist won't leave me in peace; it's not easy to free oneself of a dentist of this kind, but that's only part of the entire story!" He was nevertheless able to ordain four priests on 18 December 1951.

On 16 July 1952 the state police took action against every Catholic community in Bulgaria, arresting some forty priests, including the bishop, who was staying in a modest holiday home outside Sofia. Until his trial opened on 29 September there was no further news of him, though evidence was to emerge that he had been savagely tortured in prison. After four days during which the authorities failed to extract any confession on anti-Soviet activities from him or any of those tried with him, he, two Assumptionist religious, and a parish priest were condemned to be shot. Relatives were allowed to visit him for the last time on 6 October; they implored him to ask for clemency, but he refused, saying, "No, I know the Lord will give me the strength to accept death in accordance with his will. I have not denounced anyone. . . . I could have been free to enjoy every possible comfort, if I had wished it." He did ask for blankets, as he was made to sleep on a bare cement floor. His niece Gabriella brought him a basket of food every day until mid-November, the guard returning the empty basket. When it was returned with the food untouched on 18 November, Gabriella was told that he had been executed on the 11th. Confirmation of this reached the Vatican only in 1975, when the Bulgarian Head of State, Todor Zhikov, had an audience with Pope Paul VI, who asked him directly what had happened to Bishop Bossilkov and was told that he had died "in prison twenty-three years ago." His body was thrown into a common grave and has never been found.

He was beatified in Rome on 15 March 1998. The Bulgarian prosecutor general then started proceedings for his posthumous exoneration, and in May 1999 a decreee of the Bulgarian Supreme Court of Appeal found that the 1952 trial records contained "glaring violations" of justice and annulled the death sentence. This was welcomed by Mgr Blagovest Vanghelov, vicar general of the Catholic Byzantine-Rite Apostolic Exarchate of Sofia, as "a clear moral exoneration."

Much of the above derives from a letter sent to all Passionists for the beatification by the superior general, José A. Obregozo, C.P., dated 25 January 1998. See also *Osservatore Romano,* weekly edition, 18 March 1998, p. 2; *The Tablet,* 29 May 1999, p. 758, on the posthumous exoneration. On the background see J. Rothschild, *East Central Europe Between the Two World Wars* (1974); R. J. Crampton, *Eastern Europe in the Twentieth Century* (1994). His niece Gabriella's testimony for the process of beatification is given on a website prepared by Fr Victor Hoagland, C.P.: www.crypton.org/cpexams/bossilkov/bio.html.

14 November

St Nicholas of Sibenik and Companions, *Martyrs* (1391)

Nicholas Tavelic was born at Sibenik in Dalmatia during the first half of the fourteenth century and became a Franciscan at Rivotorto, near Assisi. He was sent on a mission to Bosnia, where a sect called the Bogomils was preaching a heretical version of the Faith, which even some bishops were said to have accepted. The task of restoring the true Faith was given to the Dominican and Franciscan friars. Nicholas was particularly successful. He worked in Bosnia and on the Dalmatian coast for twenty years before being sent on a mission to Palestine.

In 1219 St Francis of Assisi (4 Oct.) had undertaken a personal mission to the Holy Land. Appalled at the dissoluteness and self-seeking of the Crusaders, he had passed through the enemy lines at great danger to himself, demanding to see the Sultan, and had secured for the Franciscans the custody of the Holy Places. By the time Nicholas went to join them the eighth and last Crusade was long over and Jerusalem was in the hands of the Saracens.

Nicholas studied and prayed there with three other Franciscans, Peter of Narbonne, Deodatus of Rodez in Aquitaine, and Stephen of Cuneo from Genoa. This little group—a Croat, two Frenchmen, and an Italian—came to the conclusion that Christ's injunction to go and preach to all nations was to be taken literally and that they must take the gospel to the Muslims. On 11 November 1391 they went to see the Qadi, the civil judge of Saracen Jerusalem. "We have come here," they told him, "not sent by any man, but by God, who has deigned to inspire us to come and teach you the truth and the way to salvation." The Qadi was at first amazed and then angry at what he saw as the effrontery of infidels, especially as they did not mince their words on his religion: "You are in a state of eternal damnation since your law is not the law of God nor given by God nor even a good law; in fact it is evil indeed. . . . [It] contains many lies, impossibilities, laughable matters, contradictions, and other things which lead men not to good or virtue but to evil and a great many vices." They were equally scathing about the person of Mohammed, calling him "a libertine, a murderer, a glutton, a despoiler who put man's end in eating, whoring, and wearing expensive clothes." The Qadi ordered the four to recant on pain of death. They refused, saying that they were ready to suffer any torture and to die for the Catholic Faith. They were flogged, then thrown into prison, and four days later publicly burned at the stake.

Fr Gerardo Calveti, their superior and the Custodian of the Holy Land from 1388 to 1398, recorded their names and their words in a moving testimony to the facts of their martyrdom. Their canonization was expected to be promulgated in 1941, when the thirteen-hundredth anniversary of the conversion of Croatia was to be celebrated, but the Second World War made this impracticable. The decree was eventually proclaimed by Pope Paul VI on 21 June 1970.

The citations are from the text of an official ecclesiastical inquiry held on 20 Jan. 1392, in P. Durrieu, "Procès-verbale du martyre de quatre frères Mineurs en 1391," in *Archives* 1 (1881), pp. 539-46; Eng. trans. in F. E. Peters, *Jerusalem* (1985), pp. 459-61. Wadding, 9, pp. 118-20; F.B.S., pp. 853-6; *Osservatore Romano*, 2 July 1970; *N.S.B.* 1, pp. 40-1; *Bibl.SS.*, 12, 148-51.

Appendix

A COMPARISON OF CALENDARS OF SAINTS' DAYS

The left-hand column shows those saints who are placed first on their dates in the body of this work and in Capital Letters—those commemorated throughout the Roman Catholic Church with the rank of **SOLEMNITY, Feast**, Memorial, or *Optional Memorial*, or *those of particular importance for the English-speaking world*. The centre column shows the corresponding entry for the date in the Common Worship Calendar and Lectionary authorized by the Church of England, with the rank of **PRINCIPAL FEAST, Festival**, Lesser Festival, or *Commemoration* (the use of **BOLD CAPS., Bold**, Roman, and *Italic* is as used in the Common Worship Calendar). The right-hand column shows the corresponding entry in the Calendar of the Church Year of the Episcopal Church in the United States of America.

Dates in parentheses in the centre and right-hand columns indicate corresponding dates in *Butler's*: if the date is the same, the entry in *Butler's* is not the leading one for the day.

JANUARY

1	**THE MOTHER OF GOD**	The Naming and Circumcision of Jesus	The Holy Name of Our Lord Jesus Christ
2		Basil and Gregory *Seraphim of Sarov*[1] *Samuel Azariah*[2]	Basil and Gregory
7	*Raymund of Peñafort*		
9			Julia Chester Emery[3]
10		*William Laud*[4]	William Laud
11		*Mary Slessor*[5]	
12		Aelred of Hexham (12 Jan.)	Aelred of Rievaulx
	Benedict Biscop	Benedict Biscop	
13	*Hilary of Poitiers*	Hilary of Poitiers *Kentigern* (13 Jan.) *George Fox*[6]	Hilary of Poitiers
17	Antony	Antony *Charles Gore*[7]	Antony

291

18			Confession of St Peter (= St Peter's Chair)
19	*Wulfstan*	Wulfstan	Wulfstan
20	*Fabian and Sebastian*	*Richard Rolle* (29 Sept.)	Fabian
21	Agnes	Agnes	Agnes
22	*Vincent of Zaragoza*	*Vincent of Saragossa*	Vincent of Saragossa
23			Phillips Brooks[8]
24	Francis de Sales	Francis de Sales	
25	**Conversion of Paul**	**Conversion of Paul**	**Conversion of Paul**
26	Timothy and Titus	Timothy and Titus	Timothy and Titus
27	*Angela Merici*	John Chrysostom (13 Sept.)	John Chrysostom
28	Thomas Aquinas	Thomas Aquinas	Thomas Aquinas
30		Charles[9]	
31	John Bosco	*John Bosco*	

1. Monk and spiritual guide (1833)   2. Bishop in South India, evangelist (1945)
3. Missionary in the Pacific region (1922)   4. Archbishop of Canterbury (1645)
5. Missionary in West Africa (1915) 6. Founder of the Society of Friends (1691) 7. Bishop, founder of the Community of the Resurrection (1932) 8. Bishop of Massachusetts (1893)
9. King Charles I, martyr (1649)

FEBRUARY

1	*Brigid of Kildare*	*Brigid of Kildare*	Brigid (Bride)
3	*Blaise*	*Anskar* (3 Feb.)	Anskar
4	*Gilbert of Sempringham*	*Gilbert of Sempringham*	Cornelius the Centurion (2 Feb.)
5	Agatha		Martyrs of Japan
6	Martyrs of Japan	*Martyrs of Japan*	
8	*Jerome Emiliani*		
10	Scholastica	*Scholastica*	
11	*Our Lady of Lourdes*		
13			Absalom Jones[1]
14	Cyril and Methodius	Cyril and Methodius	Cyril and Methodius
15		*Sigfrid* (15 Feb.)	
		Thomas Bray[2]	Thomas Bray
17	*Seven Founders of the Servite Order*	Janani Luwum[3]	
18			Martin Luther
21	*Peter Damian*		
	Robert Southwell		
23	Polycarp	Polycarp	Polycarp
24	Ethelbert of Kent		**Matthias** (14 May)
27		George Herbert[4]	George Herbert
28	Oswald of Worcester		

1. Priest (1818)   2. Founder of S.P.C.K. and S.P.G. (1730)   3. Archbishop of Uganda, martyr (1977)   4. Priest and poet (1633)

MARCH

1	*David of Wales*	David of Menevia	David of Menevia, Wales
2	*Chad*	Chad	Chad
3	*Katharine Drexel*		John and Charles Wesley[1]
4	*Casimir*		
7	Perpetua and Felicity	Perpetua, Felicity, and Companions	Perpetua and Companions
8	*John of God*	Edward King[2] Felix[3] Geoffrey Studdert Kennedy[4]	
9	*Frances of Rome*		Gregory of Nyssa (10 Jan.)
10	*John Ogilvie*		
12		Gregory the Great (3 Sept.)	
13	*Agnellus of Pisa*		
16	*John de Brébeuf*		
17	*Patrick*	Patrick	Patrick
18	*Cyril of Jerusalem*	*Cyril of Jerusalem*	Cyril of Jerusalem
19	**JOSEPH**	Joseph of Nazareth	Joseph
20	*Cuthbert*	Cuthbert	Cuthbert
21		Thomas Cranmer[5]	Thomas Ken[6]
23	*Turibius of Mogrovejo*		Gregory the Illuminator (the Enlightener; 30 Sept.)
24		*Walter Hilton[7]* *Oscar Romero[8]*	
25	**ANNUNCIATION OF THE LORD**	**ANNUNCIATION OF THE LORD**	Annunciation of Our Lord
26		*Harriet Monsell[9]*	
27			Charles Henry Brent[10]
31		*John Donne[11]*	

1. John: priest, founder of Methodist movement (1791); Charles: priest and hymnwriter (1788)   2. Bishop of Lincoln (1910)   3. Bishop, apostle to the East Angles (647)   4. Priest and poet, known as "Woodbine Willie" (1929)   5. Archbishop of Canterbury, Reformation martyr (1556)   6. Bishop of Bath and Wells, Non-juror, hymn writer (1711)   7. Mystic writer (1396)   8. Roman Catholic archbishop of San Salvador, martyr (1980)   9. Founder of Community of St John the Baptist, Clewer (1883)   10. Bishop of the Philippines and of Western New York (1929)   11. Priest and poet (1631)

APRIL

1		Frederick Denison Maurice[1]	Frederick Denison Maurice
2	Francis of Paola		James Lloyd Breck[2]
3	Richard of Chichester		Richard of Chichester
4	Isidore		Martin Luther King, Jr.[3]
5	Vincent Ferrer		
7	John Baptist de la Salle		
8	Julie Billiart		William Augustus Muhlenberg[4]
9		Dietrich Bonhoeffer[5]	Dietrich Bonhoeffer
10		William Law[6] William of Ockham[7]	William Law
11	Stanislaus of Cracow	George Augustus Selwyn[8]	George Augustus Selwyn
13	Martin I		
16		Isabella Gilmore[9]	
19		Alphege (19 Apr.)	Alphege
21	Anselm	Anselm	Anselm
23	George	**George**	
24	Fidelis of Sigmaringen	Mellitus (24 Apr.)	
25	**Mark**	**Mark**	**Mark**
27		Christina Rossetti[10]	
28	Peter Chanel	Peter Chanel	
29	Catherine of Siena	Catherine of Siena	Catherine of Siena
30	Pius V	Mary Ramabai[11]	

1. Teacher and priest (1872) 2. Priest (1876) 3. Civil Rights leader (1968) 4. Priest (1877)
5. Lutheran pastor and martyr (1945) 6. Spiritual writer (1761) 7. Friar, philosoper, and
teacher (1347) 8. First bishop of New Zealand and bishop of Lichfield (1878)
9. Deaconess (1923) 10. Poet (1894) 11. Translator of the scriptures (1922)

MAY

1	Joseph the Worker	**Philip and James** (3 May)	**Philip and James**
2	Athanasius	Athanasius	Athanasius
3	**Philip and James**		
4	Martyrs of England and Wales	English Saints and Martyrs of the Reformation Era	Monica (27 Aug.)
7	John of Beverley		
8		Julian of Norwich[1]	Julian of Norwich
9			Gregory of Nazianzus (Nazianzen; 2 Jan.)

294

12	*Nereus and Achilles*		
	Pancras		
14	**Matthias**	**Matthias**	
16		*Caroline Chisholm*[2]	
18	*John I*		
19	*Dunstan of Canterbury*	Dunstan of Canterbury	Dunstan
20	*Bernardino of Siena*	Alcuin of York (19 May)	Alcuin
21	*Godric of Finchale*	*Helena* (18 Aug.)	
23		*Petroc* (4 June)	
24		John and Charles Wesley	Jackson Kemper[3]
25	*Bede the Venerable*	Venerable Bede	Bede, the Venerable
	Gregory VII	*Aldhelm* (25 May)	
26	Philip Neri		Augustine of
			Canterbury (27 May)
27	*Augustine of Canterbury*	Augustine of Canterbury	
	John Calvin[4]		
	Philip Neri (26 May)		
28		*Lanfranc*[5]	
30		Josephine Butler[6]	
		Joan of Arc (30 May)	
31	**Visitation of the B.V.M.**	**Visit of the B.V. M. to**	**Visitation of the**
		Elizabeth	**B.V.M.**

1. Spiritual writer (c. 1417) 2. Social reformer (1877) 3. First missionary bishop in the United States (1879) 4. Reformer (1564) 5. Archbishop of Canterbury and scholar (1089) 6. Social reformer (1906)

JUNE

1	Justin Martyr	Justin	Justin
2	*Marcellinus and Peter*		The Martyrs of Lyons
			(2 June)
3	St Charles Lwanga and	*The Martyrs of Uganda*	The Martyrs of Uganda
	Companions (martyrs of Uganda)		
5	Boniface	Boniface	Boniface
6	Norbert	*Ini Kopuria*[1]	
7	*Willibald*		
8		Thomas Ken[2]	
9	*Ephraem*	*Ephrem of Syria*	Ephrem of Edessa, Syria
	Columba of Iona	Columba of Iona	Columba of Iona
11	Barnabas	**Barnabas**	**Barnabas**
13	Antony of Padua		
14		*Richard Baxter*[3]	Basil the Great (2. Jan.)
15		*Evelyn Underhill*[4]	Evelyn Underhill
16		Richard of Chichester (3 Apr.)	
		Joseph Butler[5]	Joseph Butler

17		*Samuel and Henrietta Barnett*[6]	
18		*Bernard Miseki*[7]	Bernard Miseki
19	*Romuald*	*Sundar Singh of India*[8]	
20	*Alban*		
21	Aloysius Gonzaga		
22	*John Fisher and Thomas More* *Paulinus of Nola*	Alban (20 June)	Alban
23	*Etheldreda*	Etheldreda	
24	**BIRTHDAY OF JOHN THE BAPTIST**	Birth of John the Baptist	Nativity of John the Baptist
27	*Cyril of Alexandria*	*Cyril of Alexandria*	
28	Irenaeus of Lyons	Irenaeus of Lyons	Ireneaus of Lyons
29	**PETER AND PAUL**	Peter and Paul	Peter and Paul
30	*Martyrs of Rome under Nero*		

1. Founder of the Melanesian Brotherhood (1945) 2. *See* note to 21 March 3. Puritan divine (1691) 4. Spiritual writer (1941) 5. Bishop of Durham, philosopher (1752) 6. Social reformers (1913 and 1936) 7. Apostle of the MaShona and martyr (1896) 8. Sadhu (holy man), evangelist, and teacher (1929)

JULY

1	*Oliver Plunkett*	*John and Henry Venn*[1]	
3	**Thomas**	**Thomas the Apostle**	
4	*Elizabeth of Portugal*		
5	*Antony Zaccariah*		
6	*Maria Goretti*	*Thomas More and John Fisher* (22 June)	
11	Benedict	Benedict	
13	*Henry II*		
14	*Camillus de Lelis*	John Keble[2]	
15	Bonaventure	*Bonaventure* Swithun of Winchester (2 July)	
16		*Osmund of Salisbury* (4 Dec.)	
17			William White[3]
18		*Elizabeth Ferrard*[4]	
19		Gregory of Nyssa (10 Jan.) and Macrina (the Younger; 19 July)	
20		*Margaret of Antioch*[5] *Bartolomé de las Casas*[6]	Elizabeth Cady Stanton, Amelia Bloomer, Sojourner Truth, and Harriett Ross Tubman[7]

21	*Laurence of Brindisi*		
22	Mary Magdalen	**Mary Magdalene**	Mary Magdalene
23	*Bridget of Sweden*	*Bridget of Sweden*	
25	**James**	**James**	James
26	Joachim and Anne	Anne and Joachim	The Parents of the B.V.M.
27		*Brooke Foss Westcott*[8]	William Reed Huntington[9]
29	**Martha**, *Mary, and Lazarus*	Mary, Martha, and Lazarus	Mary and Martha of Bethany
30	*Peter Chrysologus*	William Wilberforce[10]	William Wilberforce
31	Ignatius of Loyola	*Ignatius of Loyola*	Ignatius of Loyola

1. Priests, evangelical divines (1813 and 1873) 2. Priest, tractarian, and poet (1866) 3. Bishop of Pennsylvania (1836) 4. First deaconess of the Church of England, foundress of The Community of St Andrew (1883) 5. Martyr (fourth century) 6. Apostle to the Indies (1566) 7. Social reformers and champions of women's and slaves' rights (1902; 1894; 1883; 1913) 8. Bishop of Durham and teacher (1901) 9. Priest (1909) 10. Social reformer (1833)

AUGUST

1	Alphonsus de'Liguori		Joseph of Arimathea (31 Aug.)
2	*Eusebius of Vercelli*		
4	John Vianney	*Jean-Baptist Vianney*	
5	*Oswald*	Oswald	
7	*Sixtus II, Agapitus, Felicissimus, and Comps.*	*John Mason Neale*[1]	John Mason Neale
8	Dominic	Dominic	Dominic
9		Mary Sumner[2]	
10	**Laurence**	Laurence	Laurence
11	Clare of Assisi	Clare of Assisi *John Henry Newman*[3]	Clare of Assisi
13	*Pontian and Hippolytus*	Jeremy Taylor[4] *Florence Nightingale*[5] *Octavia Hill*[6]	Jeremy Taylor
14		*Maximilian Kolbe* (14 Aug.)	Jonathan Myrick Daniels[7]
15	**The Assumption of the B.V.M.**	**The Blessed Virgin Mary**	Mary the Virgin
16	*Stephen of Hungary*		
18			William Porcher DuBose[8]
19	John Eudes		
20	Bernard	Bernard *William and Catherine Booth*[9]	Bernard

21	Pius X		
23	*Rose of Lima*		
24	**Bartholomew**	Bartholomew	Bartholomew
25	*Louis of France*		Louis of France
	Joseph Calasanz		
27	Monica	Monica	Thomas Gallaudet and Henry Winter Syle[10]
28	Augustine	Augustine	Augustine
29	Passion of John the Baptist	Beheading of John the Baptist	
30		John Bunyan[11]	
31		Aidan of Lindisfarne (31 Aug., *but see* Dec. Suppl.)	Aidan

1. Priest and hymn writer (1866) 2. Foundress of the Mothers' Union (1921) 3. Priest and tractarian (1890) 4. Bishop of Down and Conor and teacher (1667) 5. Nurse and social reformer (1910) 6. Social reformer (1912) 7. Seminarian and Witness for Civil Rights (1965) 8. Priest (1918) 9. Founders of the Salvation Army (1912 and 1890) 10. Minister to the deaf (1902); first deaf person to be ordained in the Episcopal Church (1890) 11. Spiritual writer (1688)

SEPTEMBER

1		*Giles of Provence*[1]	David Pendleton Oakerhater[2]
2		*Martyrs of Papua New Guinea*[3]	Martyrs of New Guinea
3	Gregory the Great	Gregory the Great	
4		*Birinus* (5 Dec.)	Paul Jones[4]
6		*Allen Gardiner*[5]	
8	**Birthday of Our Lady**	Birth of the B. V. M.	Constance, Nun, and Companions[6]
9	*Peter Claver*	*Charles Fuge Lowder*[7]	
13	John Chrysostom	John Chrysostom	Cyprian (16 Sept.)
15		Cyprian	
16	Cornelius	Ninian (16 Sept.)	Ninian
	Cyprian	*Edward Bouverie Pusey*[8]	
17	*Robert Bellarmine*	Hildegard of Bingen (17 Sept.)	Hildegard
18			Edward Bouverie Pusey
19	*Januarius*	*Theodore of Tarsus* (of Canterbury; 19 Sept.)	Theodore of Tarsus
20	*Andrew Kim, Paul Chong, and Comps., martyrs of Korea*	John Coleridge Patteson and Comps.[9]	John Coleridge Patteson and Comps.
21	**Matthew**	**Matthew**	**Matthew**

298

25		Lancelot Andrewes[10]	
		Sergei of Radonezh	Sergius
		(Sergius; 25 Sept.)	
26	*Cosmas and Damian*	*Wilson Carlile*[11]	Lancelot Andrewes
27	Vincent de Paul	Vincent de Paul	
28	Wenceslas		
	Laurence Ruiz and Comps.		
30	Jerome	*Jerome*	Jerome

1. Hermit (*c.* 710) 2. Deacon and missionary (1931) 3. (1901 and 1942) 4. Bishop and peace advocate (1941) 5. Missionary, founder of South American Missionary Society (1951) 6. "The Martyrs of Memphis," died of yellow fever (1878) 7. Priest (1880) 8. Priest and tractarian (1882) 9. Bishop of Melanesia and his comapnions, martyrs (1871) 10. Bishop of Winchester and spiritual writer (1626) 11. Founder of the Church Army (1942)

OCTOBER

1	Thérèse of Lisieux	*Remigius of Rheims*	Remigius
		(13 Jan.)	
		Anthony Ashley Cooper[1]	
3	Thomas of Hereford		
4	Francis of Assisi	Francis of Assisi	Francis of Assisi
6	Bruno	William Tyndale[2]	William Tyndale
7	Our Lady of the Rosary		
9	*John Leonardi*	*Denys of Paris and Comps.* (9 Oct.)	
		Robert Grosseteste[3]	Robert Grosseteste
10	*Francis Borgia*	Paulinus of York (10 Oct.)	
		Thomas Traherne[4]	
11		*Ethelburga* (12 Oct.)	
		James the Deacon[5]	
12	*Wilfrid*	Wilfrid of Ripon	
		Elizabeth Fry[6]	
		Edith Cavell[7]	
13	*Edward the Confessor*	Edward the Confessor	
14	*Callistus I*		Samuel Isaac Joseph
			Schereschewsky[8]
15	Teresa of Avila	Teresa of Avila	Teresa of Avila
16	*Hedwig*	*Nicholas Ridley and*	Hugh Latimer and
		Hugh Latimer[9]	Nicholas Ridley, and
			Thomas Cranmer
	Margaret Mary Alacoque		
17	Ignatius of Antioch	Ignatius of Antioch	Ignatius of Antioch
18	**Luke**	**Luke**	**Luke**
19	*John de Brebeuf and Comps.*	Henry Martyn[11]	Henry Martyn
	Paul of the Cross		

23	*John of Capistrano*		**James of Jerusalem** (the Less; 3 May)
24	Antony Mary Claret		
25	*Forty Martyrs of England* *and Wales*	*Crispin and Crispinian* (25 Oct.)	
26		Alfred the Great[11] *Cedd of Lastingham* (26 Oct.)	Alfred the Great
28	**Simon and Jude**	**Simon and Jude**	**Simon and Jude**
29		James Hannington[12]	James Hannington
31		*Martin Luther*[13]	

1. Earl of Shaftesbury and social reformer (1885)   2. Translator of the scriptures and reformation martyr (1536)   3. Bishop of Lincoln, philosopher, and scientist (1253)   4. Metaphysical poet and divine (1674)   5. Companion of Paulinus (seventh century)   6. Prison reformer (1845)   7. Nurse (1915)   8. Bishop of Shanghai (1906)   9. Reformation martyrs (1555)   10. Translator of the scriptures, missionary in India and Persia (1812)   11. King of the West Saxons and scholar (899)   12. Bishop of Eastern Equatorial Africa, martyred in Uganda (1885)   13. Reformer and translator of the scriptures (1556)

NOVEMBER

1	**ALL SAINTS**	**ALL SAINTS**	All Saints
2	All Souls	Faithful Departed (All Souls' Day)	All Faithful Departed
3	*Martin de Porres*	Richard Hooker[1] *Martin of Porres*	Richard Hooker
4	Charles Borromeo		
6		*Leonard* (of Noblac; 6 Nov.) *William Temple*[2]	
7	*Willibrord*	Willibrord	Willibrord
8	*John Duns Scotus*	Saints and Martyrs of England	
9		*Margery Kempe*[3]	
10	Leo (the Great)	Leo the Great	Leo the Great
11	Martin of Tours	Martin of Tours	Martin of Tours
12	Josaphat		Charles Simeon[4]
13		Charles Simeon	
14	*Laurence O'Toole*	*Samuel Seabury*[5]	Samuel Seabury
15	*Albert the Great*		
16	*Margaret of Scotland* *Gertrude the Great and* *Mechtildis of Helfta* Edmund of Abingdon	Margaret of Scotland *Edmund of Abingdon*	Margaret of Scotland
17	Elizabeth of Hungary *Hugh of Lincoln*	Hugh of Lincoln	Hugh of Linclon
18	*Philippine Duchesne*	Elizabeth of Hungary (17 Nov.)	Hilda of Whitby (17 Nov.)

300

19		Hilda of Whitby	Elizabeth of Hungary
		Mechtild of Magdeburg[6]	
20	*Edmund*	Edmund	Edmund
		Priscilla Lydia Sellon[7]	
21	*Presentation of the B.V.M.*		
22	Cecilia	*Cecilia*	
23	*Clement I*	Clement of Rome	Clement
	Columbanus		
25		*Catherine of Alexandria*[8]	
		Isaac Watts[9]	James Otis Sargent Huntington[10]
28			Kamehameha and Emma[11]
30	**Andrew**	**Andrew**	**Andrew**

1. Anglican apologist and teacher (1600) 2. Archbishop of Canterbury and teacher (1944) 3. Mystic (*c.* 1440) 4. Priest, Evangelical divine (1836) 5. First bishop of the Episcopal Church of America (1796) 6. Mystic and spiritual writer (1280) 7. Restorer of the religious life in the Church of England (1876) 8. Martyr (removed from Universal Calendar in 1969; fourth century) 9. Hymn writer (1748) 10. Priest and monk (1935) 11. King and queen of Hawaii (1864; 1885)

DECEMBER

1	*Edmund Campion*	*Charles de Foucauld*[1]	Nicholas Ferrar[2]
2			Channing Moore Williams[3]
3	Francis Xavier	*Francis Xavier*	
4	*John Damascene*	*John of Damascus*	John of Damascus
		Nicholas Ferrar	
5	*Sabas*		Clement of Alexandria
6	*Nicholas (of Myra)*	*Nicholas of Myra*	Nicholas of Myra
7	Ambrose	Ambrose	Ambrose
8	**IMMACULATE CONCEPTION OF THE B.V.M**	Conception of the B.V.M.	
9	*Seven Martyrs of Samosata*		
11	*Damasus I*		
12	*Our Lady of Guadalupe*		
	Jane Frances de Chantal		
13		Lucy (13 Dec.)	
		Samuel Johnson[4]	
14	John of the Cross	John of the Cross	
17		*Eglantine Jebb*[5]	
21	*Peter Canisius*		**Thomas** (3 July)
22	*Frances Xavier Cabrini*		

23	*John of Kanti*		
26	**Stephen**	Stephen	Stephen
27	**John**	John	John
28	**Holy Innocents**	Holy Innocents	Holy Innocents
29	*Thomas Becket*	Thomas Beckett	Thomas Becket
31	*Silvester I*	*John Wyclif*[6]	

1. Hermit in the Sahara (1916) 2. Missionary bishop in China and Japan (1910) 3. Deacon, founder of Little Gidding Community (1637) 4. Moralist (1784) 5. Social reformer, foundress of "Save the Children" (1928) 6. Reformer (1384)

The publishers would like to express their gratitude to S.P.C.K. Publishing for making the information contained in the Common Worship Calendar and Lectionary freely available.

General Index of Entries

References in Roman are to the first printing of the twelve volumes. Dates in *Italic* under the same name refer to reprinted volumes—January, February, and November at the time of going to press (Dec. 1999). Where there is no second line for these entries, either the reference is the same or (in a few cases) the entry has subsequently been dropped. All new entries in reprints to date are also in the December Supplement and indexed here as such. Where there is only a date with no page number given under a Dec. Suppl. entry, the entry is not yet in a reprint of that volume.

Consultant Editors

DAVID HUGH FARMER. Former Reader in history at the University of Reading. Author of *St Hugh of Lincoln* and other biographical studies of saints. Author of *The Oxford Dictionary of Saints*. General consultant editor.

REV. PHILIP CARAMAN, S.J. Author of numerous biographies of saints and chief promoter of the cause of the Forty English Martyrs (canonized in 1970). Consultant on English Martyrs. Died in 1998.

JOHN HARWOOD. Librarian of the Missionary Institute in London and course lecturer on the Orthodox churches. Consultant on Eastern and Orthodox saints.

DOM ERIC HOLLAS, O.S.B. Monk of St John's Abbey, Collegeville, Minnesota, and director of the Hill Monastic Manuscript Library in Collegeville, where he also teaches theology at St John's University. General consultant, U.S.A.

PROF. KATHLEEN JONES. Emeritus Professor of Social Policy at the University of York. Author of many books and articles on social policy and mental illness. Honorary Fellow of the Royal College of Psychiatrists. Translator of *The Poems of St John of the Cross* (1993). Consultant on social history and abnormal behaviour.

DOM DANIEL REES, O.S.B. Monk of Downside Abbey and librarian of the monastery library. Bibliographical consultant.

DR RICHARD SHARPE. Reader in diplomatic history at the University of Oxford. Author of *Medieval Irish Saints' Lives* (1991), *Adomnán of Iona. Life of St Columba* (1995), and numerous articles on Celtic saints. Consultant on this subject.

REV. AYLWARD SHORTER, W.F. Long experience of African Missions and author of many books on the subject. Former President of Missionary Institute, London, now Principal of Tangaza College, Nairobi. Consultant on missionary saints.

DOM ALBERIC STACPOOLE, O.S.B. Monk of Ampleforth Abbey. Fellow of the Royal Historical Society. Secretary of the Ecumenical Society of Our Lady. Editor of several works, including *Vatican II by Those Who Were There* (1985). Engaged on a study of St Anslem. Consultant on feasts of Our Lady.

DOM HENRY WANSBROUGH, O.S.B. Monk of Ampleforth Abbey, currently Master of St Benet's Hall, Oxford. Member of the Pontifical Biblical Commission. Author of numerous works on scripture and Editor of the *New Jerusalem Bible* (1985). Consultant on New Testament saints.

SR BENEDICTA WARD, S.L.G. Anglican religious. Lecturer at Oxford Institute of Medieval History. Author of numerous works on hagiography, spirituality, and mysticism. Consultant on Middle Ages and age of Bede.